SMARTER
THAN THE
STREET

INVEST AND MAKE MONEY IN ANY MARKET

GARY KAMINSKY
with Jeffrey Krames

New York   Chicago   San Francisco   Lisbon   London   Madrid
Mexico City   Milan   New Delhi   San Juan   Seoul
Singapore   Sydney   Toronto

The **McGraw·Hill** Companies

First Edition

1 2 3 4 5 6 7 8 9 10   DOC/DOC 1 5 4 3 2 1 0

ISBN: 978-0-07-174922-0
MHID: 0-07-174922-5

This publication is designed to provide accurate and authoritative information in regard to the subject matter covered. It is sold with the understanding that neither the author nor the publisher is engaged in rendering legal, accounting, securities trading, or other professional services. If legal advice or other expert assistance is required, the services of a competent professional person should be sought.
—From a Declaration of Principles Jointly Adopted
by a Committee of the American Bar Association
and a Committee of Publishers and Associations

McGraw-Hill books are available at special quantity discounts to use as premiums and sales promotions or for use in corporate training programs. To contact a representative, please e-mail us at bulksales@mcgraw-hill.com.

This book is printed on acid-free paper.

Library of Congress Cataloging-in-Publication Data
Kaminsky, Gary.
    Smarter than the Street : how to invest and make money in any market / by Gary Kaminsky.
        p. cm.
    Includes bibliographical references and index.
    ISBN 978-0-07-174922-0 (alk. paper)
    1. Investments.   2. Investment analysis.   I. Title.
    HG4521.K247   2011
    332.6—dc22   2010029783

I dedicate this book to Lori—my wife of 21 years, my best friend, and the only woman I could imagine who would put up with all the nonsense I bring into our marriage every day. I also dedicate the book to our three sons, James, Tommy, and Willy, who are unique, clever, and capable, each destined to accomplish whatever he desires in life.

CONTENTS

FOREWORD

By Joseph V. Amato, President, Neuberger Berman

Investing is hard work. Smart investing is even harder. Explaining how to invest presents a different kind of challenge. In *Smarter Than the Street*, Gary Kaminsky has drawn upon his knowledge and met that challenge: he has taken a complex subject and translated it into plain English.

In a way, that's what Gary has done throughout his career in the investment business. When Gary worked with us at Neuberger Berman, he was a leader on Team Kaminsky, one of our largest and most successful investment teams, serving as a key voice to clients and the outside world. It's that unique and commonsense voice that's on display in these pages.

As president and chief investment officer of Neuberger Berman, dealing with our talented money management teams is a core part of what I do every day. It would be hard to find anyone more passionate about investing than Gary. During his tenure here, Gary was also a believer in our partnership culture—a research-based, bottoms-up investing culture that has served the firm so well since our founding in 1939.

At Neuberger, Gary played a key role in building Team Kaminsky. He worked to develop a tight-knit team with a strong sense of camaraderie. Every member of the team felt they were important to the team's overall success. This in turn contributed to the group's strong track record—clearly, when you get the most out of all your people, you make success happen.

Gary understood as well as anyone that, at Neuberger Berman, the client always comes first, and he made sure that he lived that proposition every day. Even during brutal market environments such as the dot-com crash of 2000–2002, he was able to focus on capital preservation, a hallmark of any successful money manager.

Gary was also an "out-of-the-box" thinker. He always sought out investment opportunities that went against the "herd mentality." He had great instincts and an understanding of a wide range of asset classes.

What made Gary flourish at Neuberger Berman was an innate ability to relate to anyone, no matter how sophisticated—or unsophisticated—about investing, and no matter how senior or junior. This is evident in his approach to writing this book.

Gary's *Smarter Than the Street* should enable almost any reader to become more knowledgeable and disciplined, and ultimately, a more *effective* investor. Even those with only a passing interest in the financial markets will find this book valuable. Whether a novice investor or a seasoned professional, you will absorb important ideas that will help you approach the markets in ways you might not have imagined.

In Part One of *Smarter Than the Street*, Gary puts the volatility of the past decade in meaningful context and educates the reader as to the significant challenges all investors face in the decades ahead. In Part Two, he gives specific advice on effective stock picking in these uncertain markets.

It's rare to encounter an investment book that's also a good read. In the case of *Smarter Than the Street*, I am confident that you will take away some valuable lessons that will serve you well in the years ahead.

INTRODUCTION

This is a book that has been many years in the making. The reality is that I wanted to write this book many years ago, but since I was a full-time money manager, I could never find the time. What has driven me to write this book now? It certainly had nothing to do with money or fame or any of the other trappings that successful book authors receive. The truth is that I felt I *had* to write this book. That's because in the nearly two decades that I managed other people's money, I had a front-row seat for the scores of injustices designed to keep the individual investor down. That's why I wrote this book. I felt that once investors were made aware of how the great Wall Street marketing machine is designed to trip them up, they would have a chance to compete with even the biggest Wall Street players on a level playing field. The goal of the book is crystal clear: to demystify the sausage making on Wall Street and give every investor the tools he needs to make money in every market.

In the more than 200 times I have appeared on CNBC's top-rated programs—*Squawk Box* (top-rated morning program), *Closing Bell* (afternoon show), and *Fast Money* (evening show hosted by Melissa Lee) and my 2010 show, *CNBC's Strategy*

Session—I have developed a reputation as one of the Street's most successful, straight-talking money managers. As a managing director of the investment house Neuberger Berman, my team, known as "Team K," routinely outperformed the market, often by more than 200 percent of the returns of the benchmark S&P 500. And we achieved that in every kind of market, up, down, and sideways.

Here are some examples: from the lows of 2002 to the highs of 2008, my team delivered a stunning return that outpaced the performance of the S&P by more than 100 percent. Passive investing—that is, buying some sort of index fund—delivered anemic returns in comparison.

Since we will be focusing on the S&P index so often throughout the book, it is important that we are all on the same page as far as the definition is concerned. According to Standard & Poor's, the S&P 500 is a capitalization-weighted index of 500 stocks designed to measure the performance of the broad domestic economy. S&P solely decides which stocks are in and out of this index.

Another example of my team's performance: between 1999 and 2008, assets under my team's management grew from approximately $2 billion to just under $13 billion. Between June 30, 2007, and June 30, 2008, the annualized return on the S&P was 2.88 percent. During the same time period, equity returns for my team were in excess of 11 percent. That translates into a return of about 400 percent that of the S&P 500. Those are the kinds of returns that would thrill every investor (see Figures I-1 and I-2 for a complete list of annual and annualized returns). And we didn't do it by magic; we did it constructing a specific strategy and adhering to that strategy, regardless of the investing climate. It is a strategy that almost anyone can learn. One of the primary goals of this book is to reveal this strategy, step by step, to individual investors. But, as I will discuss throughout the book, it requires investors to be vigilant and proactive.

Annualized Returns
(for periods ending June 30, 2008)

	2Q08	YTD	1 Year	3 Years	5 Years	10 Years	Since Inception 12/31/96
Total Portfolio Return (Net of Fees)	3.92	-2.66	-0.98	10.09	12.43	7.89	11.24
Equity Only Return (Gross of Fees)	5.55	-3.05	0.59	13.34	16.76	11.08	14.50
Russell 300® Index	-1.69	-11.05	-12.69	4.73	8.37	3.51	6.85
S&P 500 Index	-2.73	-11.91	-13.12	4.41	7.58	2.88	6.60

Annual Returns
(for periods ending Decembr 31)

	2007	2006	2005	2004	2003	2002	2001	2000	1999	1998	1997
Total Portfolio Return (Net of Fees)	10.54	14.47	11.68	18.02	21.33	-10.39	-2.43	1.28	27.43	19.31	28.38
Equity Only Return (Gross of Fees)	14.46	18.58	15.29	24.29	31.46	-14.89	-4.04	1.84	35.92	29.18	31.06
Russell 300® Index	5.14	15.72	6.12	11.95	31.06	-21.54	-11.46	-7.46	20.90	24.14	31.78
S&P 500 Index	5.49	15.79	4.91	10.88	28.68	-22.10	-11.88	-9.11	21.04	28.58	33.36

Figure I-1 Investment Performance (for periods ending June 30, 2008).

	Composite			Benchmarks			Composite			
	Composite Total Return (Gross of Fees) %	Composite Equity Only Return (Gross of Fees) %	Composite Total Return (Net of Fees) %	Russell 300® Index %	S&P 500 Index %	No. of Accounts	Market Value (millions)	Group Composite AUM (millions)	Total Firm Assets (billions)	Asset Weighted Standard Deviation
YTD Jun 08	N/A	-3.05	-2.66	-11.05	-11.91	2,730	4,780.1	5,153.1	N/A	N/A
2007	N/A	14.46	10.54	5.14	5.49	2,699	4,936.1	5,296.3	148.5	5.0
2006	N/A	18.58	14.47	15.72	15.79	2,524	4,430.9	4,692.7	127.0	4.9
2005	12.61	15.29	11.68	6.12	4.91	2,199	3,664.5	3,664.5	105.9	5.6
2004	19.01	24.29	18.02	11.95	10.88	1,618	2,662.9	2,662.9	82.9	6.1
2003	22.37	31.46	21.33	31.06	28.68	1,264	1,933.3	1,933.3	70.5	7.9
2002	-9.56	-14.89	-10.39	-21.54	-22.10	898	1,203.7	1,203.7	56.1	6.2
2001	-1.48	-4.04	-2.4	-11.46	-11.88	729	905.8	905.8	59.0	10.8
2000	2.30	1.84	1.28	-7.46	-9.11	661	864.2	864.2	55.5	13.8
1999	28.96	35.92	27.43	20.90	21.01	42	53.3	53.3	54.4	10.1
1998	20.86	29.18	19.31	24.14	28.58	9	8.5	8.5	55.6	4.0

Figure I-2 Investment Performance (for periods ending June 30, 2008).

I felt that one of the reasons my investment team was so successful was the degree of discipline we employed in managing other people's money. Our investment methods and principles have proven themselves in up, sideways, and down markets. In other words, if you follow our methodology, not only will you make money in most markets, but you will lose much less money when those around you are losing their shirts.

The unfortunate reality is that most investors do not have the kind of discipline that they need if they are to equal or outperform professionals. However, just about all investors, regardless of their level of skill or knowledge, have the ability to master a set of investment principles that will help them to level the playing field with investment professionals.

However, investors must recognize that passivity is the enemy when markets are going nowhere, despite the multi-hundred-million-dollar Wall Street marketing campaigns that try to prove otherwise.

One of the other aims of this book is to help teach readers that investing is more like chess than like checkers. They need to stay ahead of the curve if they are to outperform their peers. Every investor needs the proper mindset and emotional discipline to win. To obtain that all-important mindset, investors need to understand what motivates different constituencies and figure out what is happening behind the scenes. One of the major goals of the book is to instill in investors the same types of reflexes, principles, habits, and investment strategies that have helped me and my team outperform the market for so many years.

However, I will show you how to achieve these kinds of superb returns by devoting just three to five hours of research to the stock market each week, not the hours that professional money managers put in. In less than an hour a day, you will be able to make the same kinds of decisions that top money managers make on a routine basis. Once I tell you *what* to look for—

and *where* to look for it—the rest of it will come relatively easily, regardless of your level of investing knowledge starting out.

Taking personal control of your financial future makes more sense now than ever before. That's because research shows that in the last two-plus decades, the percentage of money managers that beat the S&P 500 is down by a significant margin over the percentage for the decades prior to 1987.

Lastly, this is going to be a book that is rich in stories that will take readers behind the scenes and give them a sort of backstage pass to all of the things they don't see behind the great Wall Street curtain.

Smarter Than the Street is not merely an investment book; it is a manifesto and a revelatory book that demystifies Wall Street, makes bold predictions, and tells investors what Wall Street and other money managers don't want them to know. That's because the vast majority of money managers don't care if their clients make money. How can that be? Because most money managers work for investment firms that have multiple constituencies, and their highest priority may not be growing individual investors' portfolios.

For example, investors who have already made money are interested in capital preservation. But brokers and money managers generally make their money when people buy more stocks and financial products, not less. So it is not uncommon for the goal of the individual and the goal of the institution to be at odds with each other. Your personal desire may be to "zig" when the institution wants you to "zag."

Among those who do manage other people's money as their primary job, many care more about how they perform as measured against the benchmark S&P 500 than they do about absolute returns. Today, many "active money managers" are really "closet indexers" in disguise. (I helped to popularize that phrase on CNBC.) That means that they are buying so many blue chip stocks that their performance merely mimics that of the S&P 500. Recognizing how money managers operate is the first step in executing a plan for achieving absolute returns in a world that is focused on relative performance.

Here's an example that reveals something about the psyche of the typical money manager: If the S&P loses 20 percent while the manager's fund loses only 10 percent during that same period, the manager considers that a great year. In that situation, money managers can advertise to the investing public that they have outperformed Wall Street by two to one. Under the rules of the game that I established and played by as a money manager, that scenario is simply unacceptable. In my world, losing money is *never* an acceptable outcome.

Another misperception about investing is that you should always avoid paying a fee of any kind when buying a mutual fund or purchasing any other investment vehicle. This rule is a bit trickier. With those closet index money managers, paying any kind of a "load" or fee is definitely throwing good money after bad. That's because, as we discussed, their returns are likely

Losing money is never an acceptable outcome.

to come in at about the same as the benchmark S&P 500—and anyone could buy that index in the form of an exchange-traded fund (ETF: ticker symbol SPY) for less than the cost of a New York City movie ticket (in fees).

I will explain why investors need to be original and look elsewhere for investment ideas. It is silly to make an investment decision because an analyst on CNBC upgrades or downgrades a stock.

However, there are places on the Internet that investors can turn to in order to become much better investors. In Chapter 9 of the book, I will describe what investors should be looking for on each of the Web sites that I will recommend they turn to every day (the same ones that I look at every day).

In addition, there are company Web sites that will also provide a great deal of help as you look to "up" your game. And finally, there are several key Wall Street blogs that I also consider to be proprietary that I will recommend to investors. I won't give away their identities here, but I will describe the best of them in Chapter 9 as well. Turning to these sites will help you to narrow your stock search and make you better prepared in all facets of investing.

In *Smarter Than the Street*, I also do something that no other investing book has attempted: I show individual investors, step by step, how to make money when markets go nowhere. No book in recent memory has attempted to do that. There have been great books that have been built on the assumption of a perennial strong bull market (Jeremy Siegel's *Stocks for the Long Run*, now in its fourth edition, is one), and conversely, there have been books that show investors what to do when the sky falls and all of their money comes crashing down (Peter Schiff's *Crash Proof: How to Profit from the Coming Economic Collapse* is an example of that genre).

However, I could find no book built on the assumption that both the U.S. economy and the U.S. financial markets will essentially do nothing for an entire decade. The Dow will not crash, nor will it soar. Instead, it will trade within a range. There are some very specific reasons why the Dow will be such a disappointment in the decade ahead, and I will explain them in great detail.

In Part One of the book, I will explain the specific factors that will cause our economy and our financial markets to stagnate.

Once investors see the logic, they will be eager to learn some sort of system or strategy that will help them to grow their money in zero-growth markets.

In the opening chapters of the book, I will explain why we will *not* see the kind of bull market that we saw in the 1980s and 1990s. Those investors who want evidence that we will have a prolonged lackluster stock market need only turn to recent history. In the 13-year period since Alan Greenspan's now infamous "Irrational Exuberance" speech was delivered in 1996, the overall returns on the stock market failed to keep up with the returns on relatively risk-free three-month Treasury bills. That stark reality flies in the face of much of what investors have been taught since the great 18-year bull market started in the summer of 1982.

In Part Two of the book, I show investors precisely how to make money in zero-growth markets. These are the "money chapters" that investors will use to buy the kinds of stocks that will outperform the market—and many market professionals— in the years ahead.

For those investors who question the primary assumption of the book—that the demand for stocks will weaken in the next decade—research revealed in August of 2010 underscores my thesis. The *Wall Street Journal*, citing Merrill Lynch Wealth Management Affluent Insights Quarterly, reported that people of all ages are getting far more risk averse thanks to the calamitous events of the last decade (that will be examined in depth in Part One of the book).

The key to this eye-opening research is that young investors, age 18 to 34, who have always been the most tolerant of risk (normally only 20 to 25 percent of this group is fearful of risk), have now become almost as risk averse as those age 65 and older—a stunning development. A staggering 52 percent of the younger group reported that they "have a low tolerance for risk today." Fifty-five percent of those 65 or older reported that they also "have a low tolerance for risk." For the groups in between, about 45 percent saw themselves as risk averse. How will this play out in the markets? This will surely dampen enthusiasm for stocks which will likely create a larger demand for bonds and other low-risk assets in the years ahead. I will be elaborating on these themes and other reasons behind them throughout the book.

I will also tell you how many stocks you should own at any one time, a topic that few investing books touch upon. Another topic I will tackle that few other books do is how long one should plan to hold a stock. I am a big believer in the idea that long-term capital gains create significantly more growth for individual investors. This is first and foremost an investing book, not a trading book or one for day traders. Our holding period reflects that, while giving investors the greatest chance of success at making money in all kinds of markets.

However, even more important than a stock's holding period is figuring out precisely *when* to sell a stock. It is in this area that the vast majority of investment books fall down on the job. I will include very specific guidelines as to when one should consider selling any stock position.

Another key topic I will address is whether or not you should hire an investment advisor. That's a question that individual investors pose to me all the time. The answer is not a straightforward yes or no. If you can devote the requisite three to five hours each week to researching stocks and the markets, then you probably do not need an outside advisor. However, if you don't have that kind of time, then you should indeed look to hire an investment advisor.

There are some money managers out there who can add real value to a fund or a portfolio. In those instances, paying a fee, which typically runs between 1 and 1¼ percent, makes perfect sense. The trick is to identify those elite money managers.

How will you know if you have hired the right money manager? I will arm you with everything you need to know—and precisely what questions to ask of your money managers. In other words, the book will be so comprehensive in its coverage that it will contain everything that investors need to know if they are to oversee their money manager and make sure that she is helping them to achieve their financial goals.

There will be dozens of examples throughout the book that will help this material come alive for the reader. It is one thing to simply espouse an investment principle. It is quite another to illustrate how to put that principle to work in a sideways market. Using some of our greatest stock moves, along with other vivid examples, I will show investors that they do not need a Ph.D. to become a superb stock picker.

However, and this is key: the strategies that are presented in Part Two of the book will help you to buy and sell stocks and make money in *all* markets, not just sideways markets. I believe in these techniques so strongly that I contend that by following them, you will be able to amass a portfolio that will do well even if the overall market does not go up. You just need to develop the habits, tactics, and strategies presented in the book and stick to them. I will show you all of that in Part Two of the book.

Part One

WALL STREET EXPOSED

1

THE LOST GENERATION OF INVESTORS

The two major market meltdowns of the last decade have created a new phenomenon that I call the "lost generation of investors." When I use the phrase *lost generation*, I mean the people who left the market between 2000 and 2009 and will not be coming back anytime soon as a result of their experiences during that very difficult period. I will use the phrase *lost decade* the way the *Wall Street Journal* does, to signify the period from 2000 to 2009, in which markets went nowhere. During the lost decade, millions of investors left the stock market and have never come back. Both of these phenomena occurred chiefly as a result of the two market disasters of the first decade of the 2000s, which some have called the "zeroes."

The first market debacle—the bursting of the dot-com bubble—started in 2000 and caused the Nasdaq to crumble from a high of over 5,000 in the first quarter of 2000 to a low of about

1,200 by late 2002. Since major market crashes don't happen very often, after this collapse, most investors thought that all was well with the markets and drove the Dow to top 14,000 in 2007 (while the Nasdaq has never come close to approaching 5,000 again).

During the lost decade, millions of investors left the stock market and have never come back.

Let's look at the year-by-year performance of the stock market for the decade 2000–2009 (see Figure 1-1). Please note that all the stock charts in the book use month end numbers. They may not look exactly like the charts you may see on other Web sites, which are likely more volatile because they use *daily* closing numbers. These percentages represent annual actual returns of the S&P 500:

2000: –9.1%	2005: 4.9%
2001: –11.9%	2006: 15.9%
2002: –22.1%	2007: 5.5%
2003: 28.7%	2008: –37.0%
2004: 10.9%	2009: 26.5%

As we contemplate the lost generation of investors, we will widen our analysis to include larger and larger segments of time so that we can see how the overall markets performed over the long haul. However, before we widen our lens, let's take a closer look at what the returns of the last decade tell us.

- **First, we had a horrible start to the 2000s, with three down years in a row and each loss greater than that of the year before.** That is uncharacteristic of the U.S. stock market. Since 1973, for example, only one out of every four years has been a down year. Of course, if we look at the entire decade, we actually had more up

Figure 1-1   S&P 10-year chart: going nowhere.

years than down ones, by a margin of six to four. But
it is, of course, the magnitude of the gains and losses
that counts.

- **The horrific 37 percent loss of 2008 virtually wiped out
  the combined gains of the previous four years.** That was
  the year of the subprime mortgage mess, and it
  blindsided investors. The stock market had already had
  its worst days in 2000–2002, most investors thought, so
  surely it was not going to crash again. Yet the subprime
  mortgage mess caused a liquidity crisis that had many
  experts talking depression. The events of the 1930s were
  at our doorsteps again, many people believed, thanks to
  the huge housing bubble that burst in 2008. That bubble
  and the ensuing liquidity crisis drove the Dow Jones
  Industrial Average from its high of 14,164 in 2007 to
  6,547 in March of 2009.
- **A $10,000 investment in the S&P 500 at the beginning
  of the decade would have left you with just over $9,000
  at the end of the decade.** That makes the U.S. stock

market the worst performing of all asset classes for the decade, worse than cash, bonds, the money market, or real estate. This negative return unnerved many investors, leaving psychological scars that we will explore in depth later in this chapter.

We also know that investors bailed out of the stock market in a big way in 2009. In fact, we now know that more than $53 billion was taken out of the stock market in 2009 by jittery investors who could not wait to get out, and 2010 started off the same way. In early March, $4.6 billion had been taken out of U.S. stock mutual funds in the first quarter of 2010, according to the Investment Company Institute (and that figure did not include ETFs, or exchange-traded funds). And if all of that is not enough to convince you of how unpopular the stock market has become, consider this: In the first nine weeks or so of 2010, world equity funds had absorbed a little less than $14 billion, while bond funds were more than four times as popular, taking in more than $56 billion. This is proof positive that investors are willing to settle for the anemic returns on bond funds rather than risk their hard-earned capital in the equity and mutual fund markets. This trend of leaving the market was sparked by what happened in the last three months of 2008. During that period, the Fed reported that U.S. households lost 9 percent of their wealth, the most ever recorded for a three-month period.

A Brief Glimpse of Historical Stock Market Returns

To understand the lost generation in context, we need to understand how the equity markets have performed over time and what most investors expect from their investment in the U.S. stock market. That is, what are the assumptions held by most "retail" investors (the 100 million individual U.S. investors with some stock market exposure), and where do these assumptions come from?

We know that there have been several watershed books that have had a major influence on the psyches of millions of investors. One such book, which many now consider a classic, is Jeremy Siegel's *Stocks for the Long Run*. First published in 1994, it contains a plethora of information on the U.S. stock market dating all the way back to 1802, when it first began trading.

Siegel explains that a single dollar invested in the U.S. stock market in 1802 would have been worth $12.7 million by the end of 2006 (assuming that one reinvested all interest, dividends, and capital gains). That's a remarkable number to ponder. Siegel tells us that the U.S. stock market has averaged a 7 percent gain each year over those more than 200 years, and 10 percent when adjusted for inflation. Siegel's book has sold hundreds of thousands of copies over the years, and it has become a favorite tool of the great Wall Street marketing machine (in early editions, tens of thousands of copies of the book were purchased by brokerage houses). It is the poster child for buy-and-hold investing, a phenomenon that was held as gospel prior to the lost generation phenomenon described in this chapter (there will be more on buy-and-hold investing in Chapter 3).

Bear Markets of the Last Half-Century

There has been some great research done on the bear markets of the last 50 years or so. Examining the percentage and length of the declines tells us quite a bit about the financial markets. Since 1957, there have been 10 bear markets in the United States. A bear market is defined as a loss of 20 percent or more of the S&P 500. Table 1-1 gives a list of all 10, along with the years in which they began and ended.

Table 1-1   Bear Markets since 1957

Year	Percentage Decline
1957	20
1961–1962	29
1966	22
1968–1970	37
1973–1974	48
1981–1982	22
1987	34
1990	20
2000–2002	45
2008	38

Source: Burton Malkiel, *The Random Walk Guide to Investing*

Now let's turn the tables and take a look at the bull markets of the last half-century (see Table 1-2).

Table 1-2   Bull Markets of the Last Half-Century

Year	Percentage Gain
1962–1966	86
1966–1968	32
1970–1973	77
1974–1976	76
1978–1981	38
1982–1987	250
1987–1990	73
1990–2000	396
2002–2007	94
2009	28

Source: Seeking Alpha.com

It is worth mentioning that there are several ways to slice up or synthesize the same information. For example, if you look at these bear and bull market tables, you will note that in some years, such as 1966, 1974, and 2002, we had both bear and bull markets either beginning or ending in the same calendar year. This reality reveals the complexity of attempting to time markets. Employing the definition of a 20 percent move as an indicator of a bull or bear market, we see bull markets that exist within larger bear markets and bear markets that exist within larger bull markets. The most noteworthy and greatest bull market in history occurred between 1982 and 2000. Yet within these incredible 18 years, which delivered a stunning return, there were several instances of both bull and bear markets (again, when using the 20 percent rule).

Back to the Lost Decade

These numbers tell me a great deal about the financial markets and how investors are likely to behave in the future. When one looks at all the numbers, the lost decade in particular is a fascinating period that reveals a great deal about the mysteries of the market. Within this 10-year period, we actually had more bull markets than bear markets, by a factor of 4 to 2. However, it is the timing and magnitude of the gains and losses that tell the real tale.

For example, after an incredible 18-year run-up, we lost almost half of the value of the S&P 500 in the period 2000–2002. Clearly, the dot-com bubble spread like cancer to the entire market. Then, later in the decade, from 2002 through 2007, the S&P 500 had a stunning 94 percent gain, which helped the market top the 14,000 level in the Dow. (The S&P 500 and the Dow generally move in the same direction. The S&P is a much better indicator, since it includes 500 stocks while the Dow has only 30, but any significant move in the S&P will always have a similar effect on the Dow Jones average as well.) However, it was the devastating loss of 38 percent in 2008 that destroyed any hopes of a positive decade. Despite the strong 28 percent gain in the final year of the decade, 2009, the S&P 500 still closed well under the level at which it opened in 1999 and 2000.

Research also shows that pension fund and other high-end money managers, who control large pools of funds, often amounting to billions of dollars, have also changed their investing habits. These managers have recently turned toward more investments in hedge funds and higher-fee investments, and, most important, have also significantly shifted their allocation from stocks to bonds.

The individual investors who were most affected by the last decade are those over 50 years of age. Even after the dot-com bubble, they felt that they still had enough time to get their money back. They did not anticipate the credit/liquidity crisis of 2008, and they watched with terror as they lost half of their investment portfolios on average (those with most of their money allocated to the stock market).

That explains the changes we have seen in investing behavior among retail investors as well. According to the Federal Reserve Board, household investments in bonds reached a record level in 2009, approaching nearly 25 percent of all personal holdings.

New research also proves that investors are leaving the market in record numbers. In 2008, the amounts of money being taken out of the stock and fund markets offset all of the inflows into those same markets during the previous four years.

This psychological scarring will play a major role in defining the decade ahead. The psychological shift will have ramifications that will dramatically affect the next generation of investors. As a result of the poor performance and return of equities in this last decade, those who had planned to retire couldn't do so. We know this from numbers that were released in 2010.

One statistic shows that the retirement age has shot up (from 65 to 70.5) because of what has happened to people's retirement savings in the last 26-month recession. In 2010, the average value of the average 401(k) was less than it had been in 2005. The researcher who came up with these numbers, Craig Copeland of the Employee Benefit Research Institute (EBRI), speculated that the retirement age could even increase to 75. No wonder pessimism is on the rise. According to the EBRI, just under 90 percent of the people it surveyed say that they will retire later. The EBRI also reported that the percentage of people with virtually no retirement savings grew for the third straight year. In 2010, it was reported that 43 percent of people have less than $10,000 in savings and, incredibly, 27 percent of workers now say that they have less than $1,000, up from 20 percent in 2009.

In addition, those families that had planned to send their children to first-rate universities or simply build up their education funds could not do so. That's why, when I look at the next 10 years, I see the same roller-coaster ride as the last 10. Stocks will go up, and stocks will go down. There will be periods of exuberance (and note that I am not echoing former Fed Chairman Greenspan's phrase, "irrational exuberance"), and similarly periods in which it looks as if the world is coming to an end.

Another by-product of the lost decade will be how specific acts of the Fed, the Treasury, and the U.S. government will be interpreted. For example, there will be periods much like those that followed the lows in 2009, when people were excited because the government had stepped in to make things better with the TARP and stimulus packages. Equity markets will react positively to these types of changes because they will view these actions as sparking productivity and increasing GDP growth. And this will be true not only in the United States, but on a global basis.

For example, in May of 2010, when the country of Greece faced insolvency, the European Union stepped in with a near-trillion-dollar rescue plan. There was such fear surrounding the Greece problem that the Dow soared more than 400 points after that deal was announced.

In other times, those same kinds of moves will be interpreted as harbingers of disaster. The reasoning during those periods will be that if the government had to take such drastic actions, then the financial outlook must really be bleak.

Investors need to inoculate themselves against the noise of the market and learn to stick to a specific buy and sell discipline. I will argue throughout the book that investors need to be just that, investors, and not traders (and God forbid day traders) that are reacting to every hiccup in the market.

Research That Proves the Tale of the Tape

One of the key assumptions of this book is that the next 10 years will resemble the last 10. And I am not alone in this belief. One noteworthy author and researcher, Vitaliy Katsenelson, has done some terrific research that backs up my thesis. He shows that despite the unprecedented events of these last 10 years, history favors a market that is likely to end the next decade (2010–2019) pretty much where we started this one.

Katsenelson explains that ever since the U.S. stock market started trading two centuries ago, every lengthy bull market has been immediately followed by a "range-bound market that lasted about 15 years." A range-bound market is one that trades between two levels, usually characterized by a relatively narrow difference. For example, in 2011, if the Dow traded between 10,000 and 11,000 one would consider that a range-bound market. He also explains that the only exception was the Great Depression. Katsenelson also notes that the bull market of 1982–2000 was a "super-sized" bull market. To give you an idea of the magnitude of that market, consider this: if by some miracle (and it would take one) the Dow repeated its great percentage increase of 1982–2000 over the next 18 years, it would hit an incredible 175,000 points by 2028.

Lastly, Katsenelson urges investors to understand the difference between a range-bound market and a bear market, and the importance of investing differently in each of those types of markets.

Many people believe that the great recession of 2008 to 2009, brought on by the housing bubble and subprime mortgage meltdown, was so severe that it makes the current situation analogous to the Great Depression. Let's take a quick look at these historical returns to gain further insight into the markets and see if this comparison holds any water.

In a 10-week period in 1929, from September 3 to November 13, Wall Street experienced the Great Crash and the market lost just under 48 percent of its value. After that, from November 14 to April 17, 1930, the market snapped back impressively with a 48 percent gain. Today, some members of the great Wall Street marketing machine are out there telling people to get back in the market with both feet so that they can enjoy the fruits of a similar bounceback and perhaps a new bull market. As is commonly declared in the world of finance, however, past performance is not indicative of future returns. The situations in 1929 and 2009 are totally different, for reasons that I have already explained, and will explain more fully throughout the book. As a result, I foresee no such snapback or new bull market occurring anytime soon. The bottom line is that the demand for stocks was far greater in 1930 than it is today.

This has a lot to do with the timing of the great bull market of 1982–2000. Referring back to Katsenelson's research, every impressive bull market has been followed by a 15-year range-bound market. Perhaps 2000 to 2010 was the beginning of that 15-year range-bound market, which would mean that we will continue to be range-bound through 2015. Alternatively, the last 10 years could have simply been a return to normal valuations following the excesses of the 1982–2000 market. If that is the case, we may be in a range-bound market from 2010 to 2025. One can make a compelling argument for either scenario. One can also argue that we are going to see equities significantly underperform other asset classes, such as real estate or bonds. The scenario that seems most unlikely is that we're going to have a significant expansion of price/earnings (P/E) ratios or an increase in the multiples paid for stocks, which is the major reason that stocks increase in value over time. (The multiple, which is derived by dividing a company's market price by the company's earnings per share, is also known as a stock's P/E ratio, or simply P/E. Algebraically, earnings times the multiple will give you the share price.)

There is mounting evidence that this predicted period of underperformance could easily become a reality. This book will be filled with statistics that show that in certain periods, equity prices have stagnated for long periods of time. Let me give an apt example of a single company that will bring these concepts to life (no pun intended). Let's look at Jack Welch's GE in the 1990s. As CEO of GE, Welch made GE's stock a darling of Wall Street because he was able to achieve both an increase in earnings and an increase in the company's multiple. Year in and year out, GE's earnings increased, which helped GE's stock to rise. At the same time, because Welch was seen as a superstar CEO, investors valued the company more highly because of his management. At its zenith in 2000, GE's stock was trading at nearly 50 times earnings (a multiple of 50). In 2010, in marked contrast, the company trades at about a quarter of its once-mighty multiple, selling at only about 15 times earnings (a multiple of 15).

Is There a Right P/E Level?

Let's go back a decade to look at P/E ratios before the tech bubble burst. At the market's zenith in 2000, the average P/E ratio of the S&P 500 was 40, making stocks very expensive. If that number does not faze you, consider this: At the same time, the average Nasdaq stock was three times as expensive as the average S&P stock, with an average P/E of an astronomical 120, excluding stocks with no earnings! Compare that to the historical average P/E for an S&P stock, which is a far more reasonable median level of 15.7. At this time, tech stocks made up more than a third of the S&P 500, the highest percentage of any group in history.

The unprecedented P/E ratios of stocks at the end of the great bull market in 2000 have had a profound effect on stocks in the last decade and are likely to affect stock prices going forward.

If you use the arithmetic long-term averages as your compass, the reversion to normalized P/E multiples will feel worse this time because we're coming off so much higher a base. Investors may think that they have paid their dues with the poor performance of stocks between 2000 and 2009, but that may not be the case. Valuations were so unrealistically high in 2000 that it might very well require more than a decade for stocks to trade at more reasonable levels. This reality may prove to be yet another drag on financial markets, making any near-term bull market a most unlikely event.

The other point worth noting is that today, because of the human emotions associated with investing, it is very difficult to figure what a normalized P/E ratio should be. In some cases, investors get euphoric and buy stocks at levels way above the median of 15.7. Other times, investors get depressed and pessimistic, and sell at levels way below that figure.

There is one more key factor, in addition to investors' behavior, that makes it very difficult to calculate a normalized P/E number, and that is government stimulus. Since 2008, government stimulus packages have been the major facilitator of economic growth in the United States. The longer this continues, the more difficult it will be to figure out what the real P/E ratio should be.

I believe that investors, over time, will grow more skeptical of government stimulus and, as a result, will be unlikely to buy stocks at a premium. This will most likely bring down P/E ratios to far more reasonable levels. Put another way, the demand for equities will be outstripped by supply, causing markets to go lower or tread water at best. The next section provides more insight into why this is likely to continue for quite some time.

In the meantime, however, some harsh statistics that were released in 2010 confirm that it isn't only individuals that are altering their attitude toward stocks—pension fund managers are also becoming far more skittish about the equities market. According to the *New York Times*, companies are moving away from stocks into far more conservative investments, such as long-term bonds. But that's only part of the story. In order to get back the billions that they have lost in recent years, pension fund managers are also trying all sorts of riskier types of investments, such as junk bonds, foreign stocks, commodity futures, and mortgage-backed securities. The verdict is still out on whether or not these alternative investments will work, but there is no doubt that investing behavior has changed at the institutional level as well as the individual level.

Investor Behavior and the Scars of the Lost Decade

Regardless of where we go from here, the two disasters of the last decade have sparked a major shift in investor sentiment, with millions of investors not likely to return to the market for years to come. As mentioned earlier, investor behavior has been affected at a very deep level. One of my favorite war stories helps to provide more insight into why this happened and why it is unlikely to change anytime soon. This is a story that sums up for me the whole idea of the lost generation.

I was on a business trip a couple of years ago, and I visited a Raymond James financial retail office in western Florida. A stockbroker told me a story about two neighbors who lived on his street. In 1999, one of his neighbors decided to take his life savings and put it in the stock market, figuring that he would retire somewhere around 2012. He assumed that having a 12-plus-year time horizon would guarantee him a strong total return and that he would have no problem growing his nest egg.

During this period, both he and his wife were working, and they both decided to contribute the maximum allowed to their 401(k) plans. Taking the advice of many pundits, he put the maximum into a diversified portfolio of equities. He allocated portions of the family's funds to S&P 500 stocks, including value stocks and growth stocks (closet indexing), and he felt that he was properly diversified.

The same week, the broker's other neighbor made a very different decision. He also was still working, and he decided that he wanted to take his money and buy something that would provide much pleasure for him and his family. As a result, he bought a boat so that he and his family and friends could go waterskiing every weekend.

So one guy takes $90,000 and puts it in the stock market, and the other guy takes $90,000, buys a beautiful boat, and uses that boat to go out with his family every weekend for the next decade. Week in and week out, he takes his kids and their friends out on the boat, and they have a great time honing their waterskiing abilities.

This was a pretty small community, and it seemed that everyone knew Jack and Joe—and how Jack had invested everything in the stock market, and how Joe was the guy who bought the boat and enjoyed it every weekend with his family and friends. In 2009, these two neighbors got together after the market rebounded some. Jack, the man who bought into buy-and-hold investing and the long-term thesis of the stock market, is still working, since he was unable to retire. Not only did he have to move his retirement back several years, but we also know that he lost money, since the S&P was about 10 percent lower 10 years after he put his life savings into the market (and his stocks pretty much mirrored the performance of the S&P 500).

Joe, on the other hand, had an entire decade to enjoy his boat, and everyone in town knew it. In fact, the Jack and Joe story permeated every nook and cranny of the entire community. It seemed that there wasn't anyone who did not know the story of these two very different men and their respective choices.

The point of the story is this: Since everyone in town had a front-row seat for Jack and Joe's decisions, the next generation of investors learned about how quickly the market could go south, and it had a profound effect on their behavior. Some people were keenly aware of how they were affected by the two men's decisions, but many others were affected on a more subconscious level. Either way, Jack's lifetime investment gave stocks a bad reputation, making the next generation of investors far more hesitant to put their hard-earned money into the stock market. This creates a natural imbalance between the supply of and demand for equities. How do we know this? We know this because we have one very prominent example of a very similar scenario playing out on a huge scale, and that is Japan. Let's take a quick look at Japan's lost decade and generation.

In the closing days of 1989, the Nikkei stock index hit an all-time high of just under 39,000. At the same time, money was very much available, and many risky loans were made to businesses and individuals. As in the United States, a housing bubble played a prominent role in Japan's economic debacle. Certain elite neighborhoods in Tokyo were garnering the equivalent of an incredible $1 million per square meter (or $93,000 per square foot). After the bubble burst, amazingly, these same properties were worth only about 1 percent of their peak value. By 2004, residential homes had also experienced calamitous devaluations, being on average worth only about 10 percent of their peak values (yet at the time still the most expensive in the world).

Japan's cheap credit and subsequent real estate bubble continued to pose a huge problem for its economy. A deflationary spiral caused the Nikkei to continue to fall, and even government investment in crumbling banks and businesses could not stop the bleeding, despite a near zero percent interest rate set by the Central Bank of Japan (it called these failed businesses "zombie businesses"). In October 2008, the Nikkei 225 hit a 26-year low of just under 7,000. In early 2010, the Nikkei was trading at just over 10,000, still down about 75 percent from its 1989 high. Many people argue that Japan continues to be locked in an economic meltdown. (We will look at the Japanese bubble and the comparisons to the United States in more depth in the next chapter).

Given all of these factors, the only way to make real money in the decade ahead will be to buy the right stocks at the right time. The most accepted phrase that describes this phenomenon is a "stock picker's market." Those who have the tools and education to buy the right stocks at the right time and adopt a strict buy and sell discipline will be the winners in the next decade. We already know that the next decade is off to a very challenging start. In the first seven months of 2010, incredibly, more than $33 billion of U.S. stock mutual funds was taken out of the stock market, so reported the *New York Times* quoting the Investment Company Institute. This book will provide you with everything you need to know in order to make those all-important buy and sell decisions.

2

THE ZERO-GROWTH
DECADE AHEAD

Now that we understand why we will lose a generation of investors, we can dive deeper into the reasons why the economy and the financial markets will stagnate for the next decade.

Since investing is all about supply and demand, the demand for equities (stocks) will almost certainly go down in the years ahead. As discussed in Chapter 1, we are already seeing this scenario play out, as millions of investors have withdrawn from the stock market. This is unfortunate, since research shows that most investors leave the markets at the worst times, when markets are at their lows. For those investment firms that were keeping their money in equity markets, in 2009 and early 2010 we saw a big shift to investments in stock markets outside the United States, mostly those in Europe and Japan. However, by the spring of 2010, amid great problems in Greece and the rest of Europe, the U.S. dollar experienced a strong resurgence against other major currencies, and the U.S. stock market became the safest choice for investors around the world. How long that will continue is anyone's guess, but I still believe that the headwinds we have discussed will come to the fore and make people more skittish about putting their money in any stock market, whether it be in Asia, Europe, or the United States.

The Unemployment Factor

As we discussed in the previous chapter, following the great bear market of 2008, millions of people were unable to retire when they had planned to do so. To make matters worse, a significant percentage of these people who could not retire also could not find a job, as the unemployment rate was hovering right around 10 percent (it was 10.2 percent at the end of 2009). That's the highest unemployment rate since 1983, and many experts feel that the "real" unemployment percentage is higher—more like 17.5 percent. The disparity in these numbers is due to the fact that there is a very real possibility that there are an additional 7½ percent of workers out there who have simply given up on getting a job or have accepted part-time work when they would have preferred full-time employment. In both of these cases, these people would generally not be included in the 10 percent unemployed.

Even the lower figure does not offer any comfort to the U.S. economy. Since the recession began in December of 2007, a record number of 8.4 million jobs have been lost.

Whether the unemployment percentage is 10 percent or closer to 20 percent, we know that people without jobs are not investing in their 401(k) plans or making any other stock market investments. This weighs on the natural balance of supply and demand for equities. It is yet one more piece of evidence indicating that a significant and lasting bull market is unlikely anytime soon. However, the unemployment number, when looked at on its own, is insufficient evidence for a bear or range-bound market. Remember that we had high unemployment rates in 1982 and 1983, at the beginning of the great bull market. In fact, between 1982 and 1987, the S&P increased in value by 250 percent, even with an unemployment rate that exceeded 11 percent in 1983. But the early 1980s and the new decade that started in 2010 are different in several important respects.

For example, the number of people who were involved in the stock market in one way or another was much lower in 1983. Experts agree that only about 20 percent of American households were involved in the stock market at that time. In the 2000s, more than one in two American households had some sort of stock market exposure, which is why the losses of this decade left such an indelible mark on the mindset and the real wealth of America's investing class. While only 20 percent of the population felt the effect of the bear market of 1981–1982, more than half of American households felt the severe shocks brought on by the two crises of the last decade.

For example, as I alluded to in the previous chapter, in March of 2009, the Fed reported that households had lost $5.1 trillion, or nearly 10 percent of their total wealth, in just the last three months of 2008. In all of 2008, the wealth of U.S. households dropped by about 18 percent, or $11.1 trillion. At that time, the *New York Times* published an article that concluded that the actual damage was far worse, although the numbers had yet to catch up to the real loss in the collective wealth of the nation.

To give you an idea of the magnitude of this crash, the second worst financial disaster of the last 50 years happened in 2002, when the worth of U.S. households fell by a "mere" 3 percent as a result of the dot-com crash. "The most recent loss of wealth is staggering and will probably put further pressure on the econ-

In all of 2008, the wealth of U.S. households dropped by 18 percent, or $11.1 trillion.

omy because many people will have to spend less and save more," declared the *New York Times* in March of 2009.

There are other important differences between 1983 and 2009. The equity market had experienced a huge drought prior to the August 1982 market turnaround. For example, in early 1966 the Dow was close to 1,000. In 1982, before the bull market got underway, the Dow was in the 770s. That is a 16-year period in which the market not only did not go up but lost a good deal of ground. Very few bear markets last that long. (By strict definition, there were actually four bear markets between 1966 and the 1982 turnaround. See Table 1-1.) That is very different from the situation we have in 2010—following a great 18-year supercharged bull market and then a lost decade marred by two major crises.

The Subprime Meltdown and the Housing Crisis

The housing crisis is also an important factor that will play a key role in slowing the economy and the growth of the financial markets in the years ahead. In 2008 alone, there were 1,000,000 foreclosures on U.S. homes and an additional 1,000,000 homes on which the foreclosure process had been started. At the end of that year, many experts believed that following such an unprecedented debacle, the worst had to be over in the housing market. They were wrong. In the third quarter of 2009 alone, for example, an additional 937,840 homes received some kind of foreclosure document, whether it was a default notice, an auction notice, or bank repossession, according to a RealtyTrac report.

In November 2009, the *Wall Street Journal* reported that nearly one in four mortgages were under water, meaning that the amount of the mortgages on these properties was more than the properties were worth. Prices have plummeted to such a degree that more than 5.3 million homes have mortgages that are at least 20 percent higher than the value of the property, making any kind of sharp snapback of the economy unlikely.

The press appropriately called the third quarter of 2009 the "worst three months" in recorded history for real estate, and because the depth of the problem may actually be understated as a result of the delay in delinquency filings. Many experts now agree that we may not see any meaningful turnaround of the real estate market until 2013. In late February of 2010, it was reported that January home sales were the worst in 50 years. This followed a dismal 2009, in which home sales fell almost 25 percent from 2007. The unprecedented nature of this housing debacle makes any prediction of a turnaround no more than mere speculation. The reality is that no one really knows when these disastrous housing markets will turn around.

Before I take this too far, let me note that this is not a book on the mortgage meltdown, the housing crisis, or the liquidity crisis. By the time this book is published, there will probably have been dozens of books published on these disasters. However, it is worth taking a closer look at the events of 2008 and 2009—and the events that they put in motion—so that we can gain additional insights into the headwinds that the U.S. and other global financial markets will face in the years ahead.

The Government Steps In to Stop the Bleeding

In 2008 and 2009, the government stepped in to provide much-needed stability to deal with a number of crises that were wreaking havoc with the U.S. economy and the U.S. financial markets.

Thanks to the housing bubble and the subprime mortgage mess, several of the largest financial institutions in the United States disappeared practically overnight. Bear Stearns, founded in 1923, had survived the 1929 crash without firing a single worker. However, the circumstances were far different in 2008. Once the markets learned that the company could not be saved with a government loan, the firm was sold in a "fire sale" to JPMorgan Chase for $10 per share. A few months later, starting in September of 2008, the government stepped in and bailed out AIG by providing as much as $182.5 billion to stabilize the insurance giant. Later, former U.S. Treasury Secretary Hank Paulson said that if the government had not stepped in and had let the company fail, this could have triggered a series of events that might have made the overall unemployment rate skyrocket to 25 percent.

A month after the AIG bailout, the House and Senate passed the $787 billion Troubled Asset Relief Program, better known by its acronym, TARP. The purpose of this bailout package was to allow the U.S. government to buy bad assets from banks and other troubled financial institutions. These "troubled" assets were the result of the subprime mortgage mess, which had infected financial institutions and the U.S. economy as a whole. However, getting this bill passed was no small task. In fact, when the House failed to pass TARP on September 29, 2008, the Dow lost more than 777 points, the worst one-day point drop in history (but not the worst day in percentage terms). That one day erased $1.2 trillion in stock market value, the first trillion-dollar day in the Dow's history; it was even worse than the loss on the first day of trading following the September 11 attacks (a 685-point loss). The purpose of TARP was to permit the government to provide much-needed funds to financial institutions in order to spark lending, which had dried up almost completely as a result of the mortgage meltdown.

I was the cohead of "Team K" at Neuberger Berman when the subprime mortgage mess hit. At that time, we were managing close to $13 billion. Neuberger had been acquired by Lehman Brothers in 2003. I was not a fan of the sale, believing that the cultures of investment banks and money management firms were vastly different. From my position at Neuberger, I saw some of these events coming down the tracks like a freight train. Among concerns, I did not want my compensation to be paid in the form of restricted Lehman shares any longer. As a result, I negotiated a settlement with Neuberger Berman four months before Lehman ultimately declared bankruptcy and collapsed.

I recount these events here not to overwhelm you with big numbers or to show off my predictive abilities, but to extract lessons from these events and examine possible scenarios for how they will affect the U.S. and global financial markets in the decade ahead.

In no other period in U.S. history did the government shell out trillions of dollars to stave off an unprecedented global financial disaster. Many policy makers and pundits swore that if we did not make these trillion-dollar gambles, then we risked financial ruin on a global scale. "Spend trillions now or we will see the collapse of the entire financial system" was a popular refrain that was repeated again and again, day in and day out, on the cable news channels in 2008 and 2009.

One of the key reasons that markets face a zero-growth decade is directly related to the series of events that nearly sent the U.S. and the global economy off a cliff. As a result of all of the drastic actions taken by the Fed and the Treasury, such as the creation of TARP, the Fed was forced to print hundreds of billions—even trillions—of dollars, creating the conditions for rising inflation, which is one of the reasons that gold has appreciated so dramatically in recent years.

As a result of these actions—although they were critical and necessary measures—in my opinion it will take a minimum of five years for us to recover from these crises and probably another five before burned investors return to the stock market. And these numbers are conservative. I base them on several factors, not the least of which is the one-two punch of the dot-com crash of 2000–2002 combined with the recent Great Recession/liquidity crisis of 2008 and 2009. Investors got badly burned not once, but twice in the same decade, which had the effect of scaring off millions of investors who once believed that buy and hold was a "can't-lose" investing strategy. Millions of these investors have yet to return to the stock market. In fact, in March of 2010, it was estimated that as much as $3 trillion of individual investors' money remains on the sidelines, despite the 60 percent increase in the stock market from the lows of 2009 to the first quarter of 2010.

As we write these words in early 2010, we are just emerging from the liquidity crisis of the last 18 months. However, *we already know that there is another crisis right around the corner*. Given the drastic, unprecedented actions of the Fed and Treasury, it will be impossible to avoid one. It may be a Treasury bond bubble or a crisis ignited by the lack of purchasing power of the U.S. dollar, but there is another shoe to drop, and this will cause millions of additional investors to run for the exits.

The lost generation of investors will be far more likely to turn to fixed-income investments, or bonds, in the years ahead; thus, only a handful of stocks will add significant value to a portfolio.

On what do I base these predictions? As discussed in Chapter 1, the best comparison to the events that took place in the United States in recent years is Japan in the late 1980s. Let's return to that country and take an even closer look at Japan during its troubled era to see what the tea leaves are telling us may happen to U.S. financial markets in the years ahead.

Back to the Future in Japan

As we discussed in the previous chapter, in 1989 the Japanese market peaked at just under 39,000 before plummeting in subsequent years. As in the United States, a housing bubble was one of the primary causes of the Japanese market crash. When the price of real estate skyrocketed by a factor of 10 in 1989, Japan, in theory, according to the Ministry of Construction, had the ability to buy the entire United States four times over, despite the fact that the United States was 25 times the size of Japan. Suddenly, in 1989, the United States no longer had the world's most valuable stock market. Following its destruction in World War II, Japan was 25 times smaller than the United States and had only half its population, yet it raced past the United States to become the world's most highly valued financial market by the late 1980s.

The bubble in Japan extended from 1986 to 1991, a period in which both housing and equity prices simply spiraled out of control. The period that followed was known as the "lost decade," the first time that we heard that phrase used in the business lexicon.

Just how similar is this disaster to the one that we now face in the United States?

First, let's look at interest rates. During the building of Japan's bubble, the Bank of Japan was ordered to cut prime interest rates to post–World War II lows, similar to what happened in the United States during the liquidity crisis. Later the Bank of Japan drove interest rates to near zero, also similar to what happened in the United States in 2009. In each of these situations, rock bottom interest rates were insufficient to spark meaningful economic growth.

Next, let's turn to housing: The Japanese housing boom actually helped to finance the huge run-up in stocks, which helped the Nikkei index to triple in value between 1985 and 1989. At that time, the average Japanese stock multiple expanded to an unprecedented 78 times earnings, almost three times the average multiple of just a few years earlier.

How bad had things gotten? Nippon Telephone and Telegraph, or NTT, which was very similar to America's AT&T, was suddenly worth hundreds of billions of dollars and had a P/E ratio of more than 300. Incredibly, that one company alone was worth far more than many smaller nations' *total* stock market values.

This was what I like to call a period of "panic buying" in Japan, in which people used other already wildly inflated assets (e.g., real estate) to finance and inflate another asset class (e.g., stocks). As a point of contrast, in early 1989 the average multiple of a U.S. Dow stock was less than 13, making the value of a share of Japanese stock more than six times that of a share of an average U.S. Dow stock during the same time period.

It bears noting that Japan was the "it" country in the late 1980s. Japan was purchasing the most prestigious U.S. real estate properties, including such gems as Rockefeller Center and Pebble Beach. Japanese management techniques were heralded as the best way to run businesses during this period. Many business schools featured Japanese management techniques in their regular course curricula, as if the United States had run out of solutions and had to look to Japan for answers. It was during this "Japan can do no wrong" era that the prices of Japanese equities ran amok. This makes sense, since huge events and bubbles seldom take place in a vacuum. Instead, they occur against a backdrop that usually provides both context and reason for things that ultimately turn out to be unreasonable.

Similarities to the United States

Japan's lost decade bears similarities to both of the U.S. crises of the first decade of the twenty-first century. The first important comparison is the huge stock run-up in Japan between 1985 and 1989 and the dot-com market that catapulted the Nasdaq to more than 5,000 in the first quarter of 2000. In many ways, both periods were fueled by assumptions that were ultimately proven false. In Japan, real estate was wildly overpriced, and investors used those valuations to drive stock prices sky high.

In the United States, the assumption that earnings did not count was proven false, and this was one of the triggers of the dot-com crash. There were hundreds of companies like eToys.com that had incredible initial public offerings (IPOs), only to fall back to earth months later when investors realized that these companies had no sustainable business models that could deliver a steady stream of earnings. Things had gotten so out of control at that time that the multiples of Nasdaq stocks *with earnings* exceeded 120, while the average S&P stock had a multiple of 40.

The valuations of U.S. stocks in 1999–2000 bore a strong resemblance to the Japanese valuations of the late 1980s.

In both Japan in 1989 and the United States in 2000, stocks had become so grossly overpriced that a bear market in each country in the near team was virtually guaranteed. The Nasdaq crash of 2000–2002 closely resembled the Japanese meltdown that started in the late 1980s.

Let's take a look at the numbers. The Nikkei, which had neared 39,000 in December 1989, had plummeted to around 14,000 by 1992. A decade later, the Nikkei had fallen to below 8,000. That was the worst performance for any stock market since the 1929–1932 crash. A dollar invested in the Japanese stock market in January 1990 was worth only 67 cents 11 years later, an annualized return of minus 3.59 percent.

Compare that to the lost decade in the United States. In Chapter 1, we saw that the S&P 500 lost nearly 10 percent of its value from 2000 to 2009. That loss isn't anywhere near as bad as the losses that mounted up in Japan. But let's look at the tech-heavy Nasdaq market. At its peak in 2000, it topped 5,000. During four periods over the ensuing decade, in 2002, 2003, 2008, and 2009, the Nasdaq traded at a level that was about 25 percent of its high. More than a decade later, in early 2010, even after an impressive bounce off the lows of 2009, the Nasdaq still traded at less than 45 percent of its high. That meant that a dollar invested in the Nasdaq market in early 2000 was worth less than 45 cents in 2010. If one looks at the Nasdaq 100—the 100 largest stocks

> *The Nasdaq crash of 2000–2002 closely resembled the Japanese meltdown that started in the late 1980s.*

traded on the Nasdaq exchange—the losses are even worse. A one-dollar investment in this index at its high in 2000 was worth only about 37 cents.

The other similarity between Japan and the United States is the huge stimulus and spending packages implemented by each country in an effort to prop up its economy and financial markets.

In the early 1990s, the Japanese government put in place a number of economic initiatives, including multiple stimulus packages in the form of work programs, in order to breathe some life into what many felt was a dead or near-dead economy. However, these stimulus packages accomplished very little. Between 1996 and 2002, Japan's per capita GDP barely budged, increasing by a mere 0.2 percent. Similarly, according to a report issued by the White House Council of Economic Advisers, the 2009 stimulus package raised U.S. GDP by about 2 percent in the fourth quarter of 2009, "relative to what it otherwise would have been." One other point of similarity is that both Japan and the United States are huge debtor nations. In 2010, the level of U.S. debt is expected to approach 100 percent of gross domestic product, while in Japan, the debt to GDP level is expected to approach 200 percent.

I find it very interesting that many of our smartest investing book authors do not believe that the United States can experience an economic and financial downturn like that of Japan in the years ahead. In researching this book, I found that many bestselling investing authors treat the Japanese bubble as an isolated event that could not possibly touch the shores of the United States. Some books allocated a paragraph or a page to the Japanese bubble and drew few, if any, analogies to the United States. To be fair, most of these books were written prior to the liquidity crisis of 2008. However, as I have described in this chapter, there are many similarities between the two countries and the actions taken by their respective governments during their most turbulent periods.

The stimulus packages in both Japan and the United States, for example, were expected to turn things around. We know that those packages had little effect on Japan's ability to grow either its economy or its financial markets. The key thing to remember about these kinds of stimulus packages is that they are an act of last resort. Since the country's private sector was too weak to bring about the desired level of growth, the politicians in each nation were forced to step in with these expensive government programs.

As I write these words in 2010, it is simply not known whether the United States will experience the continued and sustained problems that choked the Japanese economy and stock market for so long. It is simply too soon to tell. However, we do know that on a conscious and subconscious level—like the man who invested all of his money in the stock market versus the man who bought the boat—fewer people will be willing to put their hard-earned dollars into the U.S. market in the decade ahead. This will create a natural imbalance between the supply and demand for equities in the years ahead.

In late February of 2010, in testifying before Congress, Fed Chairman Ben Bernanke said that even if a recovery takes hold, it is likely to be a "tepid" one. That is a striking admission. Even after the trillions of dollars had been spent, the U.S. Fed chairman admitted that tepid is about the best we can hope for. That's not exactly the kind of prediction that breeds confidence among an already jittery investment public.

However, and this is critical, even if the United States does experience a protracted period of anemic economic growth and a stock market that goes nowhere, this does not necessarily spell doom and gloom for all U.S. investors. The recognition that the country is looking at another lost decade does not mean that you cannot profit or make money in the years ahead. It simply means that to put a winning strategy in place, you must be aware of the headwinds you are facing.

As mentioned earlier, the lost generation of investors will be far more likely to turn to fixed-income investments, or bonds, in the years ahead, and thus only a handful of stocks will add significant value to a portfolio. However, even in the disastrous Japanese market described in this chapter, there were handfuls of opportunities to make money on both the long and the short side to create absolute returns. All of this means that a general market portfolio or a closet index portfolio is highly unlikely to produce meaningful returns over any extended period of time.

An interesting footnote to this chapter: Some months after this chapter was written, *Barron's* published a fascinating article by Thomas H. Kee, president of *Stock Traders Daily*. He asserts that the stock market will be down for a period of 16 years starting from 2007. He developed a construct called the "Investment Rate," which is a "proprietary measure of normalized demand for investments in the U.S."

Kee explains that to figure out what will happen in the market, one should not study such things as interest rates, business inventories, and housing starts, which economists and market experts have obsessed over ever since such things have been recorded. Instead, the "Investment Rate measures the core of all economic activity, people."

The underlying principle is that people put much more money into the markets after they have put their children through college, or at about age 48. After analyzing certain demographics, Kee developed a model that takes the "Kee age" into account. The bottom line is that we are in a phase in which investment dollars will be shrinking, not growing. Kee suggests that we are entering a very tough period in which high deficits, social security and Medicare expenses, and the baby boomers' retirement will make it very difficult to achieve any new highs in the market until 2023 (although there is a chance that the market could find a bottom before that time). Kee back-tested his methods, and they held true from the Depression through the lackluster 1970s, and through up markets in between. In light of that, I viewed Kee's Investment Rate as one more piece of important research backing up my own theory that we will not see any significant market growth for years to come.

3

WALL STREET'S GREATEST MYTHS REVEALED

In the first two chapters of the book, I made what I hope you agree is a compelling case that the next decade will be chock-full of hurdles that will make any significant growth of the U.S. financial markets a giant uphill battle. However, I also said that there will be pockets of opportunity where investors can make money in the years ahead if they are given the right information, tools, and techniques that can lead them in the right direction.

The purpose of this chapter is to reeducate investors by show-ing them that many of the things they have been taught about the stock market either are outright misrepresentations or are no longer applicable. Either way, these "truths" must be exposed if investors are to have a real chance of achieving the kind of returns that the best money managers achieve.

My goal is to get you so familiar with the mythical nature of the following concepts that recognizing it will be second nature to you. Only then will you have the necessary foundation in place so that you can move on to Part Two, where the specific details of how to make money in sideways markets will be revealed.

Myth 1: The Majority of Money Managers Are Great Stock Pickers

This may be the greatest myth of all. As I mentioned in the introduction of the book, there are some money managers who do indeed do great research and pick great stocks. But I believe that these asset managers are in the minority. The bulk of money managers are what I call "closet indexers." Rather than doing fundamental research, going out and meeting with companies, trying to understand new business models and new competition, and developing a long-term investment strategy, these "benchmark huggers" are simply trying to buy enough of the types of stocks (e.g., perhaps 100 or more) that will allow them to equal or just surpass the performance of the S&P 500. One story from my early days on Wall Street tells the tale.

When I was one of the managing directors running the private banking group at Cowen in the mid-1990s, there was one hardworking money manager who was an extremely nice guy. I always assumed that he was a very good stock picker who did tons of research. One afternoon, I went into his office after the market closed, and I looked at his portfolio. He was doing his end-of-the-day portfolio analysis—and he was looking at a sheet of paper that seemed foreign to me. That sheet was basically a description of his portfolio—95 to 100 stocks with information on each stock and the sector to which it belonged.

For example, if he owned IBM, it was in the S&P information technology sector. If he owned Pfizer, it was in the S&P pharmaceutical drug sector. Every night he would review the performance of his portfolio and compare it to the performance of the S&P 500. Did he underperform or outperform the S&P?

That was all he seemed to care about. He didn't appear to care whether or not his investments were actually good investments that made money for his clients.

That was a revelation to me at the time, and it has stayed with me all these years. Over the last decade of zero growth in equities, I had the epiphany that for the most part, "active managers" (money managers who select individual stocks for their portfolios) aren't true active managers (money managers who do their homework and conduct research). The more I traveled, met with money managers, and attended conferences, the more convinced I became that most money managers were closet indexers. If they could outperform the S&P 500 by even half a percent, they were pleased with their performance and declared themselves to be very successful (this outperformance looked good on their marketing materials).

Myth 2: The Compensation System for Wall Street Money Managers Is, "If I Make *You* Money, I Make *Myself* Money"

I am still shocked that most individual investors think that the compensation structure for Wall Street managers is based on the premise, "If I make *you* money, I make *myself* money." Now in the hedge fund world, a performance-based world in which hedge fund managers receive anywhere from 15 to 20 percent of the performance profits, that statement might be true. That segment of investing is designed for investors to pay for performance. But even in that world, hedge fund managers take a 1–2 percent management fee.

However, when you buy a mutual fund, and thus give money to a money manager, that manager's compensation is most likely tied to growth in assets, which isn't necessarily correlated with growth in performance. For example, take a money manager who works for a mutual fund family with a great marketing machine behind it. If he grows the assets he manages from, say, $1 billion to $2 billion, his compensation will go up, because it's directly tied to the growth of assets under management. Let's also assume, as with most mutual funds, that you are paying that mutual fund money manager a fee to manage your portfolio. Finally, let's assume that the S&P increases by 7 percent, but the fund loses 2 percent in the same time period. Even in that situation, in which both relative and total performance are in negative territory and the manager loses you money, his compensation package may double simply because assets under management doubled.

While it is worth noting that the great bulk of the compensation structures at asset managers and mutual fund companies are partially correlated with individual performance, they're much more highly correlated with the profitability of the firm, asset growth, and other such things. These are things that are not transparent to most investors, although they may be mentioned in the fund prospectus, which few investors read. So when you see an advertisement for a mutual fund or see a fund manager on CNBC asking you to invest your hard-earned money, she isn't telling you how she is compensated. That's why it is so important that you recognize that your interests and the interests of the money manager may not be aligned.

Myth 3: Money Managers Care about *Absolute* Performance

This myth is related to the first two, but it is so important that it is worth discussing on its own. It's not that no money managers care about the absolute performance—actual returns, not returns compared to an index—of the funds or money that they manage. Indeed, many fund managers care a great deal. But if you read the marketing materials of many mutual funds, the claim you find most often is that they are going to try to achieve *relative* performance by outperforming the market (most often the S&P 500). That's their objective.

You may believe that their objective is to make you money. Obviously, that's what they hope to accomplish. But when you invest with a money manager, you should expect him to report that he has, in essence, achieved remarkable things when he does better than the market as a whole or a portion of the market.

This is really where Wall Street goes off the rails. I can think of no other profession that adopts this type of performance measurement. If you go to a doctor and have a heart operation, the doctor and the hospital measure their success by a successful outcome of the operation. They don't say that they are successful simply because you are not as sick as the heart patient in the next bed.

The crazy thing about Wall Street is that you can invest with several different money managers, and they can all lose you a big percentage of your money, but each will still claim that she did a great job because she beat the market. It makes no sense, but that's just how it is, and you need to be aware of how money managers measure their performance. I feel that the key to successful money management is to achieve absolute positive returns. Losing money is losing money, and I feel that any money management or mutual fund company that measures its performance based on relative returns does not deserve your hard-earned dollars. That's because it is these kinds of companies that give themselves the most wiggle room in describing their performance. Let me give you an example of an extreme case of this.

Let's say that you invest in a socially responsible fund because you believe in investing in companies that do good things for people and for the planet. You read the fund prospectus, and it says that the fund will be benchmarking its performance against the S&P 500, but that there are certain sectors that it will avoid (such as liquor and tobacco stocks). A year goes by, and the S&P has a strong year: up by 12 percent. You also learn that in the second quarter of that year, there was a development out of Washington and the tax on liquor and tobacco was reduced by a significant margin. As a result, liquor and tobacco were the strongest performers of the S&P, up 35 and 40 percent, respectively, which helped fuel the strong performance of the benchmark S&P index.

Now here is where things get interesting. Although your socially responsive fund was down by 2 percent that year (versus the 12 percent increase in the S&P 500), the managers of that fund might tell you, "We outperformed." You scratch your head and ask, "How can that be? You lost money." They respond by telling you, "If you take liquor and tobacco, which represented 85 percent of the S&P's 12 percent rise, out of the equation, we actually outperformed because our fund beat the remainder of the S&P by almost two percentage points."

This kind of thing goes on every day at almost every asset management company. Almost all companies can come up with some excuse for why they did not add value to the benchmark. So you must be careful and pay attention to how the game is played so that you are not swayed by ridiculous claims that bear little resemblance to reality. The transparency—which most companies must live by—is just not there with many Wall Street products. Once again, Wall Street, unlike most other businesses, has its own set of rules, which often tend to obscure reality rather than reveal it. The same is not true in other consumer businesses. If you buy, say, a box of cereal, you know exactly what you are getting. You can look on the box and know the calorie count, the number of grams of protein and fat, and other such information. In the asset management business, you don't have that level of transparency.

Wall Street . . . has its own set of rules, which often tend to obscure reality rather than reveal it.

Here's one more example, taken from the Internet. Turn to the home page of T. Rowe Price, the investment management company, and what comes up in great big letters is the following claim:

Over 75% of our funds beat their Lipper averages.

Lipper, which is owned by the business reporting firm Reuters, gives the average level of performance for mutual funds of all types.

Dig deeper into the T. Rowe Price Web site by clicking on the "Learn more about our approach" button, and this is what comes up first:

Explore the T. Rowe Price difference.

Our disciplined, time-tested approach has proven successful for over 70 years in a variety of market conditions. In fact, for each 3-, 5-, and 10-year period ended 12/31/09, over 75% of our funds beat their Lipper average.*

The asterisk here refers to this statement at the bottom of that page of the Web site:

Based on cumulative total return, 123 of 169 (73%), 116 of 145, 118 of 133, and 56 of 71 T. Rowe Price funds (including all share classes and excluding funds used in insurance products) outperformed their Lipper average for the 1-, 3-, 5-, and 10-year periods ended 12/31/09, respectively. Not all funds outperformed for all periods. (Source for data: Lipper Inc.)

Now you see why I have never been a fan of asterisks.

Myth 4: An Index Fund Is the Best Way to Invest

It is well known among readers of books on investing that about nine out of every ten money managers tend to underperform the benchmark S&P 500. In light of that compelling statistic, many great investment figures, such as Warren Buffett and Vanguard Group founder John Bogle, have argued that individual investors are best off placing their money in index funds—that is, low-cost funds that mimic the performance of a benchmark index, like the S&P 500 (the most popular), the Russell 2000, or even the entire stock market (that is the ultimate index fund, one that allows you to buy the entire stock market).

Index investing is also called *passive investing*, since it does not involve a money manager selecting stocks for his fund. Instead, the stocks that make up an index fund are predetermined by their size and their place in a particular pool of stocks (the Russell 2000, for example, is "2,000 of the smallest securities based on a combination of their market cap and current index membership," so says Russell Investments). I feel that an index fund, especially over the next decade, is exactly the wrong place for an investor to put her hard-earned money. Advertisements that tell you the opposite are, in my view, false marketing. For example, an investor who decided to place her money in an S&P 500 index fund in 1999 lost money over the next 10 years, as we saw in the examples given in the last two chapters. That means that not only did she have no return on her money, but she had a negative return. That person would have been better off keeping her money in a CD or a savings account, even if the returns on these investments were only a few percentage points over the decade.

The basic premise of investing in an index fund is the notion that the law of averages is on your side, since, after all, 90 percent of asset managers do not beat the index and do not add value. However, that's hardly the whole story. As we discussed earlier, many money managers don't add value because they aren't even trying to do so; they are just trying to "hug" the benchmark. So we would have to discount a good percentage of money managers, since their actions place them closer to the passive investing camp than the active investing camp.

The other big problem I have with an index fund is that when you just put your money in an index fund, you're not taking advantage of the lucrative investment opportunities that present themselves all the time. Instead, you're tying up your money in a fund that I believe will go nowhere for a long time.

That means your money is held hostage when markets go down, and you are, in essence, limiting your returns when markets go up. If you actively manage your investments the way I show you in Part Two of this book, then you will increase your chances of achieving a long-term positive return that outperforms the markets and the average benchmark returns.

When I actively managed money, I typically beat both the market averages and achieved positive results for my clients— not just relative returns, but absolute returns. I always focused on absolute returns because I felt that if I was not delivering positive returns for my investors, I was not doing my job. Don't get me wrong; one can't always achieve positive returns. There are stocks that surprise even the best of money managers. But if you can bat about .600, then you can do what I did and achieve a positive net result most of the time.

But what about those people who argue that index investing is the low-cost way to invest? Aren't they right? Well, they are right in that index funds can be purchased very cheaply.

However, that misses the point. When you manage your own money successfully, you do not have to lose as much on the downside when markets fall, and you can make more money when markets go up. And let's not forget the key premise of this book: You can make money when markets go nowhere. Even though you are managing only your own money, you can be among the one out of ten "managers" on average that add value to your own portfolio.

Myth 5: Your Broker or Money Manager Has Your Best Interests at Heart Every Time He Recommends a Particular Stock or Mutual Fund

Once again, I do not mean that every broker or money manager is an evil being who is trying to separate you from your money. However, there are certain realities of the investment business that you should be aware of so that you can properly weigh all of the advice that you receive from financial "professionals."

Let's say you live in Denver, and you invest your money with a large investment company that I will call XYZ (I won't use real names to protect the innocent). You have a local financial advisor from firm XYZ who works with you to develop your financial objectives and put together your stock and fund portfolio. You selected this firm after seeing a heartwarming TV commercial from this company that features an older couple sitting on a beach, discussing their plans to retire early and buy a gorgeous house on the water. Another ad that caught your attention was from another financial company; it featured a young girl graduating from college and another young, beautiful woman on her wedding day—in both situations accompanied by both her father and the family's financial advisor.

What is not obvious from these one-sided advertisements from "financial supermarkets"—which is what large, sprawling investment banking firms with different units and departments are often called—is that financial advisors from these firms serve a number of different masters at the same time. That's one of the dirty little secrets of the money management business, and it is more widespread than you might think. Let's dig deeper so that you can see precisely what is happening behind the scenes.

That financial advisor that you are counting on reviews the research that is generated internally at her company, talks to her company's strategists, and also talks regularly to the firm's investment policy committee—the team responsible for setting the general strategic direction and parameters of that firm's investment choices and decisions.

While you are a client of a brokerage firm or investment bank, your financial advisor is supposed to recommend investments that are in your best interests, your advisor may be serving two interests at the same time—yours and those of an outside money management firm.

Put another way, when you are a client of one of the big firms, your investment advisor, wealth advisor, or whatever he calls himself is hostage to what his firm has in its product pouch. So if your broker's firm has a selling agreement with a certain mutual fund company, then your money manager or financial advisor has to sell what's on his firm's approved or "recommended to buy" list.

So while you may think that your advisor is recommending investments that he feels meet your investment objectives perfectly, he may in fact be making recommendations based on an entirely different set of criteria. For example, Suncor Energy may be the best energy stock out there, but your advisor is not going to tell you that. Instead, his firm may have Exxon Mobil or Royal Dutch on its recommended list, so that's the stock you'll hear about. And the same is true for mutual funds. I am not saying that this is necessarily a bad thing; it's just how the sausage is made on Wall Street. When you deal with large financial institutions, you must accept the fact that you are a small fish in a large pond. Only then can you bring a healthy amount of skepticism and scrutiny to the investments that are being recommended for you and your family.

This subject is a bit tricky, because, as in any industry, there are a handful of people who abuse the system and grab all the headlines (think Bernie Madoff). However, the vast majority of the financial advisors that Team K dealt with were honest people who went to work every day trying to do right by their clients. But the fact that financial advisors serve several constituencies simultaneously is just the way the investing business operates.

Myth 6: Talking Heads Always Have Something Meaningful to Say

We have all watched so-called investment experts on every business program and channel. These pundits come from every walk of life in the investment world, from business book authors to portfolio managers to CEOs of S&P 500 corporations.

As someone who was on the air from the earliest days of financial television (I was one of the original cohosts of CNBC's successful morning program *Squawk Box*), I have always felt a deep sense of responsibility to provide a realistic and complete assessment of the true state of things—whether I am discussing a specific stock or the overall economy. I give my perspective based on information from the many financial industry people I have met over the years, in addition to other observations, such as what I have read online or in the financial pages, or what I may have watched on financial television that day or that week. I strive to keep things "real," whether I am on CNBC or being interviewed by business journalists from such publications as *BusinessWeek*, *Fortune*, or *Forbes*. As someone who often interacts with individual investors, I have some very strong feelings about what constitutes fair and ethical behavior for "experts" who impart advice on financial television. There are a few things that really bother me when I am observing experts and pundits on financial television.

My first pet peeve involves transparency, or the lack thereof: portfolio managers, financial advisors, and the like will come on television and talk about a specific strategy or a specific stock that they own. That expert might say, "I like IBM" or "I like GE." For many years, the person interviewing that expert did not even ask whether or not that person, or his firm, owned that stock. That all changed about a decade ago when certain analysts got into all kinds of trouble when it was discovered that they were gaming the system by saying one thing about a stock on the air but telling their friends something totally different in private. So that problem was solved by instituting new rules for the game.

However, I see an equally egregious problem today that no one is talking about: After that portfolio manager tells the interviewer that he owns IBM, no one ever follows up or presses the issue by asking this key question:

> What does that stock investment represent as a percentage of your total assets under management? You're making a strong argument for why you like something, well, is it ½ of 1 percent of your portfolio? Or is it 8 percent?

Not long ago, I was on CNBC's *Fast Money* program, and I mentioned the stock American Tower. I specifically made the point that my former team owns 8 million shares of this stock, priced at $40 per share. There's a world of difference between what I reported and the typical money manager, who reports only that she likes stock XYZ. What if the fund manages $100 million in assets, but owns only 3,000 shares of that stock, or less than ⅒ of 1 percent of her portfolio? I have a major problem with the whole disclosure thing. That's why I wish that people who work in financial broadcasting and as magazine journalists would act like people who are trying to manage their own money, using the information that they uncover as a source of information in making their own investment decisions.

The next issue harks back to the problem I mentioned earlier about whether or not that portfolio manager owns the stocks that he is recommending. And this is something that I find very strange. When I managed money, many prospective clients would ask, "Do you invest in your own fund?" And from where we sat, on Team K, it was a no-brainer. If you are going to give me your hard-earned money to manage, you can bet that the answer is,

"Of course we invest in our own fund." I think it would be absolutely ludicrous if you don't "eat your own cooking."

I can't tell you how many money managers I have seen on television who violate this key principle all the time. The money manager rattles off a list of the stocks she is recommending and briefly explains why she likes each of those stocks. When the interviewer asks, usually at the end of the interview, "Which of these stocks do you own in the fund that you manage?" I am flabbergasted when the money manager says, "None of them." As a viewer, I think to myself, "Why does this person have *any* credibility whatsoever?"

To me, it is "garbage in, garbage out." If you are going to make decisions based on what other people recommend, then you have to know the whole story. For example, let's say that a portfolio manager comes on CNBC and says that he owns Amazon and Google. He may not even like those two stocks, but he recommends them because he is overweighted in technology and must own some of the biggest tech stocks if he is going to stay overweighted in technology. Will that manager hold those stocks for 10 days if they go up 10 percent, or will he hold them for the long term? You often get only one dimension from that person, while investing is always a three-dimensional endeavor.

I can recall debating a few of these money managers when I ran into them. I would ask them about the "recommend" versus "own" issue. And they would come back and say, "Well, we own only these kinds of stocks in this fund, so I can't buy stocks that do not fit into those categories."

One story comes to mind as to how some money managers box themselves in by the way they classify the funds that they manage. As emphasized throughout the book, investors need to know what motivates different groups of buyers and sellers. That is, they have to understand why a certain money manager might dump tens of thousands of shares of a stock that he still likes. Investors also need to understand why a money manager may not buy a single share of a stock that he absolutely loves. Let's take a close look at an example of the latter.

One of my all-time favorite stocks, and one that I mentioned often on CNBC, is Suncor Energy (SU). I have a great story about Suncor that will illustrate why it is so important to understand what may be happening behind the scenes before making an investment decision.

I warn you that this was one of the most ludicrous things I had ever heard in my 20 years in the investing game.

I was up in Fort McMurray, Canada, which is where Suncor is based. At this point, the stock had doubled while we owned it, zipping from $30 per share to $60. At that time, the market capitalization—that is, the company's stock market worth—was roughly $9.5 billion. One of my colleagues and I got into a conversation with an analyst from another firm who was there on a company-sponsored information trip.

"Oh, do you own Suncor?" we asked. (We were sure he did; after all, why else was he there?)

We were blown away when the analyst said that he didn't.

Not a single share.

He said that his money management firm had been following Suncor closely for two years, and loved everything that the firm was doing.

"Well then, why don't you own the stock?" I asked.

"We can't buy the stock," declared the analyst. "We are large-cap growth managers, and it hasn't reached our threshold. It has to hit $10 billion in market capitalization before we can touch it."

So here is a guy who is sitting on his hands, watching that stock go from $30 to $60, and he can't touch it because of his mandate as a large-cap money manager. So you've got to know that's how this game is being played. You have to understand that when you are buying a stock from somebody or selling a stock to someone else, the person on the other side of the transaction may be buying or selling not because he thinks the stock is going up or down, but because of certain ridiculous idiosyncrasies of the investing game.

Put another way, money managers are often boxed in by their own labels. Large-cap money managers can't buy stocks until they reach a certain level. To succeed, investors and money managers need to "unwrap the box" so that they are not bound by stupid labels that limit their investment opportunities. Similarly, small-cap money managers cannot hold on to a winning stock once it is no longer a small-cap stock, even if that company is doing everything right. These are the kinds of strange "rules" that investors need to take note of in order to understand Wall Street's underbelly.

In my opinion, no one should ever recommend any stock or security that she does not herself own, either personally or in the fund that she manages, or both.

Myth 7: All Sell-Side Analysts Do Original Work and Research

Before you ask, "What is a sell-side analyst?" let me define my terms. A *sell-side analyst* works for a brokerage company like Merrill Lynch, Morgan Stanley, Goldman Sachs, or Raymond James, and makes specific recommendations to the firm's clients on which stocks to own and how they should be rated.

A *buy-side analyst* works for a mutual fund company or a pension fund, and makes recommendations to the firm's money managers on which stocks to own. His research is only for people *inside* the company and is not revealed to people outside the firm.

Let me make the distinction between the two even clearer. Let's take the health-care company Johnson & Johnson (J&J). There is an analyst at the investment company First Boston who follows J&J. Her job is to send out research to First Boston's clients on what is happening at J&J. She may send out a report right after

J&J issues its quarterly report, identifying what she considers to be the key issues facing the company, outside factors that are important, financial statement analysis, and more. She might issue a buy, sell, or hold opinion about what clients should do with the stock. That's roughly the job description of a sell-side analyst.

A buy-side analyst, on the other hand, tells the portfolio managers at his company whether a particular stock should be in a portfolio or out of a portfolio. Let's take the fund company Fidelity Investments. Fidelity has a buy-side analyst that follows J&J. He speaks directly with the portfolio managers within Fidelity about J&J. For example, the manager of the Magellan fund, which owns large-cap stocks, has an interest in J&J, as does the portfolio manager of Fidelity's Select Health Care Fund. The buy-side analyst gives his opinion about J&J—but that opinion stays within the institution.

If you are a retail investor and you are doing it yourself, you never really have access to what buy-side analysts are doing or saying. When individual investors come into contact with analysts, 99 times out of 100, what they're reading or hearing is something put out by a sell-side analyst. Buy-side analysts are working just for their own constituencies. So if the Fidelity analyst, for example, decided to internally downgrade J&J for the firm's portfolio managers to a "sell," you, the individual investor, will not know that. You may find it out a year later when you look at the mutual fund holdings and you see that J&J, which once was a top holding, is no longer in the portfolio.

Now, the myth is that a lot of sell-side analysts do a lot of original work. This is not necessarily true, and it comes back to this whole notion of relative performance. I feel that the majority of sell-side analysts are little more than reporters. What do I mean by that? What they're doing is taking the public regulatory filings, technical reports like the 10-Qs and 10-Ks (these are quarterly and annual reports, respectively, that a public company must file with the SEC that include financials and information on compensation, growth, and other such factors), earnings releases, the company's press releases about new products, new marketing agreements, and so on, and filtering this information back to their constituencies. In essence, what they are telling their clients is information that, for the most part, is readily available on J&J's Web site. They may inject a couple of new things or opinions into the report, but they seldom offer game-changing opinions or information. In the J&J example, they may report that J&J's sales were up by X percent, total pharmaceutical sales were up by Y percent, and generic product sales were down by Z percent. This represents a vast departure from the way things were done, say, 20 to 30 years ago.

In the 1980s, for example, sell-side analysts did much more original research than they do today. Back then, it was much more about doing your homework, predicting and projecting possible future scenarios for the companies you covered. Much of the change in the job performance of sell-side analysts has resulted from the regulatory changes that have taken place in the last few years. Years ago, companies could sit down with sell-side analysts and help them try to project what the future of the company might look like a year or two down the road.

Today, regulations such as Regulation FD (Reg FD) have altered the landscape and the world of investing. Adopted in the year 2000, Reg FD was put in place to make sure that no one constituency had any information advantage over any other group. It mandates that all information issued by publicly traded companies must be released to everyone at the same time. Reg FD certainly raised the level of transparency, but it also created a regulatory hurdle, so that when companies meet with analysts, they must immediately release the information they provide to everyone else in order to level the playing field. That's a good thing, but one unintended consequence of Reg FD is that it made the job of a sell-side analyst more that of a reporter than of a predictor or projector of future trends.

Thus, 20 or 30 years ago, sell-side analysts would meet with the company, try to understand its five-year business plan, build out a model in which they tried to put in certain assumptions about growth, and then try to figure out the correct valuation of the company. That's not true today.

Let's take it back to what the myth is here. The myth is that sell-side analysts do original work and add real value. However, I feel strongly that investors should never make decisions based on what they hear come from a sell-side analyst's mouth (or his pen). When you hear sell-side analysts upgrading or downgrading stocks, it's not necessarily because they've changed their opinion about that specific company or that specific stock; it may be because the firm as a whole has changed its opinion on a macro outlook. They are

> When you rely on the research of others, you know only what they know, and what they don't know is what hurts you.

just giving you back what's out there already, in essence, regurgitating information. That takes me back to one of my favorite Team K investing realities: "When you rely on the research of others, you know only what they know, and what they don't know is what hurts you."

Of course, I have come across a handful of analysts in my 20-year career who actually stick their necks out to make assumptions and bold calls about a stock. But the number of analysts who actually think outside the box is perhaps 10 to 20 percent and no more.

Myth 8: Stocks Will Always Go Up in the Long-Run

This myth sells a lot of financial products. It is also very effective in selling money management services. The statement that stocks, mutual funds, ETFs, and other such products always go up is a pretty big statement, but I feel that it is a deceptive statement. The truth is, we don't know. We know that if you look at certain time periods in which you hold nothing but equities—as opposed to other asset classes, such as bonds or cash—you will earn a better rate of return.

However, there have been long periods of time during which stocks have gone nowhere. We saw that in the late 1960s through the 1970s until stocks turned around in 1982. And we saw a similar scenario play out over the last decade, as we discussed in Chapter 1. But where is the proof that stocks will go up over the next 100 years?

There is absolutely no evidence that a "buy-and-hold" strategy will work in the future. The major assumption of this book is that buy and hold is no longer a viable investment strategy, especially with the coming range-bound market. When you ask people in the buy-and-hold camp what evidence they have that stocks will definitely go up in the years ahead, you almost never get a consistent or concise answer. A few of the typical responses include things like, "Stocks will protect you in periods of inflation," or, "Stocks with dividends and distributions, if properly invested, will provide a greater return than fixed income."

I contend that buy and hold is dead and buy and sell is alive and well. As we'll discuss in Chapter 7, buy and hold was predicated on companies' ability to maintain competitive advantages for decades. Today, with a rapidly changing global marketplace, and with information available to all worldwide market participants in real time, those advantages vanish quickly.

However, there are two ways in which you can make money on equities. First, you make money when the value of the stock goes up. However, if you choose not to sell that stock, then the additional wealth that has been created is paper wealth, not money that you can go out and spend in the supermarket. But if you buy and sell, then you have the capital gain. The second way of making money is through dividends and distributions, which we'll talk about later.

Stock prices go up because the demand for a particular stock rises by a meaningful percentage (e.g., because of anything from a new successful product launch or the hiring of a great new CEO). When demand for a given stock increases, the price of that stock likely rises as well. In that situation the multiple for that stock may expand, meaning that investors are valuing these companies more highly (e.g., investors may decide that a particular stock is now worth 25 times its current earnings rather than 20 times). However, what if for, say, the next 20 years, multiples actually go down? That is, what if, despite new innovations and favorable management changes, the multiple that people are willing to pay to own stocks actually decreases?

Earlier we established the fact that the long-term mean multiple has been about 15. When stocks trade at 10 to 12 times earnings, they are considered cheap; on the other hand, when stocks trade at 16 to 18 times earnings, they're expensive.

But who knows? Who knows if the next generation of investors isn't going to be quite content with a fixed-income return and call it a day, therefore depressing the multiple of the stocks to the lower end of the range?

Just buying stocks because over the long term they always go up is like saying, "I'm going to play blackjack every day because ultimately I'll have to have a winning hand." By the time you have that winning hand, you may be down $1,000 and down to your last $50. Look at how much money you'll have lost waiting for that winning hand.

It's that type of completely flawed thinking that's behind the philosophy that stocks always go up.

In short, in the years ahead, betting on the stock market as a whole to go up may be the worst bet an investor can make.

Myth 9: Individual Investors Can't Beat the Pros

This myth is related to several other observations in this chapter, but because it is one of the major themes of the book, it is important enough to merit its own entry here.

Several of the reasons that individuals can beat investment professionals have already been discussed. For one thing, many money managers follow the "herd mentality" by hugging a benchmark and being closet indexers.

As an individual investor, you are not constrained by many of the things that trip up so many money managers. You don't need to answer to anyone but yourself when you buy and sell securities. You don't have to worry about beating the S&P 500 or getting new investors to put new money in your fund. You can do your own research, create your own investment thesis, and act upon the events that are happening without answering to other constituencies.

Here is a case in point that proves the argument. Suppose you decide that you want to buy stock in a fast-growing retailer that sells surfing clothes for teens. You feel that the company has good growth potential, you like its strategy for identifying new markets, and you think it has a product that's unique.

An institutional money manager who is managing $10 billion also decides that he likes this company and wants to buy the stock. The key difference is that you are far more nimble when it comes to taking a position in a stock. Let me elaborate on that statement.

In this situation, you have a $200,000 account, and you decide to buy 1,000 shares at $20 per share. That stock now represents 10 percent of your portfolio. The mutual fund manager with the $10 billion fund must go out and buy 5 million shares if the stock is to make the same relative contribution to his portfolio.

If he purchases 5 million shares of the same stock at the same price, that is a $100 million investment. Let's also assume that the total capitalization of that stock is $1.3 billion. Given the large number of shares he had to buy, it probably took him two to three weeks to accumulate his 5 million shares, since there are only so many shares of each stock traded each day.

A few days after he has amassed his position, you and the portfolio manager read a *Wall Street Journal* story that says that this retailer now has new competition (a company that is expanding from a regional firm to a national competitor), and that because of this new rival, it is going to need to alter its marketing and rollout plans. In fact, it has to refocus its "old" business model. Because of this story, the company's stock price falls from $20 to $17 in a single day. The difference between you as an individual and the institutional manager is you're actually in a more advantageous position.

The reason you have a leg up on that portfolio manager is that you can sell that stock because something has changed (we're going to touch upon selling discipline in Part Two). You can unwind that position by selling all the shares in one quick trade. The portfolio manager, unfortunately, is stuck with those shares for at least a couple of weeks because it will take him that much time to sell them. As a result of that reality, he may opt to hold on to those shares rather than sell them. If he was smaller, like you, he might make the opposite decision and decide to sell the shares, or sell the shares and buy them back at a later date. But because the amounts he is dealing with are so large, the asset manager does not have that luxury. You can avoid some of the losses that an asset manager would face by getting out quickly.

This is a case in which being small means being nimble, which gives the smaller entity the edge. There are cases in which being larger is a great help, but not all of the time. Warren Buffett, the biggest fish in the sea, gets special breaks and influences the companies he chooses to invest in. But you don't need to be a Warren Buffett to be a first-rate manager of your own money.

Now you may be incredulous, saying, "Come off it; there is no way that the small guy has the advantage over the big institutional portfolio managers." However, the evidence does not lie.

Between 2000 and 2009, according to the *Wall Street Journal*, fund company Janus Capital Group lost a stunning $58.4 billion in shareholder wealth. Once heralded as one of the best fund companies around, it amassed a decade-long total return of minus 1 percent a year. Its performance was so bad that the *Journal* called Janus the worst "wealth destroyer," based on an analysis conducted by investment rating company Morningstar, Inc. And Janus was not alone. Putnam Investments lost $46.4 billion of its clients' money, AllianceBernstein Holding lost $11.4 billion, and Invesco lost $10.1 billion. The total numbers by category are even worse: large-cap growth funds shed some $107.6 billion in value, while high-tech funds surrendered $62.8 billion of their shareholders' wealth.

These are some of the biggest sharks in the investment waters, and look at their results. Surely you believe that you can do better. Let's move on to Part Two so that you can acquire the skills and strategies that will help you to beat even some of the best fund managers.

Part Two

STRATEGIES AND DISCIPLINES FOR OUTPERFORMANCE

4

TAKE THE OTHER
SIDE OF THE TRADE

To outperform the market, investors need to know precisely how to identify the most overcrowded investment vehicles so that they can not only avoid them, but buy the other side of the trade. I have always considered myself to be an investor who goes against the herd. That's because research has shown that the majority of investors are usually on the wrong side of the trade. As mentioned earlier, most investors make the wrong moves at the wrong times.

For example, when the stock market cratered in the first quarter of 2009, countless investors took their money out of the market in March, when the Dow was trading at about 6,500. Had they left their money in the market, they would have increased their holdings by more than 60 percent in a year—the kind of gain that usually comes around only once or twice in a generation. This is further proof that market timing is another failed technique of the great Wall Street marketing machine.

As another example of how the herd usually moves in the wrong direction, in November 2009, the single most over-crowded trade was shorting the dollar. (*Shorting* an investment vehicle means that we borrow shares and sell an investment that we currently do not own. When the investment decreases in value, we buy it back and return the borrowed shares to the lender, pocketing the difference in price.) This means that large institutions, hedge funds, and big-time investors were all betting that the dollar would continue to go down against other major currencies, such as the yen and the euro. This was because of all the extreme actions implemented by the Fed and Treasury that we have discussed earlier.

That is why, at the time, I urged people to purchase the U.S. dollar while the rest of the world was shorting it. In my experience, being on the less popular side of a trade pays handsome dividends. The easiest way to buy the dollar is through an exchange-traded fund (ETF). The great thing about an ETF is it allows you to buy a basket of stocks by purchasing a single security, as if you were buying a single stock. In this case, purchasing the ETF with the ticker symbol UUP allows investors to own the U.S. dollar for almost zero fees. This is a great way to hedge or protect your stock portfolio, as UUP is likely to rise when your stock portfolio falls. Here's why: if interest rates go up and the dollar rebounds, there is a very good chance that certain stocks will fall; thus, owning the dollar will provide an excellent hedge to protect your portfolio. There are many different kinds of investments (such as bonds, gold, and oil) that will rise when stock markets fall, which is why these are powerful investment vehicles that act as a hedge in a stock downturn. Hedging is an important concept that I will dive into far more deeply in the final chapter of the book.

Ten years ago, individual investors who were managing their own money did not have the ability to hedge their stock portfolios with these simple, low-fee products. We will show investors how to take advantage of the many financial innovations that have been created.

Every Time You Buy a Share . . .

One thing people always forget is that every time you buy a share of stock, somebody else is selling it to you. And every time you sell a share, somebody else is buying it. While that may seem like a truly obvious thing, it really isn't. There are very few places in commerce where that type of interaction takes place. For example, when you go into a deli and buy a sandwich, the sandwich is made, you eat the sandwich, and at the end of the experience, the sandwich is gone. There's an applicable example with food.

Let's take another example. Assume that you are about to purchase a new computer. The computer has been manufactured and shipped to a retailer, and it is now purchased by you. That computer is now off the market, as you own it.

That's what makes the capital markets so unique: There is simply no end to the transaction. Every time somebody is buying, somebody else is selling. There's no terminal value for that exchange. Each transaction is just one facet of the movement of that paper, which—barring some sort of extreme scenario, such as a bankruptcy filing or a merger or acquisition involving that company—goes on indefinitely.

Let's look at a specific case. One stock that I have followed closely is a company called Lululemon, a company that makes athletic apparel for yoga, dance, running, and other activities for men and women. I am shorting the stock, and as I write this chapter, Lululemon is selling for about $26 per share. The stock is down a little more than $1, or 4 percent, in a 24-hour period.

One of the first things we know about this stock is that there are more sellers than buyers. How do we come to that conclusion? With everything else being equal, meaning that everybody who is buying and selling theoretically has the same information, the stock is going down, so there must be more sellers than buyers. The opposite is obviously also true. If the stock price is rising, we know that there are more buyers than sellers.

When there's positive news out that may drive the price of that stock up, a seller will still be willing to sell you those shares, but only at a higher price. That's because he believes that the news that is out there has created more value in the company, and the market has reinforced that belief. And the opposite holds true as well; if there is bad news about a company whose stock you own, perhaps involving a new competitor taking market share away from that company, then the buyer will take that dislocation in the marketplace and use it to her advantage to entice you to sell her your shares at a lower price.

While this may seem simple and obvious, I argue that the majority of the time, people who are buying and selling shares are thinking only about what *they* want to do, as opposed to exploring the real underlying motivation of the person on the other side of the trade.

Let me use an analogy from the world of gambling. Great poker players don't play only their own cards—they play the cards of the other players at the table. Only the weakest of poker players plays only his own cards, and a player that does so usually ends up losing his shirt. He has dealt himself a huge disadvantage. Alternatively, a strong poker player can win even when she doesn't have the best cards at the table. By figuring out what the other players have, she may be able to bluff others out of the hand, knowing that while she doesn't have a strong hand, neither do any of the other players at the table. So her rivals may all fold their cards if she makes a really strong bet.

The game of blackjack offers a similar analogy. When you sit down at a blackjack table, you may think that you are playing only "the house." But that's not true. You need to pay attention to the behavior of the other players at the table. They are an important factor, especially if you are following a disciplined approach while at least one or two of the other players are novices who tend to do the wrong things at the wrong times.

Let me extend this blackjack example: Let's assume that your strategy is that when the dealer shows a low card (a two through a six) and you also have a low card, you will never "hit" (take another card). That's your strategy, but other players at your table are not disciplined and instead take a card even when the dealer is showing a low card. In that scenario, the probability of that dealer's "busting" (e.g., going over 21) based on normal circumstances has now gone down because the other guys are throwing probability to the wind and taking cards when they shouldn't. It's not random because you know that there are only a certain number of face cards in the deck.

Let's take the example back to investing. If you are not thinking about the factors that are motivating the sellers when you are buying, you're putting yourself at a competitive disadvantage. Obviously you are buying shares when others are selling. But the greatest way to take advantage of others' missteps is to try to identify when sales are being made for nonrational reasons.

Apple Computer offers an ideal example of why it is so important to understand the motivations of others. In January 2009, Apple CEO Steve Jobs announced that he was about to take a leave of absence because of health issues that were "more complex" than he had first thought. He told employees and sharcholders that he would return in June, but that he would "be around for major strategic decisions."

However, skeptical investors who felt that Jobs was the greatest CEO around did not believe that Jobs would be back so soon, and many thousands of them dumped their Apple shares. As a result, Apple lost about 8 percent of its value in after-hours trading on the day that Jobs made that announcement. Around five months later, at the end of June, Jobs returned to work—just as he had said he would.

Now, let's look at what happened to the stock. When Jobs announced that he was taking that leave, the stock dipped into the 80s. A year later, Apple was making new record highs, trading well above $200 per share. If you were one of the strategic investors who felt that Jobs would indeed return and that the company would not fall off a cliff in the interim, you might have viewed that announcement as a buying opportunity. Had you bought those shares, you would have more than doubled your money, achieving a stunning return in excess of 150 percent. That is why it is important to examine the motives of the guy on the other side of the trade. Let's look at another reason that shares of a particular stock move for irrational reasons.

Let's say the manager of a large-cap growth fund at a mutual fund company resigns. Another manager takes over the existing portfolio, and the new manager decides that he isn't going to take the time to even review the stocks in that portfolio. He clearly isn't interested in doing the fundamental research. Instead, he wants to sink or swim on his own stock choices. One would think that the changes in that portfolio would be made in a rational way, but that's not always the case. There are many managers who just decide, "The day I take over this fund, I want my own names in the portfolio." I learned this lesson firsthand in my first days on my first job in the business.

After graduating from business school, I took a job at J.R.O. Associates, which was one of the early hedge funds. I worked with this incredible portfolio manager, Marc Howard, one of the best traders of all time. He was one of the main reasons that J.R.O. was one of the best-known and best-performing hedge funds from the late 1980s to the mid-1990s. The principles at J.R.O. were John Oppenheimer and Marc Howard, and I learned a great deal trading and working for this duo. It was from them that I learned that portfolio managers often do a "do over" by selling everything in a portfolio. Having just graduated from business school and thinking about a stock market in a very fundamental and academic way, this was very foreign to me, and I am sure it is foreign to the majority of individual investors as well.

However, there are many days when professional money managers decide to just get everything off "the sheet," as it is called. A trader may be having a bad six months or a bad three months and may decide to just dump everything. When that happens, you may see a stock go down 4 to 5 percent with no news on that company. You check the company Web site, look at other investment sites, and assume that there has to be some reason that the stock is selling off so sharply. But it might simply be a case where a portfolio manager just wants to get out.

There are other examples of why stocks are sold for less than rational reasons. Throughout the book, we talk about the huge amounts of money that go toward index benchmarking. When, say, Standard & Poor's decides to move certain stocks into and out of the S&P 500, certain unintended consequences ensue. Once it is announced that a certain stock, say Norfolk Southern, is going into the S&P 500 index, index funds mirroring that index must purchase a certain number of shares of that particular stock. What is not known is how many money managers are trying to mimic the index, therefore creating artificial buying demand by buying shares of that same security. And the opposite holds true as well. When a stock is going out of an index, then money managers may create artificial selling demand for the same reasons, only this time, it's because closet indexers are selling shares.

One of My First—and Best—Lessons

There is another story from my earliest days on Wall Street that also illustrates why it is so important to buy when others are selling. My first day on Wall Street took place at J.R.O. in the early 1990s. Many of my friends from the school where I got my MBA went into training programs at large companies like Goldman Sachs, Morgan Stanley, Kidder Peabody, or Donaldson Lufkin Jenrette (notice that some of these firms do not exist any longer). Their experience at those firms was very different from the experience I got at J.R.O.

For example, I was told to dress casually at the hedge fund, whereas the more buttoned-up investment banks insisted on suits and ties. On my first day, I donned a pair of jeans, loafers, and a button-down shirt. About midway through that morning, one of the firm's principals, Marc Howard, said to me, "Kaminsky, I want you to go to a road show and listen to this company talk about their IPO." I didn't know what a road show was, and I was too embarrassed to ask. While I knew what an IPO was from business school, I had no idea what this event was all about.

As I was walking out the door, ready to head over to the upscale Metropolitan Club for this company presentation, hosted by the investment banking firm of Ladenburg Thalmann, one of my colleagues, Tim Grazioso, stopped me. He said, "Gary, I hope you're going to go home and put a suit on." Learning rather quickly to keep a suit in the office at all times, I made my way to my apartment on 84th Street, threw on a suit, and rushed over to the road show. The company presenting was some sort of technology database provider (this was in the pre-Internet days, when the most popular programs were Lotus 123, dBase, and WordPerfect).

Listening to the company's presentation explaining what it was going to do, I literally had no idea what the firm's business mission statement was or if the firm was ever going to make any money. I also had no idea how I would go back to the office and explain any of this to my bosses. I looked at the prospectus and saw that the company had been losing money for three years since its inception, and the analysts were estimating that the company would continue to lose money as it built out its business over the next three years (great investment, right?). Returning to the office at 59th and Lexington, I quietly walked back to my desk and tried to hide out. It was now 2:00 p.m.

At about 3:45, Marc Howard stood up in front of everybody and said in a loud voice, "Kaminsky, what did you think of that road show? Do you think we should be buying that stock?" It was while I was walking to the middle of the trading floor that I concluded that my career on Wall Street, barely one day old, was just about to end. Howard asked me what I thought about the company, and I decided I had no choice but to be honest.

I told him that (1) I didn't understand what the company did, (2) I couldn't follow its strategy, and (3) it appeared to me that the company would continue to lose money for years in the future. So I suggested, in light of these factors, that this was not a stock that the firm should even consider buying. All of a sudden I felt a rush of adrenaline and realized that my career probably would not end that day. Feeling heroic and a bit cocky at this point, I quietly walked back to my desk.

Howard waited a few minutes, then said to me, "Kaminsky, you moron, do you know what we do here? We buy stocks and we *sell* stocks!" The point of this story is to emphasize the lesson I learned that day, one that has been with me for my entire 20-year career and that stays with me to this day.

When I attended that research meeting, I went there like most investors, thinking only about buying the stock. Should we buy the stock or not buy the stock? I did not even consider any other options, since it seemed to me to be a black-and-white decision. Of course, there was another option.

I never went to another company presentation without thinking of the lesson that Howard was trying to explain to me that day, and that was that we didn't have to buy shares; in fact, we could do the opposite by shorting that stock. If we thought that the stock was bad and that the buyers were going to artificially inflate its value because it was being hyped to the rafters, we could short the stock and make money that way.

On that day, I became a believer in the advantages that one can gain by understanding that most people think only about buying a stock and never about selling it. It was Howard's comment, *"Do you know what we do?"* that proved to be the decisive factor. Based on the company's bleak outlook, we decided to short this stock the minute it became public because it was going to be artificially priced at a level that was unrealistic.

We figured that this company, whose stock would be priced somewhere between $10 and $12 per share, would continue to lose money and continue to bleed away shareholders' equity. We figured that within nine months or so, that $10+ stock would be trading for about $2 to $3 per share. In the end, the scenario played out pretty much as we had forecasted.

In that two-year period at J.R.O. Associates, we consistently made more money finding companies like this, where the equity was overvalued and the stocks were being artificially marked up with unrealistic expectations. Thinking "inside the box" makes you focus only on buying a stock and hoping it goes up. Thinking "outside the box" makes you realize that taking advantage of artificial buys and artificial sells is another avenue for creating wealth. Taking advantage of artificial buying prices and artificial selling prices is how you create excess returns.

Shorting will be an important method of making money as we approach the zero-growth decade ahead. Realizing that will give you an advantage because the vast majority of investors out there believe falsely that stocks always go up (which we disproved in the previous chapter), and because investors have an instilled philosophy that the way to make money in stock markets is to make money on the long side, or make money when stocks go up. But you don't need to be a hedge fund to make money on the short side. Today, unlike

> Thinking "outside the box" makes you realize that [there is] another avenue for creating wealth.

1990, when the only way to make money was by shorting specific company stocks or options, you've got hundreds of ways to short the market with ETFs that are linked to various industries, sectors, and commodities. So if you have a strong opinion one way or another, as a retail investor, you can go long or short a sector and have double or triple leverage without having to go out and have a futures account, which is a wonderful opportunity available to all investors.

Before closing out this J.R.O. story, let me add a footnote: At J.R.O., we had this beautiful American flag on a wall display. Potential clients or company officials who visited our offices could not miss it. Located in the reception area, it said, *"Invest in America, Buy Puts"* (puts are option instruments that allow investors to bet that a stock or an index will go down). While you may ask, "What does that mean? What does that have to do with anything?" you have to think outside the box and avoid traditional thinking.

People think that "Invest in America" means go long stocks: Buy stocks and hold them for some period of time. But you must also recognize that while buying puts theoretically will not create any new products or any new jobs, it is when you take advantage of these dislocations that you create excess returns for yourself in the market. Every time I met with a company, every time I looked at a potential investment, that sign—"Invest in America, Buy Puts"—was always inside my brain. I was always thinking, "If I'm going to buy this stock, what is the person selling it to me thinking? What is his rational reason for trying to determine the value for which he's going to sell it to me now?"

Although I cannot prove it, during my 20 years on Wall Street, if someone were able to go back and record the results, I believe that we made more money over the life of the investment when we bought stocks on down days than when we bought them on up days. You may argue that, well, that's pretty obvious. Every time you're buying on a down day, you're buying at a cheaper level. It is like buying stocks when they are on sale, but most people don't look at it that way.

When you talk to the average investor, she would say that she would be more comfortable buying a stock on an up day. People like to buy into momentum and like to buy into markets that are going up. It's a lot easier psychologically to make an investment when the stock is going up, because you think, as the buyer, "I'm making the right decision because other people are making that decision with me."

One of the keys to investment success is breaking that habit. Train yourself to have enough confidence in your investment thesis or in your investment philosophy that you want to take advantage of the opportunities created by dislocations and noise. Again, most people will tell you that this is obvious.

Many money managers tell people to dollar cost average (meaning buy the same dollar amount of shares or mutual funds at fixed intervals, like the first of every month) or to "buy on dips." To me, "buy on dips" is one of the stupidest and most overused phrases on television. If people were actually buying on dips, there would be no dips because there would be more buyers than sellers. When the Dow is down by 150 points on a given day, people don't say, "Oh, I want to buy on this dip." I never lose sight of the fact that stocks are no more than pieces of paper that people are buying and selling. If many thousands of investors were actually buying on dips, the market would not stay down, but would be up almost instantaneously. It sounds obvious, but think about it. When you break the mold of being like everybody else, that's how you take advantage of this. Later in the book, I will show you how to train yourself to think outside the box so that you can buy the kind of companies that will outperform the market. You will also learn to be a buyer of stocks when you are overwhelmed by sellers—just so long as your fundamental reasons for buying that stock remain intact. The key to putting a good plan into action is to break away from the herd mentality (as we mentioned earlier). To do that, as you will see, you need to disconnect what you feel from what you do. You need to disconnect your thinking from your action.

A One-Decision Investment versus a Two-Decision Investment

In essence, I am telling people, at least in part, to be contrarian. However, that was never a characterization that I thought worked very well. Yes, you need to buy when everyone else is selling. But "contrarian investor" is an overused phrase. Being a contrarian could mean anything. If you're a value investor, you could say that you're being contrarian when you buy a growth stock. Anyone can basically call himself a contrarian. So we don't want to pigeonhole ourselves as being contrarians. Successful investing is much more about establishing a discipline and not deviating from it.

Let's talk about buyers and sellers and a trade that I made recently. In early 2010, I believed that the run-up in Nasdaq was not about fundamentals, but rather was about money managers chasing relative performance and all buying the same large-cap tech names at the same time. That's when (after New Year's) I made the decision to short the Nasdaq. This was not a fundamental call. In fact, I didn't even care how the earnings season panned out. I made a determination that the sellers were going to overwhelm the buyers regardless of earnings. This was based on my outside-the-box thinking as to what had driven the market up in the November and December 2009 time frame.

Back to the trade: As I mentioned, I decided to short the Nasdaq through the earnings season. The key to this story is to understand that there are "one-decision investments" and there are "two-decision investments." In a one-decision investment, you've got to execute the buy trade with the anticipation that this is something you can own for a long period of time. In a two-decision investment, you've got to consider how you will execute both the buy trade and the sell trade at the same time. You've got to determine why you want to make the buy or short the stock, and simultaneously, when you make that decision, you've got to decide when you want to cover or when you want to sell.

If you go into a two-decision investment, meaning that this is not something that you're going to own for the long term (three to five years), you're attempting to take advantage of a market dislocation. At the time when you buy or short the security, you've got to make a determination about your exit strategy. The key to this story is that we tried to do something that differentiated our actions from those of the rest of the pack.

It was during the time that I was shorting the Nasdaq that I was harangued for making this trade by my fellow panelists when I appeared on the CNBC show *Fast Money*. One of the other experts characterized the trade as "crazy." It was then that I knew that I had made the right decision. When all is said and done, I made a very healthy return when the Nasdaq fell by a substantial amount in January 2010. But I am getting ahead of myself.

While we will cover the topic of developing a strong sell discipline in Chapter 11 of the book, I do want to discuss one aspect of it here. Let's take one of my all-time favorite stocks, Suncor Energy. When you own a stock like this, one that has consistently beaten the market, there are times over a 10-year period when the valuation *seems* high enough to warrant selling the stock. However, if the company's prospects continue to get better, the terminal value for the business will go up. So you can't just say, "I am going to buy this stock at $12 a share and sell it if it reaches $18." That's because when it reaches $18, it may actually be worth $25.

The point is that when you're in a two-decision stock, you've got to set out at the beginning knowing precisely when you are going to buy and when you are going to sell. Let's go back to this Nasdaq example. When I shorted the Nasdaq, or the "Qs," as it is called (the ETF ticker symbol for the Nasdaq 100 is QQQQ), it was because I wanted to be short the Nasdaq. That's because I felt that no matter what happened with the fundamental technology earnings, because of what had happened in late 2009, these were the stocks that I thought would get crushed first. I made that calculation—that there would be additional selling pressure on these stocks—not because of the fundamentals (e.g., P/E ratios), but because I knew that money managers would want to lighten up on these stocks. However, things didn't go exactly as planned.

When I went short in early January, the trade went against me at first; the Nasdaq continued to move up for the first 10 days of the month. But because I had made a determination that I was going to maintain this position with a disciplined two-decision methodology, I was undeterred. As the large-cap technology companies started reporting (first Intel, then Amazon, then IBM, and so on), the Nasdaq began to roll over—and it went down. At one point, I think it was off 9 percent from its recently reached 52-week high. I covered the short at the end of the earnings season for large-cap technology because that had been my plan going in. As an aside, the Nasdaq continued to fall as equities in general fell (after I got out of the trade and took my profits), but because success in a two-decision investment is predicated on being disciplined, you have to stick to your game plan.

This type of investment behavior, I guarantee you, will make you more comfortable and more confident in taking the opposite side of the momentum trade. Being disciplined and following these disciplines over the long run, whether you're right or you're wrong, will make you be more confident in taking the other side of the trade. When you follow a disciplined approach, you will develop the confidence within yourself to step in there and go the other way when it seems that the entire world is going against you.

5

LET CHANGE BE YOUR COMPASS, PART 1: GE

The *Merriam-Webster Online Dictionary* defines *change* in two different ways. As a verb, *change* is defined as "to make different in some particular . . . to make radically different . . . [or] to give a different position, course, or direction to." As a noun, *change* is defined as "the act, process, or result of changing . . . the passage of the moon from one monthly revolution to another; *also*: the passage of [the] moon from one phase to another."

To me, change is a dominant theme that investors must make an important part of their own investing discipline. That's because change is almost always the key signal that tells investors whether to buy or sell a stock. When something important changes within a company, investors need to take note of that change and analyze the likely ramifications of the new situation. For example, a change in management, a major acquisition, or a major shift in strategy can be an important change that signals the need for some action on the part of the investor.

When I think of change, I always try to reflect back on one of the best books I've ever read, *Ugly Americans* by Ben Mezrich, which was the true story of a bunch of "Ivy League Cowboys Who Raided the Asian Markets for Millions," as the subtitle of the book explains.

In Mezrich's bestseller, one of the main characters in the book, Dean Carney, put together eight rules of investing that have always stayed with me, so much so that I feel that they should be included here. Finding them in Mezrich's book has always served as a reminder that there is a big world out there beyond the typical prescriptive business book world. In other words, you can get great ideas from many places that at first blush would not seem like obvious good choices for the typical investor (several of these rules are paraphrased or shortened).

1. **Never get into something you can't get out of by the closing bell.** Every trade that you make, you should be looking for the exit point, and you should always keep your eye on the exit point. (pp. 68–69)
2. **Don't ever take anything at face value, because face value is the biggest lie of any market.** Nothing is ever priced at its true worth. The key is to figure out its intrinsic value and get it for much, much less. (p. 88)
3. **One minute, you have your feet on the ground and you're moving forward. The next minute the ground is gone and you're falling.** The key is to never land. Stay in the air as long as you can. (p. 88)
4. **You walk into a room with a grenade, and your best-case scenario is walking back out still carrying that grenade.** The worst-case scenario is that the grenade explodes, blowing you into little bloody pieces. The moral of the story: don't make bets with no upside. (p. 143)
5. **Don't overthink.** If it looks like a duck and quacks like a duck, it's a duck. (p. 173)

6. **Fear is the greatest motivator.** Motivation is what it takes to find profit. (p. 233)
7. **The first place to look for a solution is within the problem itself.** (p. 245)
8. **The ends justify the means, but there's only one end that really matters:** ending up on a beach with a bottle of champagne. (p. 259)

The most important thing I took away from this book that relates to change is that change is good—it means that you're alive. So many times in our regular lives, we are fearful of change—we are concerned about the impact of change on our everyday existence. This is also true in business. The number of management books published on dealing with change is in the thousands, but it is not a topic that one hears much about in the corridors of Wall Street. However, history has shown that wealth creation in equity markets is based on identifying change, riding the winds of change, and understanding the ramifications of change.

Change has been the catalyst for the greatest investments of all time. If we look back at many of the greatest investments over the last 50 years, whether they were in biotechnology, technology, financial services, or retailing, the one common denominator for all of them is that the entrepreneurs, managers, or visionaries did *something different*. And that change came in many shapes and sizes. Whether it came in the form of a new product, a new process, or a different way of delivering the same goods or services, it was change that paved the way for

> *Change has been the catalyst for the greatest investments of all time.*

significant asset appreciation. While this concept may seem simple or elementary, I guarantee you that when they are thinking about investing, many managers and traders walk away from the obvious and try to overcomplicate matters.

As I begin to present specific techniques for evaluating stocks, which I do in this chapter, it is important to reiterate a point that I made at the end of the introduction: These techniques for selecting stocks work in all types of markets. However, since I do not expect a "rising tide market" to lift all boats in the decade ahead, it is absolutely critical that you learn to master the concepts and techniques that I present in these latter chapters of the book. It is this methodology that I believe gives investors the best chance of success regardless of market conditions. This is a critical concept to keep in mind as you read and learn from the remainder of Part Two of the book. When I was managing money, there was a phrase that we always used to connote boiling down even the most complex ideas into their simplest common denominators. This phrase was not meant to be condescending or insulting, but instead was used to make sure that we were not making things tougher to understand than was absolutely necessary. The phrase was "dumbing it down."

As investors, we wanted to make things as simple as possible for ourselves. There's no reason why my 11-year-old son, William, shouldn't be capable of understanding any company's mission statement or how a company plans to differentiate itself in the marketplace. When it gets more complicated than that, I believe that's a sign that you should avoid or stay completely clear of the business. I am in good company on this idea. Warren Buffett is known to invest only in companies and industries that he easily understands, while avoiding technology stocks and anything that he does not comprehend readily. In Buffett's world, for instance, insurance and furniture are a lot easier to understand than microprocessors and MP3 players.

Where to Start Looking for Change

The first thing you do is if you're thinking about making an investment is to go online, look up the company, and pull out the last two annual reports and the last two 10-K filings. These two mandatory documents (mandatory for all publicly traded companies, that is) can allow you to familiarize yourself with a particular company, so that when meaningful change does occur, you will be able to identify it quickly. Let me take a moment to tell you the difference between the two documents.

The annual report is almost always a glossy, full-color promotional piece depicting a very happy, successful, and diverse company that fosters every good thing one can imagine—happy board members and even happier employees, great training programs, philanthropic efforts, "green" programs, and more. However, in the annual report, a company also discusses the developments over the past year. It includes a letter to shareholders from the CEO or a group of top managers, followed by the company's financials, with just about everything in between describing the company's various units and businesses.

The 10-K, on the other hand, is filed with the SEC and is typically just a financial report, with nothing other than the facts. While the annual report is more aesthetically appealing, the 10-K is where you can get the really critical information you will need in order to evaluate any company to see if it fits the criteria for inclusion in your portfolio. (I will be discussing those criteria in great detail in Chapter 6.)

Let's look at an example of an annual report and see what information we can get out of it. Let's pull up GE's 2001 annual report (finding it is as easy as Googling "GE 2001 annual report"). The first place I go is to the chairman's "Letter to Share Owners." Even before I open the report, I already know that 2001 was a tough year for the stock market. As we saw in Chapter 1, the S&P 500 was down dramatically between 2000 and 2002, including nearly 12 percent in 2001 alone. There were, of course, the horrendous attacks of September 11, 2001, which resulted in the second worst point drop in Dow history. GE, the last remaining Dow stock from the original 12 (which were selected by Charles Dow in 1896), is considered one of the bell-wethers of the entire stock market and did not escape the harsh market conditions that year.

In the Letter to Share Owners, the newly appointed chairman, Jeff Immelt, the manager who had been given the task of filling the shoes of Jack Welch (the man called the "Manager of the Century" by *Fortune* magazine), tells us that GE's stock "was down 16%, slightly more than the S&P 500."

However, GE had a very good year in 2001 when measured against two other key metrics:

- **Earnings grew by 11 percent, to $14.1 billion.** This was the highest in GE's history. It also crushed the average S&P 500 stock, whose average earnings declined by more than 20 percent.
- **Cash from operations grew to $17.2 billion.** This was up by a double-digit amount (12 percent) over the previous year.

This may leave investors asking the obvious question: if earnings were so strong, and the cash generated by the business was also quite healthy, why did GE underperform the market?

Revenues were weak that year, Immelt also reported, despite the sharp increase in earnings. However, I attribute the company's poor performance to another factor, and that was Welch's retirement. Many people felt that there was a "Welch premium" built into the stock, and everyone knew that Welch was stepping down in 2001 (he was originally slated to retire in 2000, but he stayed on to oversee the company's acquisition of Honeywell, which was eventually blocked by European regulators).

When Welch took over at General Electric in 1981, revenues were just shy of $27 billion. When he stepped down, revenues were close to $130 billion. Similarly, when he took over, the company had a market cap of $13 billion. When he stepped down, the company was worth more than $450 billion, making it the world's most valuable corporation. Under Welch, GE was a consistent out-performer in many important areas, most importantly building stock market value. But investors feared that without him, much of the management magic would be lost. In fact, I recall the story of a friend of mine meeting a senior manager of GE on a plane in 1999, and the manager explained that she and many of her fellow managers who had been made millionaires through GE stock feared for their financial futures as a result of Welch's retirement.

So here we have a textbook case of how a management change was perceived to be a real negative for the company, and the stock price reflected it. When Immelt took over the company in September 2001, the stock was trading at about $41 per share. As we will discuss later in the chapter, GE's stock has performed poorly since then—off by more than 60 percent and underper-forming the average S&P 500 stock by a staggering amount. This reality lends credence to my thesis that the Welch management change was viewed as a terrible change for the company. To be fair, there are other factors, besides Immelt, that contributed to GE's poor performance; we will look at those in the next section. But with the company trading at a multiple of only 15 or so—as opposed to multiples three times as high under Welch—there is a high probability that Welch's retirement was one of the primary reasons for the company's wretched performance.

What about the 10-K?

Let's stay with GE as we look to define and determine the value of a 10-K report for the typical investor. Even though this sounds like the most technical, wonkiest report one can imag-ine, there are important things that are included in a 10-K that merit an investor's attention. While some of the wording and language may go over your head, there are two key parts of the 10-K that deserve every investor's attention.

When attempting to figure out the change within a company that drove a share price movement, the most important element of the 10-K to review is the "Management's Discussion and Analysis" section (frequently called the MDA, which also appears in the company's annual report). In this section, the management discusses the operation of the company in detail by comparing the current period with prior periods. It's in the MDA and the "Risk Factors" portion of a 10-K that you as an individual investor can get a sense of where the management team feels the business is going, as well as the risks and rewards associated with the business plan at hand.

As we will see in the following example, the 10-K often includes a far more honest, and frankly pessimistic, view of things. It is for this reason that this report is so important to investors.

Let's start with an excerpt from GE's 10-K for the year ending 2009, filed in 2010. We will start with an excerpt from the MDA (emphasis added):

Item 7. Management's Discussion and Analysis of Financial Condition and Results of Operations.

Overview of Our Earnings from 2007 through 2009

Net earnings attributable to the Company decreased 37% in 2009 and 22% in 2008, reflecting the challenging economic conditions of the last two years and the effect on both our industrial and financial services businesses. **Our financial services businesses were most significantly affected as GECS net earnings attributable to the Company fell 80% in 2009 and 32% in 2008.** Excluding the financial services businesses, our net earnings attributable to the Company decreased 7% in 2009 and 13% in 2008, reflecting the weakened global economy and challenging market conditions. We believe that we are beginning to see signs of stabilization in the global economy. We have a strong backlog entering 2010 and are positioned for global growth in 2011 and 2012.

That is a very frank and transparent description of the company—and a stunning one. For two decades under Jack Welch, GE had increased its earnings just about every year, and its stock had dwarfed the returns of the average S&P 500 stock. Now we learn in the 10-K that GE's earnings decreased by wide margins in 2008 and 2009. In addition, net earnings for GE Capital, the company's financial services arm, fell by 80 percent in 2009 and 32 percent in 2008. To be fair, just about every company that had a large financial business got hammered during the liquidity crisis of those two years. However, the takeaway here isn't necessarily how badly the company performed (GE's stock, which had traded above $60 per share under Welch in 2000, traded as low as $5.73 per share in March 2009—an 18-year low), but rather how much more the 10-K disclosed than the company's Letter to Investors. In that letter by CEO Immelt, investors read the following sections (I will include only some of the section titles here, exactly as they appeared in the annual report; that should give you enough insight into the tone and purpose of the annual report):

- Create financial flexibility
- The GE renewal
- A simplified portfolio focused on infrastructure
- Investing in profitable growth
- We lead in growth markets
- An energized and accountable team
- Attractive growth in earnings, cash and returns

Even though Immelt started the Letter to Investors by calling this decade "The Decade From Hell" (quoting *Time* magazine), you can see how he tried to put a positive spin on every aspect of the company, including the disastrous financial services business. In fact, here is one of the ways he characterized GE Capital in his letter: *"GE Capital Finance earned $11 billion in 2008–09 and never had an unprofitable quarter during this period."* He also included this statement about the financial services part of the company and how he plans to reduce its size in relation to other GE businesses:

> We are repositioning GE Capital as a smaller and more focused specialty finance franchise. Our competitive advantage is in value-added origination and risk management. We will continue to be a significant lender for assets we know, and in markets where we are a recognized leader. We are preparing for a more highly regulated financial services market. GE Capital can still generate solid returns in this more focused form.

Comparing the Letter to Investors to the MDA part of the 10-K gives us a very clear sense of how dramatically these reports differ. An investor could learn about the earnings of the financial part of GE in the 2009 Annual Report; however, that report is a 125-page document, with the financials taking up 95 pages. Thus, you would really have to hunt down those numbers that reveal the weak performance of GE Capital (they are on page 36, by the way). The 10-K is far more up-front and, despite its daunting title, is actually easier to navigate when it comes to learning the truth(s) about a particular company.

Now let's look at the second most important part of the 10-K, the "Risk Factors" portion (which is item 1A of the report). Once again, I will include just the section heads to illustrate the difference in these reports:

- Our global growth is subject to economic and political risks.
- We are subject to a wide variety of laws and regulations that may change in significant ways.

- We are subject to legal proceedings and legal compliance risks.
- The success of our business depends on achieving our objectives for strategic acquisitions and dispositions.
- Sustained increases in costs of pension and healthcare benefits may reduce our profitability.
- Conditions in the financial and credit markets may affect the availability and cost of GE Capital's funding.
- Difficult conditions in the financial services markets have materially and adversely affected the business and results of operations of GE Capital and these conditions may persist.
- The soundness of other financial institutions could adversely affect GE Capital.
- The real estate markets in which GE Capital participates are highly uncertain.
- Failure to maintain our credit ratings could adversely affect our cost of funds and related margins, liquidity, competitive position and access to capital markets.
- Current conditions in the global economy and the major industries we serve also may materially and adversely affect the business and results of operations of our non-financial businesses.
- We are dependent on market acceptance of new product introductions and product innovations for continued revenue growth.
- Our Intellectual property portfolio may not prevent competitors from independently developing products and services similar to or duplicative to ours, and we may not be able to obtain necessary licenses.
- Significant raw material shortages, supplier capacity constraints, supplier production disruptions, supplier quality issues or price increases could increase our operating costs and adversely impact the competitive positions of our products.
- There are risks inherent in owning our common stock.

This list needs to include all of the risks that management per-ceives as having a potential negative effect on the company and its stock. Reading this report really gives you a sense of a com-pany's uncertain future. In fact, reading this list of 15 potential risks has the unintended consequence of turning off potential investors. Who would want to own GE's stock after reviewing this eye-opening list? But do not allow yourself to be over-whelmed by the risk portion of a 10-K. All companies face many risks in these turbulent times, in which a sustainable competitive advantage can disappear practically overnight. This is just one tool of many in your toolbox that will help you to identify change and evaluate the soundness of your investments and potential investments. In fact, for the record, in almost exactly one year to the day, GE's stock had tripled from its low of March 2009 to just over $18 per share in March 2010 (before dropping to $15 per share in August 2010). This swing illustrates that hav-ing many risks does not automatically translate into a bad invest-ment if you buy and sell a stock at the right time.

In the next chapter, I will reveal what I call the eight pillars of change and why they are so critical when it comes to portfo-lio construction.

6

LET CHANGE BE YOUR
COMPASS, PART 2: DISNEY

In Chapter 5, we focused on just two reports: the annual report and the 10-K. Although these reports are critical in helping you to figure out where a company has been and where it is going, there are many additional places for you to detect the kind of change that might lead you to buy or sell a stock. In this chapter, I will begin by presenting the Eight Pillars of Change that we used at Team K to identify the truly consequential types of change that would allow us to make a buy or sell decision on a stock. These eight points are critical enough that I highly recommend that you keep a running scorecard on the eight pillars and fill in the specifics when a significant change causes you to buy a stock or to rethink your position when you perceive that change to be negative or positive enough to warrant action.

The Eight Pillars of Change

In trying to identify the types of change that will result in a revaluation of a company, you begin by trying to understand what the existing business is and trying to determine what various types of change can do to that company, both in the short term and in the long run.

The GE example in Chapter 5 illustrates one of the eight pillars of change that we look for in evaluating companies and stocks, and that is management or board changes.

That was just one of eight types of change that can affect a company at any time and without any warning. In order to stay abreast of all of the key events surrounding any company that you own or are thinking of owning, you must consistently monitor each of the following eight pillars of change:

1. Management or board changes
2. Corporate restructuring
3. Changes in the capital structure of the company
4. Changes in the compensation structure
5. New products or technological innovation
6. Political or regulatory changes
7. Monetary or currency changes
8. Social or cultural changes

These may sound daunting or even academic, but I assure you that once we go through them, you will have a much clearer sense of what each type of change can mean to a company. In this chapter I will show you where to look in order to stay on top of these changes for any company that you own or are thinking of buying.

Fortunately, there is one company with a rich and historic legacy that has, at one time or another, been through each of the eight pillars of change, for better or worse. That company, founded in 1923, was first known as Disney Brothers Cartoon Studio before changing its name to the Walt Disney Studio. Today we just call the company "Disney" or "The Walt Disney Company." Let's look at the company's history over the last few decades to find examples of the eight pillars of change. One final introductory word: This is, of course, not a book about Disney. However, in order to make sure that I present enough context for each type of change, I will be including stories and anecdotes from the Disney archive, as well as from other companies. So at times it may feel like this is a book about Disney, but it is not. It is about change, and how one company dealt with change in its many forms and faces.

The First Pillar of Change: Management or Board Changes

GE was a great example of a negative management change that might have led an investor to make a sell decision had he owned the stock in 2000–2001. Let's turn this example on its head and look at an example of a positive management change that might have led investors to make the opposite decision.

Walt Disney, the genius behind the Disney company and brand, died in late 1966. That left a management void that was not filled for nearly two decades. (The death of a charismatic founder can indeed be a reason to sell a particular stock, but that is not the point of this story.) Let me include a bit of history in order to provide more insight into Disney's interesting past.

After Walt died in 1966, his brother Roy ran the company for a while until his death in late 1971. However, both brothers made the all-too-common mistake of not preparing for their successors. As a result, the company drifted for years, as Ron Grover explains in his book, *The Disney Touch*. The one person who Walt tried to prepare to run the company was his son-in-law, Ron Miller. Miller, a former professional football player, was not the right person to run the house that Walt and Roy had built. He simply did not have the "gut" or the experience.

By 1979, the company was sinking fast. The problem was that, unlike during the Walt and Roy years, there was no one at the company who could make a decision. Instead, the people running Disney were letting Walt's ghost make the decisions by asking at every pivotal point, "What would Walt have done?"

Ron Miller was named chief executive in 1983. But even Miller knew that he was not the ideal person to run the company. That was when he started to court Michael Eisner, the Paramount president who, along with Barry Diller, had turned Paramount into a cash machine with such hits as *Raiders of the Lost Ark*. But Eisner didn't want to run only the company's film division; he wanted to run the whole company.

By the 1980s, Disney was a company that was rich in assets but impoverished in management talent. In the early 1980s, corporate raiders were threatening the company's very existence. It was common knowledge that the company's assets were not being leveraged or grown in any meaningful way. What it really needed was an outsider to run the business, someone who would not be weighed down by Walt and the company's history.

Let's stay with Disney but turn the tables once again by discussing a management move that marked another important change in the company's history. Frank Wells, who proved to be a superb number two to Michael Eisner, died tragically in a 1994 helicopter accident. That left a mile-wide management gap at Disney. Eisner could not run the entire company himself. He needed to replace Wells, and he eventually decided to hire his friend, über-agent Michael Ovitz.

Ovitz had become something of a legend in the world of movies, representing many of the biggest stars in Hollywood and New York, including Sean Connery, Tom Cruise, and David Letterman. At William Morris and at CAA, Ovitz worked in environments that did not have rigid hierarchies and titles—

companies whose cultures were vastly different from that of a large, publicly traded company like Disney. Worse yet, Ovitz wanted to be a "partner" or a co-chief executive to Eisner, a man never known as one who shared power easily or willingly.

Even before Ovitz started working at Disney, his hiring created great friction within the company. Key Disney executives refused to report to Ovitz—instead, they continued to report to Eisner. However, regardless of the fights that were taking place behind the scenes, upon its announcement, the Ovitz hiring drew applause from almost every other quarter.

The *Los Angeles Times* couldn't praise the choice enough, declaring, "Ovitz Pick Ideal Choice for Global Giant," in its headline that day. It called Ovitz the kind of "globally connected executive" that Disney needed. But Eisner, Ovitz, and several key Disney executives knew that trouble had started brewing even before the press release was issued. In fact, both Eisner and Ovitz said that they might have made the biggest mistake of their careers—Eisner in choosing Ovitz, and Ovitz in accepting the job. The problem was clear from the start: Ovitz's role was never really clearly distinguished from Eisner's own role at the firm.

Once again, as with the Eisner hiring, we are not saying that this was a good thing or a bad thing, but the Ovitz hiring was enough of a change to allow investors to decide to either buy the stock or sell all or a portion of their Disney shares (or do nothing at all) as a result. One investor did act on the news. Famed investment banker Herb Allen doubled the number of Disney shares he owned, saying that the company would be far stronger in five years with Ovitz there. However, with 20/20 hindsight, we know that the culture of Disney was thrown into disarray by the Ovitz hiring. Eventually, Disney paid Ovitz $140 million just to get rid of him, making him one of the worst hires in corporate America history.

Let's move beyond Disney to discuss what other things I look for when it comes to management and board changes. This is not rocket science. And, as I pointed out earlier, these ideas do not apply only to companies in sideways markets; this change and the others presented in this chapter are worth noting and possibly acting upon in all kind of markets.

If there is a new CEO or CFO coming into the company who is a bona fide winner because he has a great track record running one or more other companies, then that is obviously a positive change. It might even be someone who is coming out of retirement to take the job. As long as that individual has created organic growth or earnings growth for another firm, that's someone you want.

The litmus test for a new board member is similar. You are not just looking for somebody who can show up at a board meeting and collect a check. You are looking for somebody who can add real value to the board because she has a specific type of expertise that will help the company.

Two examples that come to mind as model CEOs are Jim Kilts, who came out of retirement to run Gillette before the firm was sold to Procter & Gamble, and Mickey Drexler, one of the most successful merchants of all time, who had turned around The Gap and J. Crew before joining the board of Apple. What he brought to Apple was retailing experience, a major component in the Apple growth story.

What about red flags when it comes to management changes? An automatic red flag, if there ever was one—and this comes from my earliest days in the business—is the departure of a CFO. That doesn't necessarily mean that you sell the stock immediately. But typically, warning bells should go off when the chief financial officer leaves a company that you own or are considering purchasing.

An automatic red flag . . . is the departure of a CFO.

The CFO is the person who is responsible for putting the numbers together. Aside from the CEO, there is no more critical position in a company. The thing to look for is *how* that person leaves. If the CFO's departure has been discussed and telegraphed well in advance, that's a different story from a CFO who suddenly leaves "for personal reasons" or "to spend more time with family." Typically, if the CFO wants to retire or wants to leave for another job, members of the board like to let the public know this so that there is no perception that there is disagreement over accounting, revenue recognition, or how the company is generating its sales.

The Second Pillar of Change: Corporate Restructuring

The restructuring of a company can be an important turning point for that firm, and, as we saw with management changes, it can be a positive or negative development depending upon the personnel involved and the situation.

Before Michael Eisner came to Disney, Touchstone Pictures, the company's second movie label, was run first by a 27-year-old with no movie experience. By 1984, Walt Disney's movie operations were in real trouble. While its rivals were turning out hits like *Star Wars*, *Beverly Hills Cop*, and *Gremlins*, Disney had such pitiful pictures as *Country*, *Baby*, *The Journey of Natty Gann*, and *My Science Project*; the only success was *Splash*. Once on board, Eisner and his team figured that the five pictures slated for release before their arrival would lose well over $100 million.

Upon his arrival at Disney, Michael Eisner reorganized the company to give him direct control over the company's movie studios. This was a critical decision, since the company was hemorrhaging money as a result of its films' poor performance at the box office. One of the first things Eisner did was to toss dozens of scripts on the garbage heap. Eisner knew how to make money-making movies from his years at Paramount, and he was determined to reinvent the company's film operations from top to bottom.

Eisner had a multitier strategy. First, he would make the kind of movies that Paramount would make, including "R"-rated pictures, which no one at Disney would have dared to do before Eisner took over. Second, he would reinvigorate the careers of stars who had faded from the limelight, such as Nick Nolte, Bette Midler, and Richard Dreyfus. That way, Disney would be able to keep actors' salaries way down compared with those paid by other movie studios.

Eisner's strategies all paid big dividends. The first movie of the Eisner era was *Down and Out in Beverly Hills*, starring the aforementioned Nolte, Midler, and Dreyfus. The week it opened, it beat both *The Color Purple* and *Out of Africa*. That film eventually hauled in $62 million, helping Eisner to win the confidence of Wall Street. When he was hired, amid the threat of takeover, Disney's stock was trading just below $60 per share. By early 1985, the stock had risen to more than $80 per share, and in February 1986, the board voted a four-for-one stock split.

One of the effects of the reorganization of the company was that Eisner could take characters and movie themes and use them at the company's theme parks and as toys and action figures to sell in the company's stores. Licensing and cross-fertilization of the company's assets became a huge and successful strategy under Eisner and Wells, and the company achieved real synergy that other companies spoke of but never realized. Eisner was able to leverage and grow the assets of the company in a way that his predecessors were not.

Let's once again move away from Disney to discuss more general guidelines on what to look for when it comes to corporate restructuring. On a more general basis, many things could be considered corporate restructuring, but while you are doing your own due diligence, you want to find something that stands out from a commonsense perspective.

For example, let's say a company announces that it is going to restructure a significant amount of its manufacturing operations. More specifically, the company announces that it's going to outsource much of its manufacturing because it will be able to save a significant amount of money and increase its profit margins by doing so. While this restructuring may result in thousands of layoffs in the United States, the actual outsourcing of the manufacturing could, a year later, create significantly larger profits and give the company far more control over its costs because it will not be subject to the high fixed expenses of overhead, employees, building additional factories, and so on. That is a situation that warrants further review but could be perceived as positive change.

Staying with the restructuring topic, we could use that same situation as an example of negative change associated with corporate restructuring. Let's say that a company decides to take a significant amount of its production overseas. One of the long-term ramifications may be the inability to ramp up production on a hot new product because the company does not control its own production facilities. This is especially true in cyclical businesses that have short-term demand surges. This could easily lead to a product shortage at the worst possible time. Because the company doesn't control its own manufacturing, but relies on a third-party vendor, it may miss the opportunity to make certain sales because it doesn't have control over the manufacturing process. As a result, you can look at taking manufacturing outside of the company in either a positive or a negative way.

The Third Pillar of Change: Changes in the Capital Structure of the Company

Of the pillars I have presented so far, this third pillar may sound like the most difficult to get your hands around. But it sounds more complicated than it is. Capital structure simply refers to the manner in which a company finances its assets. What you need to know is that this pillar has everything to do with the way a company maintains its balance sheet, which lists all of the company's assets and liabilities. Capital structure can be examined for an entire company or for a particular division of a company or a project that it undertakes.

Going back to Disney, we will look at changes in capital structure as they pertain to a particular division and a particular project.

One excellent example of this type of change in capital structure came when Disney was in talks to create Euro Disney. Building that park was projected to cost $2 billion.

In October 1989, Disney sold shares to the public in a highly successful $1 billion stock offering that was initially priced at $13 per share. The deal was ultimately an incredible one for Disney: by putting up less than $200 million of its own money, the company owned almost half of an entity valued at $3 billion (French law does not permit foreign companies to own more than 50 percent of a French company).

The way Disney capitalized its new European park was applauded by investors. As a result of all the good press surrounding Disney's deal making and the new theme park, Disney's stock rose six points in the United States. Clearly this was a case in which investors weighed in early on, lavishing praise on the company by buying up Disney shares. Most changes in capital structure do not move a stock as decisively as this one did.

Now that we have covered Disney, let's once again open up this discussion to other situations so that you can better recognize how changes in capital structure might affect a stock going forward.

This one is straightforward. Any time a company is able to take advantage of the capital markets to make its balance sheet stronger, that's a positive type of change, but one that warrants further analysis before making a buy or sell decision on the stock.

Access to capital markets simply means that a company can sell bonds or notes and go to the institutional market and get money at a relatively low interest rate. Additionally, companies can choose to sell equity or issue new shares. Issuing additional equity is most likely dilutive. During the liquidity crisis of 2008 and 2009, the vast majority of firms had a great deal of trouble accessing these markets and raising money. While things have loosened up quite a bit in the years since then, there are still many companies that would have trouble accessing the capital markets. So this one is easy: The companies that are the most creditworthy—the ones that will be most able to get fast money and restructure their debt—are the companies that will be most attractive from a capital structure perspective. When companies cannot tap the capital markets when their debt comes due, they have no choice but to sell assets in order to meet their debt maturities. In selected cases, those companies will have to sell some of their crown jewels to keep their businesses afloat—a harbinger of bad things to come.

The Fourth Pillar of Change: Changes in the Compensation Structure

Once again, Disney offers a great example of how a change in compensation structure can be a real game changer for a company. When Walt's son-in-law became CEO, he was paid a relatively paltry salary: less than $400,000 per year, with little chance for bonuses and only a small amount of stock options. However, the salary was not really the issue. It was the absence of incentive pay in the event that the company really took off. That was just one more item that proved that Disney was not being run like the major-league entertainment conglomerate that it had become. Someone evaluating Disney stock at the time might have looked at the lackluster pay package of the CEO and asked, "If the chief executive has so little monetary incentive to grow the company, then why should I entrust my hard-earned dollars to Disney?"

In recruiting outside talent, the Disney board knew that it would have to be far more generous in its pay package if it was going to bring in the quality of management capable of turning around the company's fortunes. After all, Michael Eisner had made more than $2 million at Paramount in 1983.

Both Eisner and Wells were willing to take small salaries at Disney in return for great stock option plans. Frank Wells even told the outgoing CEO that he would take $1 a year in salary in return for a generous stock option plan.

In the end, both Eisner and Wells received modest salaries ($750,000 and $400,000, respectively), but it was the stock options and special bonuses that made their deals so spectacular. They received a stunning number of stock options—500,000 for Eisner and 450,000 for Wells. Also, the two would get a percentage of the company's net income in the event that they could grow the company at a higher rate than their predecessors. In the previous five years, Disney's growth had averaged 9 percent. Eisner would get 2 percent of any increase over that amount, and Wells would get 1 percent.

Once again, I do not want to pass judgment on these seemingly generous pay packages. That's because there are two ways one could have evaluated these compensation plans. The low salaries were a bargain by CEO standards. However, the other parts of the plans were incredibly generous—but only if the two men grew the company. One investor might have thought that the plan was a great one for investors, since Eisner and Wells would make real money only in the event that they were truly successful. A different investor might feel that the stock options and other aspects of the plan were just too much. The point is that a new compensation plan like this one represents a substantial enough change to warrant a potential purchase or sale of Disney's stock.

━━━━━━━

How will you know what to look for when it comes to a change in compensation systems at a company that you are following? Let's use this extreme example to illustrate how some compensation structures can affect a firm. Let's assume that a company decides that all its employees are going to take 50 percent of their compensation in the form of restricted stock. Initially this could be perceived as a positive, in the sense that employees will be more aligned with shareholders, and will come to work every day and do things that will help the stock go up. But conversely, as we've seen with companies like Enron, Lehman Brothers, and Bear Stearns, this principle of forcing a high level of insider ownership through the compensation structure isn't necessarily a good thing in and of itself.

What I look for in a compensation structure is something that creates a symbiotic balance between people being motivated to grow the business and being aligned with common shareholders. However, there is a real risk that when you give people incentives to grow the stock, they will make short-term decisions just to jack up the stock price on a quarterly basis.

In the wake of the 2008 financial crisis, much of the financial regulatory reform that is being discussed in Washington in 2010 is moving in the right direction—so that people are not motivated to move the stock in the short term, but instead are paid to look out for the long-term interest of the firm. Any award that gives incentives only for performance in the short term must be viewed with a healthy amount of skepticism. If a company that you are following is that short-term-oriented, then be very careful to follow the firm and continue to do your due diligence on all other aspects of the company. Legislators are looking at provisions that would allow them to take back money from Wall Street executives who have juiced the stock just for the short term. That is called a "clawback" provision, and it makes a great deal of sense to make sure that senior managers do not focus on the short term. The bottom line is this: it is much better to invest in companies whose compensation systems are in alignment with longer-term thinking and decision making.

The Fifth Pillar of Change: New Products or Technological Innovation

Once again we look to Disney to offer us textbook examples of either new products or some fresh innovation that changed the company.

This time we turn back the clock to 1985, when Disney executives negotiated a deal with MGM to use MGM's movies in Disney's new theme park, which was eventually called Disney MGM Studios. The best part for Disney was the deal it wrangled out of MGM. Disney signed a 20-year deal with MGM that gave Disney the rights to use hundreds of MGM films for a mere pittance. Disney estimated that attendance alone would add $100 million per year in revenues, and that is not even counting the food, beverage, and merchandise income. And for no additional fees, Disney was also able to use the MGM name and logo (Leo the Lion) on advertising, stationery, and posters. Disney was, of course, ecstatic. When MGM boss Kirk Kerkorian found out that the company had even given away the right to use the MGM logo, he threw a fit and tried to back out of the deal. But Disney would not budge.

Wall Street loved the deal. Before the park opened, Disney's stock was trading at about $85 per share. Within a month, Disney's stock price flirted with the $100 mark. Clearly this was one case in which a new product—albeit on a grand scale—

made the company's coffers richer. Once again we see change powerful enough to move the stock price, and investors who were savvy enough to recognize the effect of the new attraction in advance were able to capitalize on their instincts.

———

Once again, let's broaden the conversation to discuss what to look for when it comes to new products or technological innovation in a company that you might be following. This fifth pillar might be the easiest one of all to figure out.

Any time a company comes out with a significant new product, you probably won't need to go to the financial press to learn about it, because the company will be putting a tremendous amount of money behind its launch of its latest innovative product, and the news will not be restricted to the financial pages.

The most obvious example that comes to mind is Apple. Whenever it comes out with a new product—from the iPod to the iPhone to the iPad—Wall Street is watching. Since no one is better than Apple when it comes to product launches, it is not surprising that Apple's stock is worth $275 per share in the second quarter of 2010, up from about $75 four years earlier, in 2006. That is an incredible rise, and it has a great deal to do with the innovative products that the company has released during that period.

Let's cite another example, this one not a new product per se, but an example of a new service delivery system—eBay. When eBay went public in 1998, I had a friend who already loved the company because she had been buying and selling on the site. She was certainly an early adopter of the new technology, and as a result, she bought the stock the day it went public. In a matter of weeks, the stock was up by several hundred percent. This is very much the approach promoted by Peter Lynch, who argued in his book *One Up on Wall Street* that stock buyers should think as consumers: Does this new product or new technology make sense to you at that particular price point? Try not to overcomplicate things when evaluating new products, new technologies, or new services.

What about looking at a new product or innovation that can actually hurt a company? What about a company that comes out with a new product that reduces its core revenue stream? The one company that leaps to mind is Starbucks.

Several years back, Starbucks attempted to diversify its product mix by offering breakfast and lunch fare. In selling these new products, the firm took the emphasis off its four-dollar lattés and cappuccinos and tried to jam down breakfast food on its existing customer base. Anytime a company takes its eye off its core product in favor of an ancillary product (or products), it risks weakening its competitive position. That happened to Starbucks when it sold warm breakfast sandwiches. According to press reports, the smell of egg, cheese, and bacon interfered with the rich aroma of its coffee in its stores. That's when the firm decided to abandon those warm sandwiches and redouble its focus on its key, core product.

The Sixth Pillar of Change: Political or Regulatory Changes

The last three pillars are what I call "macro" changes. They do not happen inside the walls of the company; instead, they occur outside of the firm. Let's start with a key regulatory change that made a big difference to Disney.

In 1970, the Federal Communications Commission (FCC) established a new set of rules called the Financial Interest and Syndication Rules (fin-syn). The FCC created these regulations in order to prevent the big three networks from becoming more monopolistic. They were not permitted to own any of the prime-time programming aired on their own network.

However, the television landscape changed dramatically over the next decades. Fox became the fourth network and a real alternative to the big three. Cable programming also grew dramatically over the years. As a result of these big changes, the power of the three big networks was diminished, which led the FCC to do away with the fin-syn rule in 1993. That important regulatory change cleared the way for Disney to acquire ABC, and it did so three years after the FCC abolished fin-syn.

Once again, we are not saying that the abolition of fin-syn was a good thing or a bad thing. However, when fin-syn was done away with, the writing was on the wall. Companies like Disney were now free to acquire one of the three big networks. (Today, all four networks have an affiliated syndication company.) What that would mean for stocks like Disney was something that investors and potential investors had to decide for themselves.

Aside from the Disney example, what other types of change should you look out for when it comes to political/regulatory changes?

Let's include one more example of how political or regulatory changes can affect not just a company, but an entire sector. In April of 2010, Goldman Sachs was charged with civil fraud by the SEC in relation to its subprime mortgage trading. This was a clear example of a political change that affected not only Goldman Sachs (which was down 30 points or more than 15 percent off that day's high at one point), but also the rest of the financial sector and the stock market as a whole.

Two weeks later, when Goldman Sachs leaders were dragged to Washington to testify before Congress, once again the entire stock market was affected. Between the testimony playing out on live television—which made Goldman look unethical, to say the least—and the problems with falling credit ratings in Greece, the stock market fell by over 200 points in a single day. Ironically, Goldman Sachs's stock traded up that day when every other major financial stock was down by about 5 percent. Once again, we see how a single lawsuit reverberated throughout the sector and infected the entire stock market.

The Seventh Pillar of Change: Monetary or Currency Changes

Disney once again offers a great example of how changes in currency values can affect the business of a company.

When the U.S. dollar is weak versus the euro and Asian currencies, there is a good chance that a greater number of tourists from Europe and Asia will travel to the United States and visit Disney's various theme parks in Florida and California. That's obviously because the cost of traveling to America and the entrance fees to the parks, which are pricey by most standards, become much cheaper for those tourists with stronger currencies.

Of course, with the liquidity crisis of 2008 and 2009, revenues at the theme parks suffered. However, attendance at the parks was up at times. In the second quarter of 2009, for example, in the middle of a great recession, attendance at all U.S. Disney theme parks was up by 3 percent, and attendance at Disneyland was up by double digits. The decrease in revenues was caused by lower prices offered at some of the Disney hotels and a number of other promotions that the company used to lure visitors to the parks. The lower prices offset the higher number of visitors, resulting in lower overall theme park revenues (despite some of the increases in attendance). It will be interesting to see what happens when the economy strengthens: Will the euro, which dropped in early 2010 vis-à-vis the dollar, rebound, and if it does, what will be the effect on attendance at the U.S. theme parks? Will we see a large influx of European tourists to the Disney parks? Or will it not matter? Once again, we are just offering an example of the effect that changes in monetary and currency values can have on a business that has currency exposure. Investors have to decide in each case whether these changes are significant enough to change their opinion on a particular company and stock.

———

What else should investors look for when it comes to monetary or currency changes?

One of the key things to look for is companies that do business outside of the United States. Since we have one global marketplace, the vast majority of Fortune 500 companies do some business overseas. In this example, we are talking about companies that do a significant amount of business outside of U.S. borders.

While these global companies are generating sales internationally, they must then translate those sales into U.S. dollars. This is when investors really need to pay attention to the currency fluctuations. That is because sales that are profitable overseas can actually be unprofitable when the currency is calculated into the equation. More specifically, let's say a firm does 30 percent of its sales in Europe. If the euro is very weak versus the U.S. dollar, those sales may be unprofitable when they are brought back home.

This is a situation that obviously cuts both ways. We can simply turn the tables on the previous example. If the euro is very strong vis-à-vis the U.S. dollar, then those sales may actually be far more profitable when the currency is figured into those overseas transactions. This is why investors should keep an eye on the strength of the U.S. dollar, so that they can be aware of situations like these.

The Eighth Pillar of Change:
Social or Cultural Changes

In this, the eighth and final pillar of change, we return to Disney in the late 1970s and early 1980s to show how a social or cultural shift can have a profound effect on a company.

As mentioned earlier in the chapter, before Michael Eisner arrived at Disney, the company's film division had had some really terrible years. In the decade prior to Eisner's arrival, earnings at the Disney film division had been shrinking for years, despite the fact that movie prices had surged during those same years. In 1982, for example, the company had made less than $20 million in film revenues, down from $54 million in profits in 1976, and most of that was due to Disney classics that had been made years earlier. Disney author Ron Grover summed it up nicely when he wrote: "[Disney] had few ties to the Steven Spielbergs and Ivan Reitmans of Hollywood, and fewer to the likes of John Hughes and John Avildsen. Box office superstars like Eddie Murphy and Sylvester Stallone wouldn't be caught dead on Dopey Drive."

At the heart of the problem was that the taste of the American moviegoer had been shifting for years, and Disney either did not recognize it or was simply unable to change along with it. No one on the board or in senior management at Disney had the guts to transform the company by making an "R"-rated picture.

Overall, 1982 was a stellar year for movies, but not at Disney. Pictures like *Missing*, *Gandhi*, *ET*, *The Verdict*, and *Tootsie* lit up the box office while garnering best picture nominations, and Disney had nothing with which to lure theatergoers away from these huge hits. This is a classic case of a social change that had the power to move the needle for a company like Disney. The weak performance of the film division was one of the reasons that Disney earnings decreased in three out of the four years prior to Eisner and Wells taking over the company, as we see in Table 6-1.

Table 6-1	Disney Earnings (millions)
1980	$135
1981	$121
1982	$100
1983	$93
1984	$98

The slight upturn in 1984 was due in part to the movie *Splash*, which was a big and surprising hit for Disney that brought in $69 million, at the time a record for the company. But that was a movie that management simply stumbled upon. Disney board members were nervous about the minor nudity in the film and were not eager to repeat that kind of thing in later movies. That was one of the reasons why only an outside management team had the ability to pull off such a convincing turnaround of the company.

Let's enlarge the discussion of this pillar of change one last time. What should investors look for when it comes to social or cultural changes? This is an area that is chock-full of examples that will help investors think about this critical topic.

One obvious social change involves doing business over the Internet. For several years after the Internet had come into its own, there was at least one generation that was deeply concerned about transacting business online. That's a social change.

For a long time, for example, my parents never felt comfortable sharing credit card information online. There was this prevailing thought that you had to touch and feel something and buy things face to face. However, with companies like Amazon and their secure Web sites, people got over the stigma of buying things online. In fact, when more research was done, it was revealed that many people didn't like having to talk to a salesperson or sales clerk or being followed around the store. Many people actually enjoyed the experience of shopping online. There was far more privacy; people could compare prices more easily online and never leave the comfort of their own homes. Coming out of the Internet bubble, in light of this particular change, it was possible to recognize companies that were going to emerge as survivors and growers (e.g., Amazon, Google, and Priceline) and which ones weren't (e.g., eToys).

Since this pillar of change is so important, let's include one more example. Let's look at the social change associated with cell phones. When they first appeared, there was a social stigma associated with the industry because many people felt that phone conversations were meant to be made in private. Ten years ago, no one thought that people would be sitting in their homes and talking not on a landline but on their mobile phones. That represents an important social change that affected a huge industry. My three children sit at home and never talk on the house phone; instead, they talk only on their cell phones.

This discussion of cell phones begs the question: Since cell phone use has exploded, why have stocks like Verizon and AT&T been such terrible performers? One reason has to do with the large amounts of capital that were needed to maintain their traditional landline businesses. This happened while the wireless portion of the market was experiencing incredible growth. So these two firms had these dinosaur businesses that were dying and killing their profitability. They were also fiercely locked in a battle for market share that further eroded profit margins (because advertising expenditures and the capital needed to create cellular networks were so high). Verizon's performance is shown in Figure 6-1.

Figure 6-1   A 10-year chart of Verizon.

AT&T also had a rough decade, which disappointed most investors (see Figure 6-2).

The poor results achieved by Verizon and AT&T do not mean that one could not have profited from this incredible social change. There was what we call a "derivative play," which simply means investing in another company that would benefit from

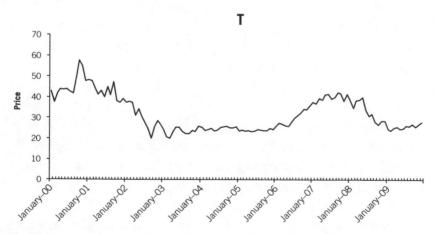

Figure 6-2   A 10-year chart of AT&T.

this type of change, but would not be as "pure" a play as Verizon or AT&T (think of it as more of an indirect play).

One of my favorite stocks that benefited from the cell phone boom was a company called American Tower (ticker symbol AMT). American Tower has been a huge beneficiary of the wireless boom, as its business is putting up the cell phone towers and other communication and broadcast tower sites. It was AMT that benefited from the Verizon/AT&T battles, as it built the infrastructure for the business that was generated by Verizon and AT&T. It is sort of like the razor blade example. AMT got the recurring revenue from all the people who were getting wireless phones. That's why its stock went from about $1.51 per share in October 2002 to top $45 by 2008.

I hope these examples will help you to recognize the kinds of social changes that are most likely to affect a company that you own or are following. The key is to recognize these changes before the rest of the world does, so that you at least have the potential to make money before other investors recognize and act on that same change.

In summary, one has to try to identify the aspects of change that will result in a revaluation of a company or higher reported earnings per share, and begin by trying to understand what the existing business is and to determine what the various aspects of change will do to that company (see Figure 6-3). Will the changes result in higher sales or earnings because the products or services are being delivered in a more efficient way, which could possibly create higher margins, stronger customer retention, or the likelihood of significant recurring revenues? Or conversely, will the changes hurt a company that you are following?

Once those questions are answered, you can then do more due diligence and at some point decide if the stock is worth buy-

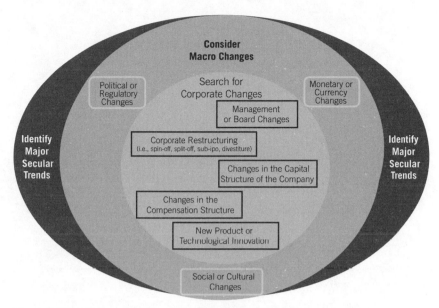

Figure 6-3   Changes that can trigger investment ideas.

ing, selling, or holding. None of this is black and white, however. Most of the time investors get to see only a world of grays, but still must attempt to determine what effect a given change will have on a company. I hope this chapter has helped you to better recognize the different kinds of changes that can affect a company so that you can recognize change and use it to give you an edge over other investors who might not be tuned in to this important phenomenon to the same degree.

7

WHAT HAS THE COMPANY DONE FOR ME LATELY?

In the previous two chapters on change, I showed that the first aspect of creating a winning strategy is to identify changes that are genuine and potentially significant. After that, the next step is to evaluate the company's execution. Execution is really the key. An investor could read a boatload of 10-Qs and annual reports and believe that change will be coming to an organization. Perhaps even the senior management team believes that positive change is on the way. However, once change has been identified, it becomes incumbent upon management to take action to capitalize on that change.

When I managed money, I tried to find the common denominator for all successful investments. Were there a handful of factors that led to a winning investment? As you know by now, I believe that there are a number of variables that can lead to better selection of stocks, better portfolio management, and so on. And I have pointed out that, while these investment strategies and tactics can improve your chances of success in any market, they become even more important when the stock market is not in rally mode or a bull market (in a rally, you could buy an index fund that would give you at least positive returns).

When you eliminate the noise, then execution comes down to what we call capital allocation. That is a formal way of referring to what a company does with the cash generated by the business (a.k.a. what have you done for me lately?). When we talk about allocating capital, we are talking about what the firm does with the cash it has left over after expenses, compensation, and expenditures on property, plant, and equipment. The way a company chooses to use its cash can make the firm a more attractive investment—a buying opportunity. On the other hand, poor cash management can be a sign that it's time to cut your losses and sell the stock.

To make this simple, there are basically five things that a company can do with the cash generated by its business operations. They are

1. Grow the business organically.
2. Pay out dividends and/or distributions.
3. Buy back outstanding shares.
4. Pursue mergers and acquisitions.
5. Nothing; just hold the cash.

Let's look at each strategy individually.

Grow the Business Organically

This tops the list of what companies can do with the cash the business generates. Here we are talking about creating new products, entering new markets, building new factories, creating new business relationships, and so on. The potential net effect is expansion of the stock's price/earnings multiple. Sometimes an investor has to really dig to get the actual percentage of organic growth versus other kinds of growth, such as acquisitions.

Overall, 10-Qs and 10-Ks are the best places to find a company's real organic growth percentage. As mentioned earlier, these are detailed reports that a company must file with the SEC, and both of them are very easy to find online. For example, I searched via Google for "Ford 10-K," and the report came right up. In item 7 of the report, as reprinted here, we get a sense of just how well the company did in 2009 when compared to 2008:

Item 7. Management's Discussion and Analysis of Financial Condition and Results of Operations (Continued)

Full Year 2009 Compared with Full Year 2008

In 2009, our net income was $1.3 billion, compared with a net loss of $1.5 billion in 2008. On a pre-tax basis, we earned $2 billion in 2009, compared with a loss of $2.6 billion in 2008.

In explaining the vast improvement in 2009 earnings over 2008, nowhere did the company say anything about a merger or acquisition, so investors can see at a glance that the earnings growth was organic in nature. The increase in the stock price reflects the strong organic earnings growth. In November 2008, the stock hit a multiyear low of under $2 per share during the height of the liquidity crisis that almost erased the U.S. car industry. But unlike Chrysler and GM, which took money from the government to help stave off disaster, Ford did not need the money. Of the Big Three, Ford was best positioned to deliver a genuine turnaround story, and it did: In December 2009, Ford's stock was up by more than 500 percent off its low, trading at about $10 in late 2009. Before the end of the first quarter of 2010, Ford's stock hit a multiyear high, as shown in Figure 7-1, outperforming the performance of the S&P 500 by a huge margin.

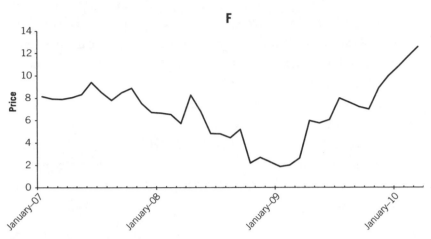

Figure 7-1   A 3-year chart of Ford.

There are other companies that come to mind as well when it comes to organic growth. One of the most prominent is one of my all-time favorite stocks, Suncor Energy, the fifth largest energy company in North America. Suncor took its process and its expertise in developing its existing resource assets and used them to increase its production of oil and other products, organically growing its business.

Suncor was originally part of Sun Oil but was spun off in 1995. It became an incredible stock because of the company's tremendous organic growth. In fact, it grew much, much faster than its original parent. From 1995 to its zenith, Suncor's stock skyrocketed from well below $3 per share to top $70 per share in 2008.

Suncor became one of the greatest stocks of my 20-year tenure as a money manager. It did so because it took all of the cash it generated and redeployed that cash to expand its daily production and grow its existing resource base. Investing in the infrastructure for organic growth is the best thing a company can do with its capital.

Another favorite name of mine when it comes to organic growth is Expeditors International, ticker symbol EXPD. I love this business because it's in the freight forwarding logistics business, where it competes with very large, bureaucratic organizations like FedEx and UPS. However, unlike those two companies, which own the planes and the trucks, these guys are asset light. Expeditors has been a very forward-looking organi-

Investing in the infrastructure for organic growth is the best thing a company can do with its capital.

zation, helping its customers with freight forwarding logistics and expanding into great growth markets like China. If you compare EXPD to UPS for a recent 10-year period, you see the power of organic growth and earnings growth. EXPD was up just under 300 percent between 2000 and 2010, while UPS has gone absolutely nowhere.

Pay Out Dividends and/or Distributions

After organic growth, dividends and distributions are the next most important thing to look for when you are evaluating a potential stock purchase. A dividend is simply a regularly scheduled cash payment made by a company to its shareholders out of the firm's profits. It is taxable in the year in which it is received.

A distribution, on the other hand, is paid when a company determines that it requires less capital and returns some of its capital to shareholders. This differs from a dividend in that it is usually an infrequent occurrence and is not taxable in the year in which it is received. Instead, it is subtracted from your purchase price, with the result that you pay a long-term capital gain when the stock is sold. Distributions are often paid by partnerships to their partners, as in the case of a real estate investment trust (REIT).

Dividends and distributions are more alike than they are different because in each case, the company is paying something to its shareholders from the operations of the business. It is the corporate structure that determines which of the two is paid. Dividends are often paid quarterly, but there are also one-time special dividends. Sometimes companies actually pay a stock dividend as opposed to a cash dividend.

Buying stocks with a rich dividend yield can be a key part of your investment strategy. The potential net effect of receiving dividends and distributions is that you are rewarded because you are getting a cash return. You've got the cash in your pocket, and you can spend it on whatever it is you want to spend it on. So assuming that the principal value of the stock doesn't go down, you're getting a net tangible and measurable return. Additionally, if the company can create a steady and growing stream of dividends or distributions, you'll be rewarded with P/E multiple growth, much as you are with organic growth. That's because any company that can grow its dividends consistently is perceived to be a healthy company (which it usually is), so the shareholders reward that company with a higher multiple. In these situations, when you hold a stock that increases its dividend every quarter or every year, you get the potential for two forms of wealth creation. The principal value of the equity investment is likely to go up, and you'll get the cash when the dividend is paid.

One of the key facts to always keep in mind is that dividends and distributions account for about half of the return on the total stock market. So when you are told that the stock market has historically delivered a 8–10 percent return, half of that return can be attributed to dividends and distributions being reinvested into the stocks that pay them. That is something that many investors either don't know or take for granted. Dividends and distributions are especially important in a sideways or range-bound market—when the stock price is not appreciating, the dividend can often provide an outsize portion of your return.

At Team K, we liked to find companies that had a capital allocation strategy that identified them as being, in our view, what are called *bond equivalents*. When we bought a bond equivalent, we would do it because we were looking not just for capital appreciation, but for total return, which, of course, includes dividends and distributions.

Typically, investors buy bonds because they want capital preservation, safety of the principal, and an income stream. In the case of a bond equivalent, you want not just an income stream or a distribution, but a *growing* dividend or distribution. If you can identify a stock that has a very predictable and growing dividend, you are likely to get a significant capital gain as well.

We defined bond equivalents to also include master limited partnerships. A master limited partnership (MLP) is a limited partnership that in many cases is an oil and/or gas company. What makes these entities different from other publicly traded companies is that they are legally organized in a way that obligates them to pay out a significant portion of their earnings as a return of capital to shareholders. One example of a highly regarded MLP is Enterprise Products Partners LP (EPD), which defines itself as providing a range of services to producers and consumers of natural gas, crude oil, and petrol chemicals in the United States, Canada, and Gulf of Mexico.

This particular MLP has performed incredibly well: for example, from March 1, 2009 to July 1, 2010, EPD's price moved from a little over $20 to about $35 (see Figure 7-2). Plus, and this is the key, it paid a distribution to its shareholders ranging from 6 to 8 percent.

Real estate investment trusts can also be considered bond equivalents. A REIT is a company whose main business is managing income-producing real estate. These firms usually manage portfolios of real estate investments. What differentiates a REIT from other entities is the industry in which it operates. REITs obviously are products of the real estate industry. However, like MLPs, they must pay the vast majority of their profits to their shareholders as dividends. While REITs underperformed during the go-go days of the 1990s, they outperformed the market by

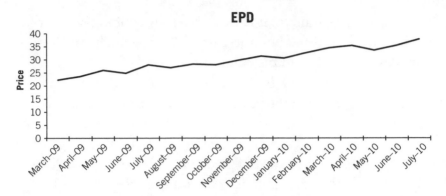

Figure 7-2   A 17-month chart of Enterprise Products Partners LP.

a wide margin in the 2000s. That's because they usually do not move in lockstep with the overall stock market. (They often go up when markets falter, which makes them a good hedge for an investor's portfolio. I will spend much more time on hedging in Chapter 11 of the book.) One example of a REIT that has performed well is Simon Property Group (SPG). Between 2000 and 2010, Simon Property, which owns shopping malls, was up some 300 percent while the S&P 500 was down slightly (see Figure 7-3). SPG also pays a dividend of about 3 percent, which is near the low end of the range for REITs.

Figure 7-3   A 10-year chart of Simon Property Group.

Another type of entity that pays a large percentage of its profits to shareholders is royalty trusts. Like a master limited partnership, many royalty trusts are involved in gas and oil production and other energy assets. For example, an investor would buy a royalty trust that owns gas if that investor expected gas prices to rise in the future. Royalty trusts also enjoy certain tax advantages because their distributions are taxed at a lower rate than ordinary income (those monies are used to reduce the cost basis of the trust, and no tax is owed until the trust is sold).

One example of a royalty trust that has done well is Sabine Royalty Trust (SBR). Sabine owns mineral, oil, and other energy assets. Since 2000, its share price has increased by nearly 300 percent (see Figure 7-4), and it has paid a dividend in excess of 5 percent.

You know by this time that I do not believe in indexing (or in being a closet indexer, which you know I abhor even more). However, this does not mean that you should not have all of the information that is relevant to a particular topic or investment. Put

Figure 7-4   A 10-year chart of Sabine Royalty Trust.

another way, just because I don't recommend something as an investment does not mean that you should not be familiar with it. Such is the case with the following exchange-traded fund (ETF).

Investors who do not want to have to choose among individual dividend-paying stocks can buy an ETF that includes a number of top-paying dividend stocks. Its ticker symbol is DVY, and its official name is "iShares Dow Jones Select Dividend Index."

For investors who do not have the time or the tools to select individual stocks, DVY gives them the option to buy a pool of stocks that all pay healthy dividends. Table 7-1 shows the top 20 percent of DVY's holdings in 2010, while Table 7-2 shows the top sectors by percentage allocation.

In the second quarter of 2010, DVY was paying an annual dividend of about 3.7 percent, which is a relatively good number. But that's only half the story. Over any real length of time

Table 7-1   Top Holdings, iShares Dow Jones Select Dividend Index

Company Name	Percent of Net Assets
Lorillard, Inc.	2.75
Entergy Corporation	2.08
Mercury General Corporation	1.98
Centurytel, Inc.	1.98
VF Corporation	1.94
Chevron Corporation	1.89
McDonald's Corporation	1.72
Kimberly-Clark Corporation	1.68
PPG Industries, Inc.	1.68
Watsco, Inc.	1.67
Percent of holdings	19.37

Table 7-2 Top Sectors, iShares Dow Jones Select Dividend Index

Sector Name	Percent of Net Assets
Utilities	24.32
Consumer goods	23.91
Industrial materials	20.72
Financial service	12.93
Consumer service	4.69
Health care	4.03
Telecommunication	3.16
Energy	3.07
Business service	2.37
Media	0.67
Percent of sectors	99.87

(two years, three years, five years, ten years), DVY has failed to keep up with the performance of the S&P 500, sometimes trailing by as much as 20 percent. This is yet one more reason why I do not recommend DVY for anyone's investment portfolio. However, DVY can be used in a different way. Once you master all of the tools I present in this book, you may want to evaluate each of the stocks in DVY's holdings. Perhaps there are gems among them, but only by doing your homework will you find out if there are one or more stocks in the DVY portfolio that are worth buying.

At this point, before moving on to the final three uses of cash, I need to reiterate the importance of the two uses discussed so far: organic growth and dividend payouts. It is critical to note that the five uses of cash are not created equal. All other things being equal, I regard organic growth and dividend payout as the best two things management can do with cash. It's not that there is no place for the other three uses of cash; it's just that we found that over an extended period of time, stocks rise further and faster if they have strong and consistent organic growth and/or a steady increase in their dividend payout. Please keep this in mind as you develop your own strategy for selecting stocks. You want to build a portfolio of companies that focus on the first two forms of capital allocation. Now we can move on to the last three uses of cash.

Buy Back Outstanding Shares

Some managers use their cash to purchase outstanding shares of their company. The net effect for that firm is fewer shares outstanding, which results in higher reported earnings per share.

There are two ways for a company to buy back its own stock. The more common is a publicly announced, ongoing share repurchase program. The second, less common way to buy back shares is more aggressive than the first method because it takes out a significant block of stock at a designated time and price and shrinks the capitalization faster. That repurchase program is called a *Dutch auction*. In both cases, the net effect is fewer shares outstanding, resulting in higher earnings per share.

Let me drill down a bit and include an example that will show the net effect of a company stock repurchase program.

Let's assume that there is a company with 200 million shares outstanding that earns $1 per share in earnings. Let's also assume that the company can buy back 40 million shares over a period of time. Finally, let's assume that the stock is being valued at 20 times earnings. So when the company earns $1 per share, the stock is a $20 stock. But once the company has bought back those 40 million shares, you now have earnings per share of $1.25 (because there are only 160 million shares left outstanding). So with the reduced number of shares, assuming the same P/E multiple, you now have a $25 stock. In this case, you've got a capital appreciation because there are fewer shares outstanding, all other things being equal. However, investing is not a science, so you can almost never assume that all other things will be equal. Let me include a real-life example to illustrate what I mean.

When it comes to share repurchases, the one company that always comes to mind is IBM. It is not a pure play in this area because it has also been very active in both engaging in mergers and acquisitions (M&A) and producing organic growth. However, it has been a very aggressive buyer of its own shares. By taking a close look at the company, we will get a chance to see the pros and cons of a share repurchase program.

Let's set the clock back a decade and look at IBM in 2000. The year before, in 1999, the company purchased some $7.3 billion of its common shares. In 2000, it reduced its shares outstanding by another 59 million shares. In 2000, IBM earned $4.44 per share. Its stock price, at its zenith in 2000, was about $135 per share. At that level, IBM had a multiple of about 30 times earnings.

"Big Blue" always struck me as a company with somewhat lackluster organic growth prospects. Part of the reason is its colossal size. In 2000, the company had revenues of more than $88 billion. It's difficult for a company to grow at 10 percent or more when it reaches that size. We know that part of the reason the company did not do all that well in 2000 was the dot-com crash, which had a negative impact on the stock market starting in the second quarter of 2000. But even discounting the technology bubble, I have always regarded IBM as a single-digit growth company. That is one of the reasons that IBM has been such an active buyer of its own shares. Knowing that its growth is not going to blow away any investors or fund managers, it has used share repurchases as a way to pump up the company stock. However, investors have seen through this, and have not rewarded the company.

As mentioned earlier, in 1999, IBM's stock hit a high of about $135 per share. In the first quarter of 2010, IBM's stock is trading at about $130 per share. Thus we have the lost decade of IBM as well, despite the company's considerable efforts in buying back its stock aggressively. In 2010, IBM is selling at less than 13 times earnings, a far cry from the multiple of 30 that it enjoyed in 2000. In light of that, I, and many other people, have wondered if IBM might have been much better off pursuing a different strategy from its aggressive stock repurchase program.

I believe that if the company had used all those buyback dollars to pay its shareholders a heftier dividend, it would be much better off today. It was as if investors had seen the stock repurchases as a ploy, albeit a failed one, to raise the price of the stock. Remember that I feel strongly that organic growth and an aggressive dividend-paying strategy are the two best uses of cash for a company. That's why I feel that IBM has consistently missed the boat on this, which is why the firm has not seen any real growth in its stock price for the last 10 years.

Let's look at one more example of a stock that has been a voracious buyer of its own shares. This is also a large-cap company that is often in the news—ExxonMobil.

ExxonMobil has been the worst-performing large-cap Dow stock for the one year following the bottoming of the stock market in March 2009 (March 2009 through March 2010). At a time when the S&P is up 60 percent from its low, ExxonMobil has basically not moved.

But, in the meantime, in December 2009, ExxonMobil announced a $41 billion acquisition of Houston-based natural gas company XTO Energy Inc. Many people believed that ExxonMobil would have been better off instituting a significant dividend increase rather than making that huge acquisition.

The point is that investing is more of an art than a science, and not much of an art either. For large companies like IBM and ExxonMobil, there are a number of different strategies that each could pursue. The market is a voting mechanism every day. Once a firm adopts a certain strategy, such as a share repurchase, there may be an immediate market reaction. But the market may have a different verdict on that company some months down the line.

Pursue Mergers and Acquisitions

Many companies, particularly those in mature industries in which organic growth is very difficult, pursue an aggressive M&A strategy. Some acquisitions are home runs that create a lot of shareholder value, and others are strikeouts. It all depends on the companies involved, the culture of the two companies, and the overlap in products and personnel. Let's look at an acquisition that I always regarded as a home run.

When GE bought RCA in 1984, it reunited two great companies that had been together before. In fact, in 1919, with the assistance of then secretary of the navy Franklin D. Roosevelt, GE helped to create the Radio Corporation of America, which it was eventually forced to sell in 1932. But when Welch saw that RCA was available, he saw the future of GE. Welch wanted GE to have a greater presence in high-growth nonmanufacturing businesses, and RCA became the focal point of that strategy. Since that acquisition, services have been a very prominent part of the GE success story, and have played a key role in helping GE to grow by double digits in the 1990s.

The $6 billion acquisition proved to be an unmitigated success, and because it was so successful, it helped GE to become a far more aggressive and confident acquirer of new businesses, which helped its stock price to consistently outperform the market for many years. However, the GE-RCA merger is the exception, not the rule. Most acquisitions fail to add any value.

According to the *Harvard Management Update*, "Most [mergers] fail to add shareholder value—indeed, post-merger, two-thirds of the newly formed companies perform well below the industry average."

Even that number seems low to me. I have always felt that 90 percent of mergers fail to add value. However, whether it's 66 percent or 90 percent, the sad truth is that most mergers fail. That is why this is such a risky growth strategy and why I rank it as number four out of the five things that a management team can do with the cash generated by the business.

Why do most mergers fail?

Noted consultant and author Denzil Rankin cites five reasons why mergers and acquisitions fail, and I will paraphrase his thinking:

- **Bad business logic.** The business model (of the acquired company) could be the wrong one. Some companies should not be acquiring at all, Rankin concludes. Managerial ego also enters into the equation. The acquiring manager gets blinded by all of those hundreds of millions or billions in additional assets and does not explore the underlying fit of the two companies.
- **Lack of understanding of the new business.** Often the acquiring company does not do enough due diligence, and this can lead to a company buying another for the wrong reason. A company must understand how the target firm makes its money. The acquiring company must also do its homework to make sure that the target company will generate the kind of value it is supposed to.
- **Bad deal management.** There are many instances in which a company gets acquisition "fever," explains Rankin. Once that happens, a firm may negotiate a bad deal by overpaying for the target company. That is why

it is so important that the acquirer get an unvarnished and honest opinion of what the business is really worth.

- **Poor integration management.** This may be one of the most prevalent reasons why acquisitions fail. Most companies do not do the necessary amount of planning for the integration. People in the acquired firm fear for their jobs, and stress levels are high. Lastly, the acquiring company fails to take the magnitude of the integration into account.

- **Flawed corporate development.** After the initial shock of the acquisition wears off, the companies must be aligned so that the two companies are maximizing the value of the new combined organization. This is where the cultural fit of the two organizations takes center stage. It is critical for managers in the acquiring company not to behave like conquerors or victors in the new organization.

Mergers and acquisitions can fail because of a combination of the aforementioned reasons or other ones as well. To succeed in the acquisition game, companies must have the right leadership team in place to make it happen, and must have extensive integration plans, contingency plans, and so on.

There is also a great deal of pressure on management to pursue acquisitions. Bankers are constantly trying to convince CEOs and other top managers to acquire companies because of all of the fees that these deals generate. One of the greatest examples of this was the famous buyout of RJR Nabisco in 1988 by Kohlberg Kravis Roberts & Co., the largest leveraged buyout up to that point (the entire greed-fest is beautifully described in the excellent book *Barbarians at the Gate*, by Bryan Burrough and John Helyar).

Many companies actually go into deals knowing that there's a 90 percent probability that a deal is not going to add value. They still do the deals because managers always feel that they're going to be the one guy out of ten who actually gets it right. I've never met a manager who doesn't go into a deal saying that he and his company are going to succeed—that they're going to be the ones who structure and manage everything just right.

However, history has shown that more often than not, mergers and acquisitions are studies in culture clashes. There is almost always difficulty integrating systems, so that the MIS systems that are basically there to help people become more of a problem. Then there is the unintended consequence of people leaving the company. At the end of the day, it's all about human capital, and when you talk to people about why they leave a company after a merger, it is almost always because of the rapport that was lost when the new management team came in. When companies take over other companies, they want to install their own people in the new company, and this has a domino effect on the firm.

The sad reality is that the M&A graveyard is full of acquisitions gone awry. Near the top of the list is the joining of AOL and Time Warner. This deal was a disaster right out of the gate: Soon after the deal was announced in early 2000, AOL's business started to falter. None of the principals ever had a sound integration plan (remember, AOL acquired Time Warner, which, in hindsight, made little sense), and any talk of synergy went up in smoke almost before the papers were signed.

Of course I am not the first person to question how these deals go so terribly wrong. Steve Rosenbush of *Business Week* summed it up nicely when he asked:

> How is it that such deals come together in the first place? In each case, managers were clearly swinging for the fences, pouring huge sums into the bet like a Vegas gambler desperate to

score a big win as he sees his chips dwindle. And bad deals often are born of fear or desperation. A rival—or potential rival—is forging a new market or making inroads into the existing one and the incumbents must respond. Sometimes there's a surfeit of confidence about what the future will hold and management's ability to stitch the various pieces together nicely. In other cases, the deal may make strategic sense but at a price that is wildly off the mark.

One more acquisition that was lambasted by Wall Street was Hewlett-Packard's acquisition of computer maker Compaq in 2001. The day before the deal was disclosed, HP's stock closed at $23.21. On September 4, 2001, the announcement of the closely guarded secret acquisition stunned investors and sent HP's stock plummeting, down nearly $4.50 per share, or more than 18 percent, to $18.87.

There are different schools of thought about whether or not this acquisition was good for HP. However, Wall Street's verdict was harsh. Between 2001 and mid-2007, HP's stock badly trailed the performance of the S&P 500. Jim Collins, the bestselling author of *Good to Great,* summed up HP's plight in the Foreword he wrote for *The HP Way* like this:

> Then in the late 1990s and early 2000s, HP veered off course, making a series of decisions incompatible (in my judgment) with the fundamental precepts that made the company great in the first place. HP brought in a charismatic CEO from the outside and embarked on a costly acquisition whose success depended largely upon a market share and cost cutting arguments, not unique technical contribution. Whether the HP-Compaq merger proves to be a success remains to be seen, although the verdict of history from similar mergers indicates low odds. Even if HP were to beat the odds and emerge with a substantial financial return on the Compaq deal, I do not think

that David Packard would have been pleased at all with the state of HP in early 2005.

So this is a situation in which one of the great business minds of our day felt that the Compaq acquisition was simply not consistent with the original precepts of the acquiring company.

The key takeaway here is that many mergers and acquisitions result in massive destruction of shareholder wealth. It is no accident that mergers and acquisitions rank near the bottom of what management could do with cash. This is especially true in sideways markets. When markets are not rising, management may be tempted to do more deals to create some excitement around the company and add to assets under management (assuming that the company has the ability to finance the deal). That is why it is so important for management to really do its due diligence before making any acquisition. Similarly, investors need to do their due diligence before considering purchasing or selling any company that pursues M&A as a major growth strategy.

To be crystal clear, I am not saying that mergers and acquisitions are necessarily a bad thing in and of themselves. I am arguing that every deal and every company must be scrutinized to make sure that the deal makes sense.

Nothing; Just Hold the Cash

The last thing a company can do is just hold cash and build it up on its balance sheet. The biggest negative of just holding cash is that the company doesn't get any of the benefits that I have described thus far. The company does not get a P/E multiple expansion, nor does it shrink the number of shares outstanding. One more potential side effect of holding cash is that activist investors may decide to target your company for redeployment of that capital. The more a firm builds up its cash for a rainy day, so to speak, the more it runs the risk of outside factors trying to influence that company's future actions. This is why I generally avoid buying companies that hold a significant percentage of their profits in cash.

One example of a company that has been attacked for holding too much cash is Microsoft. Even after paying out as much as $35 billion in regular and special dividends between 2004 and 2005, the company still had $38 billion on hand. Holding that much cash can infuriate investors and help a company to garner a great deal of negative attention in the press; for example, in July 2005, *Business Week* ran a story entitled "Too Much Cash, Too Little Innovation" and included Microsoft as one of technology's prime examples.

A quick glance at the stock chart in Figure 7-5 shows that it wasn't just the press that held Microsoft's feet to the fire—so did investors. It is clear that one did not want to have one's money tied up in Microsoft stock between 2000 and 2010, since the overall return would have been negative.

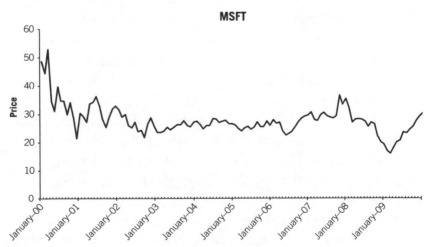

Figure 7-5   A 10-year chart of Microsoft.

Most attractive

Top Five Uses of Cash	Potential Net Effect

1. Grow the business organically
   – New factories
   – New products
   – New markets
	• P/E multiple expansion

2. Pay dividends and
   distributions
	• Shareholders rewarded with
	  cash in hand
	• P/E multiple expansion

3. Share repurchases	• Higher earnings per share (fewer shares outstanding)

4. Mergers and acquisitions
   (M&A)
	• Majority of M&As fail
	  – Clash of corporate cultures
	  – Difficulty integrating systems
	  – Personnel departures

5. Hold cash	• Pressure from investors to redeploy

Least attractive

Figure 7-6   What has the company done for its shareholders lately?

To recap, here is a summary of the five uses of cash in order of importance (with the first being most important, of course). A summary is also given in Figure 7-6.

- **Grow the business organically.** Here we are talking about new factories, new products, and new markets. The net effect of organic growth is price/earnings multiple expansion. Organic growth tops the list of things that companies can do with their cash on hand.
- **Pay dividends and distributions.** This ranks second on the list of the best uses of a company's cash. The result is that shareholders are rewarded with cash disbursements, and this can also lead to price/earnings multiple expansion.
- **Repurchase shares.** This will increase the earnings per share, since there will be fewer shares outstanding following a company's share repurchase program.
- **Pursue mergers and acquisitions.** This ranks near the bottom of things that a company can do with its cash. That's because the majority of mergers and acquisitions

fail as a result of a clash of corporate cultures, the great challenge of integrating systems, and having the best people walk out the door in search of a better position.

- **Hold cash.** This is probably the worst thing a company can do with its money—just hold it. It does not help the company, and it also invites various constituencies, such as the company's shareholders, to pressure management to spend its cash.

8
PICKING STOCKS
FOR ALL MARKETS

Many people buy stocks for the wrong reasons. They may buy stocks because a broker, analyst, or money manager advised them to do so. Listening to the advice of talking heads—rather than doing one's own due diligence—is almost always the wrong reason to buy a stock. Many analysts recommend stocks that they themselves don't even own, making the entire notion of taking their advice silly (remember, up to 90 percent of money managers fail to outperform the S&P 500 over extended periods of time). Additionally, it is always important to remember that many recommendations that you may hear about are based on a *relative* performance metric.

For example, an analyst talking about restaurant stocks might recommend the Cheesecake Factory as the best performer in the group. He might also rate the rest of the group that he covers as underperformers because of higher input costs. The key takeaway here is that while he is recommending Cheesecake

Factory, he is comparing it only with the rest of the restaurant sector. The overall group of restaurant stocks—including Cheesecake Factory—may have negative returns, but you have no way of knowing that from the analyst's recommendation. That's because sell-side analysts deal with only one sector or industry. It is important to understand this distinction.

Bestselling author Charles Ellis called investing a "loser's game" in *Winning the Loser's Game*, his book based on the assumption that investors and institutions are unable to beat or time the market. However, one of the key assumptions of my book is that it is indeed possible to beat the market if you know precisely how to do it. You can pick winners in what Ellis and others have called a loser's game.

In baseball, if you hit .300, you end up in the Hall of Fame. In investing, you need to have a batting average of between .600 and .700 percent to be a consistent winner.

In the previous two chapters, we looked at the first two keys to selecting stocks that will outperform the market: buying opportunities based on changes in the company itself and how a company uses its cash to make the firm a more attractive investment.

In this chapter, I will show one more method of identifying stocks that have the potential to outperform in sideways markets. When all three of these techniques are used in tandem to analyze stocks, the result can be quite powerful—a stock-picking methodology that will help you to hit between .600 and .700 and amass a winning stock portfolio.

In this chapter I will look at stocks from a different perspective from that used in the previous two chapters. Here I will zero in on the five tenets of stock selection that will help you as you complete your due diligence in analyzing any stock investment:

1. Sustainable competitive advantage
2. Strong financial metrics
3. Long-term free cash flow generation
4. Shareholder focus
5. Insider ownership

If you find a stock that has all five of these characteristics, then you may indeed have found a winning investment. However, just as in the previous two chapters, you have to be thorough in doing your homework. That means bringing the principles of the previous two chapters to bear in analyzing that stock so that you can be sure that it passes all of the litmus tests that I described in those chapters.

Let's take an up-close look at each of these characteristics to give you the tools you will need to analyze prospective investments.

Sustainable Competitive Advantage

Given how quickly technology and global markets change, it is more difficult than ever to achieve a long-term or sustainable competitive advantage. Companies that enjoy this type of advantage are few and far between. That's because achieving a competitive advantage requires much more than having a business strategy in place for three months or three years; it requires a focus on key issues such as sustainable growth, management succession, employee retention, and training the next generation of leaders. These issues are even more important when we assume that economic global growth will be below the long-term averages over the next decade.

Being a company that enjoys a long-term competitive advantage requires more than just doing the obvious things like identifying new sources of customers, coming up with mechanisms for customer retention, and searching for recurring revenues. It requires thinking outside of the box, such as dealing with potential damage control before disaster strikes, thinking about how you'd counter if a competitor did something irrational to steal market share, or turning customer acquisition into a science (e.g., determining the actual costs of acquiring each new customer). Much of this is about figuring out precisely what you are willing to spend on marketing and promotion to generate additional revenues.

There was a time, years ago, when companies could basically start a business, build up enough scale to dominate the space, and not have to worry about competition. It didn't matter if the business was a retailer or a technology company. Today, with the tremendous amount of information and data available to all, even our greatest growth companies, like Starbucks, which dominated for years, now have to worry about new entrants attempting to chip away at their market share—Dunkin' Donuts and McDonald's now sell high-quality coffee at a much lower price than Starbucks.

Even the largest and most dominant companies have to worry about the competition. Another great example is Wal-Mart, the world's largest retailer, with revenues in excess of $400 billion in fiscal year 2010. Now it has to watch rivals like Costco, Kohl's, and Target to make sure that it can hold on to vital market share. These three retailers have enjoyed much success, carving out their own places in the retailing industry. For example, in the second quarter of 2010, as the U.S. economy was coming out of its Great Recession, rival company Target, a more upscale retailer than Wal-Mart, reported increases in market share, while sales at Wal-Mart were essentially flat. This was not expected, and this trend is likely to continue if the economy continues to strengthen in 2011 and beyond.

In fact, given the level playing field for information today, I can think of no company in the world that doesn't have to worry about the competition.

However, I can think of a few companies that do indeed enjoy a sustainable competitive advantage in their industry. For example, let's take online retailer Amazon.com. It is the number one seller of books via the Internet. Amazon has a long-term competitive advantage in online book sales, and no move by any rival can endanger that edge any time soon. Amazon was one of the first great companies on the Net, and from the beginning it did things that no other bookseller did. In addition to having an incredible selection that no brick-and-mortar store could equal, it also had excellent customer service and was even able to create an online community of book buyers long before social communities were all the rage. All of these factors help to explain Amazon's great success.

In mid-2010, Amazon shares—whose price had gone below $10 in the dot-com bust—were selling for more than $135 per share, or close to 80 times current earnings (see Figure 8-1). A sustainable competitive advantage is a real key to choosing the right stock to buy, but that alone is not sufficient reason to own that stock. There are four other criteria that are almost as important.

Figure 8-1 A 10-year chart of Amazon.

Strong Financial Metrics

This, too, is a criterion that requires little thought. An investor always wants to own stocks that have strong financials, epitomized by the fact that the company is self-financing.

The goal of this book is not to make you an accountant. It is to try to teach you to be able to identify a company that is self-financing. A self-financing company does not need to borrow money or issue any new stock to be financially sound. The last decade has shown us that companies that have to rely on capital markets to execute their business plans can, at times, be in real trouble. Capital markets shut down, and capital markets get frozen. The lesson that I came away with from the liquidity crisis is that companies should strive to generate enough cash from the daily operations of their business to execute their growth strategies.

That is why we want to find companies that don't have to rely on capital markets. But finding self-financing companies is no simple task. We want to own companies that can move with both lightning speed and cost efficiency if they need to ramp up production at a moment's notice.

Let's look at a favorite company of mine that is strong enough to self-finance: Expeditors International (EXPD). EXPD is an air and freight carrier that competes with UPS and FedEx. However, unlike its two rivals, Expeditors does not have its cash tied up in heavy equipment like trucks and planes. Instead, the company rents fleets to get the job done, allowing it to be more focused on providing great customer service. It also has a top-notch management team led by CEO Peter Rose, who has been there since 1988. The bottom line is that Expeditors is an excellent example of a company that can self-finance. Where is the proof? In mid-2010 it had zero debt and $1 billion in cash on its books. That's the kind of winning combination you should be searching for when you are evaluating potential companies to buy and own.

Long-Term Free Cash Flow Generation

This one sounds complicated, but it really isn't. Free cash flow (FCF) is basically the cash flow generated by any business minus any capital expenditures necessary for the company to grow at its current rate. This harks back to what we talked about when we discussed companies generating cash. When companies report their earnings, there is a wide array of things that they can do to dress up their earnings so that they look better than they actually are. For example, selling off a certain division could create a one-time gain that can lead to a very big earnings surprise, which in turn can create an artificial lift to the stock.

Another example: A company that needs to do research and development (R&D) to generate product growth could dramatically cut its R&D budget to generate higher reported earnings per share. While this may look good on the surface, the company is underinvesting in the very thing that its future growth depends on. This is a warning sign.

However, there are definite risks associated with taking these types of actions. As one of the founding partners of Team K and a legend in the investing business, Joe Lasser, once said, "A cash flow statement never lies."

Joe was one of the visionaries and architects of the success of Team K, and his advice here is particularly timely and useful. Rather than buy companies that do something alien to their own DNA, like cut R&D, he advocated buying companies that had, as part of their mission, a consistent focus on generating cash so that they could grow organically. He hated companies that focused on doing something in the short term just to artificially inflate their earnings.

> *A cash flow statement never lies.*

When you think of how difficult it is to generate enough cash to run a business, the one industry that always comes to mind is the airline industry. Given the massive capital expenditures necessary to constantly rebuild a company's fleet of planes, the amount of money needed for compensation to employees, and the fact that you have to advertise and promote the business aggressively, the airline industry is one of the most challenging to run profitably. And that is not only my opinion.

Bob Crandall, a former CEO and chairman of AMR Corporation (a parent company of American Airlines), once said something like: "I would never understand how anybody would buy a share of an airline stock." That was an incredible admission for an executive who was running an airline company. He also said, "We've never earned our cost of capital" (cost of capital represents the money a company needs to finance its operations and projects). It was one of those amazing things that stood out to me. Crandall was an industry visionary, having created the frequent flier program and made some very strategic acquisitions, yet here he was admitting the weak earnings of his entire industry.

Under Crandall, American became a global airline carrier as a result of good strategic management thinking. When Crandall said that he would never understand why anyone would invest in an airline stock given the fact that his company had never earned its cost of capital, he was telling investors to invest their money elsewhere. He was basically saying that his company was better off dead than alive. If a company cannot cover its cost of capital, then what is it really worth? That was what Crandall was referring to when he made his truly astonishing comments. Even during the best years and cycles for the airline industry, the company did not generate a sufficient amount of cash.

Not all airline companies are created equal. Southwest Airlines has been a real exception to the rule. Southwest has become the largest airline in the world in terms of number of passengers flown (as of 2009). What makes Southwest so remarkable is that it is the only airline company that has been profitable for 37 straight years (as of January 2010).

Another airline that has fared better than most is Jet Blue. Despite some serious customer service problems, Jet Blue has generated cash throughout its relatively brief history. Like Southwest, it weathered some of the worst years and events in its history. For example, Jet Blue had strong financial results from 2002 to 2004, just after the tragic events of September 11 that did such serious damage to the airline industry.

However, while airlines can be attractive trading opportunities, in my opinion they should never be considered for a long-term investment. The history of the industry tells you why: Eastern Airlines, gone. Pan American, gone. People Express, gone. United and Delta Airlines had to be reorganized through Chapter 11 bankruptcy, as did Continental (and United and Continental announced a merger agreement in mid-2010). All because they couldn't generate enough cash.

When viewed as a sector, the airline industry has lost billions of dollars, as have investors. Yet people continue to buy these stocks because they are trading vehicles. Why are they good candidates to trade? There is always going to be a greater fool, a new generation of investors that feel that the airline industry has finally cut enough costs and that it is on the upturn. But that conclusion simply does not stand up to history. At the end of the day, with rare exception, the airlines have never generated cash from operations. When you're holding a portfolio with a limited number of securities, you should simply avoid this industry altogether.

Ironically, a business that is very different from the airline industry is the airplane-making business. This is evident when one compares one of the leaders in the aviation field, Boeing, to any of the large, traditional airline companies. In the fourth quarter of 2009, for example, Boeing reported revenues of $17.9 billion and free cash flow of nearly $3 billion (up from a negative $2 billion in 2008). This is an impressive performance, despite the fact that the company delayed the introduction of its new 787 planes several times during the past few years.

Did Boeing's strong cash flow translate into a strong investment? The answer is an unmitigated yes. On the day Boeing reported its strong fourth-quarter earnings (January 27, 2010), the stock was trading in the high 50s. Within three months, the stock topped the $75 mark, outperforming the S&P 500 (see Figure 8-2). Many people believe that once a company reports strong earnings and rises on the results, it is too late to get in. Boeing shows that to be dead wrong. Boeing's strong earnings report, which included very strong free cash flow, helped the company to continue its strong upward stock performance.

Shareholder Focus

This is the most subjective of the buying criteria. Companies that are intensely focused on their shareholders will do all the things that are necessary to deliver value to the people who own their stock. They will strive to grow organically and deliver strong financials. They will be giving out generous dividends,

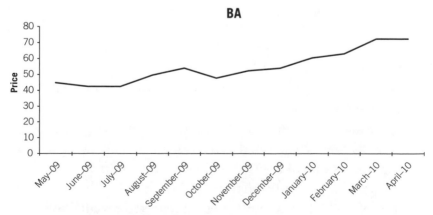

Figure 8-2   A 1-year chart of Boeing.

and in many cases buying back shares of their own stock. Shareholder focus dovetails nicely with the ideas I discussed in the previous chapter, because how a company uses the cash it generates does indicate shareholder focus, at least to some degree.

There are several other things that a company can do to show that it is shareholder focused. And this is where the subjectivity comes in. Companies can take certain actions or launch various initiatives that help shareholders, but depending upon the initiative, these companies may or may not actually be shareholder focused. It depends on the motivation behind the actions that a company takes.

For example, more people are concerned with the environment and the green movement than ever before. Is the company environmentally friendly, is it green? While being focused on the environment may mean spending more money—retrofitting equipment, paying more to do business with green suppliers, and so on—there is evidence that being green adds value and that some investors will accept those lower earnings in order to buy a socially friendly company. In this scenario, are companies being green because they believe in making the planet better, or are they doing it to appease shareholders? It is often difficult to know, but that is not a great concern. Being green is usually the right thing to do, and whatever it was that got the company to go in that direction doesn't matter. In the end, it is the actions and results that matter.

Let's look at an example of a green company. In 2009, *Newsweek*, for the first time, rated America's top 500 green companies. Surprisingly, Hewlett-Packard (HPQ) topped the list, and Starbucks came in at number 10.

HP was recognized because it was the first IT company to significantly reduce greenhouse gas emissions. If you look at a two-year chart of Hewlett-Packard between April 2008 and April 2010, its stock was up by about 18 percent while the S&P 500 was down by about 12 percent (see Figure 8-3). This was

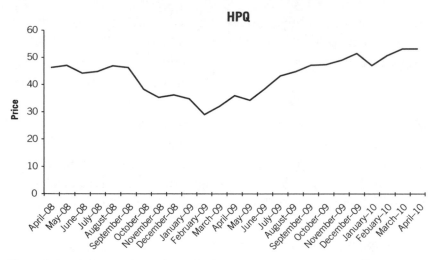

Figure 8-3   A 2-year chart of Hewlitt-Packard.

during a very turbulent time on Wall Street, as we know, since the stock market lost 37 percent of its value in 2008.

Starbucks, which has had its fair share of problems in recent years, came in at the number 10 slot on the *Newsweek* list because in 2008 it announced that it would "source products in environmentally and socially responsible ways." Starbucks vowed to encourage its supply-chain partners to protect water supplies, and it uses recycled paper products and organic coffee. Starbucks is a leader in "green" buildings as well. How did Starbucks perform since 2008? Between April 2008 and April 2010, the stock was up by about 50 percent while the S&P was down by about 12 percent (see Figure 8-4).

Another example of being shareholder focused involves those companies that make the *Fortune* and *Forbes* lists of the best companies to work for in America. Again, like being environmentally friendly, being employee focused adds to the company's cost structure: providing great health benefits, day care for workers, flexible vacation time, and many other benefits adds significantly to costs. However, once again, I have found some

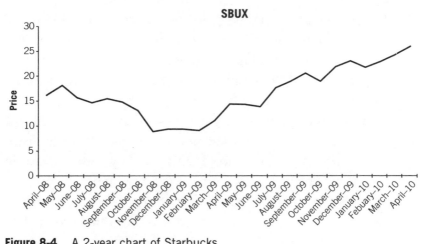

Figure 8-4   A 2-year chart of Starbucks.

correlation between those companies that top these lists and the ultimate benefit of higher stock prices for shareholders. It is worth pointing out that it may not be the fact that the company is green or that it is employee focused that boosts the stock price, but rather that if the company does good things in one area, it probably does them in several other areas as well.

In other words, if you examine the *Fortune* magazine list of the "100 Best Companies to Work For," you probably will not find the most profitable companies, but there is definitely some link between being on this list and the company's ability to out-perform its peers. I base that strictly on my own observations over a 20-year period. This does not mean that you should buy a stock simply because it is on that list, but the list is a good place to start. You should review the companies that are at the top of the list and do your homework to see if one or more of them satisfy the other criteria that I have identified in these last few chapters.

Let's look at an example of this: in 2009, *Fortune*'s number one company to work for was a company called NetApp Inc., a technology company that specializes in "enterprise storage and data management software and hardware products and services."

Let's forget how technical this company's products are and instead focus on what makes it such a great company for employees. For instance, rather than having a 12-page travel policy document, the company now tells its employees to "use your common sense" and "don't show up dog tired to save a few bucks."

Instead of asking for wonky business plans, many divisions of the company simply ask their people to write "future histories," projecting out their vision for where they see their unit in a year or two. The company didn't have any layoffs during the Great Recession, has gained market share, and had plenty of cash on hand to help it get through the liquidity crisis. And NetApp's benefits are "tops," declares *Fortune*: five paid days for employees to do volunteer work each year, more than $11,000 in adoption aid, and even autism coverage, which was used by 43 employees between 2006 and 2009 at a cost of about a quarter of a million dollars. What have all these perks done to the stock? While it is impossible to attribute the company's stock performance solely to these employee-driven offerings, it is interesting to note that in the two-year period from April 2008 to April 2010, the stock was up some 65 percent, while the S&P was down 15 percent during that same period. Just to reinforce the point, one cannot conclude that there is a cause-and-effect relationship between the company's stock price and its appearance near or at the top of these prestigious lists. It may be more of a reflection of the idea that if the company does right by its employees, it probably treats its customers in a similar fashion and executes its plans well.

This type of stock selection may seem a bit silly or unprofessional, but I have found there to be a high correlation between shareholder focus and being on a list like the *Fortune* list. Of course, this is not really something I can prove, but I have personally observed this phenomenon over the years.

This sort of investing, as I pointed out in Chapter 6, is very much like Peter Lynch's approach. Lynch was one of the first great money managers of the 1980s and wrote several bestselling investing books, such as *One Up on Wall Street*. To find the best companies, Lynch urged investors to use common sense: go to the shopping mall and see which store has the most shopping bags walking out the door. That was the Peter Lynch philosophy, a sort of eat-what-you're-cooking philosophy. I don't fundamentally disagree with Lynch, but that approach is now dated. *One Up on Wall Street* was written in a different, pre-Internet age when a company could dominate an industry and not worry that some new competitor would pop up overnight and steal market share.

Insider Ownership

This investing principle really comes down to common sense. I always have far more confidence in a company whose senior management team owns significant amounts of its own stock than in a company whose management team has little or no skin in the game. That's because companies with strong inside stock ownership have far more incentive to do good things for the company than those that don't. Put another way, how much confidence can a CEO have in her own company if she does not have much stock in the company that she leads? The good thing about insider ownership is that it is really easy to find out how many shares company insiders hold. You can learn that information on Yahoo! Finance and other popular Web sites (there will be much more on key Web sites in the next chapter). You don't need to have any kind of proprietary research or access to a technical database to learn the percentage of inside ownership of a company. Let's look at an example of how investors ignore this important investment tenet.

At a cocktail party, somebody recommends a biotechnology company to you because he heard from a friend of a friend that this company has a product in phase three, there is a high probability that the FDA is going to approve the product, and the company may announce some sort of joint development program with a pharmaceutical company. Ask yourself, how many times do you then go on to see whether the management of that biotechnology company has a significant equity position in the business? I bet you the answer is never. However, I have found over 20 years that managers who own stock side by side with you and me as investors have a much greater likelihood of practicing intelligent risk management because their shares are aligned with your shares.

Use common sense when you hear or read about managers selling shares. The article might say that the CEO is selling to diversify her portfolio or because she needs money for a family commitment or to pay her daughter's college tuition or her country club dues. Those situations are understandable as long as the executive isn't selling a disproportionate number of shares (e.g., a million shares at $50 per share).

Everybody's got to buy and sell stock at some point. But just as you don't want a CEO who never owns shares of his company's stock, because there's something wrong there, you want to find the proper balance between having a large enough amount of his capital invested in his company and proper diversification. There's no written rule here, no specific rule of thumb. It's more of a company-by-company, situation-by-situation thing. However, when you make an investment, ask yourself what percentage of your net worth you are willing to put into this idea, and then ask yourself, when looking at the insider ownership, whether you feel that management is demonstrating the same vote of confidence.

There are some money managers who believe in certain go/no-go criteria. They will say that they need to have X percent of shares held by insiders or management. I don't believe that that's the right thing to do. There are always circumstances that may make a strict rule like that not applicable.

Let's say, for example, that the CEO of a company is going through a divorce. And that divorce causes him to sell a significant number of shares, so that his ownership percentage is cut in half, and he discloses that properly. That's a lot of insider selling, but there's a reason behind it, and the CEO is transparent in his disclosure of that reason. There are some money managers who have rigid rules about what the inside ownership has to be in order for them to buy and hold that security. But, like so many things we have discussed so far, you need to think outside the box, and be aware of the reasons why insiders may be selling.

As with a lot of things we've discussed up to this point, you have to be aware of those types of things and be prepared to move quickly when a situation like that presents itself.

This is a perfect case in which you want to buy when others are selling. Those investors and money managers may be selling for the wrong reason, and you can take advantage of that dislocation because the insider selling has nothing to do with the company's fundamentals or its long-term ability to generate cash.

Let me get more specific by highlighting an actual example of what I have discussed thus far. A lot of funds set up their marketing propaganda to say things like, "We own only securities in which insider ownership represents 7 percent of shares outstanding." So an asset manager may sell a great stock from a growing firm on a technicality of insider ownership—not a great strategy, if you ask me.

There was one situation that came up at Team K involving a company in the food industry. There was a significant amount of insider selling when its CEO was going through a divorce. The company hadn't disclosed the reason for his selling, so there was a lot of misinformation in the marketplace about what was happening.

We sat down and had a conversation with management, and later found out that the CEO's wife wanted a quick divorce settlement. Since this information was not widely known, the company's stock price had experienced a 15 percent hit based on misinformation, rumor, and innuendo, and we took advantage of it. The key here is that we knew why the CEO was selling his stock, and because we were paying attention to the company's inside sales disclosures, we were able to profit on the news. As an investor, you want to look out for similar situations that could be exploited for gain with misinformation in the public domain.

I should end this section on a cautionary note: insider ownership is a hard metric to figure out, especially if you isolate it as a single construct or variable. Some companies that failed, including Bear Stearns and Lehman Brothers, had strong insider ownership. Some companies force insiders to own a significant percentage of their stock. That's why one should never make a buy or sell decision based solely on this factor.

9

DO YOUR OWN
DUE DILIGENCE

Doing your homework is one of the most critical aspects of choosing stocks; it will help you to take complete control of your investments. By mastering all of the skills and principles in this book, you will know what to look for before buying any stock. Doing your own research will help you to outperform others and the overall market. You cannot rely on others to do your due diligence for you.

As you have seen in the last several chapters, I have some very specific rules for buying stocks. The only way to follow them is to consistently search out new investment ideas by monitoring both the macro (e.g., the outside environment) and the micro factors (e.g., specific stocks, their management strategies, and so on). This means spending about 30 to 40 minutes a day online visiting the Web sites that I look at every morning. Not only will this help you to come up with new investment ideas, but it will help you to find and analyze the stocks that will out-perform the market over an extended period of time.

Why not just listen to some smart people on TV or in mag-azines and newspapers tell you about the stocks that they are buying? As I pointed out in Chapter 3, when you rely on the research of others, you know only what they know, and it's what they *don't* know that hurts you. Here is a perfect example: Dur-ing the dot-com bubble, when the Nasdaq was melting down from its peak of 5,000+ to a low of about 1,200, there were dozens of analysts who appeared on business programs urging investors to either "stay the course" or double up on their investments by buying more technology stocks. This so-called averaging down is a loser's game that the Wall Street marketing machine pushes on investors.

When the Nasdaq plummeted to 3,000, those same "experts" told investors that this was merely a "correction" and that things would turn around soon. Millions of investors listened, and then watched in horror as nearly two-thirds of their Nas-daq investments went up in smoke (and that was after that benchmark index had already sunk from 5,000 to 3,000).

Many of these "investors" were short-term traders or day traders who were desperate to get back the huge amounts of money that they had already lost. Others were long-term, buy-and-hold investors who believed that markets eventually always go up. They bought the stupidity that was being espoused almost daily by failed money managers or talking heads with little or no skin in the game. They believed in the "New Economy," and that "this time it's different." In the New Economy, profits no longer mattered. As long as there were revenues or clicks on Web sites, profits would always follow, and stocks would eventually have to go up. We now know, with our perfect 20/20 hindsight, that the dot-com bubble was like any other bubble. Correction: it was far worse, since about 75 percent of Nasdaq market worth—trillions of dollars—disappeared in two unprecedented, horrific years.

In this chapter, I will explain with great specificity the kind of research that I do to make sure that I am staying at the top of my game and making the best possible investment decisions. However, there is one reality about research that investors must understand from the outset. Unlike investment banking firms such as Goldman Sachs or Morgan Stanley, individuals do not have access to company management. Individuals are not invited to sit down and listen to CEOs and other C-level executives give presentations about new products or management strategies.

However, investors can take advantage of all the incredible tools and information that they *do* have access to on the Internet. And while having access to management gives institutions an advantage over individual investors, I will tell investors where they need to look for the kind of information that will help them to make their own investment decisions—information that will allow them to come far closer than ever before to leveling the playing field between individual investors and large institutions. The goal of this chapter is to help you determine why a stock is selling at a particular price. The stock price is based on a number of factors, including what is happening in the overall economy, in the operating environment, or to a particular company. You are trying to take a snapshot of that company, a snapshot not of yesterday or tomorrow, but of today. You are trying to figure out what outside factors are affecting today's price of that stock. You have to forget where things were and where they may be.

Once you have studied the macro elements that might be affecting the stock, then you need to look inside the company. What actions has management taken that might be affecting the price? Has a new CEO come in and changed the capital structure of the firm? Has the company just done a 180 and changed its long-stated strategy to something "new and exciting"? (When it comes to management strategy, I will almost always choose boring and steady over new and exciting.) These are things we will take a closer look at in this chapter, because it is how well—

and how quickly—you discern these changes that will determine your ultimate batting average as an investor.

After I left Neuberger Berman in 2008, I was forced to get information the same way any retail investor would: via the Internet. As mentioned earlier, I no longer had access to CEOs and company management teams. Nor could I call up any brokerage or research firm in the world and request its information. I could not call a firm and ask an analyst to call me back, or request an invitation to a company meeting or road show. However, this new reality helped me to learn that there are hundreds, even thousands, of sources of information and data that I could use to come up with a wish list of the names I wanted to analyze and buy. This is vastly different from the world of investing that I entered 20 years ago.

Where I Get My Investment Ideas

Being a retail investor has given me the ability to back-test certain ideas and assumptions. All individual investors can back-test their ideas because they have so many tools; they are not at the disadvantage that so many people perceive themselves to be. What I found is that not having the access to what I did before has forced me to impose a certain discipline upon myself in gathering information. That's because it is very easy to expose yourself to too much information, which once again results in garbage in, garbage out. You can create a situation in which you're reading so many newspapers and Web sites and spending so many hours researching that you start missing the forest for the trees. The key is to be efficient in sifting through the data and figuring out the kind of information that will be of most use to you as you manage your own money.

I must confess from the outset that I am a morning guy. I start my mornings somewhere between 4:30 and 5:00 a.m. I know many of you probably like to sleep late. I can't really help you with that. Why I sleep four to five hours a night, I don't know. I wish I could sleep more, but I can't. You will have to develop your own habits and timing for when you do your homework, but developing a winning stock market strategy does not mean that you have to take caffeine pills. There is no correlation between getting up at the crack of dawn and buying winning stocks. However, I think it does help to begin doing your research before the U.S. stock markets open at 9:30 a.m. on the East Coast (those on the West Coast obviously need to be the earliest risers).

The six key sites for you to check out each day are FT.com, CNBC.com, WSJ.com, NYTimes.com, eWallstreeter.com, and Yahoo! Finance. Remember that you are trying to identify something that you didn't know before, so that you can develop a macro view of the economy and the financial markets while also developing a micro view of the companies that might be the buy (or sell) candidates of the future. I should add a note of caution: Obviously, none of these Web sites alone will drive you to make an investment decision. However, they are a great place to start and will help you to formulate your overall strategy and to determine if any change is meaningful enough to alter your opinion about a stock.

> The six key sites for you to check out each day are FT.com, CNBC.com, WSJ.com, NYTimes.com, eWallstreeter.com, and Yahoo! Finance.

The Financial Times

The first thing I do when I come down to my office every weekday morning is click on FT.com. The reason I look at the *Financial Times* is that it's important to get a broader, global perspective, and the *FT*, a newspaper published in the United Kingdom, will tell you what has happened in Asia overnight and what is happening in Europe every morning.

So I'll typically look at the front page first, then click on the company section just to see if there's something that may be of interest that hasn't made it to the front page (however, most of these Web sites have matured and grown, so that any substantial news is "published" on the front page). You are not typically looking for new ideas on this site, but trying to figure out if something has happened from a macro perspective that might cause you to sell a stock that is already in your portfolio.

I should also point out that while a limited amount of the content on FT.com is free, you'll need to register in order to get access to the free content, and eventually you'll have to subscribe. However, it isn't much money, and it's well worth it.

Another feature of the *FT* site that I look at regularly is the "Lex" column. This is an opinion piece related to some company or some industry that will usually give you something thought-provoking. Always look out for articles that are forward-looking and not just the ones that regurgitate the day's news.

For example, in the spring of 2010, there was a piece on the front page of FT.com entitled: "Business Apps Help Sales of Apple Devices." This was a forward-looking article that predicted that Apple's new iPad would threaten the BlackBerry in a few short years. While one should seldom make a buy or sell decision based on one article or prediction, that prediction is worth keeping in mind, and combined with other news, it may lead to a valuable insight. As mentioned earlier, Apple has had an incredible track record with its new products, which is one of the reasons that the stock doubled between April 2009 and April 2010. Apple's consistency in releasing category-killing products (think iPod), along with other new things you may learn in the next few days, might provide sufficient evidence to help you make a buy or sell decision regarding either Apple or Research in Motion (RIMM), the maker of the BlackBerry. Why might you buy RIMM in light of these new developments? What if Apple's iPad sends RIMM's stock down, say, 10 percent? You might think that this is an overreaction, and decide that RIMM will maintain its huge advantage in this market because so many companies use BlackBerries for their employees' needs, and therefore the company is a good long-term investment. On the other hand, you may feel that Apple is the better choice given its superb track record of launching new products. Once again, I almost never recommend that investors make a buy or sell decision based on one article or event in the marketplace. Instead, I suggest that you consistently evaluate the stock involved, using the criteria I presented in the last three chapters.

For example, I found one recent article about the company Caterpillar, the maker of high-end farming equipment and construction, mining, and forest machinery. The article included the following: "Caterpillar is considering relocating some heavy equipment overseas productions to a new U.S. plant, part of the growing movement among manufacturers to bring manufacturing back home, a shift that will spark fierce competition . . . [for] manufacturing jobs."

This move by Caterpillar, which is at least in part politically motivated, is all about bringing production back to the United States and in turn bringing jobs back to America. There are a number of things happening here. Moving some manufacturing facilities back to the United States may have a financial impact on the company. However, the financial impact is not immediately clear. Caterpillar will now be manufacturing in U.S. dollars, but it's selling a good percentage of its products overseas and receiving foreign currencies for its products. So, if the dollar is strong, Caterpillar may see demand for its goods go down because those companies buying in foreign currency will not be able to buy as much. The opposite is true if the dollar gets weaker—demand may go up. That's the first thing. The second thing we're going to talk about is social change.

Here we have Caterpillar getting some nice political/social credit by moving jobs back to the States. So this is a possible change. Perhaps Caterpillar will see a boost in sales from U.S. firms using stimulus money, since recipients of these funds are required to buy American-made products. This is the kind of thing you want to explore, but you should also investigate further to see what other change(s) might affect the company in the near future.

CNBC.com

The second site we'll visit is CNBC.com. A must-read is my daily blog (some shameless self-promotion), Kaminsky's Call, on the Strategy Session portal. Here you will be able to keep up with my daily thoughts, opinions, and commentary on the markets. There are many unique and interesting articles featured on the Web site. One of the other great features of the site is that you can click on any ticker symbol and see if any portfolio manager or analyst has commented on the stock; you can then read that commentary and attempt to determine whether any of it is important enough to warrant further analysis.

Let's take the Caterpillar example mentioned earlier. We just read about Caterpillar's bringing more jobs onshore and discussed potential consequences of that decision. I then went to CNBC.com and typed in Caterpillar's ticker symbol (CAT), just to see if there was anything there. In this instance, I did not find anything new in terms of commentary on the stock, just an Associated Press article that reported much of what I had seen in the first article I read.

We can now formulate an opinion such as the following: the story on Caterpillar definitely constitutes change. We know it may be monetary change, we know it may be social change, and in fact it may somehow end up being regulatory change. How can it result in regulatory change? There has been much rumbling in Washington under the Obama administration that there might be greater taxation of offshore operations and tax subsidies for bringing jobs back to the United States. If that ever becomes law, Caterpillar will definitely benefit and will be that much ahead of the game. So this story warrants future monitoring to see if these proposed changes ever become law.

However, we must always be sure to keep things in perspective. That story on Caterpillar will probably not move the stock today. But since we're trying to identify change, we now go back to our scorecard and mark this as something that will require further analysis in the future.

WSJ.com

You can get a brief free trial on this site, but after that period has expired, you have to pay a fee for full access, although some articles are still free. I feel this is a good investment. In addition to all of the great articles and information you now have access to, the *Wall Street Journal* is also an interactive site that allows you to plug in stock symbols and be kept abreast of the news surrounding specific stocks and companies that you are watching. It also allows you to put in upside and downside price parameters and be notified via e-mail when the stock hits those targets. I have found these features to be extremely helpful.

I go to the *Journal* site after visiting FT.com. The two sites will have several articles in common, so I am looking for new things in the *Journal*. That's why I usually jump to Section C ("Money and Investing"). That is the key part of the paper because it features company-specific stories. The "Heard on the Street" column (also in Section C) is very helpful. I also find the rating changes on a company's debt to be very helpful in detecting any meaningful changes in that company's creditworthiness. If time permits, I also play defense by searching for any articles about any of the companies I already own to make sure that there is nothing there that will require me to rethink my thesis for holding on to any of these stocks.

I'll then play offense and go back to Sections A and B to try to identify some story about a company that I may not have heard about or a company that is doing something truly different (so that its actions qualify as authentic change). At each site you visit each day, you are looking for new information or more detailed articles on something that you might have read earlier.

NYTimes.com

After I look at FT.com, CNBC.com, and the *Wall Street Journal* site, I'll go to the *New York Times* for the same reasons. However, while there's a lot of duplicative coverage (from the *Journal* and FT.com), you will occasionally find something that you can find nowhere else. That is why you are checking multiple sources. At the time of this writing, the content on the *Times* site is free if you register on the site, but there has been talk that it is going to start charging for its content.

Let's assume that by this time, you have spent about 20 minutes online. In those 20 minutes, you should have gotten a very good sense of what's happened in the capital markets overnight, how the market is setting up in the United States, and the key events that are taking place in the macro environment. You should also have identified one or two companies that may warrant further investigation.

eWallstreeter.com

At this point, I'll be ready to get my second cup of coffee, and I'll start checking out what I'll call nonbusiness-dedicated sites for stories. One of my favorite Web sites is called eWallstreeter.com. You may ask yourself, *isn't* that a business site? It is not. In fact, eWallstreeter.com is a blog that is compiled each day by a gentleman named Mitch Brown. Mitch is a retired capital markets sales trader for Goldman Sachs and Credit Suisse First Boston. This is a free Web site that anybody can access. The great thing about this site is that it helps you navigate through all the research and noise that is generated each day on the Net. Mitch has boiled down the hundreds and thousands of articles and blogs that come out each day and features a few of the pivotal stories on his site. It might be a money manager talking about something she's done in her portfolio, or something more technical. The end result is that he does hours of research for you and filters it all down to a few powerful and compelling stories about companies, the financial markets, and what is happening in the marketplace.

So I highly recommend this site, because it lets you try to come up with new ideas while also highlighting key changes that could be significant enough to warrant a change in your portfolio (as long as you do the requisite follow-up research). Mitch is able to do this because he created a program that uses keywords to go through Google Reader, and inputs words that are likely to trigger the types of change that we talked about. He generates just the kind of unique material that will give nonprofessional investors the kind of information that they need if they are to come up with new investment ideas. He has access to letters from portfolio managers, quarterly reports, and more.

This is a site I look at every day. And there is a great amount of diversity in the articles that Mitch has on his site. For example, on one day in 2010, I found a piece by James Surowiecki from *The New Yorker* magazine (April 19, 2010) entitled "Timing the Recovery," in which he cautions investors on calling the end of the recession too soon. There was also a piece that made the case for an improving stock market. In a piece by Bill Swarts in *Smart Money* (April 12, 2010) entitled "The Case for Higher Stock Prices," the author quotes Yardeni Research as saying that as long as the Fed does not raise interest rates, this period of rising stock prices could continue.

There are also articles that are very interesting that fall outside the domain of strict business. For example, in a very provocative article in *Forbes* (April 8, 2010), writer John Maeda discusses

"Your Life in 2020" (talk about gaining a macro perspective—this article certainly does that). In the piece, the author makes some very interesting comments about what he expects the world to look like in 2020. Here is an excerpt from that article:

> Rather than be content to accept corporate anonymity, we will rediscover the value of authorship. In 2020 technology will continue to enable individual makers to operate in the same way that once only large corporations could do. Witness the growth of individuals as "brands-of-one" in the social media space, broadcasting their news in the same fashion as major media outlets, or in software apps marketplaces, where "Bob Schula" can hawk his wares right next to "Adobe Systems," and it's just as easy to buy hand-stenciled napkins from a seller on Etsy as it is to buy them from Crate & Barrel. You might say it is a return to learning to trust individuals again, instead of relying on an indirect connection to a product through trust in its brand. Certainly our trust in those brands is already being tested right now.

An article like this may not help you to make an investment decision today, but it might get you to see some important things from a different perspective, or to think about something in a new light. That is why it is so important to at least take a quick look at all the articles on this site.

Yahoo! Finance

This is another free Web site. What I like about Yahoo! Finance is that to get there, you can go through the Yahoo.com portal and see what is happening outside of the world of business (which, as mentioned earlier, is a good thing). By this time, if you have followed my advice and visited all the sites I have presented thus far, you've already seen all the top stories. The key to navigating this site is to investigate all the companies that are on your radar screen. If you have an investment in, say, Alcoa, and you have seen a key story about Alcoa on the *Journal* and CNBC sites, a story that signifies genuine change, you go to Yahoo! Finance to see how widely that story has been disseminated. You want to see if that information has gone global, so to speak.

You're trying to ascertain or determine whether what you have already read is now widely known and widely disseminated, or whether it was something that was proprietary to just one or possibly two of the other sources you've already seen. You'll go to Yahoo! Finance, type in that stock, and look at the headlines, and that will quickly tell you, because Yahoo! Finance takes data feeds from all sources from all over the world. If you see that bit of information or the same story repeated on Yahoo!, this is a confirmation that the information that you may think is proprietary is in fact global (or vice versa). If the story has gone global, you may not have the advantage that you thought you had.

———

Completing all of this research has taken me between 30 and 45 minutes. Because you are not day trading, not looking to make a quick buck, and not unduly influenced by short-term phenomena, I suggest that you identify and absorb all of this information. As I said earlier, I think that it is a good idea to write down all of the stocks you are considering buying and keep a sort of scorecard of change. In the next two chapters, we will discuss portfolio construction and developing a sell discipline, and in those chapters, I will be much more specific as to what you do with this research and information. What you *don't* do with it is read something, call up your stockbroker or go to your computer, and impulsively make a buy or sell decision on a stock.

Your information gathering does not have to end in the morning. Several of these sites will e-mail you for free if a stock that you own or are watching reaches a certain target point that you choose (either on a big upward move or on a big downward move). This happens only every so often, but if you set yourself up with one of the free services that are available, at least you will be notified via e-mail that something substantial has happened to one of the stocks that you own or are considering buying.

I check in with CNBC.com a couple of times during the day with my mobile device because you can check on your phone or BlackBerry just to see if something big has happened. However, this is something that you do while you are in transit, or in between what you do on a regular basis. It's not going to necessitate your doing anything other than being able to access mobile information.

Lastly, I would be remiss without mentioning the television network where I now spend my days, the cable news network CNBC. Even if I were not working with it, I would recommend the network for anyone who is managing his own money. The network does a remarkable job of covering many of the issues and companies that we have discussed in this chapter (e.g., the macro and the micro). The only difference between TV and the various online media we have discussed is that you cannot control the schedule with TV (whereas you can access the online sites 24/7).

In summary, the Internet has made access to information affordable and readily available to anyone. So between the sources that I've identified in this chapter and the access to company data such as annual reports, 10-Qs, and 10-Ks, there is always a wealth of information at your disposal.

What we've tried to do here is provide a framework for the investor who wants to attempt to manage her own portfolio, utilizing my 20 years of experience to uncover the greatest sources of information. You want to make sure that the information you get is focused, value-added, proprietary whenever possible, and global in nature.

By no means should you consider the list of Web sites in this chapter exhaustive or complete. It is only a microcosm of what is available to any and all investors. This is just a quick review of my morning routine. It is important for you to determine what works best for you, given the incredible amount of free information available. If simply accessing two or three sites allows you to feel comfortable that you have done enough due diligence, then kudos to you. The important thing here is to be disciplined, develop a routine, and not deviate. This is a seven-days-a-week practice. Don't think of this routine as a chore. Instead, think of it as thought-provoking and an interesting exercise. If you love the challenge and excitement of the equity markets, this will help to satiate your hunger for gobbling up ever greater amounts of research and information. At the end of the day, make it fun. I know it is fun for me. I look forward to getting out of bed every day, hitting my computer, and finding out all sorts of new things. Hopefully, you will share my enthusiasm and look forward to this as much as I do.

10

HOW MANY STOCKS SHOULD I OWN?

or as long as I can remember, there has been a raging debate regarding the optimal number of stocks in a portfolio. Many experts believe that it takes hundreds of stocks to have a truly diversified or well-balanced portfolio. John Bogle, the founder of the mutual fund company Vanguard, believes that even 500 stocks are not enough! He does not believe that owning the S&P 500 index is sufficient for investors. He thinks that investors should own the entire stock market—which is about 10,000 stocks—so that their portfolios move in lockstep with the entire market.

Determining the right number of stocks for a portfolio has become one of the most controversial aspects of stock market investing. Whether you are reading investing books or talking to money managers, there is no shortage of opinions on how many stocks one should have in a portfolio. There are literally hundreds of opinions on the right number of stocks in a "diversified" portfolio.

Don't be fooled by being too diversified. Diversification—in this context, the act of reducing the risk in a portfolio by holding several different kinds of stocks—is a marketing tool that can pull you in the direction of becoming a closet indexer. You need some diversification, of course, as everything is interconnected, and generally you don't want to hold too many investments of the same type (although there is one exception to that, which I will explain shortly). But there is no specific top-down approach for diversification. It is a fallacy of the Wall Street marketing machine.

It is far more important for you to be flexible and dynamic—to be constantly willing to change. Stock portfolios should be dynamic, not static.

Also, as an investor, you should not be constrained by the labels placed on different types of stocks. You should not just look at large-cap or small-cap stocks, but should be willing to purchase *any* type of stock. We call that "unwrapping the box," since that is what will free you up to choose any stock, regardless of its classification.

In order to outperform in a zero-growth market (or any market, for that matter) investors should own between 20 and 30 stocks. A portfolio of between 20 and 30 stocks is the ideal number to outperform the averages. Any fewer than 20 and you are rolling the dice and exposing your portfolio to excessive risk. Any more than 30 and you risk becoming a closet indexer. We have had great success over the years owning this number of stocks.

A portfolio of between 20 and 30 stocks is the ideal number to outperform the averages.

Another key question that I have been asked over the years involves the type of stocks one should own. Surely I need those 20 to 30 stocks to be spread out among different industries, lest I have too much stock concentration in one or two areas, right? No, I also disagree with the experts on this point as well.

In Chapter 8, we discussed how important it is for a company to have free cash flow. I will build on that concept in this chapter because it is such a critical concept that I really cannot stress it enough. You want to find companies that are self-financing. This particular characteristic is so important that I would recommend that you buy 20 to 30 stocks in the *same* industry if each of the companies has the ability to do this. This is also a no-brainer, especially now, after emerging from the worst liquidity crisis in decades. Companies that are self-financing do not have to turn to the equity or capital markets to raise money. Many companies that were forced to do these things were dead in the water in 2008 and 2009 when liquidity was almost nonexistent. That's why it is so important to search out those companies that can grow their business with their own cash.

The Team K approach to proper portfolio management stems from the simple idea that a portfolio should be focused, and should contain a certain number of carefully selected securities.

Four key experts conducted an extensive study that shows that the benefits of diversification diminish beyond a portfolio of 20 to 25 stocks. According to the authors of this important research (John Campbell, Martin Lettau, Burton Malkiel, and Yexiao Xu), who studied a random selection of stocks from the NYSE, the American Stock Exchange, and the Nasdaq between 1986 and 1997, one does not gain any real reduction in risk by holding more than 25 stocks. Despite this research, I feel that 30 is still an acceptable number of securities to hold at any one time, but that holding more than 30 stocks at once dilutes your best ideas with mediocre ones. Once you go over 30 names, you increase your chances of just mimicking an index like the S&P 500. However, there is an endless number of money managers and institutions out there that feel that to achieve real diversification, one has to hold 100 or more stocks. In doing so, they want to create the perception that they are excellent stock pickers. What they will tell their clients is that they are great stock pickers, and they will demonstrate this by buying 100 of the S&P 500, or 20 percent of the index. These stocks will be so good, they contend, that they don't need the other 400 stocks in the S&P 500 index in order to make you money. They use that reasoning to justify the fact that they are charging five times the fee (or more) for simply buying the index in which these stocks are included. What they are not telling you is that by holding 100 stocks, they are almost assuredly going to achieve mediocre returns that are very close to those of the index.

Holding 100 stocks is yet another myth of the great Wall Street marketing machine. And it's not just money managers who play the game this way; mutual fund managers play precisely the same game.

For example, the average U.S. stock mutual fund owns about 166 different stocks in its portfolio. Of course, some will own more and some will own less. Once again, however, mutual funds that hold that many stocks are doomed to achieve average, indexlike performance.

There's no reason to own 100 names in your portfolio. Let's look at this using a combination of common sense and mathematics (not advanced calculus, so don't worry). Assume that you hold 100 names in your portfolio and that they are equally weighted. So you have 100 stocks, and each stock represents 1 percent of your total portfolio. Some of these stocks will perform great, some good, some average, and some poorly.

First, the cost of holding 100 stocks is greater than that of holding, say, 25 stocks (in the latter case, we will assume that each stock makes up 4 percent of the total portfolio, or each is "a 4 percent position"). Every time you buy shares of stock, you must pay a commission. In this day of online investing, you pay the same amount for buying (and selling) 10 shares of stock as you do for buying 1,000 shares. An investor who owns 25 stocks pays much less—usually four times less—than the investor who pays the commission associated with 100 companies.

Let's assume that one of the names in each of these portfolios skyrockets. Let's use one of my favorite holdings of all time, Suncor Energy. That stock went from $400 million to $40 billion in market cap while we held it. That's a return of 1,000 percent. In the 100-stock portfolio, the impact of such a rise in a 1 percent position is minimal at best. After all, the stock represents only a paltry 1 percent of your total holdings.

In the 25-stock portfolio, Suncor—like all the other names—represents 4 percent of the portfolio. Therefore, the exceptional performance of that stock will have 4 times the impact it will have in the 100-stock portfolio.

Put another way, if you are just striving to achieve indexlike returns, don't waste your time getting up in the morning and doing all the work we described in the previous chapter. Don't waste your time trying to identify the organic growers or the superior dividend-paying stocks. Instead, just buy a Vanguard index fund or the S&P 500 ETF (ticker symbol SPY) and call it a day.

In order to make real money in the markets, you have to have skin in the game. A 25-stock portfolio with each position making up 4 percent of the portfolio qualifies as having skin in the game. It shows that you are willing to take the risk of holding a smaller number of stocks in the hope of outperforming the index and achieving positive overall returns. The approach I am advocating will give you a chance of making money even when the rest of the stock market goes down. Even if you don't make money, you will lose less money in down markets if you have followed the disciplined approach I have outlined in Part Two of this book.

When a 4 percent position moves in your favor, this positive result outweighs the average performance in the rest of the portfolio. Again, entire books have been written about various quantitative strategies that are created to support this methodology. I have found that some investors believe in such an approach and others don't. This is another case of forgetting the nonsense and thinking of this intuitively.

If you're going to do your own work/research, you should feel comfortable that with 25 to 30 names, you have enough diversification and you have enough skin in the game. You should never own fewer than 15 names in a portfolio, even in a period when you are holding 30 to 40 percent cash. Fewer than that and you are exposing your portfolio to excessive risk.

It is worth pointing out that for an individual investor, there's really no restriction on how big a position can get. Obviously this is not the case with most mutual funds or index funds. During the great growth of the Suncor years, many retail investors felt comfortable letting Suncor become 18 to 20 percent of their total portfolios. The vast majority of investment advisors would rail against holding a position that large, arguing that it is not prudent to take on that much risk. But I strongly disagree with the conventional wisdom on this point. If a 20 percent position in a portfolio is understood to have a significantly larger weighting in terms of your overall portfolio performance and you can accept that, why sell a portion of that very successful investment and pay the capital gains taxes simply based on some arbitrary rule that has nothing to do with creating wealth?

You need to get over the idea that the size of your portfolio or the size of an individual position should be dictated by non-subjective, quantitative data. That approach doesn't work. Following a rigid approach like this means that you are constantly reducing the number of shares of stocks that are working because their price is rising and they are making up a greater percentage of the portfolio. This has the unintended consequence of having you keep the laggards, those stocks that are adding no value to the portfolio at all. So instead of keeping the winners and selling the losers, you're letting your portfolio get stale. Your process should be to look at your portfolio on a weekly basis, recognize that the winners will become abnormally high as a percentage of the overall portfolio, accept and understand that, and follow the rules of engagement when it comes to developing your sell discipline (as I will lay out in the next chapter). Your goal is to avoid any inflexible portfolio rules that force you to make nonsensical decisions, because that is a loser's game. Books and money managers who tell you that portfolio construction should have no creativity are just dead wrong.

If you're fortunate enough to identify a handful of grand slam stock ideas, be cognizant of what they represent as a percentage of your total wealth, but allow them to run. Holding on to your winners is now a well-known refrain in this book. We can't emphasize enough that if your objective is simply to get average market returns, don't buy individual stocks. Don't spend the time creating a portfolio, and don't give your money to a money manager who's going to charge you 1.5 percent to mimic the index, because you can achieve that far more efficiently by putting your money in a low-cost index fund or ETF that mimics the index.

Let's always keep this book's mission statement in mind: to create absolute, positive returns on your stock market investments, regardless of the macro environment. Remember that the next decade is going to be very difficult. The idea that stocks will just go up as they did during the 1990s and that owning almost any stock will create wealth no longer holds true. The overriding premise, as we stressed in Part One of the book, is that the next decade is going to be very similar to the last decade.

If you held a broad, diversified portfolio during the decade of 2000 to 2009, you created a 0 percent return (or worse). At Team K, we held a focused, disciplined, actively managed portfolio based on many of the principles of this book, and during that same period, we created an equity portfolio that delivered annualized returns of 11 percent compounded.

How Does a Focused Portfolio Perform in Down Markets?

One question I often get from investors is, how does the more focused approach of holding 25 to 30 stocks perform in up markets and down markets? It is a fabulous question. In 1999, for example, the S&P was up 21 percent. That was the final year prior to the tech bubble bursting. However, with our disciplined stock selection method, we created a portfolio that was up 35 percent that same year. In 1997, the S&P was up 33 percent while Team K's equity only return was up 31 percent, so we are not perfect. Overall, however, as we discussed in the introduction, we outperformed the S&P index more years than we underperformed, and sometimes in a dramatic fashion.

Here is another example. Let's assume that in December 1998, you started with $1,000 in investments. If that $1,000 was invested in the S&P 500, you came away with $1.22 for every dollar invested in an S&P 500 index fund (or a total of $1,220).

However, if you had given that same $1,000 to Team K at Neuberger Berman, you would have come away with $2.80 for every dollar invested, or $2,800, as Figure 10-1 illustrates.

That is a dramatic difference, and it shows just how well the focused strategy performed during that lackluster decade in the stock market.

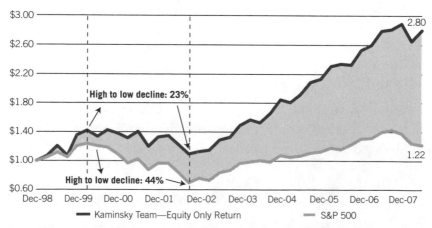

Figure 10-1   Hypothetical value of dollar invested. (For complete investment performance information see Figures I-1 and I-2.)

If you look at the down years, our focused approach also preserved much more of your capital than you would have achieved had you held your money in an index fund. In fact, one could argue that it is during the down years that our results were the most impressive.

For example, Figure 10-1 examines our performance from December 1998 through December 2007 in both up and down periods. During that period, we outperformed the market just over 70 percent of the time. This is proof positive that a focused portfolio can help to save you money when markets are weak—assuming, of course, that you have developed a disciplined approach and adhered to it consistently.

Let's dig deeper and look at some specific years to see how we did versus the averages. First, 2002 was the worst year for stocks before 2008. In 2002, the S&P was down 22 percent. The Team K portfolio was down 14 percent. Part of the reason for our success was having skin in the game, as we discussed earlier in the chapter. Having skin in the game allows you to raise cash more quickly because you have fewer stocks to choose from.

For example, when the market sold off sharply from 2000 to the low reached in mid-2002, we were able to raise cash more quickly than other money managers who had 100 or more names in their portfolios. Again, that's just common sense. In a focused portfolio with a quarter of the names, it is easier to figure out which companies are better able to compete, maintain their operating margins, continue to pay increasing dividends, and so on.

This was even more evident in 2008, when the market was down a stunning 38 percent because of the liquidity crisis and the shutting down of the capital markets. When you have 100 names to research, it is obviously going to take you a lot longer to figure out which one to sell first. When you have a focused portfolio and you've been following the stocks by doing your due diligence, it's much easier to do. You can raise cash more quickly because you know your businesses better. And that shows up clearly when we look at the numbers. From the high in 2000 to the low in 2002, the S&P was down 44 percent. We were able to sell stocks more quickly and raise cash more quickly, and as a result, the high to low decline on the Team K portfolio was 23 percent.

What that basically tells you is that when the market started to rebound in December 2002, the indexed dollar that we started with in January of 2000 was now worth only 66 cents. In the Team K portfolio, that same dollar was worth $1.40 at the height and held most of its value through those two tough years.

A story that I used to tell to highlight the power of compounding came from my middle son, Tommy Kaminsky. Tommy, believe it or not, was a natural when it came to investing and is now 15 years old. He started to manage his own portfolio when he was 10, and that's when he came to me with this story.

"Dad, I was reading a story, and this is the craziest thing. If somebody said to you, I could give you a penny a day doubled each day for 30 days, or I can give you $10,000 a day for 30 days, which would you prefer?" That's obviously a trick question, and when you tell this story to investors, the typical response is: "I know there's some kind of trick here, but what is it?"

The $10,000 a day for 30 days yields $300,000. The penny a day doubled with interest compounded is $5.4 million. I have always used that story in the context of compound interest. Overdiversification won't allow you to get to that $5.4 million. A portfolio with 100 or more stocks dilutes your best ideas— your home-run stocks. The secret behind the curtain isn't that much of a secret at all. Let the power of compounding work in your favor. Don't let your portfolio get away from you so that you dilute your best ideas. Don't be frightened by the huge mutual funds and their marketing machines into thinking that you need hundreds of stocks to make money. You have the tools and the resources and the access to information to monitor the investments you make so that you can let the upside attribution work in your favor.

Overdiversification is, for lack of a better phrase, a "CYA" mentality. When you give your hard-earned money to a money manager and she buys 100 securities for your portfolio, that always gives her a way to justify her performance. For example, she may say, "Your portfolio is down 6 percent, yes, but the market is down 5 percent, so you're pretty much in line with the market." That's a CYA mentality, because she's setting up the portfolio to reflect the benchmark. If you are picking good investments, keeping the winners, selling the losers, and keeping the portfolio focused, you can come out far ahead of that money manager with the long laundry list of names in your portfolio.

How Much Money Do You Need to Invest?

People ask me this question all of the time. "Gary," they say, "you invested billions. Surely I cannot do all the things that you recommend in this book if I have only, say, $10,000 or $20,000." My answer to that is unequivocal. You can indeed purchase and manage a portfolio of stocks with $10,000. Perhaps 20 years ago, before the Internet, you would not have been able to do this, but today the investing world is a very different animal. Back in the 1980s and before, you had to pay a full-service broker a couple of hundred dollars commission on a couple of hundred shares. But today you can buy thousands of shares of stock for less than $10 with discount brokers like TD Ameritrade, E*TRADE, and Scottrade.

There is no shortage of naysayers who will tell you that you can't invest in individual stocks with only $10,000, and that with so little money, you must put it into a mutual fund. Once again, that is a myth. It is a fallacy to believe that you need $100,000 or more to achieve proper diversification. Today you can be cost-efficient with a $10,000 portfolio as long as you aren't going to be actively trading like a day trader.

Another question people ask me involves the time horizon. How long do I need to hold on to the stocks I buy in order to give me the best chance of success? What if I have $10,000 today, but I may need the money a year from now because one of my children is getting married and I may need that money for her wedding? In that situation, you have no business placing that money in the stock market in any form (either individual stocks or a mutual fund). The experience of 2000 to 2002 and 2007 to 2009 showed us that if you have to cash out at an inopportune time, you could lose your shirt. However, had you invested in 2005 and cashed out in 2007, you would have been in great shape.

So here is what I recommend in terms of time frame. Because markets are so volatile, it is impossible to time the market. My philosophy is that you should not invest in equities if you feel that you are likely to need that money back in the foreseeable future. This means that you should not invest any money that you will need back within a three-year period at the absolute minimum.

However, the good thing about owning stocks, as opposed to other investments like real estate, is that there is liquidity every day. That means that you should have no problem selling your stocks if you need the money unexpectedly.

You should not invest any money that you will need back within a three-year period.

In portfolio construction, it is important to remember that there are many investments—such as certain commodities, real estate, private placements, and limited partnerships—in which you don't have daily liquidity. At least in the equity markets, you know that you can get your money back if you need it unexpectedly.

By the way, portfolio construction is an interdisciplinary topic—it's not just about portfolio construction. What we're trying to do here is dispel a lot of the bull that is put out by people who have an incentive to mislead you.

Owning stocks is risky. However, owning 30 stocks is no more risky than owning 100 stocks, unless you do nothing about it. The riskiest form of investing is not buying and holding—it's buying and *forgetting*. Buying and holding is different from buying and forgetting. I don't believe that buying and holding works—I believe in active management, which means buying and selling. But buying and holding is far better than buying and forgetting. When you buy and forget, it doesn't matter whether you own 1,000 stocks, 30 stocks, or 100 stocks, you might as well take your money to Las Vegas and risk your nest egg at the roulette wheel.

Over What Period of Time Should I Buy 30 Stocks?

I always think that this is a terrific question, although a complex one. The answer that you get depends on whom you ask. For example, if you are talking to a mutual fund manager, he might want to play it safe by telling you to invest a little bit of money in his fund each month, say, on the first of every month (the "dollar cost averaging" that we've discussed). This way, you will be buying shares of that mutual fund when it is up and when it is down. It is akin to averaging up and averaging down, depending on the share price each month.

Then there is the group of money managers who get compensated based on assets being invested. When you go to one of these asset managers and give her, say, $100,000, it is in her best interest to buy everything the next day so that the whole hundred thousand dollars is earning investment advisory fees right away. She's going to tell you, "We feel really good about the market right now, we like our names, and we want to get you 100 percent invested."

What differentiated Team K from other money management firms is that we had a unique way of looking at things. We were not swayed by the almighty buck. If someone came to us with a million dollars and we felt that we could invest only $600,000 of that million right now, we would put the balance of the money, or $400,000, in cash (where we earned zero dollars in fees).

How did this happen? Why didn't we have the confidence to invest the entire million dollars? It had nothing to do with confidence. In fact, I argue that it takes more confidence to allocate a substantial amount of a client's money (or your own) to cash. We put 40 percent of a client's money in cash when we felt that 60 percent of the names in our portfolio were trading at a fair price, and that the timing was right to buy them. We did not feel that it was honest or right to charge people money for making bad or subpar decisions. This was a unique approach and one of the reasons that we were able to outperform both the averages and our peers. Some money managers charge their clients for total assets under management, even those assets being held in cash accounts. We always thought that to be a terrible policy.

So what is the answer about how long it should take you to be fully invested in your 30 stocks? The answer is that there is no answer. If you can identify enough names that fit your criteria for selection at a given time, then you get fully invested. If you can't, you don't. This is when patience may indeed be one of your most important assets.

From a portfolio construction perspective, you should never ever buy stocks just for the sake of getting fully invested. It's one of the dumbest things an investor can do.

When we talk about developing a sell discipline in the next chapter, having some cash gives you a lot more flexibility when you are your own portfolio manager. This allows you to take advantage of opportunities when you spot them without having to sell off any names in your portfolio (assuming that you are not holding 30 stocks). If you are fully invested and holding 30 stocks, you are going to have to rip through your portfolio and sell something when that thirty-first great stock comes along.

That will always be true as long as you are following our rules of engagement and holding no more than 30 stocks. You will have to figure out pretty quickly which of your stocks is the least attractive and sell that one. That's because you need to be disciplined enough never to hold that thirty-first stock. If you develop the right discipline, you will give yourself a real edge in the market.

11

DEVELOP A STRONG SELL DISCIPLINE AND MANAGE THE DOWNSIDE

Developing a strong sell discipline has its own set of principles that investors must abide by. However, the vast majority of investors who buy a stock have no idea of the conditions under which they would sell that stock. That's a prescription for failure. As I've mentioned briefly already, investors must have a very detailed, very specific plan for determining the conditions under which they will sell a stock. Our team developed a multistep plan that explained precisely when it was time to exit a position.

As my brother, Michael Kaminsky, who is currently the chief investment officer of Team K at Neuberger Berman, once said so eloquently, selling a stock is 20 times harder than buying one. That resonates with most people, because as we've described earlier in the book, you can come up with many reasons and a thesis for buying a stock on any given day. Once you have your buying criteria in place, such as the reasons that we have described earlier, and once you have done your due diligence, it is easy to pull the trigger and take a position in a stock that you have been following. Whenever you buy a stock, you believe that you have made the right decision.

Selling a stock is a different story entirely. Sometimes, selling a stock is an admission that you were wrong. It has a different psychological effect from buying a stock. Let me use a classic example to make the point.

Keep Your Winners and Sell Your Losers

Let's say that an investor buys two stocks at $10 on January 1. By November, one of the two stocks has gone from $10 to $17, while the other stock has gone from $10 to $7. The reality is that the investor feels much better selling the stock that went to $17 and buying more of the stock that dropped to $7 a share. That's because human psychology works without any regard for the underlying stock fundamentals, technical analysis, the economy, or any other aspect of business. What we have done thus far in the book, and are attempting to do again here, is get you to break away from the psychological forces that trip up more than 90 percent of investors.

In this example, the right thing to do is to sell the $7 stock (your loser) and either hold or perhaps buy more of the $17 stock (your winner).

The goal of this chapter is to assist you to develop a discipline that will help you take the human emotion out of selling. I want you to learn to disregard the feelings that come with selling a stock for less than you paid for it. When you are faced with a loss, you automatically say to yourself, "I was wrong, I made a mistake." It's that knee-jerk response that helps to trip up many investors.

The first step in developing a strong sell discipline is determining the time horizon for holding any stock when you buy it—is this a one-decision or a two-decision stock? We've already covered this topic in Chapter 4, but it is important enough to review again in the context of developing a consistent sell discipline.

Keeping your winners and selling your losers is an oft-repeated rule that is worth living by.

Here is another example of a two-decision stock: You buy stock in a company because you know that the firm is launching a significant new product, and you feel that management will do a good job of promoting and selling that new product, and therefore that the valuation of the firm will rise. When you purchase that stock, you do so with a time frame in mind. In this case, you figure that you will hold the stock for, say, six to nine months to see how that product launch plays out. That's a two-decision stock.

In a one-decision stock, you have determined that the company has enough of the characteristics that you look for (e.g., strong organic growth and an increasing dividend stream) for you to hold that company's stock for an extended period of time. When I think of the long term, I think of a three- to five-year period. Most institutional money managers regard that time frame as an appropriate one, since that period gives an investor a chance to see how a stock will perform through an entire business cycle. In fact, in that time period, a company will usually go through at least one up period and one down period.

However, three to five years is optimal only when the company is doing well and executing well, and when your reason for buying the stock has not been altered by changes that we will identify in this chapter. At Neuberger Berman, we would stay invested until we lost confidence in the firm's management or the structure of the business had changed dramatically. Again, it's all about discipline. This is, of course, not a personal thing.

You don't lose confidence in a CEO because you do not like him personally. You lose confidence in management when it does something that runs counter to the stated strategy of the company. As we mentioned earlier, boring is a good thing when it means that management is executing on its strategy and not deviating from what it said it would do in the annual report, in any other key document, or in a public forum. It's when management does something that runs 180 degrees counter to its stated strategy that you have something to worry about. When that happens, it is usually because management has been *forced* to alter its strategy as a result of competition or the macro environment, or because the company's strategy has failed to achieve the desired results. Regardless of the reason for the change, when a company changes course that quickly, this should be a red flag for investors.

In this chapter, we will examine the five factors that could trigger a change in your investment thesis and lead to your selling a stock long before the three- to five-year period has expired. When we talk about a structured business plan, we mean that one of the following five things has affected the company above and beyond the control of management, and that as a result, management has been forced to change its business plan to deal with whatever new headwinds have come its way. These are the five things that investors must look out for because they could be game changers that could hurt the future prospects of any company. An investor should hold on to a stock until one or more of the following things changes:

1. Economic environment
2. Industry outlook
3. Company fundamentals
4. Management strategy
5. Valuation

Economic Environment

Investors need to always stay abreast of changes in the economic environment. Many stocks that are highly dependent on the economy, interest rates, or other such factors may fare poorly in a recession. That's why you need to always have your finger on the pulse of the economic environment.

There are some companies that can grow in both good economies and bad economies. However, the vast majority of companies are reliant on a strong global economy if they are to grow. While there are few things that most economists agree on, they do agree that economies move in cycles. There are up periods that can be characterized as euphoric (some people call these "booms"), and there are down periods that qualify as recessions (some call these "busts"). This is a natural part of how economies work. Things that affect the business cycle are GDP growth (growth of gross domestic product), income of households, and employment/unemployment rates. The key here is that you want to own stocks that benefit from economic growth. Conversely, you want to be very careful when you are considering buying or continuing to hold a stock that tends to tank when the economy weakens. These are stocks that you generally want to avoid. Conversely, you want to hold stocks that can achieve meaningful organic growth regardless of the phase of the business cycle.

For example, two types of stocks that generally do well during recessionary times are discount retailers like Wal-Mart and so-called sin stocks like liquor and cigarette stocks. That's because these are the companies that people turn to when times are bad. They look for bargains at Wal-Mart, and they do not stop smoking or drinking; in fact, many people drink and smoke more during tough times. The good news for individual investors is that the economic environment is one of the easiest factors for investors to stay abreast of on a consistent basis.

In mid-2010, most economists believed that global economies—following the Great Recession of 2008–2009—were experiencing a period of upswing. Many companies that had been severely punished during the liquidity crisis were benefiting from the stronger economy. One obvious group of stocks that comes to mind is those involved in industrial manufacturing. But note that these stocks are dependent on continued growth in order to do well over a long-term horizon. This is an area in which due diligence is particularly important. When you are considering a specific stock, you should pull up a 10-year chart to see how the company has fared during the last two disastrous downturns (2000–2002 and 2008–2009). If the stocks performed especially poorly during these two recessions, these are the stocks that you will probably want to sell first when the economy begins to falter again.

Industry Outlook

After the overall economy, the next thing that investors want to stay abreast of is the industry outlook. There are many things that can affect an industry, and this is one of the key things to look at when you do your daily due diligence. One of the most obvious things that can affect an industry is a political or regulatory change. For example, let's say, as a hypothetical example, that the U.S. government, in an effort to help pay down the deficit, decides to impose a value-added tax (VAT) on luxury items. Stocks that might be affected are those of companies like Tiffany (TIF), Coach (COH), and Nordstrom (JWN). Let's also assume that for any purchase north of $200, the government will add a 20 percent VAT. That is a move that can—and will—affect the profitability of the entire sector. This, of course, is not a book on politics, and I am not trying to come out on either side of this particular issue, but this is obviously a change that can be interpreted as a sell signal. It's an example of something that forces you to think about whether the structure of the industry has fundamentally changed.

Another example of something that can fundamentally change the outlook for an industry is a new competitor or a competitor that comes out with a new technology or product that can divert market share from the rest of the industry. Reaching back in history, one can look at railroad stocks, for example, after air flight became a reality in 1903. Air flight changed everything from politics to culture to war—and, yes, the existing modes of transportation like railroads.

More recently, we can point to the founding of Amazon.com in the mid-1990s as another example of something that can have a profound effect on an industry. Before Amazon, two brick-and-mortar stores—Barnes & Noble and Borders—ruled the industry. However, Amazon transformed the industry forever. Not only was the method of delivery altered, but so was the availability of hard-to-find titles. Amazon carries millions of books, whereas your average brick-and-mortar store can carry only a fraction of that number. As a result, when Amazon started to sell books, that might have been a sell signal for any of the brick-and-mortar bookstore stocks.

One last example: There are times when a merger or acquisition can affect an entire industry. For example, in May 2010, it was announced that United Airlines would merge with Continental Airlines. On the first day of trading after the announcement, most airline stocks went up, at least initially. However, in this case, investors may change their minds when they take a longer view of this type of change. That's because the United-Continental merger made the newly formed company the largest airline in the world. In the short term, investors regarded the consolidation of the industry as a good thing, but investors often react first and think second. On a long-term basis, investors may rethink this, since now there is one dominant airline in the industry. That new 800-pound gorilla could have an adverse effect on the lesser lights in the industry over the long term. So, as we have seen so many times before, some changes are more gray than they are black and white.

Company Fundamentals

There are many things that can change the fundamentals of a company—a change in its management, its markets, its capitalization, and so on. An investor must leave no stone unturned in learning everything about a company that he is holding in his portfolio. Investors need to be on the lookout for the changes that will truly have an impact on the companies in which they are invested. There is no shortage of examples that we can draw upon.

Let's go back to the example we discussed earlier of the company that outsourced its manufacturing operations. In the example, one possibility was that the company got hurt when the demand for one of its products surged and the firm could not keep up with that demand. The company had already spent its entire marketing budget to generate the demand, and the product had done extremely well. The window for making those sales is obviously finite. In this instance, the company's fundamentals are deeply affected; it has spent the marketing dollars to create demand for the product, but now it is not able to meet that demand. So here your company fundamentals have been affected in two ways. Number one, the company has alienated its customers, and that is going to have a longer-term impact on the business. Number two, the company has the expenses associated with building up demand for a product, but it is not going to realize the revenues. That's a sell signal associated with the specific company. How do you know this is happening? Because you're doing your due diligence in the morning, and that company's inability to meet consumer demand will be well reported in the media.

There will be times when you have to act after holding a stock for a single day. Let's say you bought the company that could not meet its consumer demand only one day before its inability to do so was reported in the media. The next day the stock opens 15 percent lower. That is a situation that calls for action. There's a saying, a cliché really, that once there's a cockroach in the closet, there's not just one, there are many. That's a sell signal. You want to get out of that stock. Take your 15 percent loss and get out, because these types of problems are systemic, and they seldom go away in three months. In other words, there are probably other problems with the company that will surface in the days, weeks, and months ahead. That is why you want to get out of that stock immediately, put it behind you, and move on.

There's another saying that is worth memorizing: "Your first loss is your best loss." This simply means that you need to be disciplined and not get married to a stock, and then, when something changes, try to get out in front of that change. Your first loss is your best loss is an acknowledgment that averaging down is almost always the wrong thing to do. And if you sell and take that loss, you have learned not to average down. Remember, one of the greatest things about the stock market is that you can always get out of something quickly. Liquidity is a beautiful thing. The beautiful thing about the stock market is that it opens

Your first loss is your best loss.

every day, and it closes every day, and even in the midst of a terrible crisis, such as the collapse of Lehman Brothers, the stock market functions as a clearing mechanism between buyers and sellers. Every time somebody buys, somebody sells, and vice versa. Your first loss is the best loss. When something changes, don't just sit there; take action as long as the change is significant enough to warrant action.

Let's include one more example of something that can change the fundamentals of a company. During the liquidity crisis of 2008 and 2009, there were many companies that attempted to reach out to the capital markets in order to refinance their debt but were unable to do so because the lending markets were frozen. Any company that finds itself in that situation—unable to refinance its debt—will find that its fundamentals have changed. First, its balance sheet will be adversely affected. And second, the company's credibility with investors and money managers will also suffer. So these are the kinds of changes that investors need to monitor in order to at least attempt to stay ahead of changes that can significantly damage a company's fundamentals.

Management Strategy

Many times, a company will come forward with a "bold" new strategy to announce to the world. Here I say, buyer beware. That's because when management changes strategy in midstream, often it is not because everything is going great, but because there are some real problems that may or may not be visible to outsiders. Eight times out of ten, a change in strategy is a red flag for investors. This type of change is easy to understand and identify, and it is something that I have mentioned before. When you are trying to identify this type of change, you are looking for any sudden turnabouts or changes in strategy that take place with little or no forewarning. The company that has gone on the record as saying that it has no plans to export its products to foreign markets and then suddenly does so must be looked at with a skeptical eye (perhaps it is afraid of losing domestic market share and needs to make it up elsewhere). So must the company that has vowed to grow organically and suddenly does a large acquisition, explaining that it must acquire that competing firm so that none of its rivals beats it to the punch.

You should also be on the lookout for stocks that cut their dividends because they want to change their capital allocation strategy. When it comes to dividends and distributions, we've already explained the return on capital and how it's such an important component. Any negative change in a firm's dividend policy merits your attention and is a possible sell signal.

On the positive side of the ledger, you are looking for firms that have a well-thought-out strategy and stick to their plan. You are also looking for companies that execute effectively. You will be able to find these companies by examining the annual reports and other documents that we discussed earlier in the book, and by paying attention to things like quarterly earnings reports. The best companies consistently beat their earnings forecasts. This does not mean, however, that those stocks will rise on the day they report their strong earnings. There are hundreds of examples every year of a company that comes out with great earnings, but its stock gets crushed. This could be the result of several different factors. Sometimes companies beat the estimates, but fall short of their "whisper number," the number that Wall Street has been buzzing about, which is usually higher than the actual earnings estimate. Other times it is a case of "buying on the rumor, selling on the news," meaning that many investors and money managers decide that the time to cash in their chips and sell the stock is right after the good news is reported, because things aren't going to get much better than that.

Valuation

Sometimes a stock does so well that its price goes up well beyond your expectations. In this case, you always need to know how that stock is being valued in relation to its peers and its relative performance in its industry. Most people and investing experts put valuation at the top of the list when making a sell decision. I think valuation is at best number five on the list. However, this is one of the most difficult selling disciplines to get your arms around. I truly believe that analysts who put price targets on stocks are wasting my time, their time, and your time.

This is another by-product of the Wall Street marketing machine, which insists that analysts put a projected price on a stock based on projected earnings and a projected multiple. One of the reasons I feel that price targets are meaningless is that companies are not static entities. At the end of the day, price targets should be moving targets. If you recognize that companies are three-dimensional entities, then you know that there are a number of things happening every day that can affect a company's stock price. That's why putting just one price target on a stock is like putting yourself in a box.

When it comes to valuation, my recommendation is that you should first be cognizant of what the multiple is for each of the stocks in your portfolio. You want to be aware of the price and the earnings that are giving that multiple. For each of the stocks you own, you want to know what the multiple is relative to the company's projected earnings. More important, you want to step out of the box and figure out what the earnings prospect is for this company relative to those of the market as a whole and its industry peers. You need to recognize that in many instances you will be holding stocks that are trading at multiples above that of the stock market; that's because those are the companies that are generating the best-quality organic growth, paying the best dividend in their sector, and so on.

You also need to be cognizant of the fact that there are euphoric periods characterized by bull moves in all stock market cycles. As a result, even though I do not advocate frequent trading, I do recommend "trading around positions." Trading around a position simply means selling some of your shares but holding on to a certain number of core shares. If a stock I am holding happens to reach a high valuation when measured against its peer group (meaning that it has a higher multiple) because there is euphoria in the market, I sometimes sell half the shares I am holding and keep the other half. Why hold on to half the shares?

I hold on to a core number of shares because sometimes that euphoria has a lot more running room than people realize. Euphoria can go on for months, or even longer, so you want to make sure that you have a chance to capitalize on that rising tide.

Conversely, in a case of relative undervaluation, I encourage buying around a position: buying back the position when that same security drops back down to a more appropriate level. This is not to be confused with averaging down, which we first discussed in Chapter 9. Here I am specifically talking about adding to a winning position when the stock is priced at a more reasonable level. This is closer to averaging up because you are buying additional shares when you are holding a winning stock.

I want to point out that there are no hard-and-fast rules here. You should not lock yourself in a box by creating any, either. You have to use judgment. Trading around a position was something that worked well for Team K over the years, which is why I am recommending it in this chapter on developing a disciplined sell strategy.

Figure 11-1 summarizes the material discussed so far in this chapter.

- Investment horizon ranges typically from two to five years
- Stay invested unless we lose confidence in company management, or the structure of the business has changed dramatically
- Change in investment thesis:
  - Economic environment
  - Industry outlook
  - Company fundamentals
  - Management strategy
  - Valuation (macro and micro)

Figure 11-1   Sell discipline.

Taxes and Selling

When it comes to developing a sell discipline, investors need to be aware of the tax implications when exiting any position. First, a word of warning: This is yet another area that is difficult to get one's arms around. That's because there are no hard-and-fast rules about when to sell or not to sell when taking the tax implications into account.

The first thing to look at is whether your portfolio is in a taxable or a nontaxable account. In a nontaxable account, whether it is a 401(k), IRA, or foundation, the entire issue of taxes is irrelevant and moot for obvious reasons. You have much more flexibility in trading around positions in a nontaxable account.

At Team K, we found that our greatest success came from creating long-term capital gains in stocks like Suncor or Kinder Morgan Partners. These are stocks that we held for many years. However—and this is the key takeaway from this section—you should never let the tax implications of an investment drive your investment process or predetermine how long you will hold an investment.

When one holds a stock for a full year and then sells that stock at a profit, the profits are considered a long-term capital gain, resulting in a lower tax rate on profits. Thus, it is natural for investors to want to hold any stock for a full year in order to get the tax benefit. However, this is one of the biggest mistakes investors make. Let me give you an example to show why.

You should never let the tax implications of an investment drive your investment process.

Let's say you buy a stock on April 1, 2009. On March 25, 2010, the industry leader decides that it is going to start a massive price war in the same market space that your company has benefited greatly from for three years. If you hold the stock for six more days, the gain on that investment will be taxed at a lower rate because it will be considered a long-term capital gain. But what happens in those six days could very well cost you your entire gain because that stock might fall precipitously in the wake of that fresh bad news. That's why you should never let the taxman (or taxwoman) determine how you manage your investment portfolio.

One more clarification: I am not saying that you should not be aware of the tax implications of your investments—you should. However, if one of the five triggers that we just outlined in this chapter changes the outlook for one or more of your stocks, then don't allow taxes to be a burden on making your final investment decision. This is something that we learned the hard way at Cowen. In fact, by not taking the advice that I have just given, we lost large sums of money on the company U.S. Surgical (ticker symbol USS). Let me turn back the clock so that you can see what we did and avoid making the same fatal errors.

The Perfect Storm: U.S. Surgical

The following is an example of a rags-to-riches-to-rags story that illustrates the importance of developing and sticking with a disciplined sell strategy.

U.S. Surgical was founded in the 1960s to design and manufacture products that are used in surgery, including sutures, staplers, cardiovascular products, and other such devices. Much later, in 1998, USS was acquired by Tyco. Team K got involved in the stock in the early 1990s. The reason for retelling the story here is that this is a textbook example of a great growth company that got into trouble and experienced one of the sell triggers discussed earlier in the chapter—industry outlook. It is also the best example of how we made the mistake of allowing taxes to drive the selling process.

USS sold its first product, the surgical staple, back in 1967. For a number of years, USS had the entire surgical staple market, and company growth was robust. Then Johnson & Johnson came out with the disposable staple in 1977 and crushed USS's hold on the surgical staple market. In the early 1980s, there was also a series of serious legal problems that affected USS.

In 1987, the company came out with a new, breakthrough product (called the Surgiport trocar, which began the laparoscopic surgery field). However, despite the success of this and other products, USS continued to be tainted because of SEC violations and a number of lawsuits. In 1990, it introduced another great new product, the "Endo Clip," which enabled laparoscopic gallbladder removal. (I am not, of course, trying to turn this book into a medical book or turn you into a medical student. However, I mention these new products to be as specific as possible in showing you what can drive a company's stock market value to rise—and rise dramatically.)

As a result of the successful launches of these new products, the company experienced a 50 percent sales increase in 1990 and a 75 percent increase in the first half of 1991. This made USS one of the greatest growth stories of all U.S. stocks of its day. The company's stock price followed its sales growth, and in January 1992, the company hit a high of $134.50. However, because of heated competition and a large oversupply of its product lines, the company then went into a steep decline. By September 1993, about 20 months after reaching its high, the company's stock price had plummeted to $22.50. At Team K, we had owned the stock through the entire ride up, but we were slow to sell it, as we were trying to generate long-term capital gains and allowed tax strategy to dictate sell timing, and as a result, lost a substantial amount of unrealized profits.

This example shows you how quickly a firm's fortunes can fall and why you should never let tax implications affect when you sell a stock. This is a big part of developing a strong sell discipline.

Now we move on to one of the most critical—and most over-looked—topics: managing risk.

Managing the Downside

How do we manage the downside? Many of the earlier chapters provide an answer to that. By keeping your winners and selling your losers, you will have a much better chance to beat the market. In addition, by letting change be your compass and adopting a strong sell discipline, you will also increase your chances of success while limiting your downside risk.

One of the other ways to manage risk is to invest in companies with management teams that are capable of reinvesting the firm's cash flow successfully. When you buy shares of a company, you become an owner of the business. So make sure the management team is capable of investing that money, and never attempt to manage short-term volatility relative to benchmark industries. Never allow yourself to be fooled into making a decision based on the wrong criteria. Master the disciplines and tenets of this book, and you will avoid the kind of unforced error that trips up so many investors.

Up until this chapter of the book, we've focused on various ways of playing offence. The first 10 chapters were really about strategies for creating positive absolute returns and ways to add value to your overall investing portfolio strategy based on the 20 years' experience I have had in dealing with various types of securities, markets, and scenarios. But at the end of the day, success will ultimately be determined by discipline, execution, and risk management, which is why risk management is so important in determining investment success.

Business expert and author Charles Tremper once said the following about risk: "The first step in the risk management process is to acknowledge the reality of risk. Denial is a common tactic that substitutes deliberate ignorance for thoughtful planning." That is a perfect sentiment that I subscribe to as well. Investors cannot put their heads in the sand and just hope that things will work out. Instead, investors need to be aware of the risk associated with their portfolio and take steps to mitigate it.

At Team K, when we were asked to describe our risk management philosophy, we typically told our clients, "Losing money is worse than missing the opportunity to make it." I think when you take both of these quotes together (Team K's and Charles Tremper's), the message comes through loud and clear: the first principle of investing is to protect your principal. You must recognize that you will make mistakes; all investors make mistakes. It is how they react when they know that they have made a mistake that separates winning investors from losing investors.

I have learned that denial is a very powerful emotion in investing. You cannot allow denial to freeze you in your tracks like a deer in the headlights. When you know that you have made a mistake, you must act. Companies change; businesses change. We demonstrated earlier

Losing money is worse than missing the opportunity to make it.

in the book how the best-thought-out investment strategy will be affected by certain things that are out of a company's control. How you react to it makes all the difference. So you must put denial in the garbage.

Thoughtful planning, as Mr. Tremper has said, is part of discipline. How you methodically execute your sell discipline is the single most important determinant of sound risk management. In a sense, they're almost the same. Strong sell discipline is a plan. Risk management is execution. They work hand in hand.

At the end of the day, I will argue that risk management is about human capital. Success in risk management is built on the human ability to overcome denial and not allow your own rules of engagement to be affected by human emotion. But there is no surefire way to protect your principal under all circumstances. For example, you can build the best stop-loss orders into every buy transaction, and still end up losing more money than you planned for.

How could that be? Putting in stop-loss orders could be a loser's game, because things will happen, you'll be stopped out, and human nature will not allow you to buy the stock back in. Those investors who had stop-loss orders in on their stocks on May 6, 2010 (when the market fell almost 1,000 points intra-day but recovered two-thirds of the loss before the close), understand how stop-loss orders can hurt you badly. For example, holders of Procter & Gamble (P&G) who had a stop-loss order within 20 points of the stock's $60+ price would have automatically had their stock sold on that horrific day. P&G fell by more than 20 points that day before recovering almost the entire loss. So here we have an investor who was trying to maintain a disciplined selling approach, but who got crushed by market forces beyond anyone's control. That's why there is no foolproof method or hard-and-fast rules for selling stocks. However, the following section features three things to focus on in order to protect yourself and your portfolio.

Protect Your Investment

My message in terms of risk management has never wavered, and the key to managing your downside involves protecting your original investment. This is something that almost any investor can identify with, since any investor knows how painful it is to lose money. Today there are all sorts of ways for investors to "hedge" their portfolios. Think of any investment in any shorting instrument as a cushion or, more accurately, as portfolio insurance. You insure your cars and your home, so why would you not want to spend some money insuring your stock portfolio?

Twenty years ago, the only way an individual could hedge a portfolio would be through fairly sophisticated investment instruments, like buying a put option or shorting another stock in the same sector. For example, let's say you had a large capital gain in Johnson & Johnson (J&J), but you did not want to sell the stock and realize a capital gain (for this hypothetical example only, we are allowing taxes to influence our sell strategy). However, you were afraid that J&J might begin to falter because of headwinds associated with regulatory changes in health care. The only way to hedge that specific position was to short the stock, short another closely related big health-care stock like Pfizer, or sell a call on the closely related stock. But the problem is that the correlation between what happens at J&J and what happens at Pfizer isn't perfect. In fact, there are situations in which the two stocks might have very different futures.

For example, you expected that both stocks would go down in the face of strong, negative regulation in the health-care arena. Let's assume that the regulation is passed by Congress and becomes law, and as a result J&J does indeed fall by 20 percent. However, at the same time, Pfizer announces that it has just come up with the next generation of Lipitor; it is going to be sold for half the price, and in addition to lowering cholesterol, it will grow hair on balding men. Therefore Pfizer's stock goes up 30 percent at a time when the rest of the group was going down 20 percent. Therefore, not only have you not managed risk, but you've lost money on both sides of the transaction. What you thought was asset protection turned out to be nothing more than a losing trade. However, that was yesterday. Today there are far better ways to protect one's principal.

Today, with the advent of exchange-traded funds (ETFs) and sector spiders (SPDRs, or ETFs that are sector-specific), it's very easy for individuals to go out and create their own hedges to protect their stock portfolio. How do you do this? Once you have your

20 to 30 stocks, the key is to look for common themes in the portfolio. Do you have a disproportionate amount of one type of stock, such as technology stocks, energy stocks, or drug stocks? I'd be surprised if there wasn't some ETF that you could use to short against the portfolio that would give you some real protection.

Throughout the book, I have repeatedly talked about the importance of doing your due diligence. In this context, you need to do your homework to help you to figure out which stocks you will sell and when you will sell them. However, I do not expect you to spend as much time playing defense (e.g., managing risk) as playing offense (e.g., putting together your portfolio of stocks). Instead, I expect you to spend about 80 percent of your time playing offense and only 20 percent playing defense.

In playing defense, the key is to monitor your portfolio continuously to see if you have significant overweighting in any sector or any space. If that is the case, try to identify the ETF or SPDR that tracks most closely with the group of stocks that makes up the largest part of your portfolio.

Here is a specific example. Let's say you review your portfolio and see that almost half of the names come from the drug, pharmaceutical, and biotechnology sector. Let's assume that you have chosen these stocks well and that as a group they are up by about 50 percent since you acquired them. You still like the stocks, but there is a potential regulatory change being discussed in Washington that, if passed by Congress, would have an adverse effect on this pool of stocks in your portfolio. In this situation, you can do one of two things. First, you can trade around these positions by unloading, say, half of each of the positions and keeping a core holding of the other half.

The other thing you can do is find an ETF that you can short in order to give you some downside protection if that regulation comes to pass. In this example, the sector SPDR that you want to short is XLV, the health-care SPDR, which represents just under 12 percent of the entire S&P 500. (If you don't know how to place a short order, call your online or other broker, and he will walk you through it. It is not difficult.)

Where can you go to learn about these sector SPDRs? Investors can go to http://www.sectorspdr.com/ and learn about the following nine sector SPDRS:

XLY	Consumer Discretionary SPDR
XLP	Consumer Staples SPDR
XLE	Energy SPDR
XLF	Financial SPDR
XLV	Health Care SPDR
XLI	Industrials SPDR
XLB	Materials SPDR
XLK	Technology SPDR
XLU	Utilities SPDR

Shorting one or more of these SPDRs can be a very effective vehicle to help you mitigate the risk in your portfolio. When you go to http://www.sectorspdr.com/, you can click on any of the nine SPDRs and then click on "holdings" to see the total list of stocks that are included in that particular ETF. So if you are not sure which of the SPDRs to short, then spend some time digging into each of them so that you can get a better sense of the type of stocks in each of these sector ETFs.

What if you review your portfolio and find that you have a large variety of stocks, with no apparent overweighting of any one sector? Then you have several options. You can simply short the entire S&P 500 by shorting SPY, which is the ETF for the entire S&P 500. What if you don't want to short any stock or ETF because you are simply not comfortable doing so? Then you have other options.

You can buy SDS, which is the ProShares UltraShort S&P 500 ETF. By buying this ETF, you are purchasing a terrific hedging instrument. SDS is twice the inverse of the S&P 500 (a double short on the S&P 500). If the S&P 500 *falls* by, say, 5 percent, then SDS will *rise* by 10 percent, and vice versa.

You can also buy SPXU, which is the ProShares UltraPro Short S&P 500. That's a long title for an ETF that is three times the inverse of the S&P 500 (a triple short on the S&P 500). If the S&P goes down by 5 percent, then this ETF will rise by 15 percent, and vice versa. So either of these two ETFs—SDS or SPXU—is an excellent idea to help you sleep better at night, particularly if you are like the vast majority of investors and have no short positions in your portfolio.

Another very good option for hedging your portfolio is EPV, ProShares UltraShort MSCI Europe. This ETF is twice the negative of the European stock market index (a double short of Europe). If Europe falls by 5 percent, then EPV will rise by 10 percent, and vice versa. This became a critical shorting vehicle in the late spring of 2010, when Greece faced possible insolvency and Portugal and Spain also got into financial trouble. Those investors who had this particular ETF slept a lot better than the rest of us who didn't when Europe's troubles spilled over into our markets, sending U.S. stock indexes plummeting.

The next logical question that investors might have is, "How much capital do I allocate to shorting the market?" This question arises whether you are actually shorting one of the ETFs I mentioned earlier or buying a shorting vehicle like SDS or EPV. Once again, there are no hard-and-fast rules about this. It really comes down to common sense and your comfort level. Let's use a specific example.

Let's assume that you have a basket of 25 stocks worth $100,000 with no dominant theme or sector overweighting the portfolio. You may decide to spend an additional $25,000 and purchase the SDS ETF. If the S&P falls by 10 percent (and for the purpose of simplicity, let's assume that your portfolio falls by the same 10 percent), SDS will increase in value by 20 percent. In this example, your portfolio (without figuring SDS into the equation) will fall by $10,000 to $90,000. However, with SDS, your portfolio falls by only $5,000, to $95,000, because your SDS investment will increase in value by $5,000. You now have a "risk-adjusted" loss of only $5,000. SDS has cushioned your portfolio by $5,000 (or by 50 percent of the loss). This would also assume you close out your SDS ETF position and lock in the gain and would then have $30,000 of liquid assets available to reinvest.

One of the biggest hurdles you will have to deal with when hedging your portfolio is the psychological impact if the market rises after you have purchased a shorting instrument. You have to get used to the fact that both losses and gains will be muted as a result of your taking a position in an investment of this type. You must be comfortable with a risk-adjusted rate of return, which is the return on your portfolio after you have calculated in the shorting vehicle(s) that you have added to your portfolio.

There are multiple ways to create hedges, such as derivative contracts, option strategies, and so on, but my philosophy for hedging your portfolio is to keep it simple. We don't want people trying to replicate what goes on at a large hedge fund. As I've described to you here, the greatest thing in terms of financial protection is common sense. Follow the guidelines I have described throughout the book, be disciplined, and don't make it more complicated. The system is designed to make things more complicated. It's designed to make you as the individual feel that you're at a major disadvantage. The TV commercials want you to believe that you need someone to help you structure your financial assets in a major way. The system is there to tell you that you can't do this yourself. For that very reason, I say you can.

When you are acquiring the sort of downside portfolio insurance described in the last few pages, do not short four or five different ETFs. Choose one or two that you can easily understand, and then figure out what percentage of your portfolio you would like to hedge. Theoretically you could hedge 100 percent of your portfolio, but then you would get zero return if the market rises. So you probably want to hedge only a portion of the portfolio, enough to make a real difference if your portfolio drops in value, but not so much that you have zero upside potential.

In conclusion, the keys to success are the same ones I have stressed throughout the book. Keep your winners and sell your losers. Consistently mine the portfolio by staying on top of the equities you own. The more you are able to do this, the less portfolio insurance you will require. You won't have to make it more complicated by having option strategies or trying to create macro hedges, because you'll be cleansing the portfolio through the natural research process.

For those investors who, in reading this final chapter of the book, are feeling discouraged because they have never shorted a stock or bought anything that they know will automatically go down when the market goes up, take heart. You do not need to be an investment banker to compete with the best and the brightest professionals. In fact, as I mentioned at the beginning of this chapter, in a very real sense you may have an advantage over the larger financial institutions.

How can that be?

The more capital you manage, the more difficult it is. The larger the asset pool you're dealing with, the harder it is to get into and out of things, and the more constrained you are in terms of what you can and cannot buy. As an individual, you are dealing with only a relatively small number of securities. You're actually at an advantage in many respects compared to the institution, which has a much bigger boat to turn around.

Allow me this final metaphor to make this point crystal clear.

I love the island of St. Bart's and often visit there. On St. Bart's is the harbor city of Gustavia. Over the Christmas period, many very wealthy individuals from around the world bring their super mega-yachts to the island—for example, Paul Allen, the cofounder of Microsoft; Roman Abramovich, the richest or second-richest man in Russia; Ron Perlman of Revlon fame; and so on. What's ironic is that in the harbor, everybody wanted to have a slip as close as possible to Gustavia. But at the same time, as the boats got bigger and bigger, everybody wanted to have a bigger boat. So now there is no room, and nobody can get his boat into the harbor. People buy these boats that cost $200, $300, $400 million, and they have to keep them all the way out in the Caribbean Sea, halfway to St. Martin, because they can't get the boats into the harbor. Yet the little dinghies that these huge yachts use to get to shore can get into and out of the harbor very quietly and easily. As the billionaires are building bigger and bigger boats, they still need the little dinghies to get to dinner in the town. It's good to recognize that you as the dinghy—as opposed to huge hedge fund managers, mutual fund managers, and closet indexers—have the ability to move and navigate far more easily. You are nimble and flexible, while the huge investment houses are more like the $400 million yacht that can't get near the shore. Remember, all you're trying to do is take your nest egg and be opportunistic and actively manage.

In order to win more than you lose, you must recognize that, use it to your advantage, and stay on top of things. And never think that your dinghy is too small. You can manage $25,000, and that's fine. You don't have to have a million dollars to beat the professionals at their own game.

SOURCE NOTES

Chapter 1: The Lost Generation of Investors

The data indicating that a dollar invested in the stock market in 1802 would have been worth $12.7 million by the end of 2006 come from Jeremy Siegel, *Stocks for the Long Run*, 4th ed. (New York: McGraw-Hill, 2008), p. 6.

The data on the bear markets of the last half century come from Burton G. Malkiel, "The Size and Shape of Bear Markets," *The Random Walk Guide to Investing* (New York: W.W. Norton & Company, paperback edition, 2007), p. 29.

The information on the retirement age increasing from 65 to 70.5 is from the research of Craig Copeland, Employee Benefit Research Institute, as cited by Gregory Bressiger, "70.5 is the new 65," *New York Post*, February 28, 2010.

The statement that 43 percent of people have less than $10,000 in savings comes from Chavon Sutton, "43% Say They Have Less than $10k for Retirement," CNNMoney.com, March 9, 2010.

The information on range-bound markets comes from the research of Vitaliy Katsenelson, "We Just Finished One Lost Decade, and Here Comes Another One," *Business Insider*, January 7, 2010.

The research on pension fund managers trying riskier investments comes from Mary Williams Walsh, "Public Pension Funds Are Adding Risk to Raise Returns," *New York Times*, March 8, 2010.

Chapter 2: The Zero-Growth Decade Ahead

The information on U.S. households losing 18 percent of their wealth comes from Vikas Bajaj, "Household Wealth Falls by Trillions," *New York Times*, March 12, 2009.

The report that one in four mortgages were underwater comes from Ruth Simon and James R. Haggerty, "One in Four Borrowers Is Underwater," *Wall Street Journal*, November 24, 2009, p. A1, citing First American CoreLogic.

The information on Japan's becoming the world's most highly valued financial market comes from Jeremy Siegel, *Stocks for the Long Run*, 4th ed. (New York: McGraw-Hill, 2008), p. 165.

The data on Nippon Telephone and Telegraph having a P/E ratio over 300 and the data on the Nikkei falling below 8,000 come from ibid.

The research on the Japanese market falling to only 67 cents on the dollar, or an annualized return of minus 3.59 percent, comes from William Bernstein, *The Four Pillars of Investing* (New York: McGraw-Hill, 2002), p. 67.

Thomas H. Kee's "Investment Rate" and "Kee Age" come from Thomas H. Kee, "For Stocks, 16 Lean Years," *Barron's*, March 15, 2010.

Chapter 3: Wall Street's Greatest Myths Revealed

"Explore the T. Rowe Price Difference" and the cumulative returns cited were excerpted from the home page on the T. Rowe Price Web site, May 17, 2010.

The information on Janus losing nearly $60 billion in shareholder wealth and being the worst "wealth destroyer" firm, along with Putnam and AllianceBernstein, came from Sam Mamudi, "Wealth Creators vs. Wealth Destroyers," *Wall Street Journal*, March 3, 2010, quoting a study from Morningstar, Inc.

Chapter 5: Let Change Be Your Compass, Part 1: GE

Dean Carney's eight rules for investors come from "The Eight Rules of Carney," quoted in Ben Mezrich, *Ugly Americans: Ivy League Cowboys Who Raided the Asian Markets for Millions* (New York: HarperCollins, 2004), 68–69, 88, 143, 173, 233, 245, 259, and back matter.

The information on GE's 2001 performance and the chairman's Letter to Share Owners is excerpted from GE's 2001 annual report.

GE's "Overview of Our Earnings" for 2009 was excerpted from Management's Discussion and Analysis of Financial Condition and Results of Operations, taken from GE's 10-K, filed in 2010.

The list of subject heads starting with Create Financial Flexibility was taken from the Letter to Investors in GE's 2009 annual report.

The statement beginning, "We are repositioning GE Capital as a smaller and more focused specialty finance franchise" comes from GE's 2009 annual report.

The list beginning with "Our global growth is subject to economic and political risks" is excerpted from the Risk Factors section of GE's 2009 10-K.

Chapter 6: Let Change Be Your Compass, Part 2: Disney

Many of the facts given in this chapter regarding Disney and the Michael Eisner era come from Ron Grover, *The Disney Touch* (New York, McGraw-Hill, 1991).

Eisner and his team figuring that the film division of the company would lose well over $100 million comes from ibid., p. 84.

Information on Disney's successful $1 billion stock offering, in which it sold 86 million shares, comes from Michael Eisner with Tony Schwartz, *Work in Progress* (New York: Random House, 1998), p. 269.

Michael Eisner's earning more than $2 million at Paramount comes from *The Disney Touch*, p. 50.

"[Disney] had few ties to the Steven Spielbergs and Ivan Reitmans of Hollywood" comes from *The Disney Touch,* p. 82.

Chapter 7: What Has the Company Done for Me Lately?

The discussion of Ford's 2009 net income as compared with 2008 net income under Item 7, Management's Discussion and Analysis of Financial Condition, is taken from Ford's 2009 10-K filing.

The five reasons why mergers and acquisitions fail—beginning with "bad business logic" and ending with "flawed corporate development"— are excerpted from the work of noted author Denzil Rankin.

"How is it that such deals come together in the first place" comes from Steve Rosenbush, "When Big Deals Go Bad—And Why," *BusinessWeek*, October 4, 2007.

"Then in the late 1990s and early 2000s, HP veered off course" comes from Jim Collins, in the Foreword to the book *The HP Way* (New York: Harper Paperbacks, 2006).

Chapter 8: Picking Stocks for All Markets

Charles Ellis, *Winning the Loser's Game*, 5th ed. (New York: McGraw-Hill, 2009).

The discussion of *Newsweek*'s ranking of the greenest companies in the United States came from Daniel McGinn, "The Greenest Big Companies in America," *Newsweek*, September 21, 2009.

Fortune magazine's ranking of the Best Companies to Work For and the new number one ranking of NetApp came from Christopher Tkaczyk, "A New No. 1 Best Employer," *Fortune*, January 22, 2009.

Chapter 9: Do Your Own Due Diligence

The article cautioning investors on calling the end of the recession too soon came from James Surowiecki, "Timing the Recovery," *The New Yorker*, April 19, 2010.

The article on improving stock prices came from Bill Swarts, "The Case for Higher Stock Prices," *Smart Money*, April 12, 2010.

The quotation beginning, "Rather than be content to accept corporate anonymity, we will rediscover the value of authorship" comes from John Maeda, "Your Life in 2020," *Forbes*, April 8, 2010.

Chapter 11: Develop a Strong Sell Discipline and Manage the Downside

Some of the specific details and information on U.S. Surgical came from FundingUniverse.com.

ACKNOWLEDGMENTS

This book could not have been written without the support and friendship of many great people who provided much assistance along the way. I'd specifically like to thank two people who helped to make this book a reality. I would like to offer my sincere thanks to Jeffrey Krames, who cold-called me some three years ago and suggested that we do a book together. I wasn't sure if Krames was calling me because he was mad at me for touting some terrible stock on CNBC or if he genuinely wanted to talk to me about a book project. It didn't take long for me to figure out which. Krames kept the lines of communication open for many years, and we have now become great friends. I respect everything about how he's been able to put this project together, and we've both learned a tremendous amount about each other since that first fateful call.

I also want to specifically cite CNBC's fireball Susan Krakower, who has been a tremendous supporter of the project over the last year. Susan is also my new "boss" and challenges me every single day at CNBC to get it right, to have fun, and to make things better than the day before. Susan is the first person I've ever met who gets up earlier than I do and has more energy.

Next, I would like to cite the contributions of members of the great firm of Neuberger Berman. Much of the information and strategies that have been discussed in this book were a collaborative effort by all the members of the team, who were responsible for creating the performance track record and many of the charts investment themes that you have read about in this book. I would like to thank the following members of Team Kaminsky: Navira Ali, Alex Bacu, Yana Berman, Tamara Calendar, Ralph De Feo, David Fecht, J. J. Gartland, Anthony Gerrits, Mary Ellen Herron, Randi Hyman, Gerry Kaminsky, Michael Kaminsky, Joe Lasser, Susan McKay, David Mizrachi, Jacqueline Rada, Avi Safei, Mindy Schwartzapfel, Kent Simons, David Wechsler, Richard Werman, and Caroline Witte.

In addition to "Team K," there are certain current Neuberger Berman people whom I would like to mention. These include Jason Ainsworth, Joe Amato, Brad Cetron, Meg Gattuso, Carolyn Golub, Charles Kantor, Ken Rende, Sevan Sakayan, Rick Szelc, George Walker, and Randy Whitestone. I would also like to recognize some former Neuberger Berman colleagues and good friends: Brian Gaffney, Jeff Lane, Bob Matza, Avi Mizrachi, and Keith Wagner.

Let's not forget my colleagues at my new home, CNBC, including CEO Mark Hoffman, whose leadership and vision are inspiring; my cohost of *Strategy Session* and friend of more than 20 years, David Faber; and our senior producers, Mary Duffy and Max Meyers. My appreciation also goes to Andy Barsh, Maria Bartiromo, Josh Bieber, Nick Deogun, Jenny Dwork, Jason Farkas, Beth Goldman, Herb Greenberg, Dan Hoffman, Kate Kelly, Joe Kernen, Melissa Lee, Steve Liesman, John Melloy, Jeremy Pink, Matt Quayle, Carl Quintanilla, Becky Quick, Brian Steel, Joe Terranova, and Samantha Wright. And an extra special shout out to Brian "Beeks" Kelly and Joe "The Liquidator" Terranova for their invaluable help reviewing the manuscript.

My friends in the "industry" who have played such an important role in my life and career include Shelly Bergman, Nils Brous, Mitch Brown, Liz Claman, Joe Cohen, Frank D'Ambrosio, Marge Demarrais, Donald Drapkin, Robert Feidelson, Jeff Greenfield, Marc Howard, Ron Insana, Rob Kapito, Steve Lipin, Nat Lipman, Paul Marsh, George Mattson, Jeff Moslow, Bob Olstein, John Oppenheimer, Scott Page, David Pelton, George Raffa, Mike Santoli, Russ Sarachek, Anthony Scaramucci, Ben Thompson, and John Ziegler. Also Timmy Grazioso and Marni Pont, who were tragically killed on September 11, 2001. And the late Seth Tobias.

I would like to thank my family and friends (and yes, despite what some consider my oversized ego, I still manage to have a few friends): the Altmans, Steve (Eugene) Anderson, Dick Bieber, the Blaus, Buster and Donna, the Dossicks, the Gladstones, the Grieffs, the Kaplans, Marian and Bobby, Marty and Nancy, the Mayos, Peter G., Peter and Judy, Raul, Richard and Rhonda, Tony Silva, a.k.a. "Tony D.," Howard Simowitz, the Spiegels, my brother Michael, Taylor, Katie, and Charlie, the Wermans. And special thanks to Jackie and Gerry (Mom and Dad), for tolerating me for the last 46+ years.

Finally, Krames ("dude") and I could never have completed this project without more than a few great meals, so let me take this opportunity to call out Chris at Matteo's, Hector at Cippolini's, and Kerrie Anne at Toku. These people took special care of us, and I am so grateful that they did (mostly because Krames threatened to boycott the book if I did not feed him his three squares a day).

INDEX

Note: Boldface numbers indicate illustrations.

ABOUT THE AUTHOR

During the last two decades, Gary Kaminsky has been one of the Street's most successful money managers. From 1990 to 1992, he was an analyst at J.R.O. Associates, a New York hedge fund. In 1992 he joined Cowen & Company as a portfolio manager in the Private Banking Department and became a partner in 1996. Assets coadvised by Mr. Kaminsky rose from $200 million to $1.3 billion between 1992 and 1999. Cowen & Company was sold to Société Générale in July 1998.

In May of 1999, Mr. Kaminsky and his team joined Neuberger Berman LLC. Under his comanagement, "Team K" grew from approximately $2 billion under management to approximately $13 billion at the time of his retirement in June 2008. Mr. Kaminsky is the cohost of the highly successful CNBC show, *Strategy Session*.

Mr. Kaminsky is a 1986 graduate of the Newhouse Communications School at Syracuse University, where he received a B.S. in TV/Radio/Film Management. He later completed an MBA in Finance from the Stern School of Business, New York University, in 1990.

Gary resides in Roslyn, New York, with his family. He is an active runner, having finished five New York marathons. In the last several years, he has completed two triathlon sprints and successfully climbed to the summit of Mt. Kilimanjaro in

Tanzania, Africa. He always considered himself a great skier, but in recent years the reality set in that his sons are better than him on the slopes.

THE DEADLY ACKEE

and Other Stories of Crime and Catastrophe

*Other Five Star Titles
by Joan Hess:*

Death of a Romance Writer and Other Stories
Big Foot Stole My Wife! and Other Stories

THE DEADLY ACKEE

and Other Stories of Crime and Catastrophe

Joan Hess

Five Star • Waterville, Maine

First Edition
First Printing: December 2003

Published in 2003 in conjunction with Tekno Books and Ed Gorman.

Set in 11 pt. Plantin.

Printed in the United States on permanent paper.

Library of Congress Cataloging-in-Publication Data

Hess, Joan.
    The deadly ackee and other stories of crime and catastrophe / by Joan Hess.—1st ed.
        p. cm.
    Contents: Caveat emptor—A little more research—The Maggody files—All's well that ends—The deadly ackee.
    ISBN 1-59414-079-0 (hc : alk. paper)
    1. Detective and mystery stories, American. I. Title.
PS3558.E79785D373 2003
813'.54—dc22   2003049535

THE DEADLY ACKEE

and Other Stories of Crime and Catastrophe

Table of Contents

Introduction

Rereading these stories, some of which were written more than a decade ago, both amused and bemused me. Amused, I suppose, because I had to resist an urge to grab a pencil and start fiddling with the prose, snipping here and using a more concise word there. This is not to say (and I never, never would unless I was offered a great sum of money) that I found them poorly written. Each of them sparkles in its own way, but my writing style has evolved over the years.

And now I'll move on to bemused, in the gentle sense of causing to muse. My novels come with, for want of a better phrase, a set of bylaws involving recurring characters, points of view, genteel violence, a bawdy or satiric voice, and rather wacky plots. Short stories, in contrast, have provided me with the chance to explore other structures and radically different narrative tones. Some of them, if published anonymously, would never be attributed to this little ol' comedic Southern writer of what are generally considered to be cozy novels. And each story came from a very small idea that would not suffice as the basis for a novel.

"Caveat Emptor" had been floating around in the back of my mind for a long while. I was at various times in my life a tenant, a landlord, a home buyer, and a real estate salesperson, and I learned the perils of each role (as well as the profound significance of the Latin phrase). I'm not sure where the narrator came from, but I wish she lived across the street from me. She's disabled, not well-educated, not intuitive, and by no means a candidate for sainthood; her appeal comes from her compassion.

"A Little More Research" is certainly one of my most bizarre stories. When I first started writing in hopes of actually making money, my children were four and seven. I continually told them that when I was in my office, I wasn't to be disturbed unless there was smoke, blood, or a strange man at the front door. Even the most timid "can I have an apple?" would obliterate my train of thought, as if said train had plunged into a dark tunnel with no glimmer of light at the end. My children are now twenty-three and twenty-six. They still don't get it.

As for "The Maggody Files: Time Will Tell," I was once married to a man who over the years became increasingly oblivious to the concept of time. Time is relentless; it cannot be put on hold for personal indulgences—and most people don't like to be kept waiting. Some years ago, I did a casual poll of my friends and acquaintances, posing this question: if you and I agreed to meet for lunch at 1:00, how many minutes after the hour would you feel horribly late and guilty? Most people said five or ten minutes. My daughter called her father, who said twenty minutes. Having forgotten to get a degree in psychology, I arrived at no conclusions. It's interesting, though.

"All's Well That Ends" is pretty obvious. After a lengthy televised trial, a celebrity was found not guilty of murder, after which he offered a lucrative reward for the apprehension of the perp. I wasn't impressed. What if, I started wondering, someone with nothing to lose . . . say, someone with a terminal disease . . . someone who wanted to provide for the family . . .

Finally, "The Deadly Ackee," a novel despite its inclusion as a story. Okay, so I went to Jamaica with a group of friends, and we rented a villa overlooking Montego Bay. The living room furniture looked as though it had been purchased from a house of ill-repute. The cook was surly, the maid was clueless, and the pool boy took off in our car one night, obliging us to climb the fence and then send a commando up onto a balcony to get inside the villa. I was intrigued by the fact that ackee (cooked with salted fish) is a national dish, yet fatal when unripe and the cause of many deaths. So maybe I paid a kid to climb a tree and fetch me a couple so I could examine them, then left them on the kitchen windowsill—to the cook's vocalized consternation. Our days were spent by the pool or at a hotel beach, and our evenings on the terrace, with bottomless pitchers of rum punch and strolling musicians who could be lured up the driveway for a few dollars. It wasn't an obvious scenario for a murder, but it did allow me to write the trip off on my taxes as a business expense.

I regret to say that this is Theo Bloomer's second and final appearance (the first, "The Night-Blooming Cereus," was reprinted last year by this same publisher). Then again, the situation may change and I'll be off to do research in New Zealand, Alaska, and other semi-exotic places. You just never know.

Joan Hess

Caveat Emptor

The first time she came walking across the street, I pegged her for a whiner. Her shoulders drooped like she thought she was carrying a goodly portion of the world's woes in a backpack, and from her expression, I could tell right off that she didn't think it was fair. I had news for her: nobody ever promised it would be. If it were, I'd have been playing pinochle beside a pool instead of watching soap operas while I ironed as the world turned.

She came onto the porch. "May I please use your phone?"

"Long distance?" I said cautiously.

"I need to call Mr. Wafford. He was supposed to have the utilities turned on by today, but nothing's on."

I took a closer look. She was at most in her late twenties, with short brown hair and a jaw about as square as I'd ever seen. Her eyes were sizzling with frustration, but her smile was friendly. Smiling back, I said, "You bought the house over there."

"I'm Sarah Benston. I signed the papers last week, and Mr. Wafford promised to arrange for the utilities to be on when we got here. It's after nine o'clock. My son and I have been on the road for fourteen hours, and there's no way we get by without water and electricity. I was hoping that he could still do something."

"You bring your son inside and let me give him a glass of juice," I said. "You can call Wafford if you want, but you're welcome to camp out over here. How old's your boy?"

"Cody's ten. I guess it's too late to call Mr. Wafford. He won't be able to do anything at this time of night."

I still wasn't sure what to make of her as she brought in a listless child, rolled out a sleeping bag for him in a corner, and kissed him good-night.

"So you bought the Sticklemann house?" I asked her as we sat down at the kitchen table.

She took a sip of coffee and nodded. "It seemed smart, even though my ex can't remember to send his child-support payments. I never finished my degree, so I decided to move back here and take classes. I was going to rent an apartment, but then Mr. Wafford explained how I could buy a house and build up equity. After the three or four years it'll take to graduate, I can sell the house and make a small profit. Cody's used to having a yard."

"How long since the divorce?" I asked.

"A year." Sarah put down her cup. "I know this is an imposition, Mrs. . . . ?"

"James, honey, but you call me Deanna. I know what you're going through. My daughter got divorced four years ago, and she had a real tough time before she threw up her hands and moved back in with me. Now she has a job, a good one, at an insurance office in town. She's dating a real polite boy she knew back in high school. Her daughter Amy's eight, so she's in bed. It's not a good idea having three generations of women in the same house, but we do what we got to do. You have a job, Sarah?"

"As a teacher's aide," she said with a shrug. "It's minimum wage, but the house payment's not much more than what I'd be paying in rent. Mr. Wafford is financing the sale privately, since I probably couldn't have qualified for a loan. Even if I had, I'd have been charged closing costs of more than three thousand dollars. This way, I only had to put down five percent, which left me enough to pay for the rental truck and the utility deposits."

"It'll work out," I said soothingly, although I had my doubts. My daughter had needed food stamps and welfare and everything else she could get until she'd found a job. I would have helped her out, but all I had were my monthly disability checks.

I made her a bed on the sofa, then sat and gazed out my bedroom window at the Sticklemann place, wondering just how much Jeremiah ("Call me 'Jem' ") Wafford had told this nice young woman.

Not nearly enough, I suspected.

I watched her from the porch the next day. I would have liked to help her haul in suitcases and furniture, but my back wasn't up to it. Her boy did what he could, trying to be the man of the family; finally, Perniski from up the road took pity on her and carried boxes, mattresses, bed frames, and mismatched chairs inside the house. All the same, she did most of the work, and I could see she had spirit.

Cody proved to be a mannersome child, and he ended up most weekday afternoons with Amy, watching movies on the television. Sarah tried to pay me for looking after him. I refused, saying that he was no trouble. He wasn't.

A month after she moved in, she came knocking on my front door. I could tell right off that she was upset, but I pretended not to notice and said, "You have time for coffee?"

"What's the deal with the water lines?" she said, close to sputtering with outrage. "The toilet backed up and flooded the bathroom. The plumber says that all the houses out here have substandard pipes from the nineteen-fifties, and there's nothing he can do short of replacing everything from the house to the main sewer line. Where am I going to find a thousand dollars?"

I sat her down on the porch swing. "There are some things Wafford didn't tell you, honey. After he bought the house, he slapped fresh paint on it and put down new linoleum—but it's still an old house. Don't be surprised if the roof leaks when it rains. Mrs. Sticklemann had to put pots and pans in every room."

Sarah stared at me. "What can I do? I called Mr. Wafford, but he reminded me that he recommended I pay for an inspection. It would have cost three hundred dollars. All I could hear him talking about were the possibilities for flower beds and a vegetable garden, and how Cody could play in the creek."

"Don't let him do that," I said. "Clover Creek may sound charming, but it's downstream from a poultry plant. Some government men were out here last spring, trying to figure out why all the fish bellied up."

"Anything else I should know?" she asked grimly.

I hoped she wasn't the sort to blame the messenger. "There's been some trouble with the folks in the house up at the corner. A couple of months ago the cops raided it and arrested them for selling drugs. One's doing time in the state prison, but two of them are back. That's why I walk up to where the school bus lets the children off in the afternoons. I've warned Cody about them too."

"Thanks, Deanna. I'd better go check the mailbox. Maybe this is the year I win a million-dollar sweepstakes."

We didn't talk for a long while after this, but only because she was busy with her job and her late-afternoon classes. Cody always kept a watch for her out the window, and as soon as her car pulled into the driveway, he'd say good-bye and dart across the road to help her carry in groceries. She and my daughter were friendly enough, but they didn't really hit it off. Amy, on the other hand, was crazy about Cody; he returned her affection with the lofty sophistication of an older man.

Sarah continued having trouble with the house. When I asked Cody about an exterminator's van, he said the carpet in his bedroom had fleas and showed me welts on his legs. On another day, he told me that his mother had called Mr. Wafford and then banged down the receiver and apologized for using "naughty" words.

She had spirit all right, I thought. Too bad she hadn't had common sense as well when she signed the papers in Wafford's office. It wasn't hard to imagine how he'd conned her, though. He was a slick one behind his hearty laugh and grandfatherly face. He'd owned half the houses along the road at one time or another. Most of the folks who'd fallen for his "equity" pitch had discovered a whole new side to him when they fell behind on their payments. There was a reason why he drove a flashy Cadillac.

"You're not going to believe this," Sarah said one evening while we watched Amy and Cody play on a tire swing in the yard. "There are bats in the attic. I saw them streaming out from under an eave last night."

"You have mice in the garage, don't you? Bats are nothing more than mice with wings."

She shuddered. "I called Wafford, and he said the same thing, then gave me a lecture about how they eat insects. From the way he carried on, I thought I was expected to thank him for providing mosquito control. What if one gets downstairs?"

"Mrs. Sticklemann kept a tennis racket in the hall. I don't

think she ever had to use it, though."

"That's comforting," she said dryly. "I was waiting for you to say she died of rabies."

"Nothing like that," I said, then stood up and raised my voice. "Amy, you need to get busy on your spelling words for the test on Friday. Go on in the house and get out your book."

Sarah gave me a look like she knew darn well I was tip-toeing around something, but she called to Cody and they left. I felt bad not telling her, but she had more than enough problems. Sometimes when you buy a lemon, you can squeeze it till your face turns blue, but you still can't make lemonade.

Later that evening when the telephone rang, I answered it without enthusiasm, expecting my daughter to give me some cockamamie story about how she had to work late.

"Deanna," Sarah said abruptly, "go into your living room. Don't turn on the light. There's a man out on the road, staring at my house. He's been there for at least half an hour. Should I call the police?"

"Hold on." I put down the receiver and did as she'd asked, then came back and picked it up. "I see him, honey. You say he's been there half an hour?"

"That's when I first noticed him. Could he be confused and think I'm our neighborhood drug dealer?"

"No," I said, "that's not his problem. You call the police if you want, Sarah, but I don't think it'll do much good."

"Do you know who he is?"

"Yes, I do. You come over tomorrow after you get home from work and I'll tell you about him. In the meantime, just ignore him. He'll go away before too long."

"Who is he?" she demanded. "How do you know he'll go away? What if he breaks into the house?"

"He won't come any closer than he already is," I said. "You and Cody are perfectly safe. I'll see you tomorrow."

I hung up and went back to the window. The figure was still there, all slouched over with his hands in his pockets, looking like a marble statue in the glow from the streetlight. I felt bad about making Sarah wait, but it was going to take a lot of time to explain it all in such a way that she wouldn't get too panicky.

"Damn that Jem Wafford," I said under my breath.

"Who is he?" Sarah demanded as soon as Cody and Amy ran around the corner of the house.

"Gerald Sticklemann," I said. "It's a long story. Are you sure you don't want coffee or a glass of iced tea?"

"Just tell me—okay?"

"Well, Gerald never was what you'd call normal. I knew the first time I laid eyes on him that there was something wrong. That was thirty years ago, when Hank and I bought this house. Gerald was close to the same age as my boys, but he never rode a bicycle or came over to play baseball in the summers. A little yellow bus came every day to take him to a special school for children that couldn't learn like they were supposed to. I made sure none of my children ever teased him, but there were some teenage boys up the road who used to call him ugly names and throw rocks at him when they rode their bicycles past the house."

"That doesn't explain why he was here last night."

"I'm getting to it," I said. "Mr. Sticklemann died not more than two years after we moved in, leaving his wife with a small income from a life insurance policy. She cleaned houses and made enough for her and Gerald to get by. There wasn't any question of him getting a proper job after he finished with that school. The only times I saw him were when he went walking down that path that leads down to the creek."

"This is all very touching, Deanna, but I need to fix dinner and get Cody started on his homework."

I held up my hands. "I'm just trying to make you understand about him. Over the years, families came and went, but the Sticklemanns stayed the same, like a soap opera without a plot. Eventually, she got too old to work and spent a lot of time with her vegetable garden. Wafford tried on occasion to convince her to sell him the house. I'd see him on the porch, his hat in his hands, grinning like a mule with a mouthful of briars, but I don't think he ever made it into the living room."

Sarah looked at her watch. "Will you please get to the point?"

"Mrs. Sticklemann died five years ago. Nobody knows exactly when because Gerald never said a word to anybody and kept doing what he always did, day in and day out. It was at least six weeks before one of her old friends came out to find out what was going on. I was in my yard when the woman came stumbling back outside, as bug-eyed and green as a bullfrog. I brought her over here so she could use my telephone, and while we waited for the police, she told me that Gerald had left his mother's body in her bed. It was in the late summer, and the flies and the stench were something awful."

"Did she die of natural causes?" Sarah asked in a tremulous voice.

"Oh, yes, there was never any question about that. The real question was what to do about Gerald. The only crime he'd committed was not notifying anybody when his mother died. He ended up in some sort of sheltered home with others of his kind. A distant cousin who was managing Gerald's affairs sold the house to Wafford. The problem is that Gerald slips out every now and then and comes back here, looking for his mother. He doesn't mean any harm."

Sarah stared at the house, her mouth so tight her lips were invisible. After a long moment, she said, "This is too much. Wafford not only forgot to tell me about the faulty plumbing, the fleas and bats, the rotten floorboards under the linoleum, the drug dealers up the street, the contaminated water in the—" She broke off and rubbed her face as though she could erase the sight of the house across the street. "I can't believe he didn't warn me about any of this! I don't have enough money to move to an apartment and put up two months' rent and a security deposit. It's all well and good for you to say this middle-aged child won't try to come into the house some night when we're asleep, but you can't be sure."

"As long as you lock your doors and windows before you go to bed, you and Cody will be all right," I said with more confidence than I felt.

Sarah swung around to look at me. "Wafford knew all about Gerald, didn't he? Doesn't his failure to tell me constitute fraud?"

"You'll have to ask a lawyer, but I wouldn't count on it. Wafford first sold the house to a nice young couple with a baby. They weren't any happier than you when they discovered all the problems, including Gerald. Wafford and the husband had such a heated argument in the driveway one afternoon that I almost called the police. Not long after that the couple packed up and left. The next day Wafford put a 'For Sale' sign in the yard. He was whistling."

Cody and Amy came running into the front yard with a bird's egg they'd found and we changed the subject.

"A policeman came to our house last night," Cody confided in me as he, Amy, and I walked back from the bus stop a week later.

"He did?" I murmured.

"He went into the kitchen with my mother. They talked for a long time, but I couldn't hear what they said."

"Did he arrest her?" asked Amy.

Cody made a face at her. "No, nitwit. They just talked, and then he left. My mother was mad, but she wouldn't tell me why."

I knew why, having seen Gerald at the edge of the road when I went into the front room to find my reading glasses. I'd considered calling Sarah to remind her to check the locks, but then I'd seen her in an upstairs window. Her face had been as pale as Gerald's.

I didn't say anything, and by the time we reached my house, Cody had forgotten about the policeman and was telling Amy about pirate ships. Sarah called an hour later and asked if I could give Cody supper.

"Glad to," I said. "You going to the library to study?"

"I have an appointment with Wafford. He wasn't happy about it, but I told him that if he wouldn't see me at his office at six o'clock, I'd go to his house and stand in the street until his neighbors started calling the police."

I let Amy and Cody eat in front of the TV set while they watched an old swashbuckler movie from the forties. It may have been considered gory in its time, but it wasn't nearly as violent as the Saturday-morning cartoons Amy watched religiously.

Sarah knocked on the door just as the movie ended. I sent the children to Amy's room, then set a cup of coffee on the table in front of her.

She ignored it. "I'm so mad that I can visualize myself buying a gun and shooting that man right between his beady eyes. Better yet, I could tar and feather him, then tie him to the back bumper and drag him through town. I don't suppose you have any tar out in the carport?"

21

"Sorry," I said, a little taken aback at the venomous edge in her voice.

"I wanted to slap the smirk right off his face. He kept calling me 'little lady' and 'sweetheart,' all the while assuring me that the house was a real bargain and he'd done me a favor by selling it to me at less than fair market value. I offered to let him buy it back at the same price, but he gave me a bunch of bull about his cash-flow problems. Well, I've got a cash-flow problem too—all my cash keeps flowing into that black hole across the street. There's a leak under the kitchen sink, and the door to the hall closet is so warped I can't get it open. Cody found a dead bat in the bathroom last weekend. On top of everything else, I've got to worry that Gerald may bust into the house in the middle of the night."

I patted her hand. "He never hurt anyone."

"There's always a first time, isn't there? The police won't do anything because Gerald isn't breaking the law. I talked to the county prosecutor this morning about a restraining order. He can't take action until Gerald makes explicit threats or starts waving a weapon. Or murders us in our beds. He'd be in big trouble then. Isn't that comforting?"

"Now, Sarah," I said, "Gerald's not going to do something like that. He's just confused and lonely."

"And I'm the proud owner of a house with rats in the basement and bats in the belfry." Her cheeks flushed, but she managed to get herself under control and added, "I'm not going to take it, Deanna. I've been pushed around all my life, first by my parents and then by an abusive jerk who used to hit me when his car wouldn't start on cold mornings."

"Maybe you and Cody could stay here until you can afford an apartment," I said. "I can sleep in Amy's room on a cot. It'll be crowded in the morning when we have to share the one bathroom, but—"

"No, thanks. This is my problem and I'm going to solve it. I'll think of something."

She gathered up Cody's coat and books, then called him. He appeared with a construction-paper eye-patch, a mustache drawn with a felt-tipped pen, and a piece of paper covered with pencil markings.

"I'm Long John Silver," he announced, "and I know where the buried treasure lies."

Something strange flashed across her face. "In the basement?" she said softly.

"No, down by the creek under a big tree. Tomorrow I'm going to dig it up and give you a chest filled with gold doubloons."

"Sounds good to me," she said, helping him on with his coat.

After they left, I settled Amy at the kitchen table with her geography workbook and a gnawed pencil. Most of the time I sat with her to make sure she didn't start doodling, but that evening I was too distracted to stay put.

When my daughter finally came home, I went into my bedroom and lay down, wondering just what Sarah might have in mind.

Jem Wafford should have been doing the same.

What she did a few nights later was so peculiar I almost went across the street to make sure she wasn't drunk. I was in the front room when I noticed Gerald was back. He was getting to be a familiar figure in his overcoat, his hands in his pockets, his bald head reminding me of a full moon. I glanced at the upstairs windows to see if Sarah was there, but the shades were drawn.

I stayed where I was, my fingers crossed in hopes she hadn't gone out and bought a gun. Gerald may have frightened her, but she'd have a hard time convincing a jury she'd shot him in self-defense.

I was beginning to feel relieved when her front porch light went on and she came outside. Her hands were blessedly empty, and she was dressed only in jeans and a thin T-shirt. I expected her to start cursing at Gerald, but she went down the steps and across the yard to join him. He retreated, but she kept smiling and talking like he was a neighbor from down the street. Pretty soon he stopped edging away from her and began to bobble his head. I couldn't see if he was saying anything in response—I'd have been surprised if he had—but Sarah didn't seem to notice. After a moment, she put her hand on his arm and led him toward her house. He moved reluctantly, but she kept her grip on him. Before long, they were inside and the front door was closed.

My heart was pounding so hard that I sat down in the rocking chair and forced myself to take a couple of slow breaths. I'd been the one swearing that Gerald wouldn't hurt anyone, but I had no way of knowing how his mother's death might have affected him deep down inside. Staring at the house was one thing; actually being inside it might set off all kinds of raw emotions.

I waited twenty minutes, then broke down and dialed Sarah's telephone number. I didn't know what I was going to do if she didn't answer, but she picked up the receiver.

"Is everything okay?" I asked, trying to keep the urgency out of my voice so Amy wouldn't get alarmed.

"Everything's fine, Deanna. Gerald and I are having a nice talk about when he and his mother lived here."

"I just thought I'd better . . ."

"I know," she said. "I'd do the same thing if the situation was reversed. I need to get back to my guest now. Don't worry about us."

All the same, I stayed by the window until I saw Gerald leave, and I made sure I got a good look at Sarah standing in the doorway. Rather than scared, she had a funny smile on her face. Smug.

"I saw you and your mother had company last night," I said to Cody the following afternoon after I'd softened him up with ice cream and cookies.

"Yeah," he said without enthusiasm. "She made me turn off the television and go upstairs, even though I already did my homework."

"So you didn't hear what they were saying?"

"No. May I please have some more ice cream?"

Amy snickered. "Pirates don't eat ice cream unless it's got blood and bones mixed in it."

"Says who?" he retorted, baring his teeth.

She obligingly squealed and ran out the back door, with Cody on her heels. My attempt to play private detective had flopped like a bad movie, I thought, as I set their bowls in the sink and turned on the water.

And I had a feeling I wouldn't do much better with Sarah.

Gerald appeared several times over the next few weeks, and each time Sarah went outside and escorted him into the house. Cody let drop one afternoon that Gerald had eaten supper with them the previous night and, for some reason that he wouldn't explain, solemnly swore that Gerald was descended from real pirates. Sarah smiled and waved when I saw her in her driveway, but she stopped coming over to have coffee before she fetched Cody. Some days I wanted to go across the street, grab her shoulders, and shake the truth out of her. I didn't do anything, though, except weasel what I could out of Cody while we walked home from the bus stop.

★ ★ ★ ★ ★

One afternoon while I was waiting for them, Jem Wafford's Cadillac swung around the corner and sped down the street. Years ago he'd given up trying to persuade me to sell, so he didn't bother to nod at me. As soon as Cody and Amy climbed off the bus, I hustled them to the house. Wafford was sitting in his car in Sarah's driveway. I told the children to make themselves peanut butter sandwiches, then crossed the street, and waited until he climbed out.

"Mrs. James," he said, pretending he hadn't left me in a cloud of dust minutes earlier, "how are you doing? Your back any better these days?"

"My back is none of your business," I said. "Are you looking for Sarah? She usually doesn't get home till six o'clock."

He took out a handkerchief and wiped his neck. "I dropped by on the chance I'd catch her on her day off."

"She doesn't have a day off. She's a full-time student and puts in thirty hours a week at a preschool. Weekends, she studies and does housework."

"You've got to admire that kind of determination," he said, beaming at me like he and I were the proud parents of a prodigy. "A single woman with a child, struggling to put herself through school so she can—"

"What do you want, Wafford?" I said bluntly.

"Is she still having trouble with Gerald?"

"You'll have to ask her yourself."

Wafford leaned his bulk against the Cadillac and gazed up at the second-story windows. "What about you, Mrs. James? Have you talked to Gerald recently?"

My curiosity got the better of me, so instead of stomping off, I said, "Not that I recall. Why?"

"At his request, I stopped by the group home where he

26

lives. We had a real interesting talk. I'm just wondering"—he tapped his temple—"how reliable he is."

"I couldn't say."

"He's been out here quite a bit, hasn't he?"

"What if he has?" I shot back.

"He told me that his mother was a miser, that she squirreled away a good deal of cash before she died." Wafford looked at me, his mouth curled in a smile but his eyes slitted like a snake's. "You ever get the idea she was putting away cash for a rainy day?"

Something was going on. I didn't know what, and if somebody'd offered me a million dollars, I couldn't have come up with the right answer.

"Maybe," I said cautiously. "She stayed to herself."

"Gerald seems to think she did," he said, "but he's not the most reliable witness, considering."

"Considering," I echoed. To this day I can't explain why I added, "But he's not the kind who tells tales. His imagination was never a strong point."

"No, it wouldn't be," Wafford said with a snicker. "Mr. Sticklemann's family owned all the land out this way once upon a time. They sold it off part and parcel over the years, most likely for cash. Folks like that didn't trust real-estate brokers and bankers."

"I don't suppose so," I said, still feeling like I had a role in a play. I could almost hear Sarah coaching me from the wings, but my script was too blurry to read. "Mrs. Sticklemann wasn't the kind to deal with bankers. She was real independent."

"That's what I was thinking." Wafford took another swipe at his neck, then stuffed his handkerchief in his pocket.

"She sure didn't squander any of it. She had that ancient Pontiac when she died, and heaven knows she never took a vacation or had repairs done to the house."

Just then Sarah drove up. I was waiting for her to snarl at him, so I was a little bewildered when she asked me to watch Cody for a while longer and invited Wafford to go inside for iced tea.

Wafford's car was still in the driveway long after Cody'd gone home and Amy had eaten supper. I was reluctant to do any more than watch from behind the curtain in the front-room window, and that's what I was doing when Sarah came walking across the street for what turned out to be the last time.

I opened the front door as she came onto the porch. "Everything all right?" I demanded.

"Wafford has offered to buy back the house for what I have in it and more. We agreed that I'd move out tonight and collect my furniture later. I want to thank you for everything you've done, Deanna. I'll write once Cody, Gerald, and I have a new address."

"Gerald?"

"I've agreed to take him with us to be my resident baby-sitter and handyman. He did me a favor and I owe him big. I'll swing by the home and pick him up on my way out of town."

I was afraid to go into it any further. "What about your classes?"

"I'm not sure I want to be a teacher," she said with a wry grin. "I may decide to go into real estate. I've learned quite a bit over the last few months."

"What about Wafford?"

"He's inspecting the property to make sure it's in the same condition as it was when I bought it. He'll leave before too long."

She hugged me, then turned around and went home. Over

the next hour, she and Cody loaded the car with suitcases and boxes. Wafford's Cadillac was in the shadows at the far end of the driveway, but he never emerged with an armload of anything. Not that he was the kind to help anybody.

Amy finally started nagging me to help her with her homework, so I abandoned my vigil and went into the kitchen. After she'd finished and gone to bed, I went back to the front room. Sarah's car was gone. Wafford's car was still there, and a light was on in the back of the house. I couldn't imagine what he was doing.

It was none of my business, so I made myself some popcorn and turned on a movie.

The next morning I noticed Wafford's car was gone too. I fixed pancakes, then listened to my daughter gripe about her boss before she gulped down a cup of coffee and shooed Amy out the door to drive her to school.

The ritual was familiar, but not comforting. Once I had the house to myself, I tidied up and started a load of laundry, but the window in the front room was a magnet. Why had Sarah befriended Gerald, of all people? Even odder, why had Wafford agreed to buy back the house? He'd always circled like a vulture, waiting to foreclose on hapless widows and families whose breadwinners had been fired or become disabled.

I hadn't received any great insights by three o'clock, when it was time to walk to the bus stop. I was almost there when Mr. Perniski came outside, dressed in his customary cardigan sweater and khaki pants.

"What's going on at the end of the road?" he said. "That young woman was acting mighty peculiar last night."

"Sarah?"

"You betcha. She pulled into the driveway over there"

—he pointed at our neighborhood drug dealer's establishment—"and gave that one with the beard what looked like a key. Long about midnight, he went sneaking down the road toward her house. The last thing we need out here is another criminal. My grandson found a hypodermic needle in the ditch last summer. We have—"

"Sarah and Cody moved out last night," I said, cutting him off. "Are you sure she gave him a key?"

"Hell, I ain't sure about nothing," Perniski muttered, then wandered away.

I thought about all this while I waited for the school bus, and I hadn't made much progress by the time Amy was occupied with a bag of cookies and old sitcoms on television. I finally slipped out and went across the street to what had been Sarah's house. The doors were locked, so all I could do was peer through windows at unoccupied rooms.

The police did not arrive for more than two days, and my instinctive response was to tell them nothing. After a moment, though, churchgoing woman that I am, I murmured something about the basement door, its shiny new bolt, and the possibility that Wafford's Cadillac was in a chop shop in the next county. As for Sarah Benston, I've never heard from her. I'm not real worried; as she said, she learned a lot about real estate during her brief stay across the street.

She can take care of herself.

A Little More Research

*Bart Bellicose realized time was running out. In the distance,
he could hear the whine of sirens, and he knew the police cars
were closing in on him like a swarm of killer bees. He stepped
back, then threw his two hundred forty pounds of bulk against
the flimsy door. It gave way with a shriek of pain, and Bellicose stumbled into the apartment.*

*There on the carpet lay the mortal remains of his client.
Even in death, the semi-nude body was as undulating as the
ocean, as smooth as the inner petals of a rose. He could see that
his client was as dead as the proverbial doornail, one of which
had ripped his arms in an angry slash of*

"Terry, honey, when are you gonna be finished? I'm
getting hungry, and it's almost too late to make reservations."

"I've asked you not to interrupt me. The deadline's
tomorrow morning at nine o'clock, for pete's sake, and my
editor's about to have an apoplectic fit. I can't concentrate
when you come in here every five minutes."

"I'm sorry. It's just that I get all lonesome out there by
myself. Maybe it would help if I rubbed your neck . . ."

"It would not. I'm on the last chapter and I need to get it
done tonight. Please don't interrupt me any more."

"Okay, I'll be a good little guest and wait in the living
room. All by myself."

"Thank you so very much. And shut the door, will you?"

grinning blood. It was obvious to anyone who'd ever eyed a fresh corpse that the

"Don't let me disturb you, but how about if I make reservations for later just in case you get done with your story?"

"I'm not going to get done if you don't leave me alone. I told you when you insisted on coming over tonight that I absolutely must have peace and quiet in order to concentrate."

"I happen to be speaking very quietly, my dear Hot Shot Writer."

"You also happen to be standing in the doorway, which means I'm looking at you rather than at the word processor. Go ahead and make reservations any place you want. I really don't care."

"Well, maybe I'll just do that."

It was obvious that . . . It was obviously murder. Bart could see that as he stared at the Bart frowned at the gaping Bart gasped as he spotted the hilt of the dagger protruding from the contoured chest

"Honey, telephone."

"I'm not home. Take a message and I'll call back tomorrow."

There was something about the dagger that touched a raw nerve. He'd seen it

"It's your editor, and he sounds real mad."

"Tell him I'm not here, and close the door on your way out."

"But I already told him you were home and working real hard on the story. He says he wants to talk to you right this minute."

"All right, damn it."

before. Sorry, Bart. Back in a minute. Try to remember, huh?

"Yo, Terry baby, how's it going?"

"It was going quite well until you called and interrupted me, Irwin. You do realize every time I'm interrupted I lose my train of thought?"

"Right, right. I wanted to remind you that we go into production tomorrow, with or without the last chapter. The book's gonna look pretty funny with a bunch of blank pages at the end. You promised me this manuscript. We paid a fat advance, and then waited patiently while you missed not one but two deadlines. You're in the catalogue. I've held the production people back till the bitter end, but the bottom line is that's where we are."

"And I'm not in my office finishing the book. *Au contraire,* I'm standing in the kitchen chitchatting with you. Goodbye, Irwin. I'll be in your office at nine o'clock."

"You and Bellicose, I presume."

"At this very moment Bellicose is standing over a body, and he'd like to investigate in the immediate future."

"So you finally got the plot straightened out?"

"Yes, I finally got the plot straightened out. Tomorrow at nine, okay? We can celebrate with Danishes."

"I'll get a dozen of them. Just make sure you show up for the party."

"I'm hanging up now, Irwin. Next time you get lonely, call your ex-wife."

He'd seen the dagger somewhere. Great.

Forget the dagger.

Bart stared at the bullet hole in the forehead. It was a third eye, as unseeing as the deep blue pools he'd

"Are you off the telephone?"

"No, I had the receiver implanted in my head and I'm listening to the time and weather as we speak. What is it?"

"I was trying to catch you before you started writing again to ask if you think Chinese sounds good. Or Japanese, I suppose, but not squid or tofu or anything creepy like that."

"I don't care. Do you mind? I mean, do you really mind giving me more than three minutes undisturbed?"

"I was just asking. You're acting like you've forgotten about last night. You didn't object to my company then."

"When I get this story done, maybe I'll remember. Please?"

"I'll sit in the living room and be as quiet as a mouse."

Deep blue pools of squid ink. On tofu.

Deadline. Deadline. Deadlineeeeee.

Bart recognized from the size of the wound that the bullet was of a low caliber. Could it have involved the swarthy woman with the mustache who'd come to his office yesterday, the one who'd cried and begged him to help her save her missing dauuuuuu

"What was that, damn it?"

"Don't pay any attention, Terry. I'll clean it up. After all, I don't have anything else to do."

"Clean what up?"

"Don't worry about it. It's no big deal."

"How can you say it was no big deal? It sounded like a

friggin' nuclear explosion."

"I don't remember seeing you at Hiroshima. Just go back to work and stop yelling at me like I was some kind of kid or something. I said I'd clean it up."

"Was it the plate glass window?"

"Go back to work."

"The television? My new state-of-the-art television that I have three years to pay on?"

"No and leave me alone so I can clean it up. I thought you had a deadline tomorrow . . ."

ghter. Bart stared around the room, which looked as if a nuclear bomb had gone off minutes before. The plate glass window was a spiderweb of cracks, and the television, a particularly expensive model with remote, built-in video cassette recorder, quadraphonic stereo, and one hundred thirty-seven channel capacity, was nothing more than a smoldering ruin of useless wires and busted tubes and would still suck up thirty-five more monthly payments.

But Bart warned himself not to dwell on the devastation and bent over the body. The flesh was still warm, and a ribbon of blood flowed from one corner of the mouth, which was twisted into a faint smile of surprise. So the victim had known the perp, Bart decided as he reached into his pocket and took out a pack of

"Did you take my cigarettes?"

"What?"

"I said, did you come into my office and take the pack of cigarettes I keep in the bottom left drawer for emergencies?"

"It was an emergency. I was out."

"Well, so am I. Bring that pack back."

"I smoked all of them this afternoon while I was watching this really great old movie about this debutante that falls in love with her sister's—"

"I'll read the newspaper if I want a review. Go down to the deli and get me another pack. You know I can't write when I'm out of cigarettes."

"No way. It's already late and I'm not about to get myself mugged just because you want a pack of cigarettes. It's your crummy neighborhood, not mine. If you're so desperate, go get them yourself."

Bart realized there was no time for a cigarette, not with the police moving in like a pack of vicious, slobbering wolves. Despite the sense of panic that could be appeased only by a cigarette, by a long deep satisfying lungful of carbon monoxide flavored with nicotine, he reluctantly turned back to the body, keenly aware that the evidence before him could lead to the identity of the murderer.

The clue was there before his eyes. He could almost see it, almost touch it, almost smell it, that acrid redolence of smoldering

"I smell smoke. What the hell's burning?"

"Nothing, Terry."

"Don't give me that. I smell smoke. I smell cigarette smoke, damn it! I thought you said the pack was empty."

"Don't short out your pacemaker over it. There was one cigarette left in the pack, that's all."

"The pack that you stole from my office? Is that the pack we're talking about? I cannot believe you would not only steal the pack from my desk, but then lie and say it was empty while sneaking the last cigarette!"

"If you keep huffing and puffing like that, you're gonna

blow the door down. I am sitting in here on the sofa holding my breath so I won't disturb you, and it seems to me you're the one bellowing and snorting and carrying on like a baby who wants a lollipop. It's like you've got some kind of oral fixation or something."

"First you steal my emergency pack, then you—"

"This is very childish. Perhaps you might worry a little less about me and a little more about the deadline tomorrow morning?"

The lingering smoke meant nothing, Bart thought with a snarl. No, the clue, the goddamn clue

No, now he could see what must have happened in the seedy apartment. The jagged corner of yellow paper beside the body was the exact same shade as the scrap he'd found at the nightclub. And that explained it. Yes! Yes!!! It was the link to the woman who'd lost a daughter, and it was the link to the strange fellow in the fedora who'd been following Bart for all those long days while he'd been on the case. It was as if the sun had finally broken the horizon after so many long weeks of arctic winter.

Bart smiled as the police stormed the room, their revolvers aimed at his heart. He knew he could explain

"Terry, I made reservations at that Thai restaurant everybody talks about all the time. We need to leave pretty soon if we're going to get there on time."

"Screw the Thai restaurant."

Bart held up the scrap of paper and said

"They're always packed, and the only reason we got the reservation is because a bunch of Shriners got drunk in the bar and refused to eat."

"Screw the Shriners."

Bart said screw the shriners oh hell come on bart you know who did it and who that fedora dude is and the scrap of yellow paper come on bart bellicose don't forget you can remember you had it a minute ago and it was good bart it was good and it was tight and it was right up there with brilliant and
it is gone finito ciao adios arrivederci

"Is everything okay, Terry? You're making an awfully funny noise in there."

"Don't worry about me. See, here I am in the kitchen and I'm just fine. As soon as I find a certain something in the drawer, I'm coming in the living room. Why don't you fix us a nice drink?"

Bart Bellicose left the police station, trying not to strut as he remembered how deftly he'd wrapped up the case in a pink bow to hand over to the detectives. They had listened in awe as he'd explained how his client, an errant husband with a fondness for exotic dancers, had blackmailed the sultry, smoky-eyed postal carrier who moonlighted at the Turkish Bazaar. The chump had opened the door to sign the yellow slip for a registered letter. Now his coffin and the case were closed.

There would be another case tomorrow, another chance to outwit the police. But for the moment, Bart savored this victory. If you wanted a case solved—and you wanted it solved right—then you called Bart Bellicose, by damn.
The end.
Yahoooooooooooo

"Yo, Terry, what time is it? Lemme get the light. Jeez, it's after midnight and I got to face the production guys in the morning."

"Stop at the bakery on your way to work, Irwin. Bart Bellicose has pulled it off again."

"It's done? You got it done? Lordy, I was sweating in my sleep for you. I'm not kidding; my pajamas are sticking to my armpits. All those glitches in the plot, those false starts and stops . . . I can't believe it."

"I'll admit I was having trouble with it. I just couldn't get a handle on the corpse sprawled on the living room floor. I couldn't see him, if you know what I mean. I couldn't touch his body, smell his blood, analyze his expression of surprise and fear."

"But you figured something out, huh?"

"With a little help from a friend."

"Well, I'm glad to hear it. Hey, I've got a bottle of twelve-year-old scotch I've been saving for my son's wedding. Now he says he wants to be a priest. Hop a cab and come on over to celebrate. Bring your friend."

"A fine idea, Irwin, although I'm afraid my friend's not up to a small party. I'll stop at the deli for a pack of cigarettes and be over shortly."

"Then be careful. You may write the hardest boiled private eye series in the industry, but you look more like a genteel lady librarian from Phoenix. Too bad Bart can't come along as your bodyguard. So tell me the truth—how'd you pull it off so quickly?"

"I realized that all I needed to do was a little more research. That's what it took—a little more research."

The Maggody Files: Time Will Tell

"Mary Frances was so excited I could barely get her hair rolled," Estelle Oppers said as she reached for the basket of pretzels on the bar. "She was as jumpy as a long-tailed cat in a room full of rocking chairs, and I finally had to threaten to get a towel and tie her down."

Ruby Bee Hanks smiled as she envisioned Mary Frances Frank, who wasn't even five feet tall but had more energy than one of those nuclear power plants. "Well, you got to admit being named Teacher of the Year is an honor. I don't know how she's faced those teenagers every morning for forty years and tried to get them interested in poetry when they were more interested in one another's britches. Back in my time, we sat on opposite sides of the room, and—"

"The award is gonna be presented at the cafeteria this Friday evening. I told her to come by that morning and I'll recomb her hair for free. She was real pleased." Estelle nodded smugly at her reflection in the mirror, real pleased by the undeniable generosity of her own gesture.

Harrumphing under her breath, Ruby Bee came out from behind the bar to take another pitcher of beer to the only customers, a trio of truckers in the back booth. Business at Ruby Bee's Bar & Grill was slow these days, but so was everything in Maggody, Arkansas (pop. 755). These days, at least, everybody knew where Arkansas was on the map on account of the new president (*not* between Oklahoma and Texas, as the old president had said), and Ruby Bee was hoping that tourists might start flocking like cowbirds now that summer was approaching. Jim Bob Buchanon seemed to feel the same, since he'd repaired the dryers at the Suds of Fun Launderette and put a fresh coat of paint on the front of Jim Bob's SuperSaver Buy 4 Less. This very morning she'd watched Roy Stivers setting out brass lamps and cracked washbowls in front of his antique store, and Brother Verber down at the Voice of the Almighty Lord Assembly Hall had changed the letters on the portable sign to read: STRANGERS WELCOME; FREE ADMISSION TO HEAVEN. This wasn't to say the collection plate wouldn't be passed under their noses several times, but at least he wasn't selling tickets at the door.

"I already knew about all the details concerning the ceremony," she said disdainfully as she returned. "Benjamin called me yesterday to say he wants to have a surprise party afterward at their house. He was supposed to come by at two to talk about the menu." She consulted the neon-trimmed clock behind her. "It's already after four. I wonder if he's still coming."

Estelle snorted. "I wouldn't hold my breath. Poor Mary Frances had to wait most of an hour before he picked her up. I'd have been hotter than a pepper mill, but she said she was used to it after all these years. She admitted he was always late when they were dating in college and she should have known there was no way to change him. The only reason she didn't wait at the altar was that she told him the wrong time for the wedding. He was at the hospital when Sara Anne was born, but Mary Frances was in labor so long her mother had time to drive down from Saint Louis. When Ben Junior was born, he didn't get there until she was back in her room and the baby was in the nursery. Imagine it taking him more than three hours to get to the hospital!"

"She's a saint to put up with him all these years. Maybe I

ought to call him at his office and remind him about our meeting. Do you recollect the name of his insurance outfit in Starley City?"

Estelle did, and pretty soon Ruby Bee was asking to speak to Benjamin Frank.

The secretary's sigh hinted at years of frustration. "He's not here yet, Mrs. Hanks. He called more than an hour ago to say he was on his way, so I'm hoping he'll be here before Mr. Whitbread gets fed up and leaves. There's a lot of business at stake." She sighed again, but most likely not for the last time.

"It don't take an hour to get to Starley City," said Ruby Bee, feeling sorry for the secretary and the unknown Mr. Whitbread. "I could be there in fifteen minutes."

"Mr. Frank has good intentions, but he'll think of errands along the way and pretty soon he'll be on the other side of the county talking to a client or over at the cafe drinking coffee. He won't even notice that he's late."

Ruby Bee asked her to remind him of the meeting, then hung up and mentally adjusted Mary Frances's halo. "How can someone be like that?" she asked Estelle. "If I was Mary Frances, I'd have long since ripped out my hair and taken to wandering around town in my underwear like Cornwallis Buchanon did before they packed him off to the county old folks' home."

"She said they've never heard the opening hymn at church or seen the credits at the picture show. She used to invite folks for supper, but she finally stopped on account of Benjamin getting home about the-time everybody was saying good night. Last year they were supposed to visit Ben Junior all the way up in Alaska, but they got to the airport late and missed the flight. She cried for a week because she was gonna see their new grandbaby for the first time and Ben Junior had booked them on a three-day cruise as a Christmas present. Of

42

course the airline wouldn't refund the money for the tickets because it wasn't their fault, and Ben Junior lost the deposit."

"There ought to be one of those twelve-step programs for folks like that," Ruby Bee said with a trace of tartness, "but they couldn't hold their meetings. Everybody'd show up too late."

They were busy commiserating with Mary Frances when the door opened and Benjamin Frank came striding across the dance floor. He was a big man, his face crinkled, his gray hair clipped short, his grin stretching from ear to ear, his teeth as white and even as could be bought anywhere. He had an unfortunate fondness for plaid and polyester, but the overall effect was dapper, if not chic. "How're the two prettiest ladies in Maggody today?" he called. "I keep waiting to hear you've both eloped with handsome millionaires from Farberville. If Mary Frances didn't keep me on a short leash, I'd be showing up on your doorsteps with flowers and candy to beg for a peck on the cheek."

Ruby Bee gave him a pinched frown. "You said you were coming at two o'clock, Benjamin, and your secretary was expecting you an hour ago."

He winked at Estelle as he sat on the stool beside her. "You sure worked magic on Mary Frances's hair this morning. You ought to open a hair salon in New York City and run those fancy boys like Vidal Sassoon right out of business."

Estelle patted her own festive red beehive. "That's right kind of you, Benjamin," she said, unable to stop herself from simpering. "A lot of folks don't realize that cosmetology is an art, and—"

"About the party," inserted Ruby Bee. "What kind of food do you want me to fix?"

He beamed at her. "Everybody knows you're the best cook

west of the Mississippi, Ruby Bee. You decide on the menu, and don't think twice about the price. I'm so proud of Mary Frances for being the Teacher of the Year that I get misty just thinking about it. I want this party to be real special. The ceremony starts at seven, so we'll most likely leave by six-thirty. You can bring the food then and get everything all set out in the dining room. I'll leave some balloons and crepe paper streamers in a sack on the back porch and be eternally grateful if you could tape 'em up."

"We'd be delighted," Estelle said just as if she were the one catering and not just tagging along out of habit. "Mary Frances will be downright thrilled when she steps through the door."

"But we aim to be at the high school at seven," said Ruby Bee. "Mary Frances won't get her award until everybody's done making speeches, but I don't want to miss a minute of it." She paused to give him a piercing look. "And you don't, either."

"I'll be sitting in the first row," Benjamin said as he slid off the stool. "I promised her I'd be home and in the shower by six o'clock, and ready to escort her whenever she's finished getting gussied up. I guess I'd better head on to my office. My secretary gets irritable if I'm late."

Ruby Bee waited until he was gone before she said, "I'd get homicidal, myself. Do you realize he never once apologized for being late?"

They resumed commiserating with poor Mary Frances, who'd taught countless teenagers to recite poetry but couldn't seem to teach her husband how to tell time.

I'd given up trying to whittle a chunk of wood into something remotely resembling a marshland mallard and was dozing away the day in the Maggody PD, where I was the one and only P. Once upon a time I'd had a real live deputy, but now I had a beeper. I also had an answering machine, but I'd quit checking messages after I realized the only person using it was my mother, Ruby Bee, and every last one of her messages began with a treatise on how much she disliked talking to a machine. What I really needed was voice mail, I decided as I monitored the progress of a spider across the ceiling. "To gripe about my schoolmarm hair, Press One. To gripe about my aversion to lipstick, Press Two. To gripe about my lack of a social life, Press Three." It would never work; there weren't enough buttons to handle Ruby Bee's litany of my sins.

The telephone interrupted my whimsical reverie. After a few scowls in its direction, I picked up the receiver and reluctantly conceded that the caller had reached the PD.

"Arly, this is Mrs. Jim Bob," said a familiar but not welcome voice. "I am fed up with those junior high boys cutting across the back of my yard on their way to Boone Creek. Not five minutes ago they tramped right through my begonias, and when I went onto the porch and told them to get off my property, one of them used an obscenity."

"No kidding?" I said with the proper degree of incredulity. "Do you want me to shoot 'em? I've still got four bullets in a box in the back room."

"No, I want you to go down to the creek and give them a lecture about trespassing and disrespect for their elders. I'd do it myself but I have to fix a green bean casserole for Eula Lemoy, whose back is bothering her. It won't keep me from watching for your car to go down the road within the next five minutes, Miss Chief of Police."

"I'll probably go ahead and shoot 'em," I said, albeit to the dial tone. Mrs. Jim Bob's a royal pain, but Jim Bob's the mayor and therefore, at least technically, my boss. In order to avoid a tedious lecture at the next town council meeting, I hung the CLOSED sign on the door and drove down Finger Lane to the swimming hole to see if I could persuade the miscreants to find another shortcut.

Said miscreants had moved on. I gazed at the bubbly brown water, remembering some moonlit nights of my youth when hormones had bubbled as loudly. The sun was warm, the breeze laden with earthy rawness of spring, the birds twittering and flitting in the branches, the squirrels nattering at me. Manhattan, where I'd led a tumultuous married life, has art galleries and opera, but there are some scenes that are a sight more elegant.

It occurred to me that I needed to stake out the swimming hole for an hour or two, just in case the miscreants returned. In order to survive the ordeal, I needed provisions along the lines of a ham sandwich, potato salad, a bag of cookies, and a big cup of iced tea. All of this was available at the SuperSaver deli, where I could also find a tabloid filled with wondrous stories of alien lobbyists and sexual aberrations.

Such are the exactitudes of law enforcement in a town where nothing ever happens, I told myself as I parked in front of the store and started inside. I detoured to greet the figure almost hidden behind a cart piled high with sacks of groceries.

"Congratulations, Mrs. Frank," I said, resisting the urge to scuffle my feet and duck my head as if I were telling lies about uncompleted homework. She hadn't been a tyrant in the classroom, but even fifteen or so years later, with white hair and faded blue eyes, she radiated a measurable dose of the same authority.

"Thank you, Arly. I must say I'm tickled pink, although I don't know if I'm more excited about the award or my retirement. Forty years is a long time to attempt to instill a lively interest in dead poets."

46

I couldn't argue with that, "Well, congratulations again," I said, edging toward the door.

"Forty years of bells and tardy slips," she continued in a musing voice, "to be followed by who knows how many years of waiting for Benjamin. That's what I'm doing now. My car's in the shop, so I'm at his mercy. Do you know how long I've been standing here?" Her voice tightened and her eyes narrowed as she regarded the rows of parked cars. "Over half an hour, that's how long. Benjamin promised to pick me up at four sharp, which is why I went ahead and bought ice cream and frozen orange juice."

"Would you like me to give you a ride home?"

"That's thoughtful of you, Arly, but surely Benjamin will be here before too much longer. It simply never occurs to him that other people dislike waiting for him. I've grown accustomed to it after all these years, but now that I'm retiring, I wonder if I'll be able to handle it."

I was eager to get back to the creek, take off my shoes, and let the mud slip between my toes, stuff my face, read about two-headed babies in the Amazon rain forest. "I'll be clapping for you on Friday," I said in one last attempt to extricate myself from the conversation.

"But Benjamin won't," she said, talking more to herself than to yours truly. "It won't matter how many times I tell him how important this is, how many times I beg him to be there at seven o'clock. He'll cross his heart and swear he'll be there, but he won't, and he'll be wondering where everyone is when he arrives two hours later. This may be the most important event in my life—an acknowledgment of all my years of teaching and the beginning of what's supposed to be our golden years together. He really should be on time." She took an orange from a sack and squeezed it until the skin burst and juice dribbled down her white fingers. "He really should."

47

Something was dribbling down my back that wasn't a source of vitamin C and I was ready to forget about my picnic and flat out flee to my car. I'd known Mary Frances Frank for a good many years, but this was my first glimpse of her as a vindictive Munchkin. "I'm sure he'll make it this one time," I said.

"He'd better," she said. "Otherwise, he'll be very, very sorry . . . this one time."

By Friday I'd corralled the miscreants and bawled them out, cleaned the back room of the PD in a paroxysm of seasonal madness, and given some consideration to dust-busting my efficiency apartment above the antique store. Only my penchant for chicken-fried steak and cream gravy saved me, and I was devising ways to idle away the afternoon as I went into the bar and grill.

"Thought you said you'd be here at noon," Ruby Bee said in an unfriendly voice.

I didn't much worry about it, in that she's no more predictable than the weather—and this was hurricane season, after all. "Did I say that? I could have sworn I said I'd be here around noon." I appropriated a stool and gave her a beguiling smile. "How about the blue plate special and a glass of milk?"

"How about you learn to be on time?" muttered my mother, although she did so while stomping into the kitchen.

I sat and waited, listening placidly to the wails from the jukebox and the conversations from the booths along the wall. Now that it was no longer legal to shoot helpless birds and hapless mammals, the hot topic seemed to be the slaughter of largemouth bass and crappies. At least it was preferable to brands of toilet bowl cleaners.

Estelle sat down beside me as Ruby Bee came through the kitchen doors. "I guess we're all excited," she said.

"I guess we are," I said, although I had no idea what she assumed was exciting us. I myself was a little choked up at the sight of the plate Ruby Bee was carrying, but I'm a patsy in such matters.

Ruby Bee banged down the plate in front of me. "Has Mary Frances decided what she's going to wear tonight?" she asked Estelle.

"Her beige linen suit. She wanted to buy a new dress, but her car's still at the shop and Benjamin didn't get home yesterday in time for her to drive to Farberville. I wouldn't have liked to have been him when he finally got there. Mary Frances's eyes were flashing when she told me about it this morning, and I can imagine what all she said to him. They may have been married for forty years, but his lateness is starting to get on her nerves."

"I heard something interesting," Ruby Bee said. She glanced at me to see if I was listening, then moved down the bar so she and Estelle could share the big secret. The two often mistake me for someone who cares. "I heard," she continued with the muted subtlety of a chain saw, "that Mary Frances made up with her brother just two days ago. After all these years of not speaking, she upped and called him, and then borrowed Elsie's car for the afternoon and went to visit him."

"She didn't say one word to me," Estelle said, clearly stunned by the magnitude of the revelation. "Not one word, and there I was recombing her hair for free!"

"Elsie promised not to tell anyone, but we were talking about the award ceremony tonight and she let drop that Mary Frances invited her brother and his wife."

"What about the credenza?"

Ruby Bee nodded somberly. "She gave it to him. Here they've been fighting like dogs and cats over it since their mama died ten years ago, refusing to speak to each other at the family reunions, paying lawyers to file lawsuits, and sitting on opposite sides of the church at weddings and funerals. All of a sudden she's willing to give him the credenza just to make peace with him. He went to her house and picked it up last night. I was flabbergasted when I heard that."

I halted a forkful of mashed potatoes halfway to my mouth. "I don't understand why you're treating this like the collapse of the Soviet Union. Maybe she wants to begin her retirement without any lingering feuds."

Estelle pondered this while she ate a pretzel. "Nope, this credenza is mahogany and it's been in the family for three or four generations. We're not talking about a sewing box or an end table worth a few dollars. Roy Stivers appraised it back when Mary Frances and her brother were dividing the estate, and he said he hadn't come across a nicer one in all his born days."

In that I wasn't sure I'd recognize a credenza if it nipped me on the butt, I resumed eating.

Ruby Bee resumed gossiping. "Elsie was miffed when Mary Frances brought the car back all covered with mud. It seems her brother is working on that new stretch of highway that's supposed to replace Highway 71 if they ever finish blasting through the mountains. Mary Frances wanted to hose off the mud, but Else said not to bother on account of it wasn't right for the Teacher of the Year to be washing cars. They almost had an argument over it, but Mary Frances insisted Elsie come over for coffee and homemade doughnuts this morning. Elsie ain't all that hard to mollify."

"Mary Frances is gonna be real-hard to mollify if Benjamin's not on time tonight," Estelle said. "She told me she was going to teach him a lesson once and for all. Do you reckon she'll say something in her speech?"

"She can't say anything folks don't already know."

The discussion wandered at this point, and so did I. Not off to the trenches, mind you, or even off to determine the dimensions of the credenza and delve into the mystery of why a woman might want to make peace with her brother after ten years of estrangement. The grapevine was more than capable of producing a tidy solution sooner or later.

Where I wandered was out to the skeletal remains of Turtle's Esso station, where I could run a speed trap to make a little money for the local coffers and, more importantly, read a magazine. At five o'clock, I went back to the PD and tucked away my radar gun, called the dispatcher at the sheriff's office to find out if I'd missed anything newsworthy (I hadn't), and was halfway out the door when I noticed the blinking red rat's eye of the answering machine.

Approach-avoidance reared its ugly head. Was it the man of my dreams offering an escape to a Caribbean island? Was it a lawyer in Manhattan calling to tell me my ex-husband was so overcome with remorse that he was sending the money he owed me? Or was it the Pope?

I pushed the button.

"This is Ruby Bee Hanks, and I don't know why I bother to call over there when all I ever get is this rude machine. I don't know what the world's coming to when people can't bother to answer their own telephones." There was a sharp inhalation before she took off once more. "Estelle and I are going out to Mary Frances's house just before the ceremony to get everything ready for the party. We won't get to the cafeteria until right at seven, so you need to go over early and save us seats on—"

The machine cut her off before I could, although it was close. I locked up and walked across the road to my apartment having been warned much earlier that Ruby Bee's Bar &

Grill would not be serving supper to the likes of me or anyone else. I could survive on a can of soup, since I'd be having chocolate cake and champagne punch within a matter of hours, I assured myself as I showered and changed into a skirt and blouse in honor of the honoree.

I figured I'd best get to the high school fifteen minutes early in order to secure the best seats. Would Benjamin Frank be thinking the same thing? From what I could gather, the only place he'd get to on time was his own funeral—unless Mary Frances Frank did indeed teach him a lesson as she'd vowed. The adage about old dogs and new tricks came to mind, along with her comment that he would be "very, very sorry."

Abruptly I got it—credenza and all. My fingers felt numb as I finished buttoning my blouse, grabbed the car keys, and sprinted down the stairs and across the road. Mary Frances had not been making peace with her brother; she'd been making a deal. It was nearly six-forty, which meant Ruby Bee and Estelle were in as much danger as Benjamin Frank, and if my car balked, all three were in for one helluva surprise party.

I squealed out in front of a pickup truck and jammed down the accelerator. The Franks lived in a farmhouse several miles out of town on a passable county road. Six-forty-two. Ruby Bee and Estelle might already be there, taping up streamers and setting out the punch bowl. Benjamin might be there, or still at his office in Starley City. Six-forty-five. Mary Frances had no idea Ruby Bee and Estelle might be in the house. Six-forty-eight.

I turned off the highway and tightened my grip on the steering wheel as I bounced down the road. Six-fifty came and went. Biting down on my lip, I went even faster and therefore came within inches of crashing into the back of Ruby Bee's car in the middle of the road. Dust caught up with me as I leaned my forehead against the steering wheel and waited for the adrenaline to abate.

Ruby Bee stood up on the far side of her car. "What in tarnation's going on?" she squawked. "You liked to kill the both of us! Driving like a madman on a narrow road!"

I got out of my car and clung to the antenna until my knees quit knocking. "Where's Estelle?"

"As any fool can see, I had a flat tire. She went on ahead to see if Benjamin can come help us change it and get all the party food into the house. At this rate, there's no way we'll be at the cafeteria on time."

Six-fifty-eight. "How far is it?" I demanded.

"You're antsy this evening," she said, her hands on her hips and a disapproving look on her face. "It's nearly a mile further, and Estelle's wearing high heels, but she should be getting there by now. If you'd stop gawking and loosen these lug nuts, we won't need Benjamin's help."

"Is he there?"

"Now how on earth should I know a thing like that?"

We both turned and looked up the road a split second before an explosion rocked the sky, the sound reverberating across the valley like distant cannon fire. Black smoke and an orange haze appeared above the trees. It was seven o'clock.

Mrs. Jim Bob stood behind a podium, her hands clutching the edges as she leaned into the microphone. "And our only hope for the future lies in the moral education of our youth, who need to learn about respecting their elders and staying out of their begonias," she was saying as I came into the room.

"Excuse me," I said, "but there's been an accident. I need to speak to Mrs. Frank." Scanning the faces in the audience, I hurried up to the front row as Mary Frances Frank stood up. I asked her to accompany me to the back of the room.

"There was an explosion at your house," I said, then stopped, ignoring the murmurs of uneasiness and Mrs. Jim Bob's shrill comments about being interrupted.

"I thought I smelled gas," she said without hesitation. "I mentioned it to Benjamin this morning, and he said he'd call the gas company. It's a good thing nobody was home."

"Then your husband is here?"

"Well, I believe he ought to be on his way by now. He called from his office at six and assured me he'd go by the house to take a quick shower, then come right here. I made a point of reminding him how important it was for him to be here at seven, then arranged for Mrs. Jim Bob to give me a ride." She regarded me with a level expression. "He may be running a few minutes late, but he should be here any minute."

"It's already seven-thirty," I said. "I had to wait at your house until a sherrif's deputy arrived to take over. The volunteer fire department is on its way, but I'm afraid there won't be anything to save. It was a powerful explosion. My first thought was dynamite."

"Why were you out that way?"

"I went to warn Ruby Bee and Estelle to be away from the house at seven o'clock. Benjamin arranged a surprise party for you after the ceremony, and they were delivering the food on their way here."

Her face turned as white as her hair. "Oh, no . . . I didn't know. I had no idea. Were they injured?"

I gave her the look she'd given me years earlier when I'd tried to explain that my dog ate my term paper. "You're damn lucky they weren't. Ruby Bee had a flat a mile from your house, and Estelle went ahead to ask Benjamin to give them a hand. If she hadn't lost a heel, she might well have lost her life."

"Thank God," she whispered.

"Benjamin's car was in the driveway," I continued coldly. "He must have been running late. If he'd been here as he promised, no one would have been hurt in the explosion."

She looked up at me, her eyes welling with tears, her lips trembling. "I told him over and over how important it was that he be here at the cafeteria at exactly seven o'clock. I really did."

I believed her. I really did.

All's Well That Ends

Jack was looking at the flickery television set on a shelf above the bar when the woman sat down next to him. Her gender was hard to overlook, but he wasn't into specifics, having long since given up hope of being approached by a gorgeous young actress in search of a passionate one-night sexathon. His sixtieth birthday had passed without such a phenomenon taking place. Not much had happened since, for that matter. He was older and grayer, although not especially wiser. For years he'd come to the corner tavern to have a beer, maybe two, and a little conversation. Depending.

"Can you believe that guy?" he said without turning his head. "It's like he thinks this is gonna change our minds about his guilt. The only people in this country who believe he's innocent are the twelve jurors. Where do they find wimps like those to serve on juries, anyway? I'll bet not one of them's ever read a newspaper. Hell, I'll bet not one of them knows how to read."

"You're Jack Julian, aren't you?" she said.

Now he looked at her. She had drab hair, yellowish skin, and dark, puffy circles under her eyes as if she hadn't slept in weeks. Her stained sweatshirt and lack of makeup suggested she wasn't a hooker, but he wasn't sure. Hookers were about the only women who came on to him—and they were usually junkies.

"Yeah," he said. "Who are you?"

"Someone who made a point of reading your pieces in the

56

newspaper. You were good."

"I suppose I was." Jack beckoned to the bartender. "Give the lady whatever she wants to drink."

"Nothing, thanks," she said. "I'd like to talk to you about Spider Durmond. You wrote as much as anybody about the case. You forgot to write about me."

"What should I have written?"

"Maybe I'll have a club soda." She took a tissue from her purse and wiped her forehead, even though it looked to be as dry as parchment. "Let's begin with the proposition that we both know he did it. This big, beautiful blond jock had a history of beating women, of roughing up photographers, of drinking too much and driving too fast and doing too many drugs. He bought off his one known rape victim. On the night of July fifteenth, he went to his estranged wife's rented beach house and stabbed her to death. His alibi was laughable—he was home, alone. Spider never went to bed alone." She took a shuddery breath. "You didn't seem to buy that in your articles about the case."

Jack glanced at the television, which was currently depicting some event in which everyone wore shorts and ran incessantly. "And a few minutes ago, while the cameramen jostled for room and the reporters knocked each other into the bushes, Spider staged a press conference and promised to pay five million dollars for evidence leading to the conviction of the real killer. I used to think those of us in the media had ethics—you know, a common moral ground. No more than a fraction of an acre, perhaps, but a little bit. I retired just before that bus veered, crashed through the rail, and nose-dived into the river."

He took a final swallow of beer. "Spider's a wonderfully photogenic guy, broad smile, dimples, not too bright, helluva great basketball player and paid accordingly. Endorsements for everything from athletic shoes to cat food. The money pumped up his brain, made him think he was invincible. Shit, maybe he thought he was invisible, too. He went to Suzanne's house, killed her, and then got all teary-eyed and claimed he was home with a cold. Jesus!"

"You think he did it," the woman said. "I know he did. I was there."

"Sure you were. Go peddle your story to a tabloid, baby. The trial's over, the jury's reached a screwball decision, and it's too late for you to make any money off this. You'll have a better chance with alien abductions in New Mexico or cattle mutilations in Iowa."

"The two of us can make five million dollars," she said, then slid off the stool. "Think about that while I visit the ladies' room."

Although Jack had been planning to leave, he sat. And thought. And got nowhere. She wasn't a hooker, and she didn't sound as if she was recently released from an institution guarded by burly men in white coats. Then again . . .

He didn't leave, though he wondered if he should have known better. "How'd you find me?" he asked the woman when she returned.

She took a sip of club soda. "You wrote a column about this place. I thought it might be your local hangout. I've been coming for the last few days, hoping to spot you."

"But you waited until tonight to speak to me."

"The jury came in this afternoon."

"And so they did," Jack said bitterly. "The trial lasted five months, and jury deliberations lasted two days. The evidence was so friggin' obvious—his blood on the scene, her hysterical phone calls to her friend, his car spotted a block from her house when he swore he was home. The woman walking her dog at midnight when she heard his garage door open." He waved to the bartender to refill his glass. "Why should I have written about you?"

"I'm one of Spider's ex-girlfriends."

"One of many. So what?"

The woman sighed. "Three years ago, I met Spider at a party. I was a model then, doing layouts for magazines like *Playboy* and *Vogue*. Spider came on to me, and I liked it. We looked really good together, like a pair of tawny lions. He promised to introduce me to movie producers. Most models see themselves as the next Audrey Hepburn."

Jack regretted his decision to linger. Pulling out his wallet, he said, "And then he dumped you and now you want revenge. It won't play in Peoria. It won't even play in Long Beach."

"It went further than that. He was escorting me to clubs, taking me with him on road trips, making sure I was seen on his arm when he deigned to bless nightclubs with his presence. He took me to the Oscar awards."

He tried to imagine her on the cover of a magazine, or even posing in a designer gown. As for a centerfold, no way. Her breasts hung like deflated balloons. Her lips were as sensual as earthworms. "I'm having some trouble with this," he admitted. "Spider made a point of being seen with good-looking women. Maybe you would have liked to—"

"My name is Abbie Cassius."

Jack's wallet fell onto the bar as he rocked back to stare at her. He knew the name quite well. He'd seen photographs of her. And there was a resemblance beneath her unhealthy, gaunt demeanor. The cheekbones were unattractively defined, but the nose was still straight, the green eyes wide-set and unblinking as they searched his.

"Abbie Cassius?" he said numbly. "I'm sorry for not recognizing you."

"But you recognize the name," she said, smiling. "I was a number with the so-called Spiderman. Now I'm ready to bring him down, at least financially. You game?"

Jack shrugged. "Were he a PT boat and I a torpedo. I know he did it, Abbie. All but twelve human beings on this planet know he did it. He not only got away with it, but he's trying to win back supporters with this five-million-dollar offer for the conviction of a nonexistent person. Pretty damn safe, isn't it?"

"You and I can screw him. It'll take the both of us, but it can be done. Why don't we find a more private place to talk?"

He looked at her for a long moment, not sure how to assess her. She was ill, obviously; whether or not she was paranoid or schizophrenic or whatever would have to be determined. He'd covered the investigation and snooped where he could, but had never found definitive proof that Spider Durmond had murdered his wife. If this washed-out woman could make the case, so be it. Screwing Spider did not appeal, except in the literal sense. And that appealed very much.

"Okay," he said at last, "why don't we move to a booth? If you have information, I'll listen. You want something to eat?"

"All I want is to teach Spider a lesson he won't forget," she said, heading for a corner booth. She waited until Jack had positioned himself across from her, then continued. "I don't know what you remember about me. I dated Spider for several months, and there were rumors that we might get married. What never came out was that I have a son, now ten, his biological father out of the picture. Ben's different; the clinical term is 'autistic,' and what it means is that he can't relate in a normal fashion. He tries to love me as best he can, but there are episodes when all I can do is remind myself of that. At the time Spider was around, Ben was spending weekdays at a residential facility and weekends at home with me."

"This created a problem?" said Jack, hating himself for lapsing into his old habits.

Abbie gave him a wry look. "Pull out a notebook if it'll make you more comfortable, or take notes on a napkin. Yes, Spider was pissed. He wanted Ben to idolize him like every other kid in America did. Ben was more concerned with astronauts and the space program; he couldn't have told you which day of the week it was, but he always kept track of the current shuttles and wanted to talk about Mir and the space telescopes. It made Spider crazy."

"How crazy?"

"Spider brought Ben a basketball for Christmas. When Ben reacted indifferently, Spider slapped him around. I became hysterical, and the whole thing erupted to the point that a neighbor called the police. I was ready to accuse Spider of everything from assault to child abuse when he made it clear that if I so much as pointed a finger at him, something bad would happen to Ben. Spider said that he had plenty of friends who enjoyed hurting little boys." Abbie teared up, looked away. "So when the cops came, I told them that everything was okay. Spider swore that he'd give me enough money to get Ben the very best treatment—if I kept quiet."

"But he didn't," Jack murmured.

"Ben lost hearing in his right ear, and he lost a lot more than that. Spider has never given us a nickel. I tried to talk to him, to remind him of his promise, but he hung up when I called and pushed me aside when I came up to him in public. Eventually he got a restraining order that barred me from attempting to make any contact or setting foot on his property. When I violated it, I was sent to the state mental hospital for evaluation. Thirty days in a snake pit. I don't recommend it."

"I know the story. You didn't have any way to make him pay you off. Why didn't you just let it go?"

"You remember how I used to look? Curves in all the right places, firm muscles, golden hair?" She paused until he reluctantly nodded. "And you didn't recognize me when I sat down. It seems I have something called plasmocerciasis, caused by a microscopic worm found in the lakes and rivers in Brazil. It's exceedingly rare in this country. At first I thought I had the flu, but when it got worse, I started going to doctors. A specialist at Walter Reed finally made the diagnosis, but the prognosis is grim. Antibiotics are ineffective. Odds are I'll be dead in a year, maybe less."

"How'd you get infected?"

"A fashion magazine wanted an exotic background for a layout. The money was good. One of the teachers at Ben's school took care of him for the ten days I was there."

Jack considered offering sympathy, then decided she wouldn't be receptive. "Okay, let's go back to something you said earlier. You were at Suzanne's house when Spider killed her? That's hard to swallow, Abbie."

"I know," she said. "After I was released from the hospital and threatened with jail time if I violated the restraining order again, I stayed away from Spider. Then I learned how sick I was. I can't even hold down an office job, and I don't have enough money to make sure Ben will be taken care of after I'm dead. I went on welfare, which gave me lots of free time to stalk Spider, but this time from a prudent distance. I watched his house. I followed his car. I couldn't afford tickets to his basketball games, but I was always parked nearby when he left the arena. When he and Suzanne were married, I was in the crowd on the sidewalk across from the church. I sat outside restaurants while they ate lobster and drank champagne. I called his house from pay phones, but hung up if anyone answered."

"Planning to accomplish what?"

"I don't know. I guess I hoped he would somehow sense my presence and worry that I might blow him away when he turned his back. I wanted him to feel just a fraction of the anxiety I feel about the future." She took a deep breath and exhaled slowly. "But let's talk about the day Suzanne was killed. I was there that afternoon, parked down the street, when Spider drove to her house and stayed for about half an hour. When he came out onto the porch, I could see he was turning on the charm, smiling, nodding at her, probably making promises to take her to Paris and the Riviera when the basketball season was over. He's a very slick performer."

"He admitted he went to her house that day," Jack said. "According to his story, that's when he scratched his arm on the screen door and dripped blood on the carpet. How do I know you didn't read it in the newspaper?"

"I can describe her house."

"The address was published, as well as photographs of the house and street. Newscasters did broadcasts from the sidewalk out front. There was footage of the jury as they were escorted inside. Ninety percent of the people in this tavern can describe the house, Abbie. You'll have to do better than that to convince me that you were there."

"Which is what I'm going to do," she said. "Spider testified that on the night of her death, he went out to dinner, then went home. If anyone had asked me, I could have backed up that much of his testimony, since I was following him. He parked in the driveway. After a few minutes, all the downstairs lights went off and shortly thereafter the light in his bedroom came on. I was about to leave when I heard a car door slam. Seconds later he drove out the gate, his headlights dark. I followed him, naturally, and realized pretty quickly where he was headed."

Jack felt a chill, as if the air conditioner had been turned up. "Suzanne's?"

"Forty-five minutes later he turned onto her road. I parked behind a grocery store and walked the half mile to the house. His car wasn't there, but the lights were on and the front door was open. I was standing in the shadows, wondering if I ought to go home and say a prayer for her, when headlights came on further down the road. I jumped behind some shrubs as Spider drove by."

"You're sure you recognized the car?"

She laughed contemptuously. "Yes, I'm sure; my hobby was such that I could have spotted his car in a blizzard. I figured he'd tried to insinuate himself back into her good graces and she'd thrown him out. The open door bothered me, though, so I waited. An hour later, the door was still open and the same lights still on. I finally decided to go into the yard to get a better look. I ended up in the living room. She was on her back on the floor with the knife in her chest. There was blood all over the place, but I made myself feel for a pulse. She was dead."

"And you didn't call nine-one-one."

"Obviously," she said. "I'd been warned that if I had any further contact with Spider, including following him, I'd face felony charges. I couldn't prove he'd been there. My word against his, and I'd spent thirty days in a mental institution for stalking him. Crazy woman versus insanely popular athlete. No, I didn't call nine-one-one or anyone else. Would you have?"

Jack regarded her soberly. "If what you're saying is true, you committed a felony by failing to report the crime."

"What's your point?"

"Okay, okay," he said, almost ashamed of himself. "Then what happened?"

"I took her wedding ring off her finger. Maybe it was an awful thing to do, but all I was thinking was the last thing she deserved was to be buried as the wife of a monster. I didn't try to sell it or anything. I've still got it, as well as my blood-stained shoes and trousers. I was in such shock that I stuffed them in the back of a closet. Now I'm glad I did, since they're proof that I was at the scene."

"Not proof that you killed her, though," Jack said. "The detectives determined early in the investigation that you weren't a suspect. You told them you were home, and since you hadn't bothered Spider for over a year or ever threatened Suzanne, they crossed you off the list."

Abbie shrugged. "Here's what is going to happen. When Spider was found innocent, you started thinking about other possibilities. Tomorrow, you'll come to my apartment and interview me. You leave with some troublesome ideas. You reread all the police reports and talk to your pals who were on the case, then return to interview me. I break down and admit that I went to Suzanne's house to convince her to resist Spider's sweet-talk. I describe how she realized who I was and became verbally abusive, how I grabbed a knife from a drawer and stabbed her, then yanked out the knife and later threw it out the car window while driving up a canyon road. I'll tell this to the prosecuting attorney, and to the judge when the time comes. No excuses, no insanity plea. I expect to get twenty-five to life, but that's not a concern. Later, you hold your own press conference and say that because you feel sorry for me, half the money is going into a trust fund for Ben." She stared at him. "I've arranged for a lawyer to draw up the papers and administer the trust. You'll keep half of whatever's left after taxes. Not a bad day's work, is it?"

"What if your doctor tells the press that you have this terminal disease?"

Abbie looked at him as though he was particularly dim-witted. "For one thing, he's bound by doctor-patient confidentiality, and I'm not about to give him permission to ever mention I was a patient. For another, he took a sabbatical and is in Brazil working with tropical disease experts there. If I'm questioned about my health, I'll just say that my consuming guilt ruined my appetite and prevented me from sleeping. There won't be a trial. My lawyer will negotiate a sentence in exchange for my full cooperation. All you have to do is play your part."

Jack envisioned himself at the precinct, telling the detectives that he strongly suspected Abbie Cassius, scorned ex-girlfriend and known harasser, had not only killed Suzanne Durmond but also retained evidence of her complicity in the crime. No matter how skeptical they were, they'd feel obliged to talk to her.

To add the icing to the cake, Spider's expression when he learned of her confession would be worth more than five million dollars. If he admitted his own guilt, double jeopardy would protect him from a second criminal indictment, but expose him as a easy target for a civil suit by his victim's family. That could cost him ten times as much.

"Do you have absolute faith in me?" he asked. "What if I forget about the trust fund?"

"When you come to my apartment, you're going to sit down and write a letter disclosing your role in a conspiracy to commit fraud, obstruct justice, and engage in theft by deception. You used to be a good reporter, Jack. I know you'll be able to capture the essence of this conversation, as well as describe your subsequent intentions to lie to the detectives and prosecutors. This letter will be in your own handwriting, of course. You'll then hand it over to me, and get it back as soon as Ben's share has been deposited in the trust account."

Jack was becoming impressed with her attention to detail. "What if Spider claims he's broke and refuses to cough up the money?"

"At the press conference he said that he can raise it by selling his mansion and his ranch in Colorado. He's on record, and you can sue him if necessary. Poor old Spider will be broke, without any expectations of multimillion-dollar basketball contracts and lucrative product endorsements. No more glitzy parties, movie premieres, celebrity tennis tournaments, television talk shows, complimentary suites in Vegas. He won't end up in prison, but a crummy one-bedroom apartment might begin to feel a little bit like a cell."

"One last question," he said. "Why me?"

"Why not?" she murmured, then wrote an address on a napkin and shoved it across the table. "Come over tomorrow morning and we'll get the show on the road."

Within a matter of weeks, Abbie Cassius had been transferred to a federal penitentiary, her prediction of twenty-five to life uncannily accurate. Spider Durmond had called a press conference during which he claimed to be pleased by this triumph of truth and justice, but his eyes had blazed with enough fury to melt a camera lens. Jack had been badgered by the media as well. Public sentiment had rumbled against him until he'd announced plans to establish a trust fund for the innocent, emotionally disabled boy.

The furor abated for several months, then flickered briefly when Spider publicly presented a check to Jack on the steps of the courthouse. Battling nausea and feeling no sense of virtue, Jack had accepted it with a grimace. Only then had he made the four-hour drive to visit Abbie behind the foreboding gray walls. She'd adjusted to the routine, she said, and was allowed to call Ben once a week. When her calls stopped, she doubted he would notice.

The day after he finalized the trust, a messenger delivered a thin package. Inside was his handwritten letter; there was no indication anyone had tampered with the sealed envelope. He burned it, then gathered the ashes and flushed them down the toilet.

It was three months later, while sitting beside a pool in a luxurious hacienda in Baja California, sunburned after a day of deep-sea fishing and on his third margarita, that Jack wandered across the article buried within the back pages of the *Los Angeles Times*. Researchers at a hospital in Rio had found an antibiotic that could reverse, or at least impede, the debilitating symptoms of plasmocerciasis, a disease virtually unknown outside of certain regions of the Amazon rain forest.

He thought back to Abbie's confession at the sentencing hearing, when the judge had required her to describe the particulars of her crime before accepting her guilty plea. She'd either embellished her fantasy with the polished skill of a best-selling horror novelist, or the twelve jurors had been right. Hard to know. In either case, Abbie had gotten what she wanted, and justice had been served, albeit lukewarm and difficult to digest.

He decided to send a postcard to Abbie the next day. "Wish you were here," he'd write.

Why not?

The Deadly Ackee

Chapter One

"Theo? I do hope I'm not interrupting, but I simply must discuss a rather minor situation that has arisen. Minor, but, well, slightly major."

Theodore Bloomer stared at the telephone receiver in his hand, perplexed by his sister's wheedling tone. It was unlike her to even consider the possibility she might be interrupting him, which might imply his time was of more value than hers. Unthinkable.

"I was in the greenhouse, checking on seedlings," he admitted cautiously. "The tomato hybrids seem to be coming along nicely."

"Really? Charles, Dorrie, and I do so enjoy your little offerings each summer. But I have a problem, Theo, and I must resolve it briskly. I have a bridge game at the club, and Pookie's picking me up in less than five minutes. Do you have any vital social engagements next week?"

"The horticulturists' club is planning a tour of the local azalea gardens," Theo said, still eyeing the receiver uneasily. "I had considered the wisdom of repotting several of my—"

"Well, that much is settled. I fear I must ask a small favor." Nadine Caldicott took a deep breath to recover from what must have been a painful sentence. "The whole thing is quite my fault; I accept full blame for it. But you know how very headstrong Dorrie can be, a trait I often suspect might have been inspired, if not blatantly encouraged, by her doting Uncle Theo."

"This involves Dorrie? What has she done now?"

"She and a group of her friends have arranged for a villa in Jamaica for their spring break next week. There will be Dorrie, her fiancé, Biff, a friend of his named Beachy or Sandy or something like that, those adorable red-haired Ellison twins, and one of Dorrie's suitemates from Wellesley. Let me think . . . Biff's at Amherst, the Whitcombe boy's at Annapolis, Mary Margaret Ellison is with Dorrie and the Bigelow girl, and her brother is between schools at the moment, I believe. You may have met some of them at the house; they're forever hanging around the pool when they're not at the club. They absolutely romp through the wine cellar, which drives Charles crazy."

"I can imagine," Theo said. "I'm sure Dorrie and her friends will have a lovely time in Jamaica. However, I hear water running in the greenhouse, and I'd better check on it. If you'll excuse—"

"All of them come from very good families, of course, and the villa is fabulous, simply fabulous. Four bedrooms, fully staffed, private pool, view of the Caribbean. It's going to be a delightful little vacation. Doesn't it sound delightful, Theo?"

"Delightful," Theo echoed obediently. "But I fail to understand how it involves me, Nadine, and I'm afraid I must hang up now. I must have left the hose running in the green-house, and—"

"I need you to chaperone them."

"Out of the question. The last time I accompanied Dorrie, I was blown down a mountainside by Israeli terrorists. It was most distressing, and I have no intention of—"

"It was quite good of you, Theo. Have I ever properly

thanked you for retrieving Dorrie from that dreadful communist cell?"

"No, nor have you allowed me to complete one sentence without—"

"Oh, dear, Pookie's honking in the driveway and she is utterly impossible if she's kept waiting. I'll have Dorrie call with the travel information. I shall insist on paying for your expenses, although I might point out that you'll be having a lovely vacation while the rest of us are literally sloshing through Connecticut slush."

"I am not going to chaperone Dorrie and her—"

A dial tone buzzed in Theo's ear. Sighing, he replaced the receiver and returned to his greenhouse, where the hose had flooded the concrete floor. He moved several clay pots out of the water, picked up a trowel, then put it down with another sigh. His sister, Nadine, was a force that required more resistance than he could usually produce. She had teethed on the Junior League, then moved through charitable fund-raisers to the fully ripened post of president of the Hospital Auxiliary. She had not done so by evincing weakness. On the contrary, had she been the *Titanic* (not an improbable analogy), the Atlantic would have been dotted with crushed ice.

Theo was still puttering in the greenhouse when the telephone once again disturbed him. He went into the kitchen to wipe his hands on a dish towel, then warily picked up the receiver. "This is Theo Bloomer."

"I'm so glad I caught you, Uncle Theo. I absolutely have to go to the library and do a midterm paper; I've put it off for months now, and all of a sudden it's due tomorrow. It's as if Simmons gave us all this time to perspire over it, knowing perfectly well we'd have to stay up all night to get it finished. *C'est-a-dire,* having it dangle over my head has made my life a living hell."

"I'm sorry to hear that," Theo said mildly.

"Thank you," Dorrie said, graciously accepting the perceived sympathy. "Did Mother call you about Jamaica?"

"It's out of the question, Dorrie. I am sixty-one years old, and far too old to spend a week on a Caribbean beach with a group of college students. I have appointments next week, and some very time-consuming chores in the greenhouse to prepare for the planting season. I'm sure you and your friends can find another chaperone for your trip."

"But we can't. Mother agreed to go along, but then she realized that a year ago she had promised Pookie they would play in the women's pairs in the Greater Connecticut Bridge Tournament that very same week. We'd already mailed in the nonrefundable deposit at that point."

"There are several of you going," Theo pointed out, "and surely one of the other parents could accompany the group."

"Not one of them. We've absolutely pleaded with them, but they're all being totally beastly about it. But it's all right, Uncle Theo. We'll forfeit the deposit—which rivals certain Third World countries' gross national products, I might add. I'll just spend the week studying in my dorm room. With everyone else off on meaningful trips, the building will be a dark, dusty, creepy old mausoleum, and I can work on a term paper or something equally thrilling. Perhaps I'll try a strawberry rinse on my hair, or a new shade of fingernail polish . . ." Several delicate sniffles ensued as she envisioned the scene.

Theo was not impressed. "Come now, you don't have to spend your vacation in the dorm. You can stay at home, and spend the time with your friends."

"If the trip collapses, I won't have any friends. I realize it's my senior year and my last spring break ever, but I truly don't mind that it will be the most wretched week of my entire life.

Please don't waste a single second worrying about me, Uncle Theo."

"Why don't you go without a chaperone, my dear? After all, you're all college seniors and quite capable of taking care of yourselves. You'll have a much better time without a gray-haired nursemaid to remind you to eat your vegetables and—"

"This is hardly the sixties. We have standards now, and it simply wouldn't look right for a group of very attractive singles to stay in a villa in a foreign country without a proper chaperone. It could lead to all sorts of tacky gossip at the club. Biff's grandmother would be so appalled she might change her mind—and her will—and let his younger sister get her pudgy little hands on the Hartley sterling collection, which was probably made by Paul Revere or someone like that."

"Then hire someone to accompany you."

"We need a proper chaperone, not a Kelly Girl." A paper rustled, and a sly note crept into her voice. "There are more than three thousand varieties of flowering plants in Jamaica, and eight hundred of them are found nowhere else in the world."

"Dorrie, as much as I would like to chaperone you and your friends, I cannot leave during the spring planting season. I'm testing a new tomato hybrid that is purported to be blight-resistant, and it's almost time to put in snap beans and peas."

"Two hundred species of wild orchids. Sixty of bromeliads, and five hundred fifty of ferns."

"Two hundred species of wild orchids?" Theo heard himself saying, despite his better sense.

"Yep. You can do almost thirty a day, Uncle Theo. I'll personally go to the botanical gardens with you and make appreciative little noises over each and every blossom, even if it means sacrificing peak tanning hours on the beach."

She continued to extol the botanical treasures found exclusively in Jamaica as Theo gazed through the glass doors at his greenhouse. Even if deprived of water for a week, he suspected his tomato seedlings were made of sterner stuff than he. Then again, very few species were Caldicott-resistant. Science was not yet that advanced.

Sangster International Airport was crowded with tourists, porters, businessmen clad in lightweight suits, and small children darting about like water skimmers. Weary parents pleaded without success as the omnipresent public address system crackled without clarity. It was, Theo decided, precisely like every other international airport he'd been in, despite the proximity of romantic Montego Bay. The humidity, noise, litter, flies, and grime were not romantic.

The crowd milled around him as he stopped for a moment to slip off his jacket and carefully fold it over his arm. No one gave a second glance to the tall, balding man with the neatly trimmed beard and bright blue eyes behind thick bifocals. Had anyone bothered to study him, he would have been categorized and dismissed as the essence of mildness, a genteel retiree, perhaps inclined to bore listeners with a harmless hobby or two. Cats, African violets, model trains. Certainly nothing too eccentric, exotic, or expensive. Theo had discovered many years ago that his nondescript demeanor served him well, and he took pains not to contradict the image.

His niece and namesake, Theodora Bloomer Caldicott, was hardly nondescript. She was a tall, graceful girl, equipped with wholesome preppie enthusiasm and a goodly dose of Connecticut snobbery. Her long blond hair usually bounced around her, but today it was up in a ponytail as a concession to the heat. Theo watched her fondly as she strolled through the airport. Caldicotts looked neither left nor right, nor at the floor, where one might inadvertently see something rude. They looked straight ahead, ever mindful of posture. The less fortunate were expected to move out of the way. For some inexplicable reason, they did.

Dorrie stopped abruptly and clapped her hands. "Isn't that quaint?" she demanded of no one in particular. "A little band of local musicians playing island music! It is so completely cute I cannot believe it. Give them a dollar, Biff."

Biff (*a.k.a.* Bedford James Hartley II, reputed to be Dorrie's fiancé) smiled indulgently. "Now, Dorrikin, we don't want to disrupt the island economy by passing out American dollars to every native who can pound some obscure instrument or dresses in polyester print."

"But they're playing calypso, just like Harry Belafonte. I think it's absolutely quaint, and I think we should encourage them to maintain their traditions. It's terribly important in a depressed economy for the natives to have a continuity with their heritage. It helps them keep their minds off poverty and things like that."

A blond-haired boy retraced his steps to join them. "Don't be an ugly American, big guy," he said to Biff, punching him in the arm. "Give them some change and let's find our luggage. I'm ready to do some beach and brewskis."

Alexander "Sandy" Whitcombe was Biff's oldest and dearest friend, Theo had learned on the flight, although somewhat of a pariah since he attended the U.S. Naval Academy at Annapolis rather than one of the more traditional ivy-coated schools. Dorrie had mentioned that said midshipman's father was some species of admiral and very adamant about family traditions, and that personally she found uniforms appealing. Well, not on doormen, of course, and only if they were dress whites and not khaki, which was primitive, especially if one were to perspire. Not that she meant chinos, obviously, since they were *de rigueur* in the summer. Or unless one was doing Kenya, in which case one simply had to wear those darling safari outfits from Banana Republic, complete with pith helmets, no matter what havoc they wrought on one's hair.

It had been a long flight. Dorrie had insisted on sitting with her darling Uncle Theo to keep him company since he was being such a super good sport to come with them. The fact that Biff had sat with another of the girls had warranted not a few catty comments interspersed in the nonstop chatter. A very long flight, indeed.

Even before boarding the plane (weeks ago?), Theo had noted that Sandy's hair was more closely cropped than the norm, and his posture reminiscent of the military, which was hardly surprising. His freckles were neatly aligned. Biff, on the other hand, had aristocratically elegant features, stylishly shaggy dark hair, and the slouch that seemed to accompany the burden of old money. However, they were dressed identically, from their sock-less loafers through their madras shorts to the discreet little alligators on their knit shirts. The uniform to end all uniforms.

As Biff hesitated, visibly aggrieved, Theo took out a dollar and dropped it in a hat in front of the band. "I enjoyed the music," he murmured.

The four black men gazed back. "No problem, mon," the guitarist said, flashing white teeth.

"Now look what you've done!" Dorrie said to Biff. "The others have gone ahead, and I don't see any of them. If you hadn't pulled this silly little Scrooge routine, we wouldn't have lost them."

Biff's ears turned the precise shade of pink Theo hoped

the fruit of his hybrid tomatoes might prove to be. "If you hadn't stopped to behave like some undergrad sociologist, we wouldn't have lost them, either."

Sandy draped arms around the combatants' shoulders. "Children, children, let's not get blown out over this. We're on spring break. We're supposed to relax, enjoy ourselves, work on those tans, and bask in the moonlight of Montego Bay. We'll catch up with the rest of the gang at the luggage terminal. Then right on to the limo, the villa, and the beer!"

Dorrie tucked her arm through Biff's and fluttered her eyelashes contritely. "Dorrikin didn't mean to snap at Biffkin. She's sorry."

Biffkin kissed Dorrikin's sweet little nose.

Theo trailed after the three as they went through the airport. The small spat between his niece and her fiancé was disturbing, and he wondered what had provoked it. He then dismissed it from his mind. With six young adults under his supervision, he suspected they had only just begun.

The other three were waiting for their luggage. The male half of the "adorable Ellison twins" was leaning against a pillar, a cigarette dangling from his lips in true Bogart fashion. He had carefully styled red hair and hooded green eyes that seemed more closed than open. He arched an eyebrow as Dorrie, Biff, and Sandy joined him.

"Trouble in paradise?" he said, smirking at their flushed faces. "Is it possible Ken and Barbie will not discover bliss under the tropical stars?"

"Stuff it," Dorrie said. She wheeled around and took refuge with the distaff half of the adorable Ellison twins. Mary Margaret raised an eyebrow, but it took her quite a while longer to manage the effort. Her red hair was lighter than her brother's, and tumbled down her back in artistic disarray. Her body was voluptuous enough to catch and retain the eye of every male in the area. Superglue could not have been more effective than her brief white shorts and translucent blouse.

"Is Trey being abominable?" she drawled. "Hardly surprising."

The final member of the sextet appeared from the direction of the ladies' room. Bitsy (Elizabeth Angelica O'Conner) Bigelow was petite, from her pert little nose to her pert little feet. Her short brown hair jiggled with each step, as did parts of her anatomy. "Trey once modeled for a Yen' poster," she said, smiling sweetly at the object of her barb. "They couldn't use it, though. Too gruesome."

"You flatter me," Trey said.

"Were that remotely true, which it is not, it would also be completely unintentional." Bitsy proved that she, too, could raise an eyebrow.

Theo took Dorrie aside. "Is this bickering the standard behavior among your friends? We haven't even officially set foot in Jamaica, and it's already growing tiresome."

"There is a tiny amount of tension between Trey and Bitsy," Dorrie said in a low voice. "They were engaged last semester. It was announced in *The New York Times*, which was quite a coup considering that her father made his money in pet accessories. The *Times* is leery of *nouveau,* if you know what I mean. Well, to make an excruciatingly boring story short, Trey pulled something intolerable, and Bitsy was forced to call the whole thing off—the very next day after she'd had the first fitting for her wedding dress. It was dreadful."

"I can imagine."

"The lace was obviously synthetic, and the hem length unsuitable for her height. I don't know what came over her. We all almost expired when she showed us a picture of it, but not a soul in the dorm dared breathe a word of criticism."

"But if they have this unpleasant history between them, why did either of them agree to come on the trip?" Theo asked, aware he would never grasp the delicacies of dorm demeanor.

"Bitsy pointed out that her family and the Ellisons belong to the same country club, and the mothers to the Symphony Guild. It simply isn't feasible for them to feud, not with the Memorial Day tennis tournament in a couple of months and the scads of club functions and parties this summer. Everyone would have been obliged to take sides and ostracize one or the other of them. Guest lists are hellacious enough as it is, without having to remember which camp people are in. It does put a damper on the divorce rate, though." Dorrie chewed on her lip for a moment. "It's terribly sensible of Bitsy, don't you think?"

"I suppose so, in a cold-blooded way. Perhaps she didn't take the engagement seriously."

"She spent thirty-seven hundred on the dress, Uncle Theo. It sounded pretty darn serious to me."

Before Theo could respond, the conveyor belt rumbled to life and luggage appeared through the rubber curtain. Within a few minutes, all the bags had been loaded on carts, wheeled through customs for a perfunctory search, and piled on the sidewalk by obliging porters with broad grins and convenient palms.

Trey was the last to amble through the door. He gazed at a long, lumpy bag. "I say, that looks like a body bag. Did someone sneak a corpse through customs? Are we to have the pleasure of someone's dear, departed great-auntie every afternoon for pickle juice cocktails?"

"Golf clubs," Sandy said. "There are some excellent courses."

"I would have thought golf was too, shall we say, plebeian for you military chaps," Trey said, flicking cigarette ashes on the bag. "I thought you spent your idle moments spitting on your shoes or assembling weapons while blindfolded."

"Leave him alone," Biff said. "I brought my clubs, too."

Mary Margaret put her hand on Biff's arm and gave him a lazy smile. "Trey's just being vile because he's a wretched golfer. His handicap qualifies him for protection under the Equal Employment Act. I'm not bad myself. In fact, the pro at the club said I was very good."

"He was simply mad about her grip," Trey added. "He told everyone in the locker room that it was outstanding."

Mary Margaret kept her eyes on Biff. "But I could always use a lesson or two. I hope you'll help me with my backswing."

Theo heard Dorrie's well-bred growl, but could only close his eyes to avoid viewing what he feared was about to transpire. He opened them as an alarmingly pink station wagon stopped in front of them. A woman with daffodil-yellow hair leaned across the seat to roll down the window. Her lipstick matched the flamingo hue of her wagon, as did the several undulations of eyeshadow.

"Caldicott party for Harmony Hills villa?" she asked. When Theo nodded, she climbed out of the station wagon and came around to the sidewalk. She was nearly as tall as he, and moved with a professional briskness that sent him back a few inches in an instinctive retreat. Her dark brown eyes and broad smile did much to soften her squarish, blunt features. She was, Theo concluded, not unattractive.

"You look tired from your flight," she announced. "I'm Geraldine Greeley, the leasing agent with whom you've corresponded. The villa's ready, so why don't you pop all your luggage in the back and pile in the station wagon."

The group gaped at her as if she'd suggested selecting a wardrobe on the basis of sixty-second blue-light specials. Theo sighed, introduced the stunned group, then said, "I'm Theo Bloomer, Ms. Greeley. For reasons that now seem obscure if not insane, I'm the chaperone. Might it be possible to persuade a porter to load the luggage?"

"Call me Gerry, honey." She turned shrewd eyes on his charges. "It'll be a tight squeeze, but the villa's only a couple of miles away. You can survive, can't you?"

"Certainly," Mary Margaret said, her fingers still wrapped around Biff's arm. "We'll just snuggle in like little old peas in a pod. You don't mind if I sit on Biff's lap, do you, Dorrie?"

Dorrie shot Biff a bright smile as she moved toward the front door of the station wagon. "Why on earth would I mind? You two little sweet peas can snuggle your little pods out."

"I am not sitting on his lap," Bitsy said, indicating Trey with a flip of her chin. "I'd rather walk."

Trey flipped his cigarette over his shoulder as he gave her a facetiously sympathetic look. "It might not be a bad idea, Bitsy. It might even take a few ounces of cellulite off those buttocks."

"My cellulite is none of your concern! I, for one, fit very nicely in my pantyhose."

Sandy took Bitsy's elbow and pulled her aside for a whispered conversation. By the time they returned to the car, the luggage had been arranged in the back. Dorrie sat between Gerry and Theo in the front seat, her jaw extended to its utmost and her lips clamped. The others had managed to find adequate space in the backseat. Gerry turned around as the final door slammed.

"Everybody comfy?" When she received no answer, she started the engine and pulled into the line of traffic inching out of the airport parking lot. "I hope you find the villa pleasant. Your cook's name is Amelia. You may find her attitude a bit difficult, but she's worked with my firm for over ten years and does an excellent job, especially with island specialties. The maid is—"

Dorrie interrupted with a shriek. "You're on the wrong side of the road, you madwoman! We're about to have a head-on collision!"

"It's the British influence, dearie. You won't get used to it in a week, but you'll be able to open your eyes in a few days."

Theo opened his eyes to a squint. "Aren't we driving too fast for this . . . ah, road?"

"It's an island tradition to drive like a bat out of hell. The Jamaicans put a dozen bodies in a little car and take off as if it were the opening of the Indy 500. Your car is at the villa, but I suggest you take great care until you've had a chance to observe the road conditions and customs. Eli will be available to drive you wherever you wish, or run errands for you. He's the lawn and pool boy, and has separate quarters in a room under the pool."

"A veritable troll," murmured Trey.

"If you say so." Gerry glanced at him in the rearview mirror with a vague smile.

"Trey's an authority on trolls," Bitsy contributed. "It was his major until he was tossed out of school for the fifth time. Or was it the sixth?"

"Darling, I didn't know you cared enough to count."

"At least I can count."

Theo gazed out the window at the lush green foliage of the landscape, wondering not for the first time why he had consented to accompany the house party, which held little promise of being the least bit "delightful." Two hundred species of wild orchids would not compensate for seven days of sniping, bickering, snarling, and whatever else arose. It was, however, too late to do much about it.

The road curved up into a sloping mountainside of villas, each protected with a high fence and gate. The yards were manicured stretches of green, shaded by towering poinsettias and royal poincianas, palms and tamarind trees, shrubs thick with bright orange flowers and explosions of scarlet. A few cars with tourists crept along the broad streets, while dark-skinned women walked purposefully, baskets balanced on their heads.

They arrived at the gate of the villa with only a few more muffled gasps. A black man who appeared to be in his early twenties unlocked the padlock and pulled back the gate, then gave Gerry a deferential nod as she drove through and up the steep driveway.

"That was Eli," she said, parking beside a short flight of steps that led to a terrace. "This is your home for the next week, and I do hope you have a lovely time. Amelia has purchased enough supplies for a day or two, then you can make a list and have Eli take her to the market. The fruit and vegetable truck will come by daily, and the fish truck every few days. You can purchase live lobsters from them if they have any after the hotel and restaurant rounds."

"And the brewski truck?" Sandy asked as he helped Bitsy out of the backseat. "Every hour, I hope."

"You'll find a complete selection of liquor in a cabinet in the kitchen and several cases of chilled beer in the refrigerator," Gerry said. "I've been at this job for twenty years, and I know what our visitors want in their first five minutes."

Dorrie snorted as she joined Theo in the driveway. "Some of our visitors seem to prefer physical contact, particularly with men who have forgotten preexisting relationships."

Gerry introduced Eli, who had followed the station wagon

up the driveway, and instructed him to unload the luggage. Theo picked up his suitcase and followed the group into the villa, which seemed to consist of at least three levels. The door from the driveway led to the main floor, with a kitchen in back and a dining room with wide French doors that opened onto a terrace. A few steps down from the terrace was a crystal blue pool surrounded by a deck. The bedrooms were presumably upstairs; the living room was on a lower level beyond the dining room. By the time Theo assimilated all the steps, the group had assembled in the living room.

"Can you believe this?" Dorrie whispered in a thoroughly awed voice. "This is a movie set, right? Early bordello—right down to the red velvet, the fringe on the drapery swags, and that absurd loveseat just begging for a hooker to sprawl across it. Mary Margaret, you are going to be in your element."

"Dorrie," Biff began reproachfully, "you shouldn't speak to—"

"Let's get the bedroom situation arranged," she continued. "I really must wash my face. Some of you may have less hygienic goals, but I can already tell this humidity is going to cause all sorts of problems with my complexion, not to mention my hair. I can almost hear my ends splitting. Come along, everyone; let's get this over with."

There were three bedrooms upstairs. Dorrie, Bitsy, and Mary Margaret took the master, which had three beds and a small balcony overlooking the terrace. Biff and Sandy took the bedroom beside the girls', and Theo found himself relegated to the smallest. Trey agreed to the room off the living room, murmuring that he did not believe in roommates unless they were also sprightly, imaginative bedmates. No one volunteered.

Theo unpacked his suitcase, hung his shirts in the closet, aligned his shoes in an esthetically pleasing formation, arranged his toiletries to his satisfaction in the minute bathroom, and then went downstairs. Dorrie joined him as he crossed the dining room, her face ominously composed. Gerry was waiting on the terrace beside the pool. A dark, thin woman with a dour expression stood beside her, a notebook in her hand.

"This is Amelia," Gerry said. "She has a list of the provisions already purchased, and will sit down to do menus whenever you wish. However, she has prepared a Jamaican chicken recipe for tonight, if that's acceptable to you."

Dorrie had spent more time with the help than she had with her parents. "Let me check the invoices against the provisions and get it done with," she said, holding out her hand for the notebook. "I'll do menus tomorrow morning after breakfast, Amelia. I dread things dangling over me."

The cook slapped the notebook in Dorrie's palm. "You find everything will match, miss. I don' cheat like some of the trash I know."

"Well, of course not," Dorrie said, shrinking back for a second as Connecticut protocol deserted her. Connecticut help did not challenge their betters—if they wanted steady employment. "I wasn't suggesting any such thing. It's simply basic procedure, like counting the silver after a dinner party."

"You can count forks if you want, miss. I got better flatware at home than they keep here." Amelia strode toward the kitchen.

Dorrie's eyelashes fluttered as she stared at the departing back. "My goodness, she's rather temperamental, isn't she?"

"But she's a marvelous cook," Gerry said. "I'll go to the kitchen with you and help you get started, then perhaps we might have a pitcher of rum punch by the pool while we discuss your plans for the week. I have brochures, maps, information about the train, names and telephone numbers for charter boats, and all that sort of thing. We'll meet your uncle out by the pool in a few minutes."

Theo agreed to the plan and went down the steps to the patio surrounding the pool. He pulled a chair under the shade of a slightly tattered umbrella, took off his bifocals and polished them, then put them on the nearby table and leaned back, his eyes closed.

When he opened them, he found himself looking at two large, white, unfettered breasts. The nipples, he noted in confused alarm, were precisely the purplish shade of the *Cattleya vio-lacea,* a rather common orchid that he had, before his retirement from the florist industry, used in many a corsage.

Mary Margaret smiled smugly as she picked up a towel and covered herself. "My deepest apologies, Mr. Bloomer. I presumed you were asleep. I never dreamed I might embarrass you."

"I was indeed asleep," Theo managed to say, suddenly realizing the necessity of again polishing his bifocals. "Although it was more of a catnap. At my age, I find a few moments will often refresh me, and I must admit the hours on the airplane were tiring. I had no idea that you—ah, you were preparing to sunbathe in a . . . a natural state. Please don't think for a second that I was perpetrating a vulgar ruse in order to . . . to behave in an ungentlemanly fashion."

"Never in my wildest fantasies, Mr. Bloomer." She picked up a straw basket and strolled toward the far side of the pool. She spread out a second towel, then lay down to expose her bare back to the sun. Her rounded rump was covered, albeit unsuccessfully, by a very small black triangle. Theo assumed it was intentional. He was not especially surprised when her hand did something mysterious and the black triangle was discarded. He admired the clarity of the water in the pool, then challenged himself to name the plants in the yard. All of them, one by one.

He had identified a cestrum, a malpighia, and a climbing vine he suspected was a cissus when Dorrie and Gerry came across the terrace and pulled up deck chairs on either side of him.

Behind them, a short black woman carried a tray with a pitcher, an ice bucket, several glasses, and a plate of crackers. Gerry introduced her as Emelda, the maid.

"Hope you like my rum punch, Mr. Bloomer," she said, her round face wrinkling as she smiled at him. "I make the best punch on the island, or so they tell me."

"I'm sure it will prove excellent," Theo said. Once she had gone, he looked at Dorrie. "Everything under control in the kitchen, my dear?"

"I suppose so, although we're having peculiar things for dinner, and I'm not sure what the others will think. Callaloo, cho-cho, peas and rice, and a chicken dish that actually may have potential." She gazed at Mary Margaret's inert form, then turned to Gerry. "It is vital, however, that I do menus immediately. I do think we'll be safer with lobster, shrimp, steaks, and that sort of thing."

"But you ought to sample the Jamaican food while you're here," Gerry said. "I'm sure Amelia will prepare ackee and salt fish for breakfast, along with fried plantains, bammies, and boiled green bananas if she can get them."

Dorrie gave Theo a look reminiscent of a lab bunny facing a twelve-inch hypodermic needle. "I'd better speak to her at once," she said as she scrambled out of her chair and hurried toward the house.

Theo took the proffered glass of rum punch from Gerry. "In one sense, Dorrie is terribly sophisticated, but in another she's as provincial as a native who's never left the island. Her parents have taken her to Europe several times, but they always stay in American hotel chains where they can count on English-speaking waiters to serve bacon and eggs for breakfast. Her father almost had a stroke when first confronted with a continental breakfast."

"Tell me about this group, Theo. They are somewhat younger than most of my clients, and they seem awfully uptight for a bunch of college kids on spring break."

He took a moment to recall what he could of Dorrie's commentary on the airplane. "Well, Sandy, the blond-haired boy, attends naval academy. His mother is solid Baltimore money, his father a stern, harrumphing sort who stresses discipline and personal sacrifice. Sandy and Biff are old prep school chums, with lots of holiday visiting and yachting in the summer."

"And Biff belongs to the red-haired girl?"

"That seems to be an issue at the moment," Theo confessed. "Biff is reputedly engaged to my niece, Dorrie, although I don't believe it's official yet and no dates have been discussed that I'm aware of."

Gerry stared at the figure across the pool. "Oh, dear, I could see the fireworks going off, but I wasn't sure why. The redhead has the moves of a hungry tigress; I can understand why your niece is storming around the kitchen."

"It's actually her normal behavior." He then explained the volatile situation between Trey and Bitsy, which earned a few ill-disguised snickers of laughter from Gerry, who was clearly amused by the complexities of the house party. "I merely intend to survive the week," he concluded stiffly.

"Marie Antoinette said the same during the French Revolution, Theo. But for now, let me show you the brochures concerning the boat and train rides, the beach parties at the hotels, the great houses and gardens, and all the touristy things in the area."

They were discussing botanical gardens when Biff, Sandy, and Bitsy, now dressed in bathing suits and carrying towels, suntan lotion, magazines, and other necessary paraphernalia to battle the sun, came out of the house and down the steps to the pool deck. Sandy and Bitsy continued around to the table with the pitcher and glasses, but Biff, after a furtive peek at the terrace, turned the opposite way and sat down next to Mary Margaret.

When Dorrie returned to the terrace, she stopped to stare at the two whispering together, their faces no more than a foot apart. For a moment, Theo thought she might stomp her foot or even snatch up an ashtray to hurl at the treacherous duo, but she gained control of herself and glided down the stairs with a serene smile. Caldicotts avoided public displays, relying on more subtle forms of vengeance. Nadine had produced more than one nervous breakdown through strategic manipulation of seating arrangements at dinner parties.

Once Dorrie had a glass of rum punch in her hand, she crossed her legs and looked at Gerry. "I had a discussion with Amelia about the breakfast menu. Are you aware that this ackee thing is poisonous if not handled properly?"

"That's what we're having for breakfast?" Sandy said from his chaise in the sun. He grasped his neck and produced a gurgling noise. "I'd rather croak with a decent tan so Mummy can have an open casket. Can't we wait until the last morning for the fateful dish?"

"I read of this ackee in the travel guide," Theo said. "It is known as the *Blighia sapida* and is now considered endemic to Jamaica, although it was introduced from Africa by slave ships in the late eighteenth century. It is only dangerous in its unripened stage, when ingestion leads to what is called the vomiting sickness. There is no known antidote. Once the pod has split, it's safe. In fact, it's the national dish of Jamaica."

Dorrie shook her head. "Amelia showed me one, and it's utterly gross-looking. The interior resembles eyeballs with shiny black centers. It was disgusting, which is by far the kindest thing I can say about it."

"It sounds scary," Bitsy said, her eyes hidden behind over-sized sunglasses that gave her the appearance of a curly-haired insect. "I don't see any reason to take chances with it. The cook may not know how to judge whether it's ripe or not, and I for one have no intention of dying outside the continental United States."

Gerry chuckled. "It is the national dish, and Amelia has prepared it all her life. The white flesh is boiled, then chopped and cooked with salted codfish imported from Canada. It tastes very much like scrambled eggs."

"Then let's just have scrambled eggs." Bitsy took a bottle of suntan oil from a denim bag and began to apply it to her legs. After a moment, Sandy took the bottle from her hand and assisted her amid little squeals of protest and giggles when his hand strayed.

"What do you think, Biff?" Dorrie called across the pool. "Shall we have poisonous fruit for breakfast, or would you prefer to live dangerously in other ways?"

Biff glanced up guiltily, then stood up and came around the pool to pour himself a glass of punch. "Whatever has put you in this tedious snit, Dorrie? It is not attractive."

"What can you possibly be talking about, Biffkin? I was inquiring in all innocence about everyone's preferences for breakfast tomorrow morning. One of us has to deal with the help, after all, and let them know what we expect of them. The little chore has cut into the peak tanning hours already, but someone has to do it. Now that it's settled, perhaps I'll change into my string bikini and wallow around on the deck like a half-naked albino walrus."

"Dorrie, that was a totally gross thing to say, and—"

"Is it time for martinis?" Trey called as he appeared on the stairs that led to the front lawn. "I have explored the territory and can claim it as my own. However, I am absolutely arid, and it is after five o'clock in the afternoon somewhere in the world."

Dorrie turned away from Biff. "Yes, darling, although we're all having rum punch. Shall I pour you one?"

"I never touch anything with fruit juice in it. My body is unaccustomed to anything remotely connected with vitamins. It drove Mummy wild. She used to tell me bedtime stories about sailors with scurvy, rickets, and zits."

"I'll run up to the kitchen and have Emelda fix up a pitcher of martinis just for you," Dorrie said. "In the interim, you can join the discussion about the breakfast menu. We're considering having this thing that's poisonous."

"I never eat breakfast, so you may all spread cyanide on your toast if you desire. And tell the woman that martinis are shaken, not stirred." Trey flopped into a chaise and gave the others a boyish smile. "I'm sending the pool boy to the hotel shop for suntan oil and a copy of *The Wall Street Journal*, by the way. If any of you chaps need anything, you'd better hop off your fannies and catch him before he leaves."

All turned their heads as a beige car roared down the driveway and squealed around the corner.

Biff gave him a withering look. "You might have let us know ahead of time, Trey. I might need something, too."

"I doubt they have cold showers in the shop at the hotel. The rooms, probably, but not the shop. Too public for words."

"Biff," Mary Margaret called, "would you be so kind as to bring me a glass of punch and help me oil my back? I can tell I'm going to turn bright red if I miss one little centimeter of flesh. I'd just die if I burned my back on the first day."

"Because you're planning to spend so much time on it at night?" Trey called back in a genial voice.

Biff glared at him, then at the terrace door through which Dorrie had vanished. His hand shook as he filled a glass with the red punch, but he managed a smile as he went around the pool and knelt next to Mary Margaret. Taking the plastic bottle, he began to dribble oil on her back.

It was intermission time. Aware that the second act would not begin until Dorrie returned, Theo looked at Gerry. "You mentioned that you've been with your firm for twenty years. You must enjoy it."

"It's amusing," she said. "We handle nearly fifty villas in this development, and lease to parties for anywhere between one week and three months. Some of the families have been coming as long as I've been here."

"And before that?" Theo inquired.

"I was a real estate agent in New Jersey. The climate here is so much more civilized, and the pace more suitable for this middle-aged body. It can be frantic when I have several groups descending the same day, but for the most part I do correspondence in the office, work in my garden, or run up to New York for travel fairs and conventions."

"I went to Jersey once," Trey said. "It was more than enough for a lifetime. Princeton, of course, but it turned out to be one of the country's most boring institutions. Where did you live?"

"Not too far from New York City. You didn't like Princeton?"

Bitsy sat up. "He was booted for what he called a practical joke. I believe the police referred to it as a second-degree felony." She oiled her forearms, then lay back.

"I didn't realize you'd transferred to the Harvard Law

School," Trey said, his voice hinting at anger for the first time. "But I might have guessed, since your literary taste leans toward epics like *Love Story.*"

"At least I can read."

Theo decided to intervene. "So, Gerry, you have a garden. Tell me, have you tried tomatoes here, or do you find the climate too hot?"

"I garden in a very modest way, Theo. I have a few bougainvilleas, azaleas, and simple things like that. I'd invite you to inspect my efforts, but I can see you'll be very busy this week."

Theo spotted Dorrie on the terrace, a pitcher in her hand. She was staring down at the couple on the distant side of the pool, and he could see the pitcher trembling. Mary Margaret was prone and glistening, but Biff stared back with a coldly defiant expression. Trey was snorting under his breath, Bitsy's latest barb seeming to have found its target. Bitsy's mouth had a self-righteous curl. Sandy was gazing at the ocean.

"Very busy, I fear," Theo agreed with a sigh. He decided to consult his travel guide for the perimeters of the hurricane season. It might provide a divertissement.

Dinner was strained, but the group had been through years of nannies, etiquette classes, parental lectures, and prep school rules, and the conversation was determinedly polite. They gathered on the terrace for coffee to allow Amelia and Emelda to clear the table. One was always considerate of the help.

Sandy took one of the brochures Gerry had left for them. "There's a beach party at one of the big resorts tonight. All the booze you can drink, wet T-shirt and limbo contests, non-stop reggae music. It sounds outrageous. Why don't we check it out?"

"It's open to the public?" Dorrie said doubtfully.

"I think it sounds marvelous," Mary Margaret said. "Don't you think it sounds marvelous, Biff? If Dorrie's too tired, I'm sure she can stay here and try to get a good night's sleep." She switched her smile to Dorrie. "You look like a raccoon, with those old dark circles under your eyes. Did all those drinks on the flight give you a nasty hangover?"

"Your concern is so totally sweet, but my mascara must be smudged. I'm not the least bit tired. I was wondering if you'd prefer to stay here and try to do something about your hair, which must be causing you no end of depression. We can thank our lucky stars that Mr. Robert isn't here to see it, can't we? But I think the party sounds marvelous."

She and the other two girls went upstairs. Biff said to Theo, "We'd be delighted to have you come with us, sir. The music may be loud, but I'm sure we can find a table toward the edge of the crowd so it won't be unbearable for you."

"How kind of you, but please go without me," Theo said hastily. "I would prefer to sit by the pool for a while, then retire at a reasonable time. I assume my presence as a chaperone is more an honorary position than a relentless responsibility. You will take care of the girls, I trust?"

"Very good care, sir," Sandy said earnestly. "As Dorrie mentioned, it is open to the public, and there is an undesirable element on the island."

Trey, who had been noticeably quiet at dinner, managed a nod.

The girls came down half an hour later, now in sundresses. Sandy announced that Eli would drive them over and wait, which meant they could all get looped, paralytic, twisted, wasted, and wrecked. It did not sound particularly appealing to Theo, but he wished them a pleasant evening and carried the coffee cups and pot to the kitchen.

Amelia snatched the tray from him. "Emelda supposed to clear the table. That be her job."

"I was on my way upstairs," Theo lied, "and it was no problem at all. Have you and Emelda made arrangements to be picked up once you've finished in here?"

"We walk to the bus stop at the bottom of the hill. Am I to fix ackee and sal' fish tomorrow morning or not? If not, I can go to the market before I come here, but I'll be late and won't have breakfast ready on time."

"I truly don't know," Theo said glumly. "I suppose you might as well fix the dish, as long as there's plenty of toast and coffee for those who are a bit squeamish."

"Whole bunch of them are squeamish," Amelia muttered. She dumped the coffee cups in the sink and splashed water on them. "Real squeamish."

"Indeed." Theo went upstairs to find his travel guide, then returned to the terrace and sat down to reread about the ackee tree and its potentially lethal fruit. After a short while, Amelia and Emelda went out the kitchen door and walked down the driveway, talking loudly to each other. Although their English had been fine earlier, Theo could understand nothing of what they said between themselves. He flipped to the section on island dialect.

The chapter was enlightening, but not enough to prevent his eyes from closing and his chin from falling against his chest. He was blissfully dozing when something caused him to open his eyes. He first suspected his unruly charges had returned home, but the house was dark and the driveway vacant. As he wrinkled his forehead, he heard voices from the villa next door.

"I'm absolutely booked solid tomorrow. I'm having lunch at a private estate in Ocho Rios. The woman has been asking me over for an intimate little luncheon for six weeks. If I simply show her a little affection, as distasteful as it may be for me, I can take her out next week for a long, profitable cruise should I encounter our friends on the high seas. However, I'm going to have to spend some time with her—even if it bores me to death." The voice was male, irritated.

"Then don't do it," a second male voice said, although it was so low Theo had difficulty making out the words. Male, definitely, and more composed than the first speaker. "I don't like this business."

"And you think I do? I'm sick of pseudo-reggae music, lunches with pudgy white ladies from New York, escorting the same to dinners where I almost puke every time I look across the table—"

"I never knew gigolos were so sensitive," interrupted the second voice.

Theo realized he was eavesdropping, an act he permitted himself only when he deemed it necessary. He coughed to announce his presence, then flipped open his book and rustled the pages. The voices stopped, although he could not help noticing a few whispers before a door closed on the far side of the fence. Within ten minutes, headlights flashed on the palm trees and a car rumbled down the driveway and into the night.

Seconds later, a car pulled up the driveway adjoining the terrace. For a moment, Theo thought Gerry might have returned with more brochures, but noted the car was a tame beige. He put down his book, wondering why a reputedly tranquil paradise seemed to have so much traffic. Eli climbed out of the car and stopped by the entrance to the terrace.

"I left the kids at the beach for a while. I'll go back for them around midnight."

"Are you sure they'll be quite safe, Eli? This is their first night in Jamaica, and they're not familiar with the local customs."

"No problem. I could see they familiar with the drinking and dancing customs. The red-haired girl was onstage trying to limbo when I left, and one of the boys had puked twice out by the water. Jamaicans don't go to the hotel parties, anyway. We go to our own places where the music is better and the rum cheaper." Eli displayed perfect white teeth. "You want to come with me some night? I can show you a good time, with lots of pretty women."

"No, thank you," Theo said, trying to imagine himself in such a place. "If nothing else, I have gathered that the political situation is causing unrest between the major parties, and a certain amount of resentment against the tourists."

"Not around Montego Bay, Mr. Bloomer. There be trouble in Kingston, where they had the gas riots couple years back. They have the demonstrations, the riots, all the fun. Here in MoBay, we just serve rum and make music for the tourists. Then we take their dollars and drink rum and make music for ourselves. No problem in MoBay."

"That's comforting to hear, Eli."

"Okay, mon. Was Mrs. Greeley here looking for me just before I came back? Sometimes she wants me to mow yards at the other villas, but I think these college kids are going to keep me busy all week."

"No, it was someone visiting next door. Mrs. Greeley intends to stop by tomorrow with tickets and information; I shall remember to tell her that you're concerned about the schedule."

"Thanks, mon." Whistling, Eli went partway down the driveway and into his quarters below the pool. After a few minutes, Theo heard reggae music drifting through the window. The music was quite pleasant to listen to as he looked at the streak of moonlight glittering on the Caribbean. After a while, the reggae was replaced with the faint strains of a Mozart concerto. If only, he told himself, he had come without Dorrie and her friends, it would have been as delightful as Nadine had promised. He caught himself wishing her ill luck in the women's pairs in the Greater Connecticut Bridge Tournament. On that petty thought, he went to bed.

The ackee argument of the previous evening proved a waste of time, since Theo was the sole diner at the breakfast table. He tasted the concoction carefully and determined that it was much like scrambled eggs. It was also quite tasty, and he said as much to Amelia as she came to clear his plate.

"What about the others?" she demanded.

"They were out very late last night, and will most likely want only coffee for breakfast. The coffee is excellent, by the way."

"Come from special plantations in the mountains. I'll bring you a pot on the terrace, and fix some more for the others should they decide to get up. I don' know when Emelda's going to clean bedrooms if they stay in bed all day."

"Surely many of the tourists who stay here overindulge," Theo said, unsure why he was defending the group. "They're on vacation."

"They drink too much, party too much, and climb in the wrong beds with the wrong people. I've even had married couples here that switched bedrooms every night. Emelda about went crazy putting on clean sheets every day."

"You don't see us at our best, do you? These kids are all college students in tough schools, and I suppose they do go to extremes when they're on vacation."

Amelia snorted as she went to the kitchen. Theo carried his coffee cup to the terrace, and was gazing at the bright flowers along the street when the pink station wagon honked at the gate. Eli appeared, went down to unlock the gate, then closed it and retreated as Gerry drove up the driveway.

She joined Theo at the table. "I just stopped by for a moment on my way to the office. I understand your group made it to the beach party last night and had quite a time."

"I was already asleep when they returned, so I've not yet heard anything about it." He studied her amused expression. "You must have heard something, however."

"Mary Margaret Ellison is well on her way to becoming an island legend. It seems she entered the limbo contest and made it to the finals. At that point, she realized her dress was impeding her performance. A limbo champion and a legend in her own time, our Miss Ellison."

"She refused to allow her dress to interfere with her limbo performance?" Theo said, dismayed. "That is to say, she felt obliged to remove the impediment on a stage and in front of a large crowd?" When Gerry nodded, he sank down in his chair. "I am failing to fulfill my duties, and I am ashamed of myself. I declined to attend this party with them last night, never considering the possibility that my absence would permit any of them to indulge in regrettable behavior. I should have gone."

"I assumed you did, but I didn't hear any gossip about a tall man in bifocals and boxer shorts attempting the limbo."

Theo pulled himself up. "Hardly. But how did you hear the gossip about Mary Margaret so quickly? It's only half past nine the morning after the unfortunate incident."

"The servants' grapevine is remarkably efficient. Some of the drivers observed the limbo finals and passed on the information in villa kitchens over coffee this morning. Maids talk over the fences while hanging out laundry. The produce men go from house to house, bargaining with the cooks in the driveways. By noon, the incident will have been analyzed for maximum amusement in every Jamaican café in MoBay."

"Oh, dear. I suppose I shall have to have a word with Mary Margaret, but I have no idea what I shall say to her. This really ought to be handled by a woman, who can offer the girl sensible female advice." He looked at Gerry. "I don't suppose . . . ?"

For a moment, she looked startled, then broke into laughter. "I'm a real estate agent, not a surrogate mother, Theo. If the rumors about the quantities of rum consumed by the Harmony Hills villa group are also true, I doubt you'll be able to have any words with anyone until late in the afternoon."

"They had too much to drink?"

"Of course they did. Everyone there did; it's standard behavior and the only hope to salvage the poor girl's reputation. Most of those present won't remember much this morning."

Dorrie staggered across the terrace and plopped down next to Theo. Her face was puffy and swollen, her eyes pink, and her robe was buttoned in a haphazard fashion that left a bumpy path up to her neck.

"Coffee, please," she croaked in a hoarse voice. "And make it snappy. I feel as if I've been put through a wash-and-wear cycle and hung out to dry."

Gerry rummaged through her bulgy straw purse and produced two tablets. "I'll get a cup from the kitchen, along with soda water so that you can take these. They're prescription, and ought to help."

"I am beyond help."

"They can't hurt," Gerry said as she started for the kitchen. "I'll be back with the soda water in a minute."

Dorrie gazed at Theo. "She meant to say Perrier, didn't

she? Please don't make me drink generic soda water, Uncle Theo. I am in no condition to deal with it."

"Perhaps your palate will excuse it this once," Theo said drily. "You do not appear to be at your peak of discernment this morning."

"This is not the time for weak attempts at humor. One more little joke and I shall throw myself over the railing."

Theo did not point out that she was likely to survive the three-foot fall. When Gerry returned with an empty cup and a glass of soda water, Dorrie obediently downed the pills with only a brief flicker of distaste. She then took her coffee cup and retreated to a shady corner of the terrace to mutter under her breath. Gerry promised to return later and gave Theo a gay little wave as she left. He did his best to reciprocate, but Dorrie merely raised a finger.

"Gerry was telling me about Mary Margaret's impromptu striptease act," Theo said once the pink station wagon reached the foot of the driveway. "I am most distressed that she would engage in that sort of behavior."

Dorrie produced a prim sniff. "Well, I wasn't surprised. Her father may own an entire insurance company in Hartford, but Daddy swears he cheats on the golf course and everybody knows he's perpetually behind on the club dues. Her mother checks into quaint little rest homes about three times a year, the kind with barbed wire fences so no one can see you while they dry you out for the next charity ball. And Trey has been always a complete wastrel, from the age of eight when he was booted out of Miss Pipkin's cotillion class to his arrest last summer when he stole John David Irwin's boat and abandoned it three miles down the coast. He said he got bored and decided to find a local pub. John David dropped the charges, but let me tell you, it made for some fabulous conversation during the Labor Day tournament."

"Why are they tolerated, then?"

"Oh, everybody's used to them, and we are talking zillions of dollars," she said, shrugging. "Is this interrogation absolutely necessary, Uncle Theo? My head is on the verge of a godawful explosion. I doubt the strain required to answer all these questions is exactly beneficial."

"I still feel obligated to have a word with her," Theo said. "Even if her parents are as uncivilized as you claim, I must insist she behave in a more decorous manner while under my supervision."

"Have at it, Uncle Theo. But you'll have to find her first." Theo felt a twinge of alarm. "She's not upstairs?" Dorrie held out her hand to study her shapely pink fingernails. "I had a manicure two days ago, and there's already a chip. It's incredibly difficult to get value for one's money these days." She curled in her claws and fluttered her eyelashes at Theo. "Mary Margaret didn't come home with us last night. The last we saw of her, she was going off with a veritable platoon of drunks. Wherever do you think she can be?"

Chapter Two

To Theo's heartfelt relief, Mary Margaret appeared at the bottom of the driveway shortly before noon, looking slightly disheveled but intact. He came onto the terrace in time to see her wave at a blue car as it sped down the hill. She then tugged at the strap of her sundress and paused to arrange a nonchalant expression before strolling up the driveway to the terrace.

"Good morning, Mr. Bloomer," she said. She sat down across from him and reached for the coffee pot.

"Good morning, Mary Margaret," Theo replied primly. "I fear you will discover the coffee is quite cold by this hour."

"Well, it must be time for Bloody Marys, then. I'm going to tell the cook to make me one. Would you like one?"

"No, thank you. I would like a word with you, however, once you've asked Amelia to make your drink."

"No problem," she said as she departed through the terrace door. It was well over ten minutes before she returned, now dressed in shorts and a T-shirt. Her hair was pulled out of her face by a barrette, and her face scrubbed to an innocent sheen.

"I was disturbed this morning when I learned you were not upstairs," Theo began in what he hoped was a sternly avuncular tone. It had yet to be successful with Dorrie, but he felt that he should make the attempt. "Also, I have heard reports that you created something of an uproar at the beach party."

"It was a stitch and a half," she agreed.

"It was hardly appropriate behavior. Should your parents

learn of it, they would be upset, to say the very least. It has been made clear that I have been remiss in my duties as chaperone. I should have accompanied the group to this party in order to provide a stabilizing influence."

"I'd have done it anyway, and it wouldn't have been all that entertaining for you—since you've already seen the prime points of my anatomy." She wiggled her eyebrows at him, then took a long drink of the Bloody Mary. "Haven't they heard of Tabasco in this place? Don't worry about my parents finding out about your dereliction of duty, Mr. Bloomer. Trey probably called this morning to tell Daddy all about it, if he could get the words out through his brays of laughter."

"You do not worry that they will be upset and perhaps demand that you return home at once?"

"Why would they do that? Mummy's in Switzerland to have her thighs vacuumed and Daddy's probably got his current girlfriend tucked in the master bed. Anyway, it wasn't as though I was at the club in front of their stodgy old banking friends. I kept my bra and panties on, for God's sake."

"And where did you sleep last night?" Theo persisted, although it was becoming obvious that she was not the least bit remorseful.

She gave him an ingenuous smile. "I'm really not sure who owned the place—isn't that a total panic? I met these guys from Dartmouth, of all places, and we went to a divinely quaint native bar, literally packed with all these black men wearing funky braids and absolutely glaring at us as if they thought we were slumming. When that got to be stifling, we piled in the Jeep and drove all over the mountainside looking for a party one of the guys had heard about."

"You and your . . . friends crashed a party?"

"As far as parties go, it was a dud. Just this older man with buck teeth and a few of his friends. Once he heard our woeful story, he let us in and gave us martinis, and everybody ended up skinny-dipping in the swimming pool. A couple of the guys had pretty quick hands, but I am capable of dealing with that sort of thing after hanging around Trey's friends all these years. I passed out in a chaise beside the pool toward morning; I suppose the flight yesterday drained me."

"Oh, my dear," Theo murmured, at a loss for further avuncular words of admonishment.

Before he could decide how best to proceed, Dorrie and Bitsy came out on the balcony. "Welcome back," Dorrie called down to Mary Margaret. "Did the boys from Dartmouth make you an honorary member of the fraternity after they'd all . . . made you?"

"You know more about the initiation procedure than I do, honey." Mary Margaret looked at her watch. "Where the hell is everybody? I'd like to hit the beach by one o'clock to do some sun. I for one do not intend to go home with a horrid white line across my back. Some people may enjoy the zebra effect, but I find it totally gross."

Bitsy smiled sweetly. "And heaven knows you're an expert in the area of total grossness. Trey and Biff are still in bed. Sandy's in the living room knocking golf balls into a plastic glass. By the way, if you wanted anything from the shops, it's too late. Dear, thoughtful Sandy sent Eli out to pick up ice, limes, and a newspaper without bothering to check with any of us. Oh, but he couldn't have checked with you because you just got in from your little drunken orgy, didn't you? How silly of me." She glanced over the fence at the villa next door, then did a discreet double-take. "Look at that example of the male species," she said, jabbing Dorrie with her elbow. "He is to absolutely die for, isn't he?"

Dorrie's mouth fell open. "Call the executioner."

Theo heard a splash, which he presumed indicated the existence of a swimming pool on the far side of the fence. The girls' expressions indicated they were observing more than a neighbor taking a dip, but he could see nothing beyond the healthy bougainvillea thick with orange flowers.

Mary Margaret pushed back her hair and, in an irritated voice, said, "Do you think it's just a tad impolite to goggle and stare at the neighbors? I swear, you two are sweating and twitching like a pair of hypoglycemics in a candy store. What time will Eli be back with the car? Has anyone decided which hotel beach to use today?"

Dorrie shook her head, her eyes still directed over the fence. "I don't know when they'll be back, Mary Margaret. Why don't you call your buddies from Dartmouth and see if they'll give you a ride?"

"I don't even know which hotel they're staying at. Besides, Biff swore he'd show me how to toss a Frisbee. He was a teensy bit worried that you might object, but I assured him that we're all too adult for that sort of petty, childish behavior. Why, you wouldn't throw a tantrum out of sheer jealousy, would you?"

"Heavens no," Dorrie said distractedly. She whispered a few words to Bitsy, who went into the bedroom and returned seconds later with a small pair of binoculars.

"I may barf," Mary Margaret said, glaring at the balcony and the two girls taking turns with the binoculars. "I really may barf."

Theo retreated to his room.

They were having lunch on the terrace when Gerry's pink wagon pulled up the driveway. Conversation had been desultory, due to the various levels of hangovers evident on the faces around the table. The girls seemed to have recovered more quickly, but out of empathy restrained themselves to a few barbs. Trey had all the liveliness of the broiled fish on his plate, and his eyes the same blankness. Sandy and Biff had eaten a few bites, although neither had produced more than a grunted reply.

Gerry joined them at the table. "I noticed nobody was awake for ackee and salt fish or boiled green bananas this morning," she said as she accepted a glass of white wine from Sandy.

Biff's face turned the greenish-yellow color of the green swan orchid (*Cycnoches chlorochilon*). "Maybe another time," he managed to say as he pushed back his chair and stumbled across the dining room for the stairs.

"Poor baby," Mary Margaret said, watching him with a smile.

"It's totally tragic," said Dorrie. "Why don't you toodle upstairs and hold poor baby's head while he tosses his cookies all over you and the bathroom floor?"

"That's disgusting." Bitsy looked at Gerry. "Who is that divine man who has the villa next door?"

"An old friend of mine, Hal D'Orsini. He's been on the island as long as I have, although he spends his summers on the Continent. He says he cannot abide the heat here, but the Riviera is hotter. I suspect it's more the influx of tourists in the off-season. The rates drop by half, and those who can subsequently afford them are not quite his crowd. He flees in a panic from the rabble into the comforting arms of the filthy rich."

Trey pulled himself out of a trance. "D'Orsini? Haven't I heard of him? Did he go to Harvard with Uncle Billy, Magsy?"

"Would you like an unripened ackee shoved down your throat?" she responded without rancor. "Call me that name one more time."

"I don't know about your Uncle Billy," Gerry said, "but I do remember something about Andover, followed by Harvard. He's merely rich and idle now."

Mary Margaret gazed speculatively at the fence. "Why, if he's an old school chum of darling Uncle Billy's, we really must have him over for a drink. He's practically family. We'd be downright remiss if we didn't give him a neighborly greeting over the fence, wouldn't we?"

Sandy looked at Bitsy, whose expression was as speculative as Mary Margaret's. "I'd hardly imagine him a candidate for the family album, Mary Margaret. We don't know all that much about him, and we don't want some elderly sort hanging around all week." He flushed as he caught Theo's eye. "Not you, sir. We're all delighted that you offered to come with us."

"We certainly are," Dorrie inserted acidly.

The others began babbling assurances that they certainly were, but Theo was not touched by their avowed, eternal gratitude. He waited until they ran out of avowals, then said to Gerry, "Sandy does have a point. What does Mr. D'Orsini do when not idling?"

"Count D'Orsini, actually," she said. "I really don't know, Theo. He has a yacht that he takes out quite often, and entertains when the right people are in residence."

Dorrie gave Bitsy a conspiratorial smile, then turned to Gerry. "Perhaps it might be more appropriate if you invited him for a drink. You could mention Uncle Billy; I'm sure he'd be fascinated to meet the niece and nephew. They are so completely clever."

"I'll stop by later in the afternoon and ask if he has plans for the cocktail hour. Where are you going this afternoon? Have you decided on a beach, or are you going to stay by the pool? If you venture out, you ought to have Eli drive you there and wait."

"I sent him on an errand," Sandy said.

"You and Trey seem to consider him your personal chauffeur," Dorrie said. "He spends a great deal of time doing errands for you two. Had you mentioned it to me, I would have asked that he pick up six and four."

"Six and four?" Theo murmured gently.

"Suntan lotion, Uncle Theo. I have plenty of sixteen for my nose and two for my back, but I'm going to have to use six on my shoulders until I've picked up some color. I want to risk four on the backs of my legs, although I may live to regret it."

"Are you using eight on your forehead?" Bitsy asked.

They commenced a long, serious conversation about numbers and anatomy, and continued it as they went upstairs. Mary Margaret announced she was going to change for the beach, and if Eli didn't get back damn *tout de suite*, she was going to be livid. Trey and Sandy wandered away, leaving Theo and Gerry across from each other.

Theo frowned as he considered the conversation he'd overheard the previous night. Something about it had sounded—well, a bit off. It had disturbed him, although he could not quite put his finger on the cause of his uneasiness. He lectured himself into a more charitable frame of mind.

"You say this D'Orsini is an old friend of yours, Gerry? You're familiar with his family and history?"

"He swears he can trace his family back to Caesar Augustus and then some, and the title to the sixteenth century. I don't believe more than a fraction of it, but I do know he's basically harmless, charming, and always willing to accept a free martini. He's also way too old for these college girls."

"I'm not sure they agree with you. They were watching

him earlier today while he was swimming, and they seemed to be interested in what they observed."

"He is attractive, and insists on doing laps in the nude. But please don't worry about him, Theo; he'll be impeccably dressed in time for cocktails. Shall I suggest that he drop by at six this evening?"

"I suppose so," Theo said, tugging at the tip of his beard as he looked over the tops of palm trees to the delphinium blue of the Caribbean. He was not delighted at the prospect of meeting Count D'Orsini, but he suspected he had little choice.

Gerry said she would call later and went to her station wagon. Before she could get in, Eli drove up the driveway in the beige car. She motioned for him to join her in the shade of the house.

"You seem to be spending quite a lot of time fetching ice from the store," she said in a cool voice. "Amelia and Emelda could pick some up in the mornings on the way to work; their bus stop is next to a store."

"I'm just doing what this group tells me, Miz Greeley. They say go here, Eli, go there, Eli, go get newspapers and suntan lotion, Eli. They have enough suntan lotion to slide this villa right down the mountainside and into the water. But I'm supposed to do what they say, right?"

"You'd better keep your nose clean if you want to keep this job. There are plenty of boys who'd gladly take over your quarters and cushy duties. You're still in a probation period, Eli, and you need to pay attention to your work. Count D'Orsini mentioned that you were skulking around his yard earlier this morning, but I see you didn't mow."

"I was working in the flower bed down by the fence, and I didn't get to it, Miz Greeley," he said with an obsequious smile.

"And in the flower bed beneath his living room window?"

"I just raked out the leaves, Miz Greeley. But no problem about mowing the grass. I do it late this afternoon, once everybody back from beach."

"See that you do. In the future, whenever you work in Count D'Orsini's yard, knock on the kitchen door and tell the cook that you're there. I will not tolerate this skulking nonsense." Gerry got into her station wagon, slammed the door, and backed down the driveway at what Theo felt was a perilous speed.

"Why, sho' nuf, Miz Simone Legree," Eli said sourly. He glanced up and winced as he saw Theo on the terrace. "Just joking, boss; she's a nice lady, real nice. When you think the boys and girls be ready for me to drive them to the beach?"

"They're upstairs changing now," Theo said. He noticed Eli's hands were empty. "Did you find whatever Sandy needed from the store?"

Eli stuffed his hands in his pockets and scuffled his feet nervously in the gravel. "No, he want today's copy of *The Wall Street Journal*. I went all the way into downtown MoBay, but all I could find was day before yesterday's. He sure is hot to see today's paper. Is he some kind of stockbroker, Mr. Bloomer?"

"He's still in school, although I have no idea about his major." Theo blinked through his bifocals at the grinning boy. "Did you go to a Jamaican school, Eli?"

"Yes, sir, I went all the way through eighth grade in MoBay. My mammy was real insistent that all her children learn how to read and write."

Amelia came through a side door, a bulging plastic trash bag in her hands. "You a liar," she said without turning her head.

"You a tight-assed old island woman," he said.

111

"I know your mammy, and I know about your school. All the way through eighth grade? Ha!" Amelia went back into the villa, allowing the door to bang closed like a crack of gunfire.

"She don' know nothing," Eli said to Theo. "I better get ready to take the kids to the beach now."

Once again, Theo found himself alone on the terrace. He was not bored, however, since he had several intriguing little puzzles to think about. Not that he presumed any of them held particular significance, but old habits died slowly, and at a certain point in his past he had been trained to notice discrepancies. There were almost as many as there were orange blossoms along the fence.

The outing to the beach required a series of shuttles. Although Theo would have preferred to visit a garden, or even to simply sit on the terrace and read, he forced himself to change into Bermuda shorts, a rather splashy floral-print shirt Dorrie had brought him from Hawaii, and a canvas hat to protect the hairless circle on the top of his head. Which was growing, he noted glumly as he went into his private bath to fetch the sole bottle of suntan lotion he owned. The bottle was dusty, and unnumbered.

When he arrived in the driveway, he found Bitsy, Sandy, and Dorrie waiting in the shade, a formidable collection of baskets and towels piled beside them. Bitsy was on her tiptoes, trying to see over the fence. Sandy looked as though he were in dire need of a nap, his eyelids drooping and his face slack. Dorrie, on the contrary, was not the least drowsy.

"I cannot imagine why we invited those insufferable Ellisons to come with us," she was saying to Bitsy as Theo approached. "They may receive their weekly allowances in Krugerrands, but they have the manners of . . . of some subspecies of primates! Not to insult the baboons, of course."

Theo deduced that Dorrie was not pleased with the seating assignments of the first shuttle. He was not especially pleased, either, although he doubted Mary Margaret would have adequate time to stir up mischief at the beach before he arrived to keep an eye on her. Whether she might have time to stir up mischief with Biff he could not say. Nor did he see any reason to ask the opinion of his tight-lipped niece.

Amelia came to the door. "I am planning to leave early tonight for church service. Emelda will stay to clear the table."

"That will be fine, Amelia," Dorrie said, her petulance replaced with a tone more suitable for dealing with the help. "Are you perfectly clear on the menus for tonight and tomorrow? I do have a few minutes if you want to go over them again with me."

"I ain't fixing ackee, miss." The door slammed.

Bitsy acknowledged that she could see nothing of interest, and sank down with a disappointed sigh. "As adorable as the petite fashions are, I do sometimes wish I were taller."

"To get a basketball scholarship?" Sandy said. "Maybe you can find a doctor to slip you some drugs, like hormones or something."

Bitsy shot him a frosty look. "No one in my family ever takes so much as an aspirin. You might consider adopting the same policy."

"This is a vacation, Itsy-Bitsy," he said. He leaned back against the house with a muted thud, crossed his arms, and made a face. "For once, I thought you might be over our old buddy Trey and ready for a little relaxation. But you pant after him so damn hard I'm surprised you don't stumble over your tongue."

"That was uncalled for," she began. Before she could elaborate (or simply berate), Eli drove up the driveway. Minutes later they were driving down the hill, swerving to avoid potholes and errant tourists, honking at dogs and children, and keeping Theo in a state of silent hysteria. He did not release his breath until they squealed to a stop in front of a sprawling resort hotel.

Dorrie was out of the car before the dust settled. "Where is the pathway to the beach?" she demanded of Eli. Her face was pink, but not, Theo presumed, from the previous day's sunbathing. Eli gestured at a walkway, and she marched away with the expression her mother used when faced with a glaring error at the bridge table. It was not a pretty sight.

Theo followed Sandy and Bitsy down the walk, across a patio with a fountain, and over an expanse of sand to a shady area under a clump of palm trees. Trey was on a chaise, his face hidden by a straw hat. Dorrie stood over him, her hands on her hips.

"Rouse yourself from this coma and answer my question. Where are they?" she demanded, kicking the leg of the chaise for good measure.

"Magsy has always wanted to parasail, so she talked Biffkin into checking out the prices with the black chap on the far side of the cove. Maybe the line will snap and she'll end up chopping sugarcane in Cuba. Then Dorrikin and Biffkin can be snuggle-bunnikins."

"Don't call me that." She stalked away to a nearby chaise and dropped her beach bag in the sand. Theo watched as she methodically oiled her body with five different preparations, settled her sunglasses firmly on her nose, and took a thick paperback from her bag. "Parasailing is infantile," she announced as she flipped open the book.

Theo found a chaise and moved it to the far edge of the shade, where he could have some protection from the bright sun, the Frisbee games, the geranium-red children armed with lethal-looking shovels, and the conversation of his charges. He then arranged his towel and book to his satisfaction, ascertained that beverages could be purchased from a concrete stand not too far away, and announced he would be delighted to bring drinks to those who would care for one. When no one replied, he strolled along the beach, bypassing the stand for the moment, in order to see if Mary Margaret was, as suggested by an unreliable source, engaging in an innocent diversion. For once.

The beach of the adjoining cove was covered with loose rocks and the remains of coral formations. There was a group at the far end, milling around a motorboat that bobbled in the shallow water. He saw Mary Margaret's red hair in the center of the group. After a few minutes, the crowd retreated and the boat roared into motion. It pulled away from the shore in a wide, curling line. Then, like a primeval jellyfish, a yellow parachute rose from the water and soared into the sky. Dangling from it was a decidedly flimsy apparatus supporting a red-haired passenger. Theo could hear her shrieks from where he stood, but he felt no flicker of empathy. She could not, he concluded, get into trouble at a hundred feet above the surface of the water.

As he turned away, a black man with shoulder-length braids nudged him. "You want to buy some ganja, mon? Super sinsemilla from the best producer on the island, but for you a special price."

"Ah, yes, *Cannabis sativa*," Theo said. "In the States I believe it is better known as marijuana, isn't it?"

The man grinned. "Yes, mon, they call it grass, pot, weed, dope, Maryjane, all kind of name. Sinsemilla is the very best, though, and grown to be very, very strong. You want to buy a nice little package?"

"Cultivation is illegal in Jamaica, as is possession. Do I

look the sort to commit a felony while a guest on your island?"

"No problem, mon. The cops don't bother nobody for a little ganja, especially not tourists. Taking it back through customs is another matter, another matter if I do say so. But Jamaican Gold sell very well in the States, and if you get it home, you could afford to buy yourself some nice new clothes."

Theo glanced down at his hibiscus-covered chest. "Thank you very much for the suggestion, but I do not believe I wish to purchase any ganja today. Perhaps another time."

He bought a cup of watery punch and returned to his chosen spot in the shade, pondering the casual encounter with the dope-seller. His travel book had mentioned the ease with which one could, if one chose, acquire the illegal organic matter in Jamaica, but he was somewhat surprised that he had been approached within his first few minutes on the beach.

He was nearly asleep when he heard Mary Margaret's high-pitched voice drawing near the cluster of chaises. She was describing the absolutely incredible thrill of parasailing, how she simply had never had such an experience, how it was almost sexual. Theo did not open his eyes. He did, however, when she added that she had met a divine man and everybody simply had to meet him or she would be devastated beyond belief.

Praying it would not be the braided dope-seller, Theo sat up and turned to look over his shoulder at Mary Margaret's new friend. The man, in his fifties or perhaps a bit older, had shaggy white hair, bushy eyebrows, and a florid but affable face. His nose was red, from either the sun or the availability of rum punches on the beach. He wore baggy khaki shorts, a T-shirt that suggested an obscene activity, and a wrinkled beach jacket. Darkly tinted sunglasses masked his eyes.

116

"Dorrie Caldicott, Bitsy Bigelow, Sandy Whitcombe, my despicable twin brother, Trey, and Theo Bloomer, who's our chaperone," Mary Margaret said, making the rounds with the ease of a hostess at a cocktail party. "You met Biff over by the boat. Everybody, this is Jackson Spitzberg. He's a movie producer from the West Coast, down here to scout locations for a wonderful new movie he's going to shoot this summer. Isn't that exciting?"

Bitsy and Sandy agreed that it was exciting. Trey muttered an acknowledgment of the introduction, but Dorrie merely fluttered a hand without looking up from her book. The producer came across the sand toward Theo, his hand extended.

"Jackson Spitzberg's the name. Nice to meet you, Bloomer," he said in a hearty voice thick with Hollywood warmth.

Theo ignored the hand. "What in blazes are you doing here?" he growled so that the others could not overhear.

"Scouting locations like the little girl said. I've got a dynamite concept for one of those old-fashioned epics, with ripped bodices, romantic rape scenes under the tropical stars, a slave revolt, a slobbering pirate or two for color, and maybe a hurricane for the climax. It's a hell of a concept, a real slam dunker if I say so myself. Don't you think the cinema public is ready for a return to the golden days of filmmaking, Bloomer?"

"You are full of it," Theo said coldly. "Perhaps the beach public is ready for the information that you're CIA, Sitermann. Perhaps I'll ask the gentleman with the motorboat to tow a banner across the sky. On the other hand, bellowing those three magic letters may just do the trick. Shall we conduct a small experiment?"

"Hey, Bloomer, don't get all riled up. Why don't we find a quiet place at the bar inside and do a rum punch or two? We'll

117

shoot the bull about the good old days together on the kib-butz, then—"

"The good old days when my niece was accused of murder? The good old days when she and I were blown down the side of a mountain by a duo of sociopathic terrorists?" Theo shook his head. "I don't think we're thinking of the same time period, Sitermann, nor do I think I wish to shoot anything, including bull, movies, or even a Magnum, with you over a rum punch. I prefer the concept of leaping to my feet to point an accusatory finger at you while shouting 'CIA?' in mock disbelief."

"Be a sport, Bloomer. I'll tell you as much as I can; I swear it on my grandpappy's Swiss bank account."

Theo took off his bifocals and polished them with a corner of his shirt. Once he had replaced them, he looked up with a disillusioned smile. "Oh, Sitermann, you spies are all alike."

Although he might have enjoyed the spectacle of Sitermann's public exposure and subsequent embarrass-ment, Theo realized Dorrie was flipping the pages of her book at an improbable rate and was apt to look up at any moment. He mentioned the possibility to Sitermann, and they retreated to the bar inside the hotel.

Once they were seated, Theo gazed across the table at the spy. "Why are you here, Sitermann? You are not a movie pro-ducer any more than I'm the winner in a J. Edgar Hoover look-alike contest."

"Vacation, old boy. Even the pricks heading the Organiza-tion allow us a couple of weeks a year to relax, and I opted for sun and fun."

"While undercover? You'll hardly return with much of a tan. The trenchcoat, you know."

"Very amusing, but what if I'm not undercover? How do you know this isn't the real me?"

"There is no real you," Theo said, shaking his head. "But I am most distressed to find you here, and I want to know exactly what you're up to. The coincidence is unnerving. You are not, and I repeat, not here for sun and fun; you are here on assignment and I insist on knowing what it is."

"But it is a coincidence—a bloomin' coincidence, if you'll excuse my little pun." Sitermann downed his drink and beckoned to the waiter for a refill. "You haven't touched your drink. Chug-a-lug and I'll spring for another—expense accounts being what they are. God bless the American taxpayers."

"I don't believe you. I wouldn't believe you if you were giving a eulogy at your grandmother's grave," said Theo. The customary mildness was gone, and the ensuing steeliness seemed to unravel Sitermann enough to wipe the amiable smile off his face. He tugged on his nose as his eyebrows met to form a bushy white hedgerow.

"Okay, okay, I can tell you want to play hardball. You've been in my shoes and you—"

"I beg your pardon. I can assure you that I've never been in your shoes, and I resent the presumption."

"Sure you do, Bloom. That's why there's a ten-foot gap in your résumé when you apparently fell off the face of the earth. I swear, one of these days I'm going to nail the agency that will admit having used you for some damn fool covert operation."

"I wish you success. Would you please continue?"

"Yeah." Sitermann sighed. "You know damn well that I can't breach security, but maybe this much will help. I'm on loan via the DEA to assist the Jamaican boys in doing a little something about the drug scene. The locals are downright ambivalent about cutting off the flow, since dope ranks right after tourism in feeding the economy. It's the number one cash crop and the number one export; rum doesn't even come close. Nearly one hundred percent of it goes to the U.S., and the street value's probably more than two and a half billion dollars. There are some plantations back in the mountains, complete with irrigation systems and private runways, that would blow your mind. I'm surprised they haven't formed a growers' association to lobby for protection."

"And this has nothing to do with my presence on the island—or my niece's?"

"Not unless the two of you are planning to smuggle a couple of pounds of sinsemilla back to the bridge club in Connecticut. I swear on my hypothetical grandmother's grave that I had no idea you were in Jamaica, Bloomer. There was not one mention of it in the briefings I received." Sitermann blinked with great earnestness. "When I saw you on the beach, I was as startled as a virgin in the backseat of a '57 Chevy, but as she was reputed to say, you never know what'll pop up. What are you doing here, old man—seeking your lost youth?"

Theo reluctantly explained his presence. "But," he added once Sitermann stopped laughing, "why are you pulling this nonsense about being a movie producer? I think I preferred you in the role of Hopalong Cassidy on the Israeli range."

"Potential starlets. It's amazing what soft young things will do for a bit part in a movie. Their honey-colored eyes just brim with gratitude when I promise a screen test back in L.A., and they can't do enough to thank me for even considering them. Why, that red-haired girl squealed louder than a BMW when I told her about the epic. I'm thinking about calling it *Desire Under the Palms*, but I seem to think it's been used. What do you think, Bloom?"

"I think it's a wonderful title," Mary Margaret said as she suddenly sat down in the chair between them. She propped her elbows on the table and gave him a soulful smile. "When will you start filming, Mr. Spitzberg?"

"Call me J.R., honey. The 'J' stands for 'just' and the 'R' stands for 'rich.' I can't say for certain when we'll go into production, but the bottom line is pretty damn quick if we want to impact the Christmas releases. I talked to Racquel's agent last night, but she's tied up with another project, very hush-hush. Mia refuses to leave the East Coast, Jane's not quite right for the concept, and I'm leaning toward someone with a little more pizzazz than Meryl. Someone with hair the color of the Caribbean sunset, with eyes the sultry emerald green of the tropical rain forest, with bazooms that just don't stop. Someone Travolta can sink his teeth into, if you're with me on this, honey."

Mary Margaret was having difficulty breathing. "That sounds totally fascinating, J.R., totally. Why don't you tell me all about your problems, and I'll rack my brain to help you out?"

Theo stood up. "Thanks for the drink, old boy. I'm going back to take a little nap in the sun while you two try to think of a way to persuade Mia to migrate. But I will keep your earlier comments in mind, and if I ever learn you were not telling the truth, I'll rack my brain, too. Or hire a skywriter. How much can three letters cost?"

As he left, he heard Mary Margaret issuing an invitation to Sitermann-Spitzberg to come by the villa for a drink that evening. To his regret, but not his surprise, he heard an acceptance. He was not convinced that Sitermann had been truthful, but there was no action dictated until he learned otherwise. Except for warning Dorrie, of course, who had met the CIA agent under less tropical conditions and would recognize him as easily as she could identify a single drop of designer perfume. From fifty feet, upwind.

He saw Dorrie standing knee-deep in the water, with Biff nearby to protect her should some presumptuous sea life endanger her petunia pink toenails. They were talking in what appeared to be a friendly fashion, which gave Theo a fragile hope that they had resolved the Mary Margaret issue and might cease the squabbling. He returned to his chaise lounge and dusted the sand off his book. He could not, however, engross himself in the description of the bromeliads indigenous to the island, and he found himself observing his niece and her fiancé with a small frown.

When the two came out of the water, Theo gestured for Dorrie to join him. "Have you and Biff arrived at an understanding?" he asked quietly.

"He says he was just being polite. I pointed out as nicely as possible—considering certain appalling recent events—that he was being obsequious and snively and oblivious to my presence. After all, I am supposed to be the center of his attention. He has no business oiling anyone but me." Dorrie permitted herself a brief smile. "He had no choice but to agree, since it was perfectly clear who was right, and he swore he would do better. We're going dancing tonight at some tremendously expensive place so that he can attempt to make amends. He also mentioned a darling little necklace that I've had my eye on for some time, so I suppose I'll be magnanimous this one time. After all, we're practically engaged."

"Congratulations. By the way, a most astonishing thing happened earlier, and I wanted to warn you, my dear."

"Mary Margaret repented, enrolled in a convent—and they took her?"

Theo told her. After a pause, Dorrie gave him a sharp look. "Did you believe him, Uncle Theo? I don't want to say anything tacky about your friend from the CIA, but I found him most unreliable. Do you recall that ghastly plaid cowboy shirt he wore one evening? And those gold-plated chains that he must have ordered from the back of a comic book? Really, he did not seem the least bit credible last summer, and I see no reason why you ought to believe him now."

"Then what would you have me believe?"

She flipped her hair back and sighed. "Good point. I certainly don't want to consider the possibility that I shall go through life being tailed by a spy in a polyester cowboy shirt."

"Nor do I," Theo said. "Mary Margaret has invited our pal Sitermann, who's currently using the alias J. R. Spitzberg, to the villa for a drink this evening, and I would imagine he does not want his true identity announced to the group. I suppose I shall comply."

"As long as he doesn't wear a leisure suit, I won't expose him. But I think you ought to keep an eye on him, Uncle Theo. There's something about him that makes me feel he's not to be trusted."

Uncle Theo agreed.

Eli shuttled them back to the villa in time to shower and dress for their guests. When Theo reached the terrace, he noted that all three girls had spent considerable time with their hair and makeup, in honor of either the count or the Hollywood producer. Or both. On the contrary, Sandy and Biff were in shorts and T-shirts, barefooted, and totally uninterested in the cocktail party, if one were to believe their pointedly bored expressions. Trey was slumped in a chair, engaged in what appeared to be an unsuccessful attempt to get an itsy bitsy spider up a waterspout.

Theo poured himself a glass of rum punch from the omnipresent pitcher and took a seat in a shady corner. He was relieved when Gerry's station wagon honked at the foot of the driveway. Eli appeared to open the gate, but before he could reclose it, a slim man with strikingly thick white hair came around the corner and up the driveway. His tanned face was in sharp contrast to his white suit, pastel blue shirt, and pale gray tie, and he walked with the air of an explorer in a cinematic jungle. His nose was sharp, his forehead high, his cheeks concave, and his smile perfectly shaped to convey the appropriate combination of charm and wry amusement. All three girls gulped. The boys settled for sneers that went unnoticed by everyone but Theo.

The apparition joined Gerry as she came up the steps to the terrace. "This," she announced, "is your neighbor, Hal D'Orsini. He is a rogue and a scoundrel, and the only reason he's not a pirate is that he doesn't want to risk ruining the crease in his trousers." She went around the group, murmuring names.

"I am delighted to meet you," he said with a small bow that produced three more gulps from the distaff faction. "I hope I shall have the pleasure of your company often during the week, and that you will feel *mi casa es su casa.* And Mr. Bloomer, how kind of you to take time off to chaperone the group. They are quite fortunate to have the benefit of your company."

His voice was carefully melodious, with a vague Bostonian undertone and a dash of British upper class. It was the voice Theo had heard, well . . . overheard, the previous evening. The voice of the man accused of being a gigolo. Theo acknowledged the introduction with a nod.

Trey roused himself to light a cigarette from the butt in his hand. "So you were at Harvard with Uncle Billy, old chap? I've heard some truly inspirational stories about the good old days and some of your pranks."

"Indeed." Hal sat down and accepted a glass from Dorrie, whose eyes were brighter than those of a stuffed animal. "Billy Bob and I had quite a time, but that was years ago when we were mischievous boys. You must tell me how you find our island paradise. Have you had an opportunity to explore the ghetto dubbed MoBay, or have you idled away your hours on the beach?"

Mary Margaret began to describe her adventure on the parasail, not failing to mention how it was, if one could imagine, almost sexual. In the midst of her breathless recitation, J. R. Spitzberg strolled up the driveway, but unlike his dashing predecessor, he was panting as he reached the terrace and his nose would have rivaled a chrysanthemum (Dark Flamingo) for redness.

Mary Margaret arranged the chairs so that she was between the two guests. She introduced her divine new friend from the West Coast, then leaned back and crossed her legs, very much the cat eyeing a bowl of cream. Or, Theo amended, the same cat eyeing a pair of plump little chipmunks. Dorrie lifted an eyebrow at Sitermann's seersucker jacket, but produced a polite smile before turning back to study Hal D'Orsini.

"Have you made any plans for tomorrow?" Gerry asked. "I was going to suggest you use the company's van for an outing to Ocho Rios. You can see Columbus Bay and climb the Dunn's River waterfall, and there's a large open-air market."

"Climb?" Dorrie echoed, zeroing in on the pertinent word. "As in scrambling up a bunch of rocks while water and moss and God knows what else drips on your head? That sounds physical."

Hal leaned across the table to pat her hand. "It's terribly touristy, but there are guides to help you and it's quite safe. I suspect you've got a firm little body under that charmingly delicate surface."

Biff growled, but Dorrie squelched any potential comments with a stern look. "I was the captain of the field hockey team at school," she allowed in a modest voice. "For three years in a row, actually. I protested, but everyone absolutely insisted and I was forced to accept the position. I do enjoy the right sports, but I'm not at all sure I want to climb places where snakes and lizards congregate."

"Or slime," Bitsy added, wrinkling her nose.

Hal gave Dorrie's hand a squeeze before settling back. "I'll tell you what, children. I've got an appointment over that way tomorrow, and I was thinking about running over in my boat. I could pick you up at the pier later in the afternoon and give you a lift back here."

"Oh?" Bitsy, Mary Margaret, and Dorrie said in unison. The three gulps brought the total to nine thus far.

"What about the van?" said Sandy. Biff and Trey nodded savagely, as if someone else's property constituted their major concern in life. Theo knew better, but he was intrigued by the new twists in the plot. As was Gerry, apparently.

"Don't worry about the van," she said. "Eli can take you to the pier, then bring the van back and wait for you here."

"What kind of boat do you have, D'Orsini?" Sitermann-Spitzberg asked suddenly.

"Nothing special, just a little seventy-foot runabout. Sleeps eight, but it's crowded with any more than that. I use it for fishing, or to flee when I feel inundated with tedious people."

"How far can you flee?"

Hal stared across the clutter of glasses on the table. "It's hardly the *QE II*, but it's adequate for my simple pleasures. Are you thinking of picking up one for yourself?"

"Yeah," Sitermann-Spitzberg said, finishing his drink and pouring another. He drank half of it, made a face, and put down the glass. "Just a little runabout to do Catalina when

126

the mood strikes. My office at the studio can be a madhouse. The writers, the directors, the actors, the endless stream of agents, lunches, openings, the whole crazy Hollywood scene —it can be migraine city, if you follow me on this one."

"Really?" said Hal, still staring.

There was an uncomfortable moment of silence. Mary Margaret swiveled her head like a weather vane, then clapped her hands. "Well, it's all settled! We'll do this waterfall thing, shop, and come back on Count D'Orsini's boat. I think it'll be fantastic."

When Dorrie and Bitsy agreed, the boys seemed to accept the inevitable. Theo, determined to keep a prudent eye on Mary Margaret, murmured that it did sound like a pleasant outing.

"Then it's a date," Hal said, standing up. "I must run along now, but I'll pick you up in Ochos Rios at four. We'll nibble on caviar and crackers, sip a little champagne, and perhaps catch the sunset on the way back. If there's anything I can do in the meantime, feel free to toss a note over the fence or give me a buzz. Until tomorrow, *ciao*."

Gerry excused herself and went with him to the foot of the driveway. Theo watched them as they halted near the curb for what appeared to be a slightly unhappy exchange.

Dorrie gave Biff a piercing look. "Well, shall we change now so we can leave as soon as we've finished dinner?"

Mary Margaret wrenched her eyes off the figures below. "Where are you going?"

"The biggest hotel we can find," Biff said, oblivious to Dorrie's darkening expression. "We thought we'd hunt up some calypso music and dance the night away. Why don't you all come along?"

"Biff," Dorrie began, "I thought—"

"Come on, honey, we'll have more fun if everyone comes

along for the ride. It'll be a blast. Trey?"

"Sure. I can't think of anything more amusing than watching Magsy pick up men in a bar. Once she graduates, she's going to open the Miss Magsy School of Seduction."

Bitsy smiled at him. "At least she'll graduate, which is more than I can say about others of us. But I guess I'll go along for the ride."

"I'm going to pass," Sandy said. "My head's still blown out from last night, and I'm going to have to pace myself if I want to get in any golf this week. Beddy-bye for this boy."

"Pooper," Bitsy said, pursing her lips. "I don't think that's very nice. But if you're going to stay here, maybe I will, too. I never go to bars without an escort; it's utterly gauche."

"Why, I'd be delighted to be your escort, Miss Bitsy," Trey drawled. "In fact, I'd be downright honored if you would allow me to have the pleasure of your company. But if you're afraid you'll have too much champagne and start crawling all over me again, you'd better stay here."

"Crawl all over you? I wouldn't even walk on you if they flattened you with a bulldozer and carpeted Tiffany's with you."

Trey wiggled his eyebrows. "So you say, Miss Bitsy, but I hear the doubt in your voice, the little whisper in the back of your mind that you might not be able to control yourself around me."

"I refuse to be manipulated by your crude remarks. I have decided to go dancing, but don't flatter yourself that you'll get within twenty feet of me. I think I'll follow Mary Margaret's lead and pick up men in the bar. As long as they're not total pigs, they'll be preferable to you!"

"Hey," Mary Margaret protested, "let's leave *moi* out of this."

Dorrie sniffed. "If only we could."

Sitermann gave Theo a look of deep sympathy. "See you around, Bloom." He told Mary Margaret he would get back to her pronto about their little agreement, then gave the group a mock salute. "*Ciao.*"

With a sense of envy, Theo watched the spy amble down the driveway. Sitermann had the freedom to spend a quiet evening with a book, or to sit in solitude and watch the stars above the dark water. He could seek out a companion for conversation, engage in a hand or two of pinochle, or even enjoy an early retirement.

Theo, on the other hand, was going dancing.

It was no more dreadful than he had anticipated, although certainly no less so. With some amount of grumbling about the tight squeeze, they managed to fit in the little car. Eli drove them to a mammoth pink hotel with a tile roof and well-lit palm trees. The bar was outside, which helped him to survive the band. Calypso it was not. Dorrie patiently explained the premise of heavy metal, then jiggled away with Biff most of the evening. Mary Margaret settled for dancing with a group of boys at the next table, but faithfully returned to both her drink and Theo's relief. Bitsy and Trey sat at opposite ends of the table, producing cold smiles and cheap shots with sporadic indifference.

By midnight the group agreed to leave. Biff went to the parking lot and returned shortly to say Eli was not waiting for them.

"But I'm ready to go right now," Dorrie said. "He was supposed to wait for us; that is what he gets paid for, isn't it?"

"I suppose we could call," Bitsy said, wrinkling her nose. "We'd have to wake Sandy, but he won't mind. After all, we can hardly walk to the villa. It's uphill."

Dorrie picked up her purse. "You call, Biff. We'll wait in front of the hotel." She then herded everyone across the patio and down a sandy sidewalk. Within a few minutes, Eli appeared in the beige car.

"Sorry, folks," he said, grinning at them, as he got out.

"You might reread your job description," Dorrie muttered as she climbed in the car. Biff came out of the hotel and obediently leapt in beside her, murmuring apologies for whatever sin he might have committed.

"Oh, I know exactly what I'm supposed to do," Eli said. "And I've been working real hard, miss."

As the others got in the car, Theo studied Eli, who beamed back with an immensely smug expression. "You haven't indulged in any substances that might impair your ability to drive, have you?" Theo asked, prudently.

"No problem, Mr. Bloomer. I'm as pure as the day my mammy birthed me. This boy doesn't do drugs." His face sobered. "I realize that drugs are a serious problem here in Jamaica, and I hate to see kids and grown men wasting their lives with tokes of ganja. Even the Rastafarians, who claim ganja is a part of their religious rituals, get a little too mellow."

"Uncle Theo, we are waiting," Dorrie said from the backseat. "I may develop serious circulation problems in my right leg if we sit here much longer. Good Lord, Mary Margaret, have your thighs always been this flabby?"

Aware that he was putting his life on the line, Theo ignored her. "I, too, am aware of the problem, Eli. For the moment, we should allow these kids to retire to their beds, but I would be most interested in continuing the conversation when we have the opportunity."

"No problem," Eli said, once again grinning as he opened the door for Theo. "And now, home, Jeeves. Park Avenue South, here we come."

Theo closed his eyes for the drive home.

The following morning they began to gather on the terrace after breakfast. Theo had equipped himself with a guidebook that explained the geological significance of the limestone that formed Dunn's River Falls, although he had little hope anyone would be particularly interested. He took his coffee to a corner to reread the section.

Dorrie came out on the balcony. "Uncle Theo, did you tell the help that we'll be out all day? Once they've cleaned, they have no reason to hang about idling. You might as well give them the afternoon off."

"Very thoughtful," Theo answered. "I shall do so before we leave."

Dorrie bent down, then stood up with a black plastic circle in her hand. "Whatever can this be?"

Trey squinted up at her. "A Ritz cracker with gangrene or a lens cap from a camera, I would guess. Have you girls been snapping photos of the chap next door—for *Playgirl* magazine?"

Bitsy looked up from a magazine. "You are disgusting. Count D'Orsini, on the other hand, is a gentleman, and we would never invade his privacy. Where did that come from, Dorrie? Has someone been in our room?"

"Let me ask Mary Margaret if it's hers." Dorrie went inside, then returned with a worried expression. "Mary Margaret didn't bring a camera. Neither did I, for that matter. It would disrupt my lines. Could this be yours, Bitsy?"

"Cameras are *a la bourgeoisie*. I wouldn't be caught dead with one. There are people who actually sit around living rooms drinking beer and looking at other people's slides, but I'd rather wear generic than bore people to death with such nonsense."

Dorrie frowned at the lens cap. "Well, it wasn't here before we went to the hotel last night, because I came out for a moment to towel-dry my hair. Mr. Robert seems to think excessive blow-drying is responsible for these insidious split ends, so I've been avoiding it whenever remotely possible. Where did this come from? Do you think someone was on the balcony last night?"

"That's a thoroughly icky thought," Bitsy said. "Do you think some sleazy sort was lurking out there to take photographs of us while we undressed?"

Sandy came through the doorway from the dining room. "Can I see the proofs?"

Dorrie held up the lens cap. "Is this yours? I found it on the balcony, and we're trying to decide if someone might have been prowling last night while we were gone."

He shook his head. "No, I didn't even bring a camera. Why should I waste my precious time taking photographs of trees and flowers, when I could utilize the time drinking?"

Theo saw no reason to mention his camera, since he was confident that the lens cap was in its proper place. He was as curious as Dorrie, however, about the mysterious appearance of the object. Looking at Sandy, he said, "You were here last night. Did you happen to hear anything out of the ordinary?"

"No, sir, not a thing. I had a couple of beers by the pool, then took a magazine to bed to study the centerfold. All quiet on the Caribbean front, so to speak."

"And the gate remained locked until we returned at midnight?"

"I guess so, sir," Sandy said, shrugging. "I didn't hear anything or see any headlights in the driveway."

"You were here the entire time?" Theo persisted. When Sandy nodded, he closed his book and stood up. "I am disturbed that someone might have gained access to the balcony. I think I shall question Eli about the key and the security arrangements, and I suggest all of you check your belongings to ascertain if anything might be missing. I shall also call Gerry and report the incident, although I imagine she can do nothing."

Dorrie again went for the pertinent word. "Missing? I didn't think to look through my jewelry! What if someone took my dinner ring or the locket Biff gave me? I would have a coronary, literally, and Daddy would be furious." She was muttering about escalating insurance rates as she disappeared into the bedroom.

Mary Margaret, Bitsy, and Sandy departed to do as Theo suggested, all three looking upset. When Biff came onto the terrace, Theo told him what had transpired.

"Good God," Biff said, staring at the balcony. "I brought a camera at Dorrie's insistence, since she wanted a few shots of herself on the beach and so forth, but I was just putting in a new roll of film and my lens cap was there. Why would someone be on the balcony, anyway? The view's okay if you like that sort of thing, but it hardly seems worth the risk simply to shoot the ocean."

"And at night," Theo said, equally puzzled. They sat in silence until the others joined them. No one reported anything missing.

"It couldn't have been a burglar," Dorrie said. "He would not have overlooked the diamond dinner ring Daddy gave me for my birthday last year. I don't know how many carats it is, but it weighs an absolute ton."

"Maybe it was a sickly burglar," Trey said. "Maybe he forgot to bring a crane to lift the thing, and was so devastated that he simply took a photograph of it for his album and slithered away."

"Or maybe he thought it was paste," Mary Margaret said, yawning. "I know I did the first time I saw it. Are you sure it's not a rhinestone, Dorrie?"

"Mary Margaret Ellison, are you insinuating that I am incapable of recognizing a diamond when I see one?"

Theo held up his hand. "Please, girls, we must decide what action, if any, we intend to take. Eli should appear with the van at any moment, and I will discuss the key situation with him. However, since nothing has been stolen, we may have to simply forget about it."

"What about that so-called gold chain you wore last night?" Dorrie said to Mary Margaret. "Are you going to claim it's anything but tinted aluminum foil?"

"I didn't want to bring any of my good stuff."

"I thought you hocked the family jewels to bail out that Hell's Angel you were so fond of," Trey said. "I did stumble across a bundle of pawn tickets one morning."

"While pawing through my underwear drawer?"

"However did you guess?"

Bitsy banged down her purse. "That's disgusting. I'm beginning to find your remarks too tacky for words."

A van pulled up the driveway before Trey could manage a counter. Theo went to speak to Amelia and Emelda, who accepted the afternoon off without argument. He then went to question Eli about security.

"I've got a key, and the office has one," Eli said. "I made sure the gate was locked behind us, and there's no way anyone could get inside the fence. But what's this about, Mr. Bloomer?"

"There was some indication that someone was prowling here last night, which is distressing for all of us. Sandy said he heard no one, yet the evidence is clear that someone went to the second floor and entered the girls' bedroom. Did you happen to come back to the villa while we were at the hotel?"

"No, sir, I just went to visit some friends. What's this evidence you mentioned?"

"A lens cap was found on the balcony. It really is puzzling, since it implies someone was taking photographs in the dark. Otherwise, the lens cap would have been noticed and retrieved. One would need a very expensive lens, but that would be a peculiar *modus operandi* for a cat burglar."

"You're right," Eli said, frowning at the balcony. "You seem to know quite a bit about playing detective. I thought I heard one of the kids say you were some kind of florist."

Theo took off his bifocals to polish them. "Yes, but I'm presently retired." He did not elucidate.

The others came outside to get in the van. After several minutes of jostling and acerbic comments about preferred seats and flabby thighs, Eli backed down the driveway and turned toward the coastal road that led to Ochos Rios. Theo noted, before he closed his eyes, that he seemed to be smiling to himself. Curious.

Chapter Three

The road curved along the coastline, cutting through villages that evoked shudders from the backseat of the van, then veering back to the rocky beaches dotted with swirls of deflated algae, birds, decaying fish, yellowish foam, and splintery skeletons of abandoned boats. A voice from the rear commented that the hotel beaches were the only *raison d'etre* for the island; another pointed out that these beaches were open to just anyone and what did one expect—Cannes?

Potholes were abundant, as were subcompacts and buses packed to the roof with Jamaicans. Speed limit signs seemed to serve only as targets for mud balls and spray paint. Chickens and children played at the edge of the road. Dogs lay in the dust, some resting for the moment and others resting for all eternity. Eli kept up a cheerful stream of chatter despite what Theo felt were brushes with death every forty-five seconds or so.

They stopped at Columbus Park to gaze at rusty cannons amid the flowers. Theo had found the pertinent page in the guidebook when Dorrie announced she was hot, thirsty, and not especially interested in a bunch of corroded war toys. Sighing, he followed the group back to the van, reminding himself that Caldicotts were intrigued with history only when it related to the trunk of the family tree. Columbus may have happened onto the continent, but the passengers on the *Mayflower* were much more relevant at the monthly DAR meetings.

Dunn's River Falls did merit a few appreciative murmurs,

however. Surrounded by a verdant hillside park dotted with flower beds, ice cream stalls, and souvenir shops, the water splashed and glittered as it spilled down a series of limestone pools. Snaking lines of tourists picked their way up the rocks, led by muscular black guides whose chests were invisible under dozens of cameras.

The girls assessed the situation and all agreed they had no intention of climbing anything, for any reason, at any time in the foreseeable future. Mary Margaret announced that she was going to the ladies' room or would simply explode. Theo joined the other two girls on a bench, while the boys went down wooden steps to the bottom of the falls.

"I cannot understand why Biff insists on this sort of reckless behavior," Dorrie said, "and I find it excruciatingly childish. If something were to happen to him, I would be left in the lurch socially all summer, and the idea of hospital visits is appalling; the ghastly shade of pea green and all those medicinal odors make me quite ill to my stomach. Anyway, I thought machismo went out with the seventies, along with pet rocks and Democrats."

Bitsy watched a plump woman in a floral print tent waddle past, then said, "Well, I cannot understand why that real estate agent thought we ought to come here, for that matter. We could have spent a perfectly civilized day shopping and having lunch at a nice hotel, but now we're stuck here for what may be hours. The people here are too tacky for words, and there are probably mosquitoes and snakes under every leaf."

"She may have overestimated your inclination for athletics," Theo said. "The climb doesn't seem all that challenging; many of the participants are less than perfect specimens, but all of them seem to be enjoying themselves."

Dorrie dabbed her forehead with a tissue. "I don't see how

they could possibly enjoy anything in this heat. They're bound to perspire, no matter how frigid the water is. Bitsy's right. This Gerry person is a loon for suggesting this trip."

"She seems quite sensible to me," Theo protested.

"Oh, she's divine. I especially like the pink eyeshadow. Have you noticed the size of her feet, Uncle Theo? She could rent out her shoes for deep-sea fishing trips."

"And that quaint little mustache," Bitsy added, "reminds me ever so much of Groucho Marx. Or perhaps Adolf Hitler."

"Don Johnson," Dorrie said, giggling.

Bitsy shook her finger. "But we mustn't be tacky. One couldn't help noticing her shoes are Gucci and that silk blouse she wore yesterday must have cost two hundred dollars. I picked up a pair of sunglasses exactly like hers in Rome for absolutely billions of lire. Daddy about died until the storekeeper did the arithmetic. You must concede she dresses well for someone who is employed." Dorrie took up the financial appraisal of Gerry's wardrobe.

Theo was nearly asleep when Dorrie tapped him on the shoulder. "Bitsy's gone to get sodas," she said, "and I want to ask you something while we're alone. I know Sitermann told you that his presence was a coincidence, but I was wondering if he might have been responsible for the lens cap I found this morning. It is rather spyish."

"That's a legitimate observation, my dear. I contemplated the same possibility, but I can't seem to resolve the problem of access to the villa. Eli says there are only two keys, one of which is always with him and the other at the real estate office. How would our CIA pal get hold of a key—and why would he be taking photographs from the balcony?"

"It was only a thought," Dorrie said crossly. "I'm much too hot to deal with details. Maybe he wanted a particular view of the moonlight and needed to get up high. Having seen the fence earlier, he bribed Eli to loan him the key. Eli left the parking lot because he knew he couldn't drive us to the villa until Sitermann brought back the key."

"The latter makes some sense, but I doubt the view from the balcony is any more spectacular than from other locales on the hillside. One could walk up the hill and achieve the same effect—without bribery, stealth, and the very real danger of getting arrested for burglary."

Dorrie shivered at the reference to unnecessary ambulation. "Then you tell me why someone was taking pictures from the balcony. If it had been light and Count D'Orsini had been doing laps, I could understand. In *vino veritas*, I might have snapped a few myself, although I'll deny ever saying that if you breathe so much as a word of it."

Theo gravely assured her he would never breathe a word of it. "I will speak to Eli once more about his key," he continued, "and try again to reach Gerry about the office copy. She was out of her office this morning. I don't think our visitor was Sitermann, though. For one thing, he has no motive, and for another, he's too well-trained to leave equipment behind. The CIA doesn't tolerate sloppiness, except perhaps in bookkeeping matters and expense accounts."

"CIA?" The bushes behind them rustled, then Bitsy appeared with three cans of soda. "Then he's not really a hot-shot Hollywood producer? Mary Margaret will just die when she finds out she's wasted all that drool over a counterfeit."

"Oops," Dorrie said under her breath.

It took Theo nearly ten minutes to convince Bitsy that she should not tell Mary Margaret, or anyone else, the truth about J. R. Spitzberg, sham movie mogul extraordinaire. Visibly disappointed, Bitsy at last agreed to save the revelation for a future time, when the information would not jeopardize the drug investigation operation.

"Where is Mary Margaret?" Dorrie asked after Theo had elicited a final, solemn vow. "Are there any vans with mattresses and curtains in the parking lot?"

"You don't think . . . ?" Theo said, dismayed.

"There she is!" Bitsy said, pointing at a line of waterfall climbers coming into view. "She's between Biff and Sandy. I hope the water doesn't pull off her bikini; it wouldn't take much."

Dorrie scowled, then abruptly forced a smile as Biff waved to her. "That bitch has gone too far," she said through clenched teeth. "And look at the way Biff keeps helping her up the rocks, as if she were some frail invalid. No one with thighs that thunderous is remotely frail. Enough is enough. This is more than anyone should have to tolerate."

Beside her, Bitsy was nodding savagely. Theo opted for a sigh.

Within an hour, they had regrouped at the van. Dorrie was smiling as she asked Biff about the climb, but her eyes were gray and her voice suspiciously bright. Mary Margaret interrupted to say that it was, if one could imagine, almost a religious experience. Theo waited for his niece to produce a scathing comeback, but to his surprise, she merely said she would have thought it was more, well, sexual than religious. If one could imagine.

Eli drove into Ochos Rios and parked across the street from the open-air market. He warned them about the higglers who would pester them unmercifully, then said he would wait near the van while they shopped. Dorrie seemed more cheerful as she led the expedition into the jungle.

Two hours later Theo followed the group back to the van and helped them unload armfuls of shirts, straw baskets, wood carvings (including an obscene one that Trey swore had cost next to nothing and would look perfect on the mantel next to Mother's needlepointed family crest), two steel drums, and a variety of other native crafts, despite labels mentioning various Asian countries. The girls seemed pleased with themselves, although Theo could see Dorrie was still simmering. The boys punched each other and bragged of the number of times they had been approached to buy ganja. According to them, the vendors had been nonstop.

"I hope you didn't actually purchase anything," Bitsy said.

"No problem," Trey said, pulling out of his pocket a plastic bag filled with dried green leaves. "We don't have to buy generic. This is designer quality, guaranteed to blow off your ears and the top of your head."

"Hey, mon," Eli said. He grabbed the bag out of Trey's hand and threw it in the van. "It's not cool to flash stuff on the street. You wouldn't like the local prisons."

"Trey would fit right in with the rats and lice," Bitsy said as she climbed into the van. "Think of all the little friends he could make."

"And we could pack a lunch for him," Sandy said. From a bag he took out several reddish objects and tossed one to Trey. "Perhaps they'll ripen during the trial, old man. If not, at least you won't languish in prison for the rest of your life."

"How thoughtful of you to worry about *moi's* baby brother. Let me see one," Mary Margaret said.

Before she could take one of the ackees, Eli grabbed the bag. "You kids are courting disaster. Ganja's not cool, and neither are unripened ackees. You sure you want to live till the end of the week?"

Theo took the ackee from Trey and handed it to Eli. "I

think we need to dispose of these in a prudent manner," he said firmly.

"I just bought them for a lark, sir," Sandy said, sounding more contrite than he looked, "but I'll trash them as soon as we get to the villa. I wouldn't want one of us to nibble on one as a midnight snack. Not even good old Trey, who'll eat anything when he's stoned."

Dorrie picked up the plastic bag and, with a sniff, dropped it in a corner. "I didn't realize people still fooled around with marijuana, but some of us never quite grow up, do we? I am ready for adult pleasures, such as the yacht, champagne, and civilization. Are the rest of you planning to goggle on the sidewalk like a bunch of freshmen rushees, or are you going to get in here so we can go?"

They went.

The pier was lined with boats of all sizes, most of them adorned with glossy hardwood, polished brass, expansive white decks, colorful canopies, coy names, and jovial sailors dressed in the precisely correct degree of casual elegance. Count D'Orsini's craft was no exception, nor was he, in white slacks, a silk shirt with a cravat, and a blue captain's hat. *Pis Aller* was painted on the bow in elaborate curlicues.

"Welcome aboard," he said, offering a hand to Dorrie. "Please make yourselves at home on my humble boat. The champagne is chilling, and the sun preparing itself for a spectacular display. You look especially lovely this afternoon, my dear. Do be careful with that step; I would be devastated if you turned one of those shapely ankles."

Dorrie acknowledged the obvious with a smile. "This is so kind of you, Count D'Orsini. If we had been forced to drive back on that ghastly road, I don't know what I would have done—but it wouldn't have been a pretty sight." She climbed onto the boat, producing a small girlish shriek as the deck rocked beneath her foot, and finding it necessary to steady herself with a hand on the count's shoulder.

Biff landed behind her. "Come on, Dorrie, you've sailed since you were six years old. Remember that little Sunfish we used to run around the island with? We won the junior division the first year we entered."

"That primitive thing?" Dorrie laughed. "It would have fit in the hull of this. Why, I do believe your new boat could fit down there, too, and leave room to stack a few cases of champagne."

Theo nudged Bitsy and Mary Margaret to climb aboard before Biff could offer his opinion about relative sizes. Sandy followed them, as did Trey. Theo then stepped onto the deck and shook Count D'Orsini's proffered hand. "This is indeed kind of you, sir," he said. "We are all looking forward to the cruise back to Montego Bay."

"You are quite welcome. Before we cast off, may I offer you champagne or would you prefer Perrier with lime?"

Dorrie had rediscovered her balance. "Perrier? Thank God. All we've been able to find the entire trip is some obscure local stuff. I told Bitsy I would rather die of dehydration than actually drink it."

"What a dreadful loss that would be," Count D'Orsini murmured.

Dorrie shot Biff a smile, but he had moved to the stern with Mary Margaret. As he made a low comment, the redhead's laughter caused several of the nearby sailors to stare over the rims of their martini glasses. Dorrie's jaw twitched, but the smile held steady in true Caldicott tradition. "Could I have just a sip of Perrier before we open the champagne, Count D'Orsini?" she said through an onslaught of eyelash flutters.

Theo retreated to a deck chair. The others arranged themselves for maximum comfort and visual effect, then permitted a cabin attendant to serve them champagne and toast triangles piled high with caviar. As the crew began to back the yacht out of its slip, Theo gazed at the jostling crowd at the edge of the market area. In the shadow of a stall was a figure with binoculars trained on the *Pis Aller*. The sun bounced off the lenses as they tracked the movement of the yacht, sending back a glare that caused Theo to squint in discomfort.

He waved at the figure, then settled back and accepted a glass of chilled Perrier and a triangle of toast. Sitermann. Sitermann showing an unnatural interest in Count D'Orsini's boat. Or in the count—or in a member of the crew—or in one of the passengers. Sitermann, who had sworn on his hypothetical grandmother's grave that he was on a mission completely unrelated to Theo and his sextet of preppies. Then again, Sitermann lied. Like a rug.

Wondering if any of the others had noticed the spy skulking in the shadow, Theo studied the group. Mary Margaret and Biff were still in the stern, shoulders a centimeter apart, laughing at some private joke while they gobbled down caviar as if they anticipated the advent of an unseasonal Lent. Trey was asleep in a chaise lounge. Sandy was listening intently to the captain in the bridge above the deck. Bitsy lay on a mat, supine and oblivious to anything but the continually replenished crystal glass in one hand. And Dorrie was sitting next to Count D'Orsini, her face rapt with admiration and her hand serenely tucked in his. Every few seconds, however, her eyes darted to the stern with the stealth of a professional shoplifter.

By this time they were too far out for Theo to ascertain if Sitermann was still observing them. He saw no glints of sun on lenses, nor did he see a flash of white hair in the surges of tourists among the stalls of the market. Not, of course, that it meant the spy had not taken a different post from which to follow the yacht as it moved across the water toward the edge of the bay and the sea beyond.

"Oh, Sitermann," Theo muttered softly.

The following morning Theo sat on the terrace, coffee in hand. There were stirrings of life in the villa, but no one had yet appeared for breakfast. Which was fine with him. The previous evening had been spent beside the pool, and had passed pleasantly enough despite the verbal strafing, which was beginning to seem normal if not mandatory. Dorrie had been cool but polite; Biff had responded with more than one comment about her cozy chat with the count. Mary Margaret had announced that she absolutely had to have a boat just like the *Pis Aller*, that it was just the right size for fun little runs to Bermuda, et cetera. There had been a remark about the Bermuda Triangle and with luck—but Theo had exited.

Emelda brought out a fresh pot of coffee. "Eli says you all came back on Count D'Orsini's boat last evening. He's something, isn't he?"

Theo did not think it prudent to mention that the count was possibly a gigolo, probably a fraud, and clearly adept at wooing pretty young things for his own purposes. "He was kind enough to offer us the ride on his boat. I fear I am not yet accustomed to driving on the left side of the road, and I find it most unnerving, to say the least. We did not have to deal with that on the water, for which I was grateful. How long has Count D'Orsini lived next door, Emelda?"

"Oh, he don't live there. He's watching the house for the Bradfords, who are visiting their grandbabies in California for two months. The count watches houses for all sorts of folks. I don't know for sure if he has a real house on the island."

"I hadn't realized that," Theo said.

Emelda wiped her hands on a dish towel. "Ain't his boat, either. It belongs to this writer man who had to go home to England for surgery. The count's been using the boat for nearly a year, taking rich widow women out to deep-sea fish and get drunk on champagne. One of my nephews cleans the boat every week, and he says the number of empty bottles is a scandal, not to mention the ganja and cocaine they does in the cabin. Why, if—"

"Emelda!" Amelia snapped, coming onto the terrace with a tray of coffee cups. "Why are you here gossiping with Mr. Bloomer? Don't you know you have to polish the furniture today?"

"I do know," Emelda said in a dignified voice. "I was merely answering some questions that were asked of me."

"So you say." Amelia gave Theo a frosty look as she went into the dining room. Emelda followed slowly, making it clear she was not intimidated by the cook's criticism.

Theo held in a smile until the kitchen door slammed shut. The chat had been enlightening, in some ill-defined way. The resulting information, which served to confirm the gigolo theory, was analyzed, then stored away until such time that it might be deemed of value, although Theo could not have predicted when that might be. He was musing in serene solitude when Gerry's station wagon honked at the bottom of the driveway.

When Eli failed to appear, she parked along the curb and opened the gate, which had been left unsecured and slightly ajar. She stopped halfway up the driveway and vanished from Theo's view, presumably to speak to Eli in his quarters below the pool. When she subsequently reappeared and came up the steps to the terrace, her expression was grim.

"I must do something about him," she said as she sat down. "He seems to spend more time running around than he does attending to his duties, and he should have locked the gate when he left. But that's my problem, not yours. Have you made plans for today?"

"There was some discussion about a train trip into the interior," Theo said. "I myself was interested, since it might provide an opportunity to see some of the indigenous vegetation. A four-hour trip, I was told, with a visit to a native market and a rum distillery."

"The Governor's Coach." Gerry took out a brochure from her large handbag and placed it on the table. "It may be better if I make reservations for you. Are all of you going?"

"The others have not yet come down for breakfast, but I think there was general agreement that all six of them would come. The girls were intrigued by the promise of further shopping, and the boys by the idea of unlimited sampling at the distillery. No one mentioned bromeliads or wild orchids." Theo shook his head, then gave himself a terse mental lecture about self-indulgence. "If you think we need reservations, you may count on seven of us."

Gerry went inside to telephone, and returned a few minutes later with a faint frown. "Amelia is quite distressed this morning. I do hope I can keep the villa fully staffed the rest of the week."

"I must apologize," Theo said. "I am guilty of keeping Emelda from her duties by engaging her in conversation. If you think it will help to alleviate tension, I shall apologize to either or both of them."

"Amelia isn't upset at Emelda. She found several unripened ackees on the windowsill in the kitchen, and was concerned that one of your group might eat one for some inane reason. If that should happen, nothing can be done. It is fatal."

"So's my hangover," Sandy said, coming out to the terrace

with a glass of water in his hand. "I'm going to stay away from rum for the rest of my life, or until this afternoon—whichever comes first. Did we really decide to go on a noisy, bumpy, jarring train into some primeval forest so the girls could stalk one-hundred-percent cotton skirts?"

"There was unanimous consensus late last evening, and Gerry was kind enough to make reservations for us," Theo said.

"You'll need to have Eli drive you to the train station in MoBay immediately after lunch," Gerry said. "This brochure has information about the time and route. I must run along to the office now; I have two groups coming in this afternoon, and I need to finalize the details. Have a pleasant trip, Theo."

"Thank you. Before you leave, may I ask you one small question concerning the security arrangements here?" When she nodded, he told her about the lens cap found on the balcony the previous morning and the implication that someone had gained access to the villa.

"I'm glad you told me," she said. "The office copy of the key is kept in a locked box, and no one could have used it. I was at the office most of the evening; I did have reason to check on another key, and I am quite sure the Harmony spare was in place."

Sandy cleared his throat. "I stayed in that night, and I didn't see anybody. But Eli's the logical suspect, isn't he?" He frowned at Theo. "What do you think, sir? I really don't like the idea of someone in the girls' bedroom. We could go down to Eli's room and confront him, but he's gone to the hotels to see if he can find me a *Wall Street Journal*. I play the market in a very small way."

Gerry looked at the balcony, then at the fence that shielded Count D'Orsini's villa. Her eyes narrowed appraisingly, but when she turned to Theo, her voice was light. "Did you ask the girls if they were doing a bit of surveillance?"

"We were all at the hotel that night, except for Sandy. Besides, Biff is the only one who brought a camera, and he certainly wouldn't have been using it in the dark to photograph our neighbor. I'm afraid there is a bit of jealousy involved. The count and my niece had a long, intimate conversation yesterday afternoon, and it did not sit well with young Mr. Hartley, whose nose was bent quite far out of shape as a result."

Gerry laughed. "Oh, I don't think the boy has anything to worry about, Theo. Hal is strictly superficial charm and wit; he wouldn't know what to do if he found a girl in his boudoir."

Sandy banged his glass down on the table. "Maybe Eli sneaked back here with a girlfriend for a little parallel parking." His face turned red as he noticed Gerry's mystified expression. "You know, ma'am, horizontal rumbling . . . or, ah, well . . ." He gave Theo a look of deep panic.

"Hanky-panky," Theo interpreted obligingly. "Sex."

"I am shocked, Ensign Pulver," Trey said as he came through the door from the dining room. "You'd better watch out if you don't want your lance to fall off, old boy. Animal life, diseases, petrification from lack of use. You never know, do you?" As he waggled a finger, the girls came onto the terrace.

"You are disgusting," Bitsy said.

"No argument from *moi*," Mary Margaret added.

"And I am forced to agree, for once," Dorrie said.

"Make it twice," Biff said.

"Good-bye, Theo," Gerry said with the deeply sympathetic look the lions might have given the Christians before dinnertime. "Have a good day."

Theo smiled faintly.

"I cannot believe I've survived this ordeal," Dorrie said as they stumbled up the dark driveway. "I mean, really—the idea of a four-hour train ride turning into a nightmare of such magnitude. An entire generation of mayflies could have been born and died in those so-called four hours. And the audacity of those people to call it the Governor's Coach! No one of any breeding or stature has ever set foot in that dingy car, much less allowed his name to be used in conjunction with it. Someone ought to report this scam to the American embassy."

Theo patted her on the shoulder. "There's no point in upsetting yourself any further, my dear. Trains do break down, even in the Washington-New York corridor, and—"

"For six hours, and in a place that could have provided the set for *Village of the Damned*? Even Baltimore's more civilized than that place. You know how I feel about poverty, Uncle Theo, and the locals acted as if they'd been invaded by minute green aliens in stainless steel quiche pans. It was hardly our fault that a hundred tourists were forced to sit around their so-called park for six hours!"

Biff patted the other shoulder. "But it wasn't that bad, honey. We had music and rum punch, and we didn't actually go into any of the little stores or have conversations with the natives. I rather enjoyed the dancing."

"I'm amazed that you remember anything, considering the quantity of that vile drink you poured down your throat. Hawaiian Punch and hundred-proof rum is not my idea of fun. Nor is having Mary Margaret sit in my lap, although you seemed to enjoy it. Sandy certainly enjoyed having her in his lap all the way back, although I was worried it might leave him permanently disabled." She ducked from under his hand. "I presume you will have Eli fired, if not executed,

Uncle Theo. His failure to pick us up at the station was the last straw. If you hadn't been able to unlock the gate somehow, we'd still be standing in the gutter like . . ." Her voice broke as she struggled to maintain her composure. "God only knows what it's done to my hair," she added in a ragged whisper.

"It was unconscionable," Sandy said, his arm around Bitsy's shoulder to encourage her to keep moving. "Eli should have found out the change in arrival time and been there. The girls are exhausted."

"My creases are simply spent," Trey said in a hollow voice, earning a dark look from Bitsy. "Sorry, darling, but it's the bitter truth. I hate to think what might happen if I even attempted to wear these trousers to the club on a Saturday night. Your mother would have a stroke."

"At least we'd notice. As for your mother—"

"I shall speak to Eli," Theo interrupted. "The car is here, and Eli is most likely in his room. If he cannot give me an adequate explanation of his failure to pick us up, I shall report the incident to Gerry."

Dorrie produced a cold smile. "The only adequate explanation is death—and it had better be his. If Amelia did not leave lobster salad for us, she can join Eli in the morgue. It is nearly midnight. I have had nothing to eat in the last ten hours except greasy potato chips, red liquefied sugar, and unsalted peanuts from the first century. My complexion is screaming in protest. I honestly think there will be a blemish by tomorrow if I don't take decisive action immediately."

"I'll look in the refrigerator while you shower," Theo murmured, hoping Amelia had done as directed. Dorrie was irritated enough to engage the firing squad and give the commands in person. The rest were grumbling, too, and clearly exhausted from the excursion. Theo, on the contrary, had rather enjoyed the forced delay in the small village while a second engine (reputedly equipped with functional brakes) was dispatched from Kingston, on the other side of the island. He had wandered into the forest, where he had happened to spot not only black and silver tree ferns (*Cyathea medullaris* and *Cyathea dealbata,* respectively), but also several epiphytes on a tree, including an orchid of the Oncidium family. The discovery had left him breathless for several minutes.

He had also struck up a conversation with a Jamaican boy, who, upon receipt of a few American coins, led Theo to an ackee tree so he might admire the upswept branches and dark green foliage that contrasted nicely with the reddish oval fruit. They had also chanced upon a streamer-tailed hummingbird and a flock of daffodil-colored parrots. All of which had been carefully noted in a small notebook for future reference. A satisfactory outing, although it had taken a great deal of fortitude to retain the edenic scene during the subsequent and incessant complaining during the remainder of the trip.

Eli's room was dark, and Theo's knock went unanswered. Theo went on to the kitchen, where he discovered a large bowl of lobster salad, several other salads, a bowl of fruit, and plates and silverware on the counter. He had transferred the meal to the terrace and was setting places when the others came back down from their rooms.

"What did Eli have to say, Uncle Theo?" Dorrie demanded.

"He was not in his room. He may have walked to a nearby villa to visit friends, and anticipated returning in only a minute or two to let us in."

Dorrie looked at Bitsy. "Did you check our room to see if anyone might have been prowling again? The very idea gives me a rash."

152

"My jewelry was where I left it," Bitsy said, wrinkling her forehead as she considered the possibility. "I couldn't tell if your things were undisturbed, since you've literally strewn them all over the place. While we're on the subject, have you seen my lime green polo shirt under your clothes? I wanted to wear it this morning with the matching shorts and visor, but I couldn't begin to find it."

Dorrie looked away. "I haven't seen your shirt, dear, but you ought to allow it to stay lost. Although it absolutely strickens me to say so, the green gives your skin a dreadfully sallow tint, as if you'd lost a battle to chlorophyll."

"Do you think so?" Bitsy flashed her teeth.

"Shall we open a bottle of champagne?" Theo suggested. "It would go nicely with the lobster, don't you think? And we've certainly earned a bit of pampering after today's unscheduled delay."

"Right on," Trey muttered. The others nodded.

They were eating when headlights flashed in the driveway next door. "I think we ought to invite Count D'Orsini over for a glass of champagne," Mary Margaret said. "I'll go ask him."

Dorrie nodded. "He was so kind yesterday, and we really must reciprocate as best we can, despite the limitations of the local help. Biff, why don't you pop over the fence and see if he's busy?"

"Because it's after midnight, for one thing," Biff said. "And I'm not especially fond of popping over fences, for another."

"You did quite a bit of popping this afternoon. You and Mary Margaret acted like two little kernels of popcorn in a pool of hot oil. It was too cute."

"Oh, I'll wander over and invite him," Mary Margaret said, pushing back her chair. She rearranged her hair so that it curled around her neck like a sinewy boa, then rewarded them with a complacent smile. "After all, he's practically family, since he and Uncle Billy were as tight as ticks during school. The stories Uncle Billy tells just leave me in stitches, if you can imagine."

"Religious or sexual?" Dorrie growled as Mary Margaret strolled down the driveway and disappeared through the gate. She dug into the hapless lobster, her fork clattering as she jabbed an errant mushroom. Her snort of satisfaction had its origins in the dawn of the species.

Several minutes later a figure came up the driveway, but it was neither Mary Margaret nor Count D'Orsini. Sitermann was in a tuxedo, his bowtie atilt like an ailing butterfly, his hair disheveled, his face more florid than an *Allium giganteum*.

"Thank the celebrity showcase you're still up," he puffed as he came onto the terrace. "My car died a couple of blocks away, and I wasn't about to walk back to the hotel. I barely made it here without being run down by some maniac on the wrong side of the road, like my old buddy Jack in *Easy Rider*."

"Poor baby," Dorrie said, handing him a glass of champagne. "But perhaps it'll make a good concept for a production."

"Good thought, sweetheart. I'll put in a call to the office tomorrow morning and let them toss it around, see if they can come up with anything." He gave her a guarded look, then sat back with a sigh. "You folks sure dine on the far side of midnight."

Theo related the highlights of the train trip. "It was frustrating to be forced to wait all afternoon," he concluded. "We did not have time to stop at the market and we had only a few minutes at the distillery. I suppose it was a disappointment for all of us."

"Then our driver failed to pick us up at the station, Mr. Spitzberg," Bitsy inserted. "One would almost suspect it was a CIA conspiracy to ruin our day. All that waiting, no shopping, a tiny paper cup of rum—and then kamikaze taxis back to the villa. Can you put that in your epic movie, Mr. Spitzberg?"

The spy glanced at Theo, who could only shrug in response. "I'll keep it in mind," he said at last. "What a great possibility you've got here. Can you visualize the camera doing a slow pan across the bay, then zooming in inch by inch for a lingering, erotic shot of the moonlight on the water?" He formed three sides of a rectangle with his thumbs and forefingers, and played camera for their benefit, making appreciative noises under his breath.

Dorrie was not interested in hypothetical camera sweeps. "What happened to Mary Margaret? She's had enough time to offer the invitation, do a striptease, and take on the entire fleet."

"That she has," Trey contributed. "I've timed her before."

Theo waited until Bitsy had deemed him disgusting, then stood up and tried to peer over the fence. There were a few lights visible, but no sound of either voices or music. "I'd better see if she . . . has, shall we say, been diverted," he said unhappily.

"Let me go, sir," Sandy said. "You might twist your ankle going down the driveway in the dark. It should only take me a second."

Theo agreed, since he wasn't sure he would be pleased with whatever he would find on Count D'Orsini's property in terms of behavior, dress, or some lack thereof. Dorrie and Bitsy exchanged sly smiles and wiggled eyebrows. With a few uneasy glances at Bitsy, Spitzberg continued to study possible camera angles through his hands, pointing out the superb juxtaposition of light and dark, of structure and nature, of purity and eroticism. Theo found it entertaining, if totally nonsensical. At least the spy was trying.

Sandy returned with Count D'Orsini, who appeared worried. "I say," he said to Theo, "did one of your gals actually say she was coming over to my villa a while back?"

"Mary Margaret went down the driveway about ten minutes ago to invite you over for a glass of champagne. It couldn't have taken her more than half a minute to arrive at your door. Are you implying she did not appear?" Theo stared at Sandy. "Could she have stumbled and fallen into the shrubbery at the foot of the driveway, perhaps hitting her head on a rock?"

Biff scrambled up. "I'll look, Mr. Bloomer. Good lord, she couldn't have gotten lost along the way. It's not more than a hundred and fifty feet down our drive and up the one next door."

"Mary Margaret is a gal of many talents," Trey said, covering a yawn. "However, she was booted out of Girl Scouts. There was something about the husband of the troop leader, a double sleeping bag, and a leaky pup tent. She was devastated when they took away her merit badge. She swore she had earned it through diligence, if nothing else."

Theo turned to Trey. "One more word from you, and you will no longer be known as an adorable Ellison. Is that clear?" After receiving a surprised nod, Theo told Biff and Sandy to take a flashlight and search the area between the two villa gates and all of Count D'Orsini's yard.

"But, Bloomer, old chap," the count said, rubbing his hands together as he paced the length of the terrace, "shouldn't we call the police or something? This makes no sense whatsoever. I know nothing of the young woman's propensities for melodramatic disappearances or practical jokes, but I really feel some sense of responsibility for her in that something might have happened to her on my property."

Theo realized he was rubbing his hands together as if in mimicry. Putting them in his lap, he said, "Let's give Biff and Sandy a chance to look for her before we take further action. I don't know her well enough to judge if she might be attempting to alarm us for her own amusement. What do you think, Dorrie?"

"I don't think she'd pull this kind of stunt. She doesn't have enough wit to think it up on the spur of the moment, and I doubt she would find it all that entertaining. Staying out all night at a party is more her style, Uncle Theo. Mooning people in the club parking lot. Leaping in the fountain at the mall. Wet T-shirt contests at the fraternity houses."

Sitermann/Spitzberg nodded. "From what she told me of her history, this doesn't seem like her idea of amusement, Bloomer."

"But how could she lose her way when her destination was less than two hundred feet?" Theo said, his voice level despite his growing sense of dread. "We heard no cries, no sounds of a scuffle, no cars in the street."

"Everything was peaceful when I walked up," Spitzberg said.

Count D'Orsini swung around, looking less boyish in the glare of the terrace lights and a good deal more battered by age. "I didn't see anyone when I returned home, and I didn't notice any unfamiliar or suspicious cars parked along the street. Mary Margaret did not knock on my door or ring the bell; I was having a brandy in the living room, and I surely would have heard her had she attempted to gain my attention in some way."

Biff and Sandy came up the driveway. Sandy shook his

head in response to Theo's sharp look. "No sign of her, sir. We checked under every bush and tree, went all along the fence, looked all over the backyard and garden, and even walked down the street a block in both directions. What could have happened to her?"

"I cannot imagine, nor can I decide what steps we ought to take at this moment. Calling the police is an option, but I'm not at all sure what, if anything, they might be able to do at this hour. They will undoubtedly point out that she is old enough to wander off, and more than capable of doing so—based on past antics. If Mary Margaret has done this as a crude joke, and subsequently is located in a local bar drinking beer and dancing, then we will look quite foolish and the police will be less than amused. However, I am responsible for her, so I fear I have no choice but to call the police and report this puzzling event."

As he went through the dining room, Dorrie caught up with him. "Do you think Mary Margaret's disappearance could have anything to do with Eli's absence?" she asked in a low voice.

"I don't see how there could be a relationship between the two. We have not seen Eli since early this afternoon, when he drove us to the train station, and he is nowhere to be found. Are you thinking his absence might be involuntary—that whoever has detained him might also have grabbed Mary Margaret while she was between the villas?"

"I don't know." Dorrie sighed. "We do know that someone—and I still suspect Sitermann—was on my balcony two nights ago, using a camera for some obscure reason. A spy appears, Eli disappears, and now Mary Margaret disappears. There is something going on, Uncle Theo; I can feel it all the way down to my cuticles."

"Indeed, my dear. Before I call the police, I think I shall

check Eli's quarters once more to see if I might find some sort of clue to his present location."

"What if his door is locked?"

Theo blinked at her from behind his bifocals. "I anticipate no problem getting inside, and the exigency excuses a bit of unauthorized entry. Would you care to accompany me? We might slip out the kitchen door and go around the back of the pool, simply to avoid arousing undue suspicion in the others, don't you think?"

They went across the kitchen patio, ducking under the ghostly fingers of laundry on the clothesline, and gingerly followed the rough flagstone path that brought them to the far side of the pool and the sloping lawn. As they came around the lower side of the pool, they heard those on the terrace conversing in worried voices. No one had yet produced a theory to explain Mary Margaret's absence, although Trey managed to introduce several possibilities that Bitsy, without missing a beat, found disgusting. Theo found them all alarming.

The door was locked, but as Theo had implied, it was not impassable. He took a small metal strip from his pocket, used it with a minimum of bother, and within seconds shooed Dorrie inside and closed the door behind them. He then took a penlight from his pocket and shined it around the room, with brief pauses on a rumpled bed, a braided rug that had been pushed partway under the bed, a pile of neatly folded shirts on a battered rocking chair, and a collection of liquor bottles. One of which was amaretto, he noted with a faint frown.

"Nice work on the door, Uncle Theo, but the window's open. We could have crawled through it rather than playing burglar."

Theo shined the light on an elaborate stereo system.

"Look at this, my dear."

"Holy Reebok," Dorrie whispered. "How much do pool boys make these days? I may forget this sociology degree nonsense and major in chlorine."

"He does seem to have done quite well, although I understood he has only recently taken this job with Gerry's agency." Theo moved across the room to a bookcase. "Christie, John D. MacDonald, Le Carré, Parker, Hess, a few Jane Austen novels, Thackeray, and Stowe, to name a few, all dog-eared and scarred from actual usage. He is well-read for someone who admitted to no more than an eighth-grade education."

"Shine the light over here, Uncle Theo. Look at this wardrobe. Brooks Brothers? Lacoste shirts? A Burberry coat? Pool boys in Connecticut do all right, since they know they're vital, but this is absurd. Honestly, how much skill does it take to vacuum the bottom of a swimming pool?"

"Apparently one commands a salary high enough to allow the purchase of some very expensive camera equipment," Theo said drily as he moved the light to a table in one corner. "This is an infrared viewing scope and costs well in excess of a thousand dollars. Here's a telephoto lens that would be extremely effective in low light, and a nocturnal lens that is decidedly state-of-the-art. A zoom, and another that is too complex for me to identify. A very nice tripod. What interesting hobbies our Eli has . . ."

"On minimum wage." Dorrie turned around slowly, her teeth cutting into her lower lip as she stared at Theo. "What does all this mean? Why would Eli have taken pictures from my balcony?"

"It is obvious that Eli is not the garden-variety of pool boy, but I'm not sure what sort of hybrid he might be," Theo said. He sat down on the edge of the narrow bed and let the penlight dance about the room. "I would very much like to speak to him. I have a vague idea of his true identity, but I must be quite sure before I say anything further. In the interim, we must do something about retrieving Mary Margaret."

"If you insist, Uncle Theo."

They went back to the kitchen and Theo placed a call to the local police station. Once he had made known the purpose of his call, there was a long silence, followed by an explosion of laughter and several comments about the unpredictability of tourists, especially the young female kind. Theo persisted, but at last replaced the receiver and turned to Dorrie with a wry expression.

"They are not impressed," he said. "I suppose it doesn't seem all that critical, and I do not blame them for that. Mary Margaret has been missing for less than thirty minutes; she was cheerful, physically fit, sober, and operating under her own power when she left the terrace. The sergeant said he would accept a report in the morning, but he seemed confident that our stray would be home and safe in bed by that time."

"In someone's bed, anyway." Dorrie chewed her lip for a moment, then shrugged. "We'd better tell the others. Then I, for one, would like to go to bed. This day has been absolutely dreadful, Uncle Theo. It's been worse than any of Mother's charity cocktail parties, when I've been obliged to be polite to her boring friends who talk endlessly about worthy causes and starving children—over brie and crudités."

"An ordeal," Theo murmured as they returned to the terrace. The group still looked worried, although they had polished off all of the food and managed to locate another bottle of champagne during the interlude.

Count D'Orsini met Theo in the doorway. "Did you call

the police? Are they coming over to initiate a search for the poor gal?"

"If she has not returned by the morning, the police have agreed to investigate, but for the moment they suggest we simply wait and see if Mary Margaret walks through the door."

"Please let me know when she returns." He nodded at the others, then went down the driveway and through the gate.

Bitsy put down her champagne glass and looked at Dorrie. "Are you going to condition your hair tonight? I'd like a few minutes in the bathroom before you lock yourself in there for three hours to squeal about split ends."

Before Dorrie could answer, Biff patted her hand. "Your hair is perfect, Dorrikin."

"It's about time you noticed that." Dorrie then announced that any conditioning would be of a purely preventive nature, and left the terrace with a sniff. Bitsy followed, apologizing for the implication, and the boys drifted away in a murmur of goodnight-sir's.

Theo realized Sitermann was sitting quietly in a shadowy corner, his bowtie undone and his hand wrapped around a glass of what appeared to be scotch, undiluted by water or ice.

"So what'd you find, Bloom?" the spy said, his free hand gesturing at the blackness of the pool and yard below, the dim street, and the lights that dotted the hillside all the way down to the inky water in the distance. "Did you search the errant girl's room for a little black book of island haunts?"

"Did you, or were you too busy devising camera sweeps for the future epic? Or perhaps you found a few promising sites in Ochos Rios, more specifically in the market?"

"I bought the damndest wood carving there. At first glance, you think it's an old codger playing a clarinet, but when you look harder, you—"

"Can it," Theo said without rancor. "Why were you keeping Count D'Orsini's yacht under surveillance?"

"Me? Oh, Bloom, you are a suspicious man. What if I were to tell you that I was shopping for gifts for my sister-in-law and her children?"

"I'd say that you were lying."

"That hurts, old man. It really does, right to my heart."

"They extracted your heart the day after they recruited you. Standard procedure, I would imagine, since I never met a CIA agent with the sensitivity of a rock. But if you're not going to tell me anything, let me see if I can make a wild guess or two." Theo formed a temple with his fingertips and smiled at the spy. "We know you're in Jamaica to help the local authorities with the drug situation, which is out of control. You're interested in not only the ganja growers, but also those who import more potent drugs from conveniently well-situated places, such as Colombia."

"The real thing, so to speak." Sitermann returned the smile.

"So to speak. Now, there are most likely two modes of transportation involved in the importation of cocaine—air and boat. Count D'Orsini, who is neither as aristocratic nor as wealthy as he would prefer to be, has a boat capable of extended jaunts into international waters, where he might, with foresight and planning, encounter another boat and transfer cargo without the cloying interference of the customs officials."

"His boat has a remarkable radar system for someone who professes to stalk only sailfish and marlin. It has a sonar device that could locate a chip of coral at two hundred feet down, a radio with which he could chat with his pals in Nice, and a fascinating storage compartment that requires

163

a microscope to find."

Theo nodded. "As I suspected. Now, if we accept the fact that you would like to meet the captain of this remarkable craft and perhaps have the opportunity to allow him to make a transaction that would end in exposure and arrest, then we might concoct a scheme in which you befriend a resident of the very next villa. That wouldn't be improbable, would it, Sitermann?"

"Gawd, you are a sly one. I sure wish I could get my hands on your dossier and figure out who your bosses were. I've eliminated the CIA, the FBI, Interpol, the British boys, and most of the resistance groups in World War II. It doesn't obsess me, but I do a little snooping when I'm not occupied."

"I am delighted to know you have a hobby. But to return to the present, let's continue with my hypothesis, shall we? It seems that Eli, the so-called pool boy, has an incredibly expensive hobby of his own—photography. He doesn't concentrate on nature shots, or even shots of girls on the beach; his equipment is more suited for undercover surveillance, such as recording unsavory moments from a discreet distance. One wonders if he is employed by someone other than an innocent real estate agency."

"You don't mean . . . ?" Sitermann polished off his drink, took a bottle from under his chair to refill his glass, then settled back with a brightly curious look.

"The local police, I would think. It's a very clever setup, actually. He goes undercover and takes a job at the adjoining villa in order to observe any possible drug deals taking place there. Only two nights ago, we obligingly left him alone so that he could sneak onto the balcony and take photographs of whatever was occurring between the count and a business associate. All these trips are most likely to his office for conferences, orders, and strategy sessions. Were you there, my friend?"

"Naw, I let the locals run this operation as best they can," Sitermann said expansively. "Gives them good experience, a chance for a little glory, and a reason to request sophisticated toys courtesy of our government. You're right about our boy Eli, of course; we even trained him in Virginia for undercover work. But what does this have to do with the red-haired girl's disappearance, Bloom?"

"I don't know. Do you have any knowledge of this, any little thing that might have slipped your eelish mind? If you do, you'd better spit it out, Mr. Spitzberg."

The spy held up three fingers in the traditional Scout salute. "All kidding aside, I swear I have no idea what happened to the girl. I didn't know Eli took pictures from the balcony a couple of nights back, and I don't know where he is at this moment in time. Look, I happened to hear the girl talking about the villa while she was waiting to parasail, and I recognized the location. I had no idea you and your niece were a part of the house party; God knows I would have run the opposite way as fast as these bony legs would carry me before I'd voluntarily tangle with you again."

Theo was not awed by the sincerity in Sitermann's voice, and he knew too many Scouts who'd mugged little old ladies. "Then what were you doing in this area tonight?"

"Classified, old boy, classified. Would you mind calling me a cab? I think I'll mosey back to the hotel and see if I can find any potential leading ladies in the bar."

Once the spy was gone, Theo instinctively carried the dishes back to the kitchen and rinsed them in the sink while he pondered Sitermann's avowal of ignorance. Afterward he climbed the stairs to the second floor and tapped on Dorrie's door.

Giggling, Dorrie opened the door a slit. "Are you going to bed now, Uncle Theo?"

"I am, yes. I wanted to be sure that you and Bitsy had found your possessions as you left them, and that nothing might be missing."

"It's all dandy," Dorrie said, still giggling although Theo had found his comments less than humorous. "You run along to bed and don't worry about Mary Margaret. See you in the morning."

Theo walked on to his bedroom, unable to prevent himself from visualizing Mary Margaret in a variety of situations, none of which enhanced his role of chaperone. In a bout of whimsy, he considered the wisdom of telephoning his sister, Nadine, to tell her what a lovely time he was having and how he did indeed wish she were there, but dismissed the heretical idea as a symptom of exhaustion. He put on his pajamas, visited the bathroom, ascertained that the villa was at peace, climbed into bed, and snapped off the light on the bedside table. He lay awake for a long while, searching his mind for a rational explanation for Mary Margaret's evanescence, which had happened in less time than it took Dorrie to list her credit cards.

He finally put it aside and forced himself to visualize tidy green rows of sugar snap peas and blossoming tomato plants, all sturdy, well-irrigated, and free from the slightest smudge of blight. Smiling, he snuggled into the pillow and closed his eyes.

Thirty seconds later the screams began.

The screaming stopped as abruptly as it had begun, but the reverberations seemed to bounce around the dark bedroom like ping-pong balls. Theo waited a few seconds for his adrenaline to ebb, then threw back the covers and scrabbled on the bedside table for his bifocals. He was tying the belt of his bathrobe when his door opened and Dorrie slipped in, her arms wrapped around herself as though she could suppress the shivers and convulsive twitches of her body, which she obviously could not. Her ashen face was streaked with black lines of mascara, and water streamed from her sodden hair. She wore a terrycloth jacket, although it had been buttoned by hasty, negligent fingers. Her feet, always shod to protect them from unsightly calluses, were bare.

"Oh, Uncle Theo," she said in an expressionless voice.

"What has happened, my dear? Here, sit down and let me bring you a towel so you can dry off. You must be thoroughly chilled."

"You would be, too," she said as she sank down on a corner of the bed, her fingers still digging into the softness of her upper arms. "I can't decide if I should scream, faint, or barf. Perhaps I ought to do all three, although I don't suppose I can do so in that order. Oh, Uncle Theo . . ." She toppled over backward and stared at the ceiling through glazed, unblinking eyes. A trickle of saliva ran down her cheek.

"Dorrie, you must tell me what happened. As much as I appreciate this melodramatic introduction, I must insist you explain what evoked those blood-chilling screams a few minutes ago."

She sat up, but immediately clamped a hand over her mouth and lurched toward the bathroom. Admittedly impatient by now, Theo waited until she was finished, then draped a jacket around her shoulders as she came back into the bedroom. He dried her cheeks with a clean handkerchief, settled her on the edge of the bed, patted her knee with avuncular tenderness, and offered her the glass of water from the bedside table. She allowed his ministrations with a few muted gulps of gratitude.

"You must explain," he said gravely.

"It was so ghastly. In truth, it was the most ghastly experience of my life. If anything like that ever happens again, I'll just—"

"What happened, Dorrie?"

"Well, since everyone had gone to bed like a bunch of middle-aged party poopers, Bitsy and I decided to go skinny-dipping in the pool. It's a perfect night—balmy, starry, redolent breeze, the exact sort of thing one reads about in romance novels. Not that I read those trashy things, mind you, but some of the girls in the dorm do and they're always reading the torrid excerpts aloud over dinner. It's enough to destroy whatever appetite one might rally for the cafeteria, better known as carbo city."

Theo bit back what could have been interpreted as an acerbic comment. "Please get to the point," he said with measured calmness. "We can discuss literary preferences at another time."

"I wouldn't call romance novels literature with a capital L, Uncle Theo. But anyway, Bitsy and I crept downstairs and went out to the pool, which was very dark since no one bothered with the lights tonight: We left our towels and things on a chaise and eased into the water so that no one would hear any splashes and come to investigate. We were giggling, of course, but very quietly. I wouldn't have minded if Biff and Sandy joined us, but Trey has both the hands and the morals of a squid, and I certainly didn't want to wrestle with him in the dark."

"Where is Bitsy at this moment?" Theo said, resisting an urge to shake the pertinent portion of the story from her. "Is she unharmed?"

"Yeah, I guess. She fainted in one of the chaises beside the pool. She didn't look as if she was going anywhere for quite a while, so I tossed a towel over her and left her there while I came up here to tell you what happened."

"Which I am optimistic that you are going to do—now."

"We were swimming around, feeling rather daring in an adolescent fashion—as if we were at summer camp and thirteen years old, zits and all. At one point we thought we heard someone in the driveway, but we decided it was a cat. Then I bumped into something in the pool. At first I assumed it was Bitsy, since it felt like an arm and she does have a pair of those. I poked her and whispered for her to watch where she was going, because I really had no intention of getting my hair wet and being forced to wash it after we finished swimming. Well, she shot back a snippy little remark—from a far corner of the pool." Dorrie gulped loudly and again clamped her hand over her mouth. After several convulsive jerks, she gained control of herself and gave Theo a shaky smile. "It scared the holy shit out of me, if you'll pardon my French. I poked this thing in front of me, and it just bobbled away without a sound. Bitsy started hissing to know what was going on, but I ignored her and swam a stroke or two to find out what it was. It was a body, Uncle Theo—a dead body."

This time she could not stop the upheavals of her stomach, and scrambled for the bathroom. Once she returned, Theo wiped her cheeks, but he kept his hands on her shoulders as he stared into her eyes. "Who was it, Dorrie?" he inquired gently.

"It was too dark to see anything, so I got out of the pool pretty damn fast and ran over to the wall to switch on the pool light. There was Eli, floating face up with his eyes wide open and his face contorted as if he'd had terrible stomach cramps or something. After we determined who it was, I turned off the light. Bitsy was screeching like a Radcliffe coed on a football weekend, so I dragged her out of the pool, slapped her a couple of times, and told her to shut up or she'd find herself eating terrycloth. That's when she fainted. You'd have thought she was Scarlett O'Hara in a twelve-inch corset."

Theo realized he had been expecting to hear Mary Margaret's name, and let out his breath. Not that this did anything to reassure him of her safety, however, he reminded himself with a wince. "Did you notice anything that might indicate the cause of death?" he asked Dorrie, still forcing himself to speak gently.

"No, but he certainly was dead. I could see that much. What do we do now, Uncle Theo?"

"I shall telephone the police. You check on Bitsy, and if she has revived herself, take her upstairs and both of you change into more suitable attire. I'll let the others know what's happened."

Dorrie stopped in the doorway and looked back at Theo, who was already reaching for his trousers. "Earlier you said you had an idea of Eli's true identity, because of the camera equipment and upscale wardrobe, but you didn't want to say anything more until you talked to him. You're not going to talk to him, Uncle Theo."

"I did have a few words with our chum from the CIA, who confirmed my theory that Eli was an undercover policeman involved in a drug operation."

Dorrie's hand tightened around the doorknob as she stared back. After a moment to digest the information, she said, "And he took the job here so that he could observe Count D'Orsini next door, right? Eli had a lovely view from the balcony, not of the ocean but of the pool and terrace on the other side of the fence. I should have figured it out myself; it's so obvious. Do you think Eli was murdered, Uncle Theo? If someone murdered him, then what does this mean for Mary Margaret? As much as I hate to say it, I am concerned about her."

"As am I, my dear, but there's no point in hypothesizing at

this moment. Eli's death is most likely an ordinary accident, brought on perhaps by a medical condition that caused him to lose consciousness or be stricken by cramps. You run along and attend to Bitsy, who may very well recover and start screaming once more. Her voice is quite piercing, to say the least, and liable to rouse all the villas on the hillside."

"All the villas on all the hillsides," Dorrie amended before closing the door.

Theo finished dressing and went out to the landing. Biff stood in the doorway of his room, a bathrobe draped over his shoulders.

"Is that you, Mr. Bloomer?" he said, squinting in the dim light. "I thought I heard a woman scream a few minutes ago. Did you hear it, too? I mean, did someone really scream—or was I imagining things? Did Dorrie just dash out of your room? Why are you dressed?"

"You heard a scream," Theo said gravely. "There's been an accident, and I fear Eli has drowned. Where is Sandy?"

"He must have gone to investigate. I had so much champagne after dinner that it took me a long time to decide I wasn't dreaming." He rubbed his temples as he continued to squint at Theo. "How did Eli drown? Is Dorrie okay? Was she the one who screamed?"

"We'll deal with your questions after I've called the police. Get dressed and go to the terrace." Theo went downstairs, but as he turned to enter the kitchen, he saw a figure silhouetted against the doorway of the terrace. "Sandy?" he whispered cautiously, sliding his hand along the wall to find the light switch.

"Mr. Bloomer?" Sandy's laugh was shaky. "Thank God. I heard a scream—or at least I thought I did, so I came downstairs to look around." He showed Theo the empty Perrier bottle he was clutching by its neck. "I wasn't sure I could

171

intimidate an intruder with this, but my golf clubs are in a closet down here. Anyway, I looked around and didn't find anybody."

"Did you check the yard and the gate?"

"Yes, sir. The gate's locked. I didn't see anything by the pool, but it seemed okay. Trey's in his room, snoring away like an electric razor. Nobody was lurking in the yard or the driveway. Eli's either still missing or passed out cold; I knocked on his door and had no answer. I guess either I was dreaming or the scream came from another villa down the hillside." He flipped on the light and, with a self-deprecating smile, put the bottle on the dining room table. "Did you come down for a glass of warm milk, sir?"

Theo assured him that there had been a scream. After instructing him to wake Trey, dress, and meet on the terrace, Theo went to the telephone and grimly dialed the telephone number of the police station.

The duty officer listened more attentively this time. Theo admitted he had no idea of the cause of death, the time of same, or any possibly pertinent facts, including proper name, home address, or next of kin. The voice on the other end promised to send officers within a few minutes. By the time two policemen parked at the bottom of the driveway and came through the gate, Theo and his charges were on the terrace. He had related what had occurred and plied them with enough coffee to produce a semblance of horrified comprehension. The pool and its unsavory contents had been left in darkness, and no one glanced in that direction.

Dorrie and Bitsy were both pale. As the two dark-skinned policemen came onto the terrace, Theo stepped forward and quietly related the events that led to the discovery of the body, hoping to head off some of the questions he knew would be directed at the girls. The policemen introduced themselves as Sergeants Stahl and Winkler, both of the Cornwall County Criminal Investigation Bureau, then went down the stairs to the pool to ascertain the validity of the narration for themselves. When the lights came on, those on the terrace tensed, but no one turned.

"How do they know it wasn't just an accident?" Dorrie asked. "It seems like they'd send patrolmen out for an accident, not sergeants. And why are they from the criminal branch?"

Biff went over to put his hand on her shoulder. "Maybe this is the only branch they have here. But it doesn't concern us, since he was simply an employee. In fact, he wasn't even our employee; he worked for that real estate woman's firm. Let's all remember to insist on the fact that this has absolutely nothing to do with any of us."

"You didn't crash against a corpse in the pool," Dorrie said, shuddering.

Sandy reached across the table to pat her hand. "It must have been a nightmare, literally. Mr. Bloomer, how long do you think he was in the pool? Could he have come back after we went to bed, or was he . . . well, was he there all along, while we were eating dinner and drinking up here? The thought makes me want to throw up. After all, he was a good chap—a little slow, but always agreeable about running errands, doing little favors. I feel really bad about not noticing him." He ducked his face and ran a hand through his stubby hair. "This is lousy, totally lousy."

"Maybe he heard Dorrie's avowal of revenge and decided to take the easy way out," Trey murmured.

"I didn't say I was going to drown him, you slime," Dorrie said, her face regaining some of its color. "I said he ought to be fired."

"Unless he was dead. I distinctly remember you saying Eli

173

had better be dead. You got that right, Dorrikin. As an oracle, you're up there with the Delphic broad."

"You might consider abandoning this unsuccessful attempt at wit and worrying a little more about Mary Margaret," Dorrie said. "She is your sister, after all, and she's been gone half the night. You do have an ounce of sibling affection somewhere in your perverted little soul, don't you?"

"She's like one of Bo Peep's sheep, darling. Leave her alone and she'll come home, wagging her tail behind her. I'm hardly inclined to lose any sleep over her."

"Do you know what you are?" Bitsy demanded shrilly.

Everyone, including an unrepentant Trey, nodded, saving her the minor effort of forming the word.

Sergeant Stahl came up the stairs. "I need to use your telephone in order to call in a report."

Theo offered to show him the way to the kitchen. Once they were there, he said, "Can you tell us anything regarding the time or cause of death? We're all feeling quite distressed about this, since it seems possible we ate supper on the terrace while Eli was below in the pool."

"The medical examiner will have to make that determination. If you're finished with your questions, I will make the necessary calls in order to start the investigation into the death of the young male in the swimming pool. Then I have questions for you and the others."

"Based on your first impressions, can you tell me if the death appears to be an accidental drowning?"

"It may have been an accident, but he did not drown. I've seen the symptoms of the vomiting sickness too many times here in Jamaica, and although this is not official, I would say with some certainty he had ingested the fruit of an unripened ackee. It is deadly."

Theo glanced at the windowsill above the sink. There were

two hard, unopened ackees on one side, both glinting darkly. He found himself wondering how many had been there in the past. The immediate past. Even yesterday, if one chose to be precise.

When the rest of the investigative team arrived, Theo and his charges were sent to the living room to wait until they were needed for questioning. The red velour furniture, although seemingly decadent, proved to be both scratchy and lumpy, and Theo gratefully accepted Sandy's offer to bring a chair from the dining room. The uncompromising back seemed more appropriate.

"He didn't just have a heart attack and drown, did he?" Dorrie asked from a lounge with an elaborate headboard, several satin pillows, and a decorative fringe that resembled thready icicles. "There are about fifty cops out there, which seems a little extreme for an accident."

Theo saw no reason not to tell them what would be common knowledge before the sun rose. "Sergeant Stahl said he recognized the symptoms of ackee poisoning."

"But Eli's a Jamaican, and a well-educated one at that; he ought to know better than to start munching on an unripened ackee. They don't look all that appetizing when they're ripe, for pity's sake."

"Well-educated?" Sandy said. "He was just a pool boy, and I had to write down the words the first time I sent him out for a *Wall Street Journal*. Maybe he was into some island voodoo club where they eat things for a thrill, or maybe he got so drunk the ackee looked ripe. He did have a fondness for cheap rum."

"Well, he ran errands for you all the time. He wasted all sorts of time to find that boring newspaper every morning," Bitsy said, "and half the time you didn't bother to glance at anything but the headlines. You left one on that nasty train today. In any case, you don't have to deal with the memories of finding his body in the swimming pool. Dorrie and I were both blown away." She touched her cheek, then gazed at Dorrie with a thoughtful expression. "Some of us absolutely fell to pieces and began doing and saying all sorts of incredibly crude things. Some of us were inhuman and totally insensitive, like a Nazi soldier."

"While others of us squealed like a chubby little pig," Dorrie responded sweetly. "But, Uncle Theo, Eli wouldn't eat an unripened ackee. Surely he knew all about the effects of one and was trained to recognize the symptoms just like sergeant what-ever-his-name-is. Someone who lives in one of those horrid shacks in the mountains might not know any better, but Eli was fairly sophisticated."

"Are we discussing the same person?" Biff said.

"Oh, he was an undercover narcotics agent," Dorrie said in an irritated voice. "You must have been too occupied with Mary Margaret's bikini to notice, but those of us with any acumen to speak of could hardly fail to realize it."

"What about Mary Margaret, sir?" Biff asked Theo, pointedly turning his back on Dorrie, who responded to the outrage with a toss of her chin and a discreet snort.

"I don't know," Theo said. "When I called earlier, the police dismissed her disappearance as self-induced. The recent tragedy makes her disappearance seem more ominous now, but I don't know what they can do until morning, even if they are more inclined to consider it relevant. She's not next door, she's not under a bush, and—well, I have no theories, myself."

Dorrie sat up. "What about Sitermann or Spitzberg or whatever we're calling him? Could he have anything to do with Mary Margaret's vanishing act—some terribly clever CIA scheme to . . . something?"

"Sitermann or Spitzberg? The CIA? Eli an undercover cop?" Sandy stood up and crossed the room to stand in front of Theo. "I don't understand what's going on, sir, but I feel that we're all entitled to an explanation. I thought we were here to party, not to get involved in some bizarre business with bodies and secret agents. I wish somebody would tell me what the hell's going on. We deserve to be told the truth."

"So do I." Theo sighed. Unable to offer any rebuttal to Sandy's argument, he provided a brief synopsis of what he knew of Sitermann's true identity and Eli's occupation. Only Dorrie seemed unruffled by the information; the others listened with shocked expressions and a scattering of interjections.

After an enigmatic look at Dorrie, Biff said, "Surely the local police department doesn't bother with assigning an officer to bust a bunch of tourists for half a baggie of ganja. Eli didn't strike me as a role model for Eliot Ness, but he must have been on something fairly important. He'd have had a good opportunity to keep a neighbor under surveillance, for instance."

"I was aware of that," Dorrie said, stretching out her hands to inspect her fingernails. "Anyone not fawning over an overstuffed bikini would have picked it up eons ago."

Bitsy shivered. "I'd sort of like to see that overstuffed bikini stroll through the door right now."

Sergeant Stahl strode through the door. "All of you will have to come to the station for questioning. What has happened is very serious, very serious indeed, and puzzling. But we will get to the bottom of it at some point, even if it requires a lengthy investigation."

Dorrie raised an eyebrow. "You may require a lengthy investigation in order to sort this out to your satisfaction, but we're returning to the United States on Saturday. We're all students and we have classes on Monday morning. I've already had to cut classes in the past, and I simply cannot miss any more this semester. You may call Simmons if you wish. I don't know her number off the top of my head, but she's in the classics department at Wellesley."

"We shall do everything possible to expedite your departure," the policeman said, retreating under the chilly blast.

"I should hope so. Besides these bothersome classes all week, I'm scheduled for a permanent on Wednesday. I doubt you can imagine how difficult it is to get an appointment with Mr. Robert, rather than having to accept some neophyte right out of beauty college, but you can believe me when I tell—"

"Let's go, my dear," Theo said. "You and Bitsy fetch your handbags while I make arrangements for transportation with the sergeant."

The sergeant, looking faintly bewildered, nodded.

The police station had the ambience, if not the vastness, of the airport. Housed in a crumbling gray building on a narrow, rutted street in Montego Bay, it clearly had been in use for several decades, and had received no benevolent attention in its lifetime. A fan whirred gently, stirring the dust but doing little to alleviate the cloying humidity and heat. Flies made lazy circles near the ceiling. An incurious desk officer pointed at a row of wooden chairs, then returned to the thick paperback novel in front of him.

"Shouldn't we call the consulate?" Dorrie whispered to Theo.

"I see no reason to become alarmed," he said, patting her knee for the umpteenth time. "We're only here to assist the police. We really don't know much of relevance or value, but I suppose we ought to do whatever we can. Eli was a pleasant individual, if not precisely what he pretended to be. He was doing his job, however, so we mustn't hold his pretense against him. I feel badly about his death." Theo took off his bifocals to polish them, earning a fleeting, impassive glance from the policeman behind the desk.

"What are you going to say about Sitermann?" Dorrie continued.

"I suspect the officers are aware of Sitermann's presence and involvement, so I think we'd better settle for the truth."

The door opened. Count D'Orsini, escorted on either side by uniformed policemen, gave those on the chairs a bleak nod as he was hurried past them and around a corner.

Bitsy let out a muted yelp. "Oh, my gawd. Do you think Count D'Orsini murdered Eli? After all, he was a dope dealer and Eli was watching him . . . If the count learned that Eli had been spying on him, he might have hired a thug to—to bump him off."

"Come on, Bitsy," Trey said from the end of the row, "you've been watching too much television. Dope dealers and thugs are passé now that 'Miami Vice' has slipped in the ratings. He might have hired a sitcom single parent to be so sensitive that Eli died of boredom, but not a thug. Jeez!"

Before Bitsy could respond, the door again opened and Gerry came into the room. Her hair was rumpled, and her makeup had been applied with haste. She gave the desk sergeant a curt nod, then came over to Theo.

"What on earth is going on?" she demanded in a low, hoarse voice. "The officer who came by my house gave me some garbled story about one of my employees, then told me to be here as soon as possible. While I was parking, I saw Hal being taken out of a police car. I'm trying to convince myself that this is a crazy dream, that I'll open my eyes and find myself in my own bed, but I have a dreadful feeling I'm already awake."

Theo told her about the unfortunate events leading to the

discovery of Eli's body in the swimming pool. When she looked as if she might topple, he stood up and insisted she take his seat.

She sank down with a distracted murmur of thanks. "Then this is not some sort of joke? Poor, poor Eli—and his family. I know very little about him, since he only applied for the position a few weeks ago, but he seemed to be a nice young man with a good mind. I believe he has a mother and several younger siblings in one of the villages. Has anyone told them about this horrible accident?"

Theo handed her a handkerchief as her eyes filled with tears. "It does not seem to have been an accident," he said gently. "Eli was an undercover policeman on an assignment, and his death is hardly apt to be a coincidence."

"He was a—what?"

Theo repeated the information, keeping an eye on the desk sergeant. "The police are taking into consideration the fact that Eli was one of them, and the death of an officer while on duty is quite naturally suspicious."

"He was a police officer," Gerry mumbled, shaking her head. "I can't believe it, Theo. It makes no sense. There's no reason why he would take a job at one of the villas. The tourists often purchase a bit of the local product, but not of any significant quantity to merit an investigation. The police quietly overlook this minor sort of indiscretion, since any harassment would have disastrous effects on tourism. You're mistaken."

"I agree that Eli was not concerned with the small usage in the villas. I must warn you that Count D'Orsini may have been involved in drug trafficking, if not in the disturbing events surrounding Eli's death."

"And don't forget about Mary Margaret," Bitsy added primly. "She's managed to have lost herself in a thoroughly suspicious manner. If Count D'Orsini killed Eli, he might have killed Mary Margaret, too."

Gerry's face sagged. Then, before Theo could realize the necessity of action, her eyes rolled back, her breath came out in a whoosh, and she slid out of the chair onto the floor. Her straw purse fell beside her, sending out a lava-like flow of wadded tissues, keys, pens, and female paraphernalia.

Dorrie glared at Bitsy. "Well, that was tactful."

"What did I do?"

"For one thing, you told her that her dear old chum might be a kidnapper and a murderer."

"That's hardly my fault, is it? I mean, it's pretty obvious that he snatched Mary Margaret and put her someplace, probably so that he could rape and torture her before cutting off her head with a machete."

"She'd enjoy some of that," Trey said.

Theo resisted the very real urge to take each one of them by the scruff of his or her neck, turn same over his knee, and paddle each until he elicited sincere promises that the bickering would end. Dismissing the fantasy with a sigh, he told Sandy to find a cup of water, and then, with Biff's assistance, picked Gerry up and put her back in the chair. The desk sergeant watched wordlessly, offering neither suggestions nor aid. By the time Sandy returned with water, Gerry's eyes had fluttered open.

"Hal is not a criminal," she said to Theo. "I've known him for twenty years, and he's simply not the sort to harm anyone."

"But you must acknowledge the possibility that he earns his living in a variety of unsavory ways. Although it was quite unintentional, I happened to overhear a conversation from his villa the first night we were here. It was—well, informative in a disturbing way."

Gerry gulped down the water and squeezed her fingers around the cup. "What did you hear, Theo?"

"A male voice making some rather unpleasant remarks about the count being a gigolo, I'm sorry to say. There were also some insinuations that led me to wonder if drug trafficking might be a secondary occupation of the men. It was none of my business, naturally, and I left the terrace immediately."

"I refuse to believe this. You must have misinterpreted what was said. Would you recognize this voice if you heard it again?"

Theo toyed with the tip of his beard as he tried to reconstruct the conversation. "I recognized Count D'Orsini's voice when you brought him over for a drink, but as for the second voice . . . I don't know. I did tell myself that there was something about it that seemed vaguely familiar, which is absurd. It couldn't have been Eli, because he drove up a minute or two later, having delivered Dorrie and her friends to the beach party." He gave his beard a final tweak. "It's nonsensical to think I had heard the voice before."

"Well, it's unfortunate that we can't locate this person in order to find out why these outrageous accusations were made, but I don't see how we could find him." Gerry looked down at the cup clutched in her hand and, with a surprised expression, slowly uncurled her fingers. "What did Bitsy say about Mary Margaret? Has something happened to her?"

"She disappeared somewhere between the terrace and Count D'Orsini's front door," Theo said. He explained what had happened, adding that the police were now more inclined to worry about the girl. "I am at a loss to decide what I ought to do, however. I should hate to alarm her father if she is indulging in some sort of prank, but I should be irresponsible

182

not to do so if she's involved in all this and in very real danger."

Trey yawned loudly. "No problem, man. Any danger she's in has to do with diseases that can be cured with a few doses of penicillin."

The desk sergeant looked up as the group hissed the word "disgusting." Everyone, including Theo, contributed to the sibilance.

As Theo and his charges straggled up the driveway the next morning, exhausted by the night of innumerable questions interspersed with frustrating idleness on the hard wooden chairs in the police station, Amelia came onto the terrace. "Mr. Bloomer!" she called, frantically waving both arms as if she were on a desert island and he were a rescue ship. "You have a long-distance telephone call. The lady keeps insisting you're here, even though I told her otherwise."

Theo gave Dorrie a wan smile. "Although this is hardly the time for parlor games, would you care to hazard a guess as to the identity of the caller? I'm not sure I'm strong enough to deal with your mother, my dear."

"Sorry, Uncle Theo, but I'm heading straight for bed. I'm so totally exhausted I'm not going to wash my hair. I may even go so far as to skip the latter half of my skin care routine, but you can bet your platinum card I'm not going to do battle with the Dragon Lady."

She darted around Amelia and vanished into the villa. The others followed more slowly, since they had not been threatened with the wrath of Nadine. No one stopped to offer any advice. Or sympathy, which Theo felt was more than justly due.

"I'll take the call in the kitchen," he said, resigned.

"That is some crazy lady on the other end," Amelia muttered sourly. She led him into the kitchen and pointed at the receiver, from which squawks erupted periodically. "Emelda and I will wait outside. I can use the fresh air."

Theo put the receiver to his ear. "Yes, Nadine?"

"Well, Theo?"

After a silence thick with tacit accusation, he took a deep breath and hurriedly said, "The villa is as charming as you'd told me it would be, and the view is spectacular. The yard is dotted with all sorts of fascinating flora, including a bougain-villea with a delicate shade of orange not unlike my night-blooming cereus."

"Well, Theo?"

"Ah, yes," he said, increasing the tempo out of some inde-finable sense of dread, "and we've been to the beach several times, and we took an excursion on a private train into the interior, where I was fortunate to find a orchid of the family—"

"I do not find these evasive tactics amusing, Theo. On the contrary, they are beneath you, although you've always had an inexplicable tendency toward deception. Even as a child, you often shirked responsibility."

"Did I, Nadine? I fear I don't recall the precise instances to which you're referring, but should you care to elucidate at some time in the future, I shall do my best to analyze them and profit from these youthful transgressions. It was nice of you to call, and I've enjoyed the conversation. If you'll excuse me now, I was on my way upstairs to—"

"Whomever you have answering the telephone in that place said all of you were at the police station. Why were you at the police station?"

"There was an incident last night—nothing that directly involved any of us. The pool boy was discovered in the pool, and—"

"We would hardly look for him in a banana tree, would we? Please stop rambling about the servants and get to the point, Theo. Pookie's picking me up any minute so that we can discuss our bidding system on the way to the tournament. She dropped me in a cue bid yesterday, just stranded me in this idiotic contract, and then had the nerve to sit there pouting—while I went down three. It was so humiliating that I seriously considered feigning a heart attack so that she'd have to play out the thing. I intend to see that it does not happen again."

"How dreadful for—"

"Even Charles was horrified, and he doesn't know a thing about bridge, much less the more subtle nuances of Blackwood. I don't know what got into Pookie; one would almost think she'd suffered a cerebral hemorrhage at the table. We were third in our section, but we'd have been first had she not made the error." Nadine snorted several times as she relived the indignities. "But that is not the reason I called, Theo."

"Do I hear Pookie's car honking in the driveway? I should hate for her to become impatient and back over the azaleas. Charles is so fond of them, as we all know, and likely to—"

"Theo, you are once more being evasive, and I simply do not have the fortitude to deal with such childish behavior today—not with two sessions of the women's pairs staring me in the face. Now, we'll overlook this business about the police station and your peculiar obsession with the servants' behavior. Simply explain the ransom note."

From beyond the kitchen door came the sound of easy laughter. The pipes rattled as showers were turned on upstairs, and a radio played a lilting reggae tune somewhere down the hillside. A doctor bird hummed above a yellow flower. A car backfired as it drove down the street. The light breeze rustled the curtain above the kitchen sink.

"Ransom note?" Theo was unable to believe the words even as they came out of his mouth.

"I assured Win that it was a mistake."

"Win?"

"Really, Theo, if I wanted to have my every word repeated, I'd invest in an echo chamber rather than CDs and municipal bonds. We are discussing Winston Andrews Ellison II, the father of those adorable twins. I assured him that the ransom note was a mistake. It was a mistake, wasn't it? I trust you haven't allowed anything to happen to Mary Margaret. The Ellisons are very old and dear friends of ours, and I would hate to think you'd permitted something to befall their daughter."

"What does this ransom note say?"

"It's an ordinary ransom note. Win was upset, naturally, and brought it over for Charles and me to examine the very minute we finished breakfast. He went so far as to consider calling Corky, but he was too distraught to face the ordeal with the overseas operator, and none of us could determine the time difference. It's either six hours earlier or six hours later, unless it's seven because of daylight savings time. I wish these Europeans would use the correct time instead of insisting on using local time. In any case, the clinic is quite strict about waking clients in the middle of the night."

"I haven't the slightest idea what you're talking about, Nadine."

"Corky Ellison is having a series of cellulite treatments at an extremely exclusive clinic in Switzerland. Although the menu is French, the staff are all German and tend to be more than a little authoritarian," Nadine said with the slowness and deliberate enunciation used for maximum communication with a non-English listener. Theo knew she had mastered the technique while doing good works at an Episcopalian home for unwed mothers of Mexican-American descent. The home had folded after the girls had fled.

"Thank you, Nadine; I am beginning to understand," he said soothingly. "But what about this purported ransom note?"

"There is nothing 'purported' about it. It came to Win Ellison this morning. It was formed with words clipped from some publication and glued down in a sloppy yet legible fashion. It implied that his daughter was in the hands of unscrupulous people, and that these people would harm her if they did not receive a specified amount of money. You can imagine how he felt."

"Did he call the police?"

"The note said quite bluntly that it would be unwise to contact the authorities. Besides, what would be the point of calling the police here? Mary Margaret is in Jamaica—under your chaperonage. If this is a joke, then it is tasteless. That's all I can say." It wasn't. After a lengthy exhalation to convey the depth of her displeasure, she continued, "If it is not a joke, then you'd best tell me what you intend to do about it, Theo."

Theo intended to sink down to the kitchen floor, lean against the refrigerator while gazing blankly at the underside of a table, and hope something would come to mind. "Ah . . . how much money was demanded for the return of the girl?" he asked.

"A million dollars, in small, unmarked bills. It was trite, to say the least. One would be inclined to think these people sat around all day watching nothing but old gangster movies. Anyway, I assured Win that the whole thing was poppycock, that he was not to worry one bit more about it—since you would see to it that Mary Margaret was returned in the same condition in which you took her on this self-indulgent, whimsical little trip of yours. I shall be at the airport in person on Saturday to pick you up, Theo, and I expect to pick up all seven of you. Do you understand?"

Before he could respond, the receiver clicked in his ear. He sat for several minutes, listening to the buzz while he tried to assimilate the conversation with Nadine. Mary Margaret's father had received a ransom note. The note demanded one million dollars. The note warned against contacting the police and implied Mary Margaret's welfare was uncertain should there be non-compliance. No one in Connecticut had any intention of compliance. He had been ordered to bring Mary Margaret home. She was to be delivered with all extremities intact.

The floor was hard, but the view not unpleasant. Theo was still there when Amelia and Emelda came through the back door.

"Are you okay?" Emelda asked, her face puckered in alarm. "Are you having a heart attack or something?"

"I was merely thinking," Theo said with what dignity he could muster. He stood up, brushed off the seat of his trousers, and replaced the receiver. "If it's convenient, I would like coffee on the terrace. I really do believe I shall continue to think out there."

"They's all crazy," someone muttered as he left the kitchen, but he did not turn back to refute the statement.

He was on the terrace, coffee in hand, when several police cars parked on the street below. Sergeant Stahl sent his men into Eli's room below the pool, then came up the stairs and sat down across from Theo.

"Do you think there might be an extra cup?" he asked wearily.

Theo poured a cup of coffee and set it down in front of the sergeant. "You've been up all night, too. The young people are in bed, but somehow sitting out here in peace seemed as appealing as sleep."

"I'll see my bed in about a week," Stahl said. "Sooner if we clear up this mess, but I don't know. The guy next door is involved—that much we know, but it's not as simple as we'd hoped."

"Then you're not convinced Count D'Orsini is responsible for Eli's death? Could it have been an accident after all?"

"It wasn't an accident. I got the initial lab reports back an hour ago. I shouldn't be telling you this, but we found a bottle of rum down in Detective Staggley's room that was laced with pulverized ackee. The only prints on it are his. No, we can rule out an accident; someone went to a lot of trouble to poison that bottle and leave it for him."

"I don't suppose he could have been experiencing some sort of personal problem and decided to . . . take his own life?" Theo asked without much enthusiasm.

"Jamaicans know how the vomiting sickness goes. It's a painful thing, and nothing anybody would choose. It takes about six hours for the symptoms to begin, but once they do, it's all over. Convulsions, coma, and good-bye." Stahl wiped his forehead as he looked down at the pool. "Staggley must have ingested the rum sometime during the afternoon, although we'll know more once we get the autopsy results. He probably went to the deck to clean the pool, was overcome with cramps, and fell into the water. There'll be water in his lungs, but it doesn't matter whether he died of hypoglycemia as a result of the ackee or from drowning. Someone caused the death. Staggley was a good officer and a good man, damn it."

"What had he told you of his investigation?"

"Not enough. We hadn't had a report in twenty-four hours, and I was planning to have him come in this morning to give us an update. He said earlier in the week that he had the goods on this D'Orsini and one of his contacts. But we don't know what Staggley had—or on whom."

Theo told him about the camera lens that had been discovered on Dorrie's balcony. "I would imagine it would be worth your while to have the film developed as soon as possible. Eli—Officer Staggley, that is—most likely was able to photograph a drug transaction next door."

"We found a roll of film in a drawer. It's at the lab, but the boys there swore it would be late afternoon before they could get to it, if not tomorrow or the next day. I let it go because we weren't sure that we'd find anything significant, but if it is what you say it is, I'll send back a uniformed officer to tell them to hustle their bureaucratic asses. I sure would like to have some solid proof that D'Orsini was dealing big quantities of cocaine. We've had an eye on him for years. We know damn well where he goes on his yacht, and we have a good idea whom he meets and what takes place. But D'Orsini's a smart chap. He was a big buddy of the governor before independence in 1962, and he still hobnobs with the more powerful political figures on the island. In fact, we're already getting pressure to release him, and we're going to have to do so if we can't find anything concrete to hold him on."

"Perhaps these photographs will be adequate," Theo said.

"If they prove the drug connection, we can hold him on that. If they're no good, we'll have to let him go. The only thing we've got is possible motive and passable opportunity, although it's a shaky case at best. There's nothing to link him to Staggley's murder."

"Have you any idea who his associates are?"

"We have a few names of Colombian dealers, but there are some gaps in the overall picture. D'Orsini doesn't bother with small, local dealers. He purchases the cocaine in significant quantities, then has it transported to the States. Somehow."

"Perhaps on jaunts to Florida?"

"It doesn't seem likely. Your Feds are real serious about what takes place in their water. It could happen, but they've kept tight surveillance on him and he's kept his nose clean. All of his close friends—and even his short-term women acquaintances—are given a thorough search at customs. The cocaine goes out and the cash comes in, just about as predictably as the tide. We don't know how."

Theo replenished the sergeant's coffee cup. "Why are you telling me all this? As much as I appreciate your candor, I find myself somewhat perplexed by it. I am, after all, a civilian."

Stahl flashed even white teeth. "That's not what your friend from the CIA says. Sitermann says he doesn't know what the devil you are, but that you've been well-trained. He didn't go into detail about what happened over in the Middle East, although he hinted that you cleared up a messy problem that baffled the police. He also said that it might be worth my while to have a quiet talk with you, Mr. Bloomer. That's what I'm doing."

"I suspected as much." Theo said with a sigh. "Sitermann has been quite generous in his willingness to provide references. It is certainly beyond the call of duty."

Sergeant Winkler came onto the terrace. "We're done with the room below the pool, Stahl. The men will be done with the pool in another few minutes. What now?"

"I think we might drive down to the lab and see how they're coming with that roll of film," Stahl said, standing up. He adjusted his sunglasses and looked down at Theo. "Have you had any word from the girl who's missing? I put out an APB on her, but I still think she's out partying and will come home sooner or later to nurse a hangover."

"We haven't heard a peep from her," Theo said, meticulously truthful if not terribly accurate in the present spirit of candor. There was a very real problem concerning the ransom note. He soothed his conscience with a promise that, should the problem not be resolved briskly, he would report the purported abduction and blame the omission on fatigue. In the interim, he could not force himself to bring more trouble on the residents of the Harmony Hills villa. They were in enough trouble as it was.

Stahl gave Theo a grin, then went down the driveway and drove away. After a few minutes, the men by the pool packed up their equipment and left, as did those in Eli's quarters below the pool. Amelia came out of the kitchen to ask about lunch; Theo told her he doubted anyone would appear before mid-afternoon. They had been up all night, he added in order to divert any unspoken condemnation.

"I heard what happened to Eli," she said, standing in the doorway with her arms crossed. "Those ackees shouldn't have been brought into my kitchen. It was asking for trouble, and trouble's what you got."

"I noticed the ackees on the windowsill. How many were brought in?"

"There was a paper bag with some in it," Amelia said. "I'm not ignorant enough to buy ackees when they're not ripe, but I hated to waste them. I put them aside to ripen. Looks like I should have wasted them."

"How many were in the paper bag?"

"Three, if I recollect. Now there's two."

"Could someone have come into the kitchen of the villa yesterday while we were on the Governor's Coach?"

She shrugged. "How do I know? Emelda and I cleaned up after lunch, folded the laundry, made salads for dinner, and left for the day. We didn't have no reason to stay around here with everybody gone.'"

"Did Eli come into the kitchen before you left?"

"I already told all this to the police, about ten times by now. Eli came back from the station, helped himself to a piece of fish and some salad from the refrigerator, told Emelda she was putting on a little weight, and generally hung around being a nuisance until we left. I hinted that he could drive us home, but he just laughed and said he was going to spend the afternoon by the pool, pretending he was rich folk.'"

Theo hesitated, unsure how to pose a particular question without offending the woman. "Ah," he said, wading in timidly, "is it possible that Eli might have helped himself to the liquor supply in the kitchen? I'm not implying any sort of theft, but might he have considered it a mere loan if he were temporarily out of his own supply?"

"I told the police what he said. I can see you'll hound me until I tell you. I got better things to do than to stand here repeating myself, but I guess it won't hurt nothing. Eli took some fruit juice from the refrigerator and said he had a little birthday present he was going to use to make a pitcher of rum punch. Some birthday it turned out to be!"

"Did the police find the pitcher by the pool?"

"Eli knew better than to leave it there, where Emelda or I would find it and have to take it inside the house. I suppose he took it in himself and washed it before . . ." Her expression hardened, but a nerve jumped in her eyelid and her voice was strained. "He cleaned up before the vomiting sickness overtook him. Put the dishes away, the glass to dry in the sink, and the ackee rind in the garbage can out back. His mama must have taught him about cleanliness being next to godliness. Too bad she didn't teach him about the sin of taking your own life."

"You think he committed suicide?" Theo asked, surprised.

"He was sure acting crazy early in the afternoon. All excited, and tighter wound up than a dreadlock. He told Emelda he was leaving right soon. She thought he meant he was taking a vacation, but she's liable to get all kinds of things wrong. Like lunch." Amelia turned away and marched into the kitchen, leaving Theo to blink at her rigid back.

Once the kitchen door slammed shut, he poured himself another cup of coffee and sat back in the chair. It was a muddle of incredible magnitude, he thought, tugging distractedly on his beard as he tried to sort things out. Things seemed disinclined to be sorted, at least to any satisfactory conclusion. Eli had photographed a transaction involving Count D'Orsini and an unknown figure, who could well be the man Theo had heard when inadvertently eavesdropping. It was possible that the count had learned of the mysterious lens cap and had taken action to see that the investigation was halted. Extreme action. But some of it made no sense, and Theo could find no way to resolve the irritating contradictions.

Mary Margaret's disappearance, although equally irritating and increasingly distressing, could be coincidental. The appearance of the ransom note hinted as much. Theo grimaced as he gave his beard a hard tweak. There was an obvious way to clear up the glaring problem of the note, but it was distasteful at best. He sat for a long while, seeking an option.

At last he ceded and went across the dining room to the kitchen. "I shall be out for lunch," he said apologetically. "The others will survive on sandwiches. Please be so kind as to tell them I shall return by the middle of the afternoon and that I hope the absence of the car will not disrupt anyone's plans."

"You going to drive?" Amelia asked with a smile that seemed faintly sardonic. "You ain't in Connecticut, you know."

"I hadn't considered it, but I suppose I shall be forced to drive." Theo went to his bedroom and put on a jacket and tie, repeating to himself that he could handle the drive with minimal peril to his vehicle and his person. If he could just remember to stay on the left, especially when entering the road and turning, he would survive. Two million Jamaicans did it daily. Tourists zipped about on motorcycles, scorning such basic protection as helmets. The local newspapers did not have lengthy lists of those maimed and killed in automobile mishaps, which surely meant most of the drivers avoided accidents.

In the middle of the mental pep talk, there was a tap on Theo's door. "Uncle Theo? Are you awake?" Dorrie whispered. He let her in and invited her to sit down. "I couldn't sleep," she said, twisting her hands together and flicking her foot back and forth in an impatient cadence.

"Are you having difficulties with what occurred in the pool, my dear? It would be understandable if you found yourself dwelling on unpleasant memories."

"Do you think my hair is the tiniest bit too ash? Bitsy said she thought it tended towards brassy, but she can be awfully bitchy when the mood strikes."

Theo tucked his wallet in his pocket and soberly observed himself in the mirror while he confirmed that his tie was straight. "A question of such importance cannot be answered without thought. Allow me to ponder the possibilities before I tender what will be an amateurish response. Hair color has not been a major issue in my life; hair retention, on the other hand, has rather occupied my idle moments."

"Oh, Uncle Theo, I know it's not all that earth-shattering."

Dorrie joined him in front of the dresser. "Besides, Mr. Robert wouldn't even allow me out of his salon if he thought it was brassy. He has incredibly high standards." She pushed back her hair and regarded him in the mirror with appraising eyes. "What did Mother have to say? Was she livid when you told her what happened to Eli?"

"A goodly part of the conversation concerned a mishap at the bridge table. I was prepared to tell her of the recent tragedy, but the conversation took another direction and I simply let it go."

"Oh?" Dorrie murmured. "And where are you going? Aren't you tired after being detained in that nasty police station all night?"

"I thought I might go to a hotel for lunch. All of you seemed apt to sleep through lunch, and I saw no reason to make things difficult for the help. Preparing lunch for one, you know, can be a bother."

"Which hotel, Uncle Theo, and how are you going to get there?"

"Any of them, I suppose; I hadn't really decided. As for transportation, I am going to take the car. I'll be back in sufficient time for you to go to the beach or do whatever you may desire."

"Let me pop on some lipstick and get my purse. I'll meet you in the driveway, Uncle Theo. I cannot imagine anything more exciting than doing lunch in a hotel with my darling uncle."

"But surely you would prefer a nap," Theo said as the door closed on her heels. "Surely you would."

"Now, remember to stay left," Dorrie said as they backed down the driveway and onto the street. "No matter how wrong it feels, it's right, so just grit your teeth and resist the urge to correct things. A head-on will feel *tres* worse. Which hotel is Sitermann in, by the way?"

"The one where we utilized the beach several days ago." Theo tightened his fingers around the steering wheel and peered down the street. No traffic approached—a good omen. "I had not considered the fact that I would be obliged to change gears with my left hand, and that the foot pedals might be reversed. It is most unsettling. I am not sure that this is wise, Dorrie. It is one thing to risk my life with this jaunt, but quite another to risk yours." After a bout of fumbling, he managed to find first gear. The car spurted forward, then sputtered to a halt. "It is clear that this is imprudent, if not reckless. I feel—"

"Just gun it, Uncle Theo. They'll get out of our way."

Despite the turtle-like pace and the occasional problem with the stick shift, Theo managed to arrive at the hotel. He parked under a palm tree and gave Dorrie an impish grin. "Quite an adventure, wasn't it?"

"It certainly was. We were almost rammed in the rear about two dozen times, Uncle Theo. Once we've done lunch with Sitermann, I'll drive us back to the villa." She twisted the rearview mirror and examined her lipstick, then opened the car door. "He does expect us, doesn't he?"

"I would imagine he does," Theo said under his breath. To Dorrie, he merely shrugged, then trailed her into the hotel lobby.

Sitermann was on a rattan couch, a drink in one hand and a rolled-up magazine in the other. He wore a white jacket over a pink T-shirt, and green trousers. The lobby was dim, but his sunglasses were firmly affixed and he seemed to experience no difficulty in spotting Theo and Dorrie. "Yo, how are you sports doing? Got time to do lunch? You know, Bloom, this little girl of yours gets prettier every time I touch base with her—and that's no hype. She ought to be in pictures."

"Can it, Sitermann," Theo said wearily. "It occurred to me that doing lunch with you might be informative, if somewhat hard on the digestion. Let's put it on your expense account, old man."

"Dynamite!" Sitermann slapped Theo on the back, then took Dorrie's arm and tucked it through his own. They went into a dining room filled with round white tables, dripping ferns, a central fountain with a discreet waterfall, and a low background of what tourists considered to be island music. Dorrie made an appreciative noise as a jacketed waiter dashed across the room to pull out a chair for her, then snapped a gleaming white napkin into her lap. A menu with the thickness of a telephone directory was placed lovingly in her hands. The waiter, who assured them that his name was Francois and that he was delighted to serve them, promised to bring cocktails immediately.

"Not bad," Dorrie said. "Is this how spies live all the time, or is this part of your cover?"

Sitermann winced. "Let's not worry about that, you gorgeous thing. Why don't you try this lobster thing for an appetizer and the scallops for an entree? I had them the other night, and they were out of sight. What looks like the thing for you, Bloom?"

"Let's start with an exchange of information. What's the prognosis for the murder investigation?"

"D'Orsini will be released by the time I eat the olive in my martini, unless that roll of film provides enough damnation to hold him. Half the bigwigs on the island have telephoned the other half of the bigwigs and insisted that D'Orsini is being treated as if he were a common criminal. High society does not acknowledge the possibility that he's a major drug dealer. Too tawdry, I suppose."

"Do you think he murdered Eli?" Theo asked.

Sitermann gazed pensively at Francois, who was introducing himself and pledging total devotion to a nearby table occupied by three well-baked women. "You know, Bloom, I don't think he did. D'Orsini may not have known Eli was a narc, but Eli sure as hell knew D'Orsini was a crook . . . and not one from whom to accept tokens of friendship. Hard to see the two of them sipping rum beside the pool, isn't it?"

"It is indeed," Theo murmured, having had the same thoughts.

Dorrie looked up over the edge of the menu. "If D'Orsini didn't do it, then who did? It had to be someone who had access to Eli's quarters below the pool. That is key, Uncle Theo."

"It is indeed."

The fickle waiter returned with their drinks and took their orders. Theo waited until he was gone, then said, "Sitermann, there is another little problem that has arisen. This is in conjunction with Mary Margaret's mysterious disappearance."

"I really don't know where she is, Bloom."

"So you say. But we'll let that go for the moment. I was informed this morning that the girl's father received a ransom note that demanded a million dollars in exchange for the hostage. Clipped words, small, unmarked bills, don't call the police—that sort of thing."

Dorrie choked on a mouthful of martini. "Is this for real? You're not making it up? A million dollars for Mary Margaret? Oh, my God, what did her father say?" She took a deep drink from the glass. "What did Mother say?"

Theo ignored her. "You do see the problem, don't you?" he said to Sitermann. "This is not an ordinary case of kidnapping."

"What problem?" Dorrie squawked.

Sitermann nodded. "You've zeroed in on the crux, Bloom. But which one of them?"

Dorrie drained the glass and barked an order in Francois's direction. "Which one of what—what?"

"Which one of your friends is involved in this supposedly professional kidnapping?" Theo said gently. "Mary Margaret disappeared last night at approximately midnight. Her father received a note this morning, not more than eight or nine hours after the fact. It's rather obvious that someone from here contacted someone in Connecticut and had that person deliver the note. There was either a great deal of foresight and planning, or collusion."

"That's the bottom line," Sitermann said.

Dorrie took the martini from Francois's tray and drank it.

"You won't say anything to the others, will you?" Theo said as he chugged up the driveway of the villa. Dorrie had been much too astounded to take the wheel, and Theo had actually begun to enjoy the thrill of driving in such a bizarre fashion. The perpetual peril had been . . . well, invigorating. "I may be wrong about the ransom note," he continued, "in that it may not involve anyone in our small group. But if I am correct, I do not wish to alert this person and cause him or her to do something foolish."

Dorrie gave him a sharp look. "Her? It's unlikely to be either Amelia or Emelda; servants are hardly capable of that level of subterfuge, unless we're discussing padding the gro-cer's account.

"I would assume you're referring to Bitsy. Come on, Uncle Theo, she has nothing to do with this. She's straighter than Pookie's nose after the plastic surgeon had a field day with it on Park Avenue—and we're talking straight. Bitsy teaches Sunday school. She's never set foot outside her bedroom without a brassiere. She squeaks when she walks."

"It is difficult to envision. But you're overlooking another distaff player in the game, my dear. It is not unheard of for the kidnap victim to be, in reality, a co-conspirator. Mary Margaret may have misjudged her father's sense of parental duty, or even the extent of his liquid assets, but she may very well be the instigator of the ransom note."

"Why would she do that? It seems like a lot of bother. Her father gives her all the money she wants, and she has enough plastic in her wallet to purchase a small European country and declare herself empress. Catherine the Great could serve as her role model, although I never bought those lurid stories. It sounded so unhygienic."

"I have no idea why she might have agreed to the scheme, much less initiated it," Theo admitted. He realized he was still clutching the steering wheel with white fingers, and forced them to relinquish the death grip. A stray image flashed through his mind, but with such haste he was unable to identify it. "Well, we made it home safely, which I find no small feat. Shall we have a celebratory coffee on the terrace?"

"I've been courting puffy eyelids too long. I'm off to nap, then see if Amelia can produce cool cucumber slices without hyperventilating. She wouldn't survive ten seconds in Connecticut."

Theo went to the terrace and gazed at the Caribbean, his lips pressed in a pensive frown. Sitermann had agreed to see what he could learn about the delivery/deliverer of the ransom note. He had not anticipated much success. They had lunched agreeably and parted on amiable terms, except for a mutter from Francois that had expressed doubt over Sitermann's ability to calculate in the delicate arena of tipping. "Joik" had not had its origins in a Parisian bistro.

Sandy and Biff were on the deck beside the pool, both

stretched out on chaise lounges and oblivious to everything but the sun. Bitsy sat in the shade of the umbrella, a magazine in her lap. A radio behind the kitchen door played Jamaican music. Dorrie appeared briefly on the balcony, ascertained Biff's whereabouts with a proprietary smile, and wiggled her fingers at Theo as she vanished back into the bedroom.

It was what he had imagined the trip would be, a peaceful scene of sunbathing, reading, enjoying the idyllic weather and lazy ambience of the island. He had hoped to see the botanical gardens, maybe even to speak to the Jamaican horticulturists about their insights into the cultivation of exotic bromeliads, for which he had a fondness. He had even dared to hope he might return to his greenhouse in Handy Hollow with a few choice cuttings to be nurtured into wondrous things that would be quite the topic of gossip at the local horticulturists' meetings.

But it was not to be, he thought as he sat down. Instead of snippets of plants and enlightening exchanges concerning temperature control and botanical diets, he was in the midst of murder. Of drug dealing, of kidnapping, of adolescent bickering. Of fraudulent aristocracy and . . .

"I say, Bloomer," Count D'Orsini called from the bottom of the driveway. "Could I be so presumptuous as to invite you over for tea or a drink? Gerry is here, and we very desperately want to talk to you."

After a quick appraisal of the poolside and the vacant balcony, Theo went down the driveway. The count was dressed in the same clothes he'd worn at the police station, and his cheeks and jaw were faintly gray with unshaven stubble. Deep lines cut into his face as if done with a blade. He had, Theo decided, rather gone to seed during the last twelve hours.

"This is good of you," he said, putting his hand on Theo's shoulder for a moment. "I know you have a low opinion of me, perhaps deservedly so. Come up to the house and let me get you something to drink, and please excuse my appearance. I was released less than an hour ago, and I must say I've had a particularly trying night."

Gerry was sitting on the patio beside the pool, a glass in her hand and a pitcher nearby on a table. "Thank you for coming, Theo. This is such a ghastly sequence of events—Eli's death, Mary Margaret's disappearance, and the knowledge that the police would like nothing more than to lock Hal up in some dingy cell until they can concoct enough evidence to convict him."

Theo sat down across from her. "But the police have released Count D'Orsini, so one must assume they have no evidence. Surely his local connections will prevent his being framed for something he did not do."

"One hopes," the count murmured as he went behind a small bar and found a bottle of Perrier. He poured a glass and brought it to Theo, then moved a chair next to Gerry. "I didn't do it, you know. Gerry tells me that you believe this rot about my possible involvement with drug traffic, and I wanted to assure you that the police chaps are mistaken. They are convinced I rove the Caribbean in the true buccaneer tradition in order to engage in wickedness." He crossed his legs and gave Theo a comradely wink. "If it were the eighteenth century, I would probably follow in the grand tradition of Edward Teach, who's always been a hero of mine. I'd like nothing more than to board a schooner aswarm with terrified virgins, my black beard flaming and my manhood in full bloom. Alas, there are no virgins aswarm anywhere these days, and the Navy takes such a dim view of that sort of adventuresome spirit."

"Virgins or cabin boys?" Gerry said drily.

"Both," he said with a second wink to Theo. "Admittedly

I do take friends out on the yacht, but I do so at their insistence. They find deep-sea fishing, or at least the premise of it, as romantic as Hemingway told them they should. The *Pis Aller* is not the *Love Boat*, alas, and most of them end up in the throes of *mal de mer* and frantic for *terra firma*."

Theo nodded. "And while these friends are conveniently below in the cabin, moaning over too many martinis, you have an opportunity to rendezvous with craft of Colombian origin, no? Your passengers subsequently and obligingly provide an alibi, should the narcotics people be so intrusive as to question the purpose of the outing."

Count D'Orsini had the courtesy to look somewhat abashed. "*Touché*, Mr. Bloomer. I may have assisted some acquaintances with the exportation of substances not exactly welcomed with open arms in the United States, but I can assure you that I am not the veritable Rothschild of the cocaine industry that the police envision me to be. They do so overestimate my impact on world trade. As for this gigolo nonsense, I have taken lonely women out for a bit of romance, but I have never requested they render payment for my attentions. If they have chosen to reward me, they have done so without any prompting on my part. I am a wastrel; there is no doubt about it in anyone's mind. I am a blackguard, a philanderer, a parasite both on my friends and on society as an entity. Were the profession feasible, I would make a dandy privateer. However, I am not a cad."

"And he's not a murderer," Gerry said. "You've got to believe that, Theo. I've known Hal for twenty years. We met at a time when my life was a shambles. My friends would not speak to me, and my relatives had scratched my name out of the family Bible. Hal helped me find myself, to sort out my life and determine who I really was and what I wanted to do with the knowledge. He is my closest and dearest friend in the world. I believe him when he says he's not a murderer."

"It is clear that you believe in his innocence, Gerry," Theo said gently. "Your faith and loyalty are admirable. I, too, would like to feel equally assured of his innocence, but I cannot. There are too many unexplained events."

D'Orsini rubbed his jaw, exposing a certain softness to his chin that belied his boyish appearance. "Permit me tell you what happened yesterday. It sounds rather damning, I'm afraid, but it is the truth. I was here by the pool all morning, catching up on correspondence and perusing the newspaper. I heard your group leave, and then I heard the car return some thirty minutes later, roughly at two o'clock. I thought nothing more about it until Eli came up my driveway an hour later, strutting as if he had wiped out the bank in Monte Carlo. It was an amazing sight, to say the least. Can I refill your glass, Bloomer?"

"No, thank you, this is sufficient."

"A bit leery of my hospitality?" Count D'Orsini laughed, then turned to look at the driveway. "Eli came up to the patio and threw himself down in a chair as if I'd suggested he wander by for cocktails. He proceeded to tell me that he was an undercover narcotics officer with the Jamaican Criminal Investigation Bureau, that he'd been observing me for several days, and that he had evidence that I'd engaged in a major transaction on this very spot. I naturally quizzed him as to the validity of his statements, and found him most convincing. Once I'd conceded his story, I asked him why he felt it proper to share the information with me—the object of his official scrutiny." He again laughed, but without sincerity. "Eli then brandished a roll of film and offered to sell it to me. He felt it would be of great interest to me—or to his superiors should I decline to purchase it."

"He was blackmailing you?" Theo said, frowning. "Did

you tell this to Sergeant Stahl?"

"Ah, not precisely. I said Eli came over to see if the lawn needed attention. I saw no reason to introduce the issue of the film."

"They came across it when they searched his room in the preliminary investigation. It is being processed now, and I should imagine they will have prints at any moment."

Gerry put her hands over her face. "I told you, Hal. It's a matter of time before they come back to arrest you. You know what you have to do."

He pulled her hands away and gave her a smile of great tenderness. "I can't, darling. If they have the film, and if it depicts what Eli said it did, then there's nothing I can do. They'll stop me before I get twenty feet off the island. All I can do is insist that I didn't poison this police chap—and I didn't. After he suggested the deal, I could only laugh and show him an empty wallet. I did tell him that I would see what sort of cash I could lay my hands on, and that I'd get back to him when I was in a position to negotiate some sort of settlement. He was willing to give me a day or two."

"You do have a basis to argue your innocence," Theo said, tugging on his beard as he pondered the count's version of the events. Eli's expensive wardrobe and penchant for imported liquor did nothing to undermine it. "If Eli agreed to give you some time to acquire the money, and it seems reasonable to suppose he would, then you would have been most foolish to murder him in the interim. He wouldn't have given you the roll of film for safekeeping; he would have concealed it in a safe place. He was more dangerous dead than alive."

"That's true." Count D'Orsini stood up and began to pace across the patio. "I pointed out that I was hardly likely to hand over twenty grand until I saw exactly what he had. He said he would develop the film, show me the prints, and pass along the negatives when we concluded the deal. We actually shook hands when he left, as though we'd finalized a merger or contracted to purchase widgets from each other. It was downright eerie, if you ask me."

"It makes sense," Gerry said, suddenly coming to life. "Hal wouldn't have done anything until he saw the prints."

"The prints that show him either buying or selling cocaine to an associate," Theo pointed out drily. "Who was it, D'Orsini? Who's the connection?"

"It's hard to say, since it rather depends on when he took the photographs. He failed to be specific, and I was too unnerved to inquire in great detail." He began to pace again, turning sharply at the pool and coming within inches of a wicker sofa. "Don't you see that, Gerry? He could have caught a fetching likeness of that swarthy Colombian chap with the dirty fingernails, or more possibly my . . . ah, shall we say, entrepreneur friend."

"Either of whom has the same motive you do," Theo said. "Eli may have approached the second person, intending to collect from the two of you."

D'Orsini paused to think, then shook his head. "Not the Colombian. We merely tossed about some ideas for future transactions, and he left the island the next morning to confer with his partners at home. Furthermore, had Eli approached him, our pool boy would have been discovered without a face. The South American business types aren't subtle."

"And the other man?" Theo prompted.

"That would be telling, old chap. If the police have ascertained his identity, then they'll be more than delighted to tell." His face grew more animated; Theo could now see why women were attracted to him. "But," he added, flashing teeth as white and even as the petals of a snowcap Shasta daisy, "the police haven't come screeching up the hill, sirens blaring, lights flashing, all that overly done sort of thing. It's perfectly quiet. I do think it's possible that this insidious roll of film was simply a threat on Eli's part." He knelt down in front of Gerry and took her hand, looking like a small, exuberant altar boy. "The roll may be a dud, darling. If so, they have nothing on me—or on anyone else. I'll be home free."

"Then you'll cease this deadly drug thing?" she asked in a hoarse voice. "You'll quit completely? You swear it?"

"And do what—work?" He turned to Theo with a self-deprecating grimace. "Harvard trained me to pull wonderful pranks, to use the correct silverware, to wear the proper clothing and say the proper things. A bit of French opens many a chateau door. All in all, it was a valuable experience, and I am quite indebted to the institution for that. But I was booted before I finished a degree, due to an unavoidable scandal that not even the dean, a liver-spotted pedant with limited imagination, could laugh away over a cigar and a glass of sherry. I'm not qualified to do anything useful. No, by damn, that's not totally accurate—I am a charming extra man at dinner parties, where I flatter the ugliest of the ducklings until they're so flustered they drink from the finger bowls. I use my talents to make otherwise lonely women feel cherished. I tend other people's houses and am meticulous about watering their plants, supervising their servants, and seeing that the lawn and the pets are groomed on a regular basis."

Gerry gave him a look of exasperated fondness. "You could work at my firm. It's not as exciting as jetting over to Nice for brunch and Paris for *le cocktail hour,* but it does keep one in groceries."

"But don't you see? I do work. It's not your perception of honest labor, but it really and truly is. Someone has to do this sort of thing. Babysitters do it on a primitive basis, tending to children. Servants do it, too, but for money. I do it for free."

He squeezed her hand so tightly she winced. "I provide a necessary service to the idle wealthy, and I ask no payment in return. I accept what is offered, certainly, but for the most part it's a meal, the use of a house or yacht, a trinket of jewelry, a ticket to the theater, a little safari. What I receive is minor in comparison to what I give so freely."

Theo suspected the count was about to wax poetic over the intricacies of providing such a selfless public service to the jet set. He put down his glass and rose. "The police do have the roll of film and are presently developing it. You must be prepared to deal with that, although I do tend to believe you are not responsible for Eli's death."

"I would never murder someone," he said earnestly, still on his knees in front of Gerry. "For one thing, I've had no experience in that kind of endeavor, and I wouldn't have the slightest idea how to go about it. I suppose one could seek suggestions from a mystery novel, but I rarely have time to finish the *Gentleman's Quarterly* and *Town and Country* every month. For another thing, I do have a vestige of loyalty to the family name and I would never do anything to add to the disgrace I've already put on it. Mother was quite right to cut me off, you know; I hardly would have expected her to have done otherwise."

Theo did not point out that a conviction for drug trafficking might be considered a whack to the family tree. He thanked the two for the drink and went down the driveway, keeping an eye on the undergrowth on the off chance he might spot Mary Margaret's foot under the spectacular ferns (Heliconia). He did not.

Theo retired to his room, hung his jacket in the closet, aligned his shoes in the closet, and lay down on the bed with his guidebook to read a section on ferns (Heliconia). When he opened his eyes, more than an hour had passed. He discovered the book astraddle his chest and placed a bookmark in it before putting it on the bedside table. He was, he reminded himself sternly, sixty-one years old and unaccustomed to spending most of the night in a police station. Count D'Orsini had described the ordeal in the police station as "trying." "Trying" was a mild term, but of course the count was at least ten years younger—and had all his hair.

He was peering in the bathroom mirror at the shiny circle on the top of his head when his door opened. "Mr. Bloomer?" Bitsy said.

"Yes?" he said, coming out of the bathroom with a slightly guilty expression. Vanity was not a mortal sin, but he did not wish to be caught in the act.

"That policeman is back, and he's absolutely frothing about the mouth. He brought a herd of men with him, and they're searching the entire house. They actually insisted on pawing through my lingerie, if you can believe it. It's nasty, and probably illegal."

Theo realized he had been hearing some activity for several minutes, although he had not assumed it came from an invasion of the magnitude Bitsy described. "I have no idea if a search warrant is required in Jamaica, but it does seem worth the bother to inquire. Where is Sergeant Stahl?"

"On the terrace. He's drinking our coffee and talking to your friend." The implicit accusation hung in the momentary silence. "I cannot bear to watch them going through my private things, so if you don't mind, I shall wait in here," she added in an indignant squeak.

Theo saw several policemen in the master bedroom as he went downstairs, but he did not linger to discuss the legality of their activity. He stopped in the kitchen to request a glass of water, but the room was uninhabited. Drawers had been pulled open; cabinet doors were ajar. Canisters had been placed on the counter—and searched, if the scattered flour and sugar were valid indications. Cases of beer had been pulled into the middle of the floor, and the contents of the refrigerator were piled on the table. Amelia and Emelda were gone, no doubt in a huff more indignant than that of the occupant of his bedroom.

Stahl and Sitermann were on the terrace, a tray with coffee and cups on the table between them. Trey sat at the far end of the table, his feet propped on the table and his hands wrapped loosely around a beer can. He appeared to be lost in his thoughts, although Theo was beginning to surmise he was merely lost.

Dorrie, Biff, Sandy, and Sandy's golf bag were lined up against the rail. Dorrie was pinker than a foxglove (*D. purpurea*); the boys' faces had the more mottled hues of a rosita lily. Dismayed by the proximity of weapons (irons, woods, and hard white spheres), Theo gave the bag a cautionary glance as he pulled out a chair and sat down. "Looking for something?" he inquired politely.

Stahl nodded with a stony expression, but Sitermann said, "The sergeant was not happy about the results from the photo lab. To be honest with you, he was more than a mite disappointed with the roll of film."

"Overexposed? Too dark?"

"No," drawled Sitermann, leaning back in his chair, "the lighting was pretty damn good for an amateur. Focus wasn't bad, and neither was the composition. One of them might win a prize in a photography contest. Of course it'd have to be sponsored by *Playboy* or one of that ilk."

"And why is that?"

"I don't think I should explain out loud, not with a fine, upstanding young lady present, Bloom." He picked up an envelope from the table and handed it to Theo. "Take a peek and you'll see how awkward it might be to verbalize the problem."

Theo took out the prints and studied them. The first was of Mary Margaret, her eyes closed and a serene smile on her face. Her breasts were bereft of any clothing. The second centered on her buttocks, which were snowy white hills of unimpeded flesh. "Oh, goodness," Theo murmured, primly moving on to the next print. It featured not only Mary Margaret's breasts, but also a totally bewildered gentleman with a balding head and scandalously wide eyes behind bifocals.

"I especially liked that one," Sitermann said. He slapped Theo on the back. "Your peepers are about to pop right out of their sockets, aren't they? That must have been some camera sweep. A right delicate close-up of something most men would kill for, in a manner of speaking."

"Uncle Theo!" Dorrie said in a shocked voice. "You didn't really stare at . . . at whatever Mr. Sitermann is snickering about, did you?"

"Right on, Mr. Bloomer," Sandy said. "You're my kind of guy."

Dorrie swiveled her head to give him a withering look. "I can assure you that my uncle is not 'your kind of guy,' Alexander Whitcombe. I find these tawdry insinuations juvenile and primitive. You may be both, but Uncle Theo is neither." She rotated her head in case Biff felt a urge to contribute his opinion. He did not.

Theo hastily put the prints back in the envelope. "May I assume they are all of a similar nature?" he asked Sitermann.

"Prone and supine. Nude, nuder, nudest, and whatever comes after that. Mary Margaret made a fine model, didn't she? I really ought to arrange a screen test for her."

"Uncle Theo," Dorrie began ominously, "is this—"

Sergeant Stahl banged down his cup. "The entire roll of

film consists of this sort of thing, Mr. Bloomer. I personally badgered the lab men for several hours to hurry them along, and will now owe favors for a long time to come. I was disappointed, very disappointed, especially since you had led me to believe we would find something of value to the investigation. I was not prepared for pornography."

"Pornography?" With an outraged expression, Sitermann bounced his hand off his forehead. "This isn't pornography, Stahl; this is art. Why, I'd gladly have one of them blown up to poster size and hung in my living room right over the mantel. Did you see the tits on that girl? Old J. Edgar himself would've had a coronary if—"

"Uncle Theo," Dorrie said, her expression as icy as her voice, "muzzle that man or I shall do it myself. He has no right to expose me to this locker room vernacular." She glared at the spy until he wilted into his chair like a dog's tooth violet in a drought.

"Yeah, watch your language," Biff said gallantly, if belatedly.

"I understand your disappointment," Theo said to Stahl. "There was reasonably credible evidence that the film was shot from the balcony and that it would implicate Count D'Orsini and an unknown associate."

"But it seems my top officer wasn't occupying himself with the investigation. It seems he had other things on his mind—and in his expensive lenses. That equipment cost a great deal of money. I didn't requisition it so that Staggley could indulge in voyeurism." He snatched up the envelope before Sitermann, whose hand was moving stealthily across the table, could reach it. "What's more, we don't have a damn thing on D'Orsini now. With the pressure we've gotten in the last eighteen hours, we wouldn't dare give him a parking ticket if he drove through a wall and parked in the middle of the police station."

Dorrie stepped forward. "I still don't understand why you've taken it upon yourself to search the villa. We certainly don't have Eli's film canisters tucked in among our panties, although it might be an appropriate place for them."

"Yeah," Biff said, nodding. "Do you have a constitutional right to do this—or a good old-fashioned search warrant? Dorrie's father has some high-power connections, and he'll be totally pissed when he finds out how your men have—"

"Sir," a uniformed officer said, coming from the dining room, "we found this in the downstairs bedroom." He held up a plastic baggie. "It's ganja, sir. About three-quarters of an ounce."

Trey flapped his hand. "Oh, that's mine. Be a good sport and put it back where you found it. I promise not to say a word if you want a little toke, but don't make a pig of yourself."

"Possession of a controlled substance is a felony in Jamaica," Sergeant Stahl said coldly.

"I told you to get rid of it," Dorrie hissed.

Trey gave her an indulgent smile. "Yes, you did, darling, and several times if I recall. But I didn't, did I? You may have enough pocket money to squander it; I, on the other hand, have been trained from birth to pinch every penny, since we all know that's why the rich stay richer. Do you think that's the reason I do so love to pinch bottoms, too? A nasty habit learned from dear old nanny?"

The uniformed man had been following the exchange with growing amusement, but he sobered when he caught Stahl's glower. "What shall I do, sir? Do you want me to arrest him and transport him to headquarters to be booked?"

"Tedious, too tedious," Trey said with a yawn.

Theo wanted to suggest tar and feathers, but instead said,

"It is a minimal amount for personal consumption, Sergeant Stahl. I hope you won't allow this young man's behavior to influence your decision."

"I think you ought to nuke him," Dorrie said. She marched through the door into the villa. Biff trailed after her, murmuring to the back of her head.

Trey held out his wrists. "Have your way with me, Sergeant. Handcuff me, swallow the key, and drag me to some filthy prison cell populated with lepers and rats. Or, if you prefer, I can trot downstairs and fetch my checkbook. I could make it out to you personally, if you prefer. That way it won't have to detour through the system."

Blinking at Trey, the officer said, "I am impressed with your obviously fervent desire to spend several more years in Jamaica, with room and board provided by the national penal system. However, I fail to understand your motivation to do so. Do you not think life will be pleasanter in your parents' home in Connecticut?"

"It's a toss-up, actually. Hanging around the family mausoleum is boring, especially if Magsy's not about to needle. My parents have always encouraged me to meet new people and try new experiences."

Stahl sighed. "I won't take any immediate action concerning the illegal possession—but I won't rule out the possibility of doing so in the future. At the moment, I'd rather find a roll of film that will provide evidence of D'Orsini's involvement. Maybe it doesn't exist. Maybe Staggley spent his idle moments photographing the young lady in various stages of undress."

"But if there is a second roll of film, why do you think it's inside the house, sir?" Sandy asked. "Wouldn't Eli have been more likely to leave it with his family or with a friend?"

"I have no expectations that we'll find it," Stahl conceded

in a wry tone, "but it seemed prudent to look around for it. I don't understand why he didn't bring it to the police lab the next morning to be developed. If he had, we would have concluded the investigation, arrested D'Orsini, picked up the associates, and handed the entire thing over to the prosecutor. Staggley knew better, damnit!"

Theo felt obliged to explain why Eli had not taken the roll of film to the police lab. He related the blackmail attempt, D'Orsini's admission of complicity, and the settlement the two had reached concerning a delayed exchange of goods and services. Once Stahl had stopped growling, Theo added, "D'Orsini did not imply he'd actually seen this roll of film, but it seems likely Eli had it in his possession at that moment. However, it is possible that it might be at a private developing service."

"I'll put Winkler on it immediately," Stahl said, standing up. "As much as I'd like to drag D'Orsini right back down to the station, I'll have to wait until we have evidence." He jabbed a finger in Trey's direction. "And as for you, you retarded little snot, keep your nose clean if you don't want to learn some of our island techniques for eliciting confessions. A checkbook won't do you any good, and neither will your family's money."

"Yes, sir." Trey made a sweeping gesture with his hand. "And have a nice day, sir. It was lovely to see you once again. Perhaps you and the wife can drop by some evening for a drink."

Theo grabbed Stahl's arm and hurried him down the steps to the driveway. "There's something I'd like to discuss with you, Sergeant."

"Capital punishment? It's not legal, but it can be arranged."

"Forget about the Ellison boy; he is, as you said so eloquently, a retarded little snot. There is a problem about the prints you obtained from the roll of film in Eli's room."

"Yeah," Stahl said, beginning to grin, "they show an old man lusting after a naked girl. Ooh, she sure does have knockers, doesn't she? We're still watching for her. My men are working their way through all the bars and parties, but there are a daunting number of them and it takes time. I don't suppose you've had any word from her yet?"

"No, not a peep. But we both know I was present when at least some of those photographs were taken. The problem is that I'm not at all sure that Eli was."

"You were too busy staring at those big round nipples to see who else was around, Bloomer." He held up his hands in mock defense. "I'm not saying that in criticism, either. I sure as hell wouldn't have been analyzing the bushes for covert camera equipment. My wife could have been standing on her head in a palm tree, along with her mother and my boss; I wouldn't have seen any of them."

Theo gave him a pained look. "I will admit that I was rather taken aback when I first opened my eyes, in that I expected to see nothing more startling than a few of the young people preparing to sunbathe in normal attire. Indeed, I was momentarily at a loss for words. But once I recovered from my initial confusion, the girl apologized and went to the far side of the pool."

"And stripped? Ooh, ooh, ooh," Stahl said gleefully.

"She did remove her bikini in order to avoid tan marks. However, I was unable to continue my nap, and I did not see Eli anywhere in the vicinity of the pool."

"Oh, Bloomer, don't tell me you spent the rest of the afternoon watching the steps from the driveway to the patio around the pool. I know damn well what you looked at—and it wasn't some ocean liner out in the pristine waters of

MoBay." Laughing, Stahl went down the driveway and drove away in a white police car.

Theo simmered in silence until he could trust himself to return to the terrace. When he did, he found Sitermann and Sandy seated at the table. The coffeepot had been replaced with a pitcher of rum punch, and the two were arguing amiably about the utility of woods on the fairway.

As Theo took a seat, Sandy looked up. "Ah, Mr. Bloomer, the policeman never showed us the actual photographs, but I gathered from what was said that they were of Mary Margaret . . . in the flesh. What do you think that means?"

Sitermann snickered. "What I'd like to know is how we can get our hands on the negatives."

"I would hate to imagine the look on the obstetrician's face the day you were born," Theo said to the spy. "But as for the odd roll of film, Sandy, I'm not sure what it means. If I hadn't been an unwitting participant, I would have presumed that Eli persuaded Mary Margaret to engage in a private session while the rest of us were occupied."

"The look on your face," Sitermann cackled, thumping Theo on the back. "Lordy, Bloom, you were about as bewildered as a nun in a soap opera!"

"To continue," Theo said, "at least some of the photographs were taken the first afternoon of our trip, not too long after our arrival. Most of you went upstairs to unpack. I went down to the pool, where I inadvertently dozed off for a few minutes. When I awoke, Mary Margaret was nearby, dressed—or should I say undressed—to some extent." He ran a finger around his collar as heat raced up his neck. "I tend to think Eli was not even at the Villa at that time, that he had gone to fetch ice or a newspaper."

"Then you think Eli was in cahoots with someone?" Sandy asked.

"You bet your time-share in Bermuda," Sitermann inserted. "And whoever it is ought to be put up for an Oscar for cinematography, or whatever you call fancy camera work."

"And you ought to be put out of your misery," Theo said testily.

Sitermann left in a flurry of crude innuendos that Theo might be more of a rogue than one might assume on first appraisal. Sandy picked up his golf bag and started for the dining room.

"I'm amazed you found the energy to play golf after such a difficult night," Theo said, shaking his head at the very idea of physical exertion. "How was the course?"

"When the uniforms swarmed in, I went to the backyard to practice chip shots," Sandy admitted. "I see too many of them at school. Biff and I are going to try to get in eighteen holes later this afternoon." His scalp turned pink under his stubby blond hair. "Is Mary Margaret's anatomy some kind of clue, sir?"

"Go polish your putter." Theo went to the kitchen in hopes that Amelia and Emelda had returned. They had not. With a sigh, he located Gerry's number on a business card taped near the telephone and dialed the number.

"North Shore Property Management," she answered list-lessly.

He identified himself, then apologetically mentioned that the residents of the villa did not have a key to the gate.

"I suppose the police have Eli's key. I'll have a copy made and have a messenger bring it over immediately. This terrible mess has left me in a walking fog, and I didn't think about the key. How did all of you get in the gate last night?"

"We managed," Theo said evasively. He went on to report that the staff had vanished, most likely because of a police invasion of the kitchen, and very well might not reappear any-time soon. He did not intend to cause difficulty, but it was—well, somewhat of a crisis, since his young people were not likely to respond well to the proposal that they all pitch in. Any inherent spirit of self-sacrificing volunteerism lay in the arena of charity functions, black ties, large orchestras, and an opportunity to display the family jewels to an audience with appreciative tastes.

"I'll call Amelia and plead," she said in the same flat voice. "You'll be leaving in two days, so I can even offer her time-and-a-half for . . . combat duty. Have you heard any-thing from the police? Did they show you the prints?"

"Yes," he said, relieved that she could not see the redness creeping up his neck, "and at this point Count D'Orsini may be safe from any kind of prosecution. The roll of film did not contain any incriminating shots of him in the middle of a transaction with this mysterious associate."

"Oh, thank God. Then the police aren't planning to arrest Hal? He would be brutalized in jail, and probably wouldn't last a month. I've got to call him and tell him. Despite his show of bravado earlier today, he was absolutely terrified of what might happen. He will be so thrilled to know he's safe."

Theo interrupted before she could say good-bye and ring off. "There's something you and D'Orsini should consider. The roll of film that the police now have may not be the only one in existence; it's possible Eli left the pertinent one with a friend. The police have searched here and in Eli's quarters, but they haven't given up yet. They're currently checking with the private film laboratories. It very well may surface somewhere."

"Oh," she said, deflating more quickly than a punctured balloon. "Then you think Hal is still in danger of being arrested?"

"I don't know." He gazed at the two ackees on the windowsill. "There is something else which you ought to discuss with D'Orsini, Gerry. This so-called associate of his might have decided to murder Eli rather than deal with the blackmail demands. Now that the film has failed to expose him, D'Orsini is the only person who knows his identity. If he has killed once, then he may decide to do so again in order to lay to rest any possibility that he might be identified in the future."

There was a very long moment of silence. Theo could hear her breath against the receiver as she considered his words. "No," she said slowly, "I think Hal is safe. I'll tell him what you said, and warn him of the possible danger. He'll be cautious until this is resolved."

"The only way in which he can be safe is to tell the police the identity of this associate."

"That would prove a little more complicated than you think. But it is kind of you to be concerned, and I will speak to Hal about taking precautions until the police can solve the murder. Now I'll telephone Amelia and see if she and Emelda can be persuaded to return for the rest of the week. It will take some bribery, but I suspect they'll agree."

Frowning, Theo replaced the receiver. The roll of film was a puzzle. The lens cap had been found on the balcony of Dorrie's bedroom, and it had been plausible to conclude someone had taken a series of photographs of occurrences next door. Now it seemed the camera had been aimed in quite a different direction, although it made little sense. Eli had told Count D'Orsini the film was incriminating. Surely Eli had known which way he was pointed—and at what subject. He had agreed to produce the prints, and it would have been more than whimsical to hope to collect any blackmail money by flourishing the study of unclad flesh. Neither art nor pornography would motivate D'Orsini into paying twenty thousand dollars.

So where was the roll of film that Eli valued and D'Orsini feared? It was not in the villa, Theo decided as his frown deepened, and not in Eli's quarters. Eli had, however, shown it to D'Orsini around the middle of the afternoon, then returned to the villa, mixed a pitcher of rum punch, and gone up to the pool to celebrate his anticipated windfall. By that time, Amelia and Emelda were already gone. The gate had been secured. There had been no hint that Eli was working with someone else.

"Drat," Theo said to himself, permitting a euphemism for a more volatile word. The situation warranted as much. He spent a few minutes cleaning up the kitchen, then went upstairs and knocked on Dorrie's door. He flinched only a bit when she opened the door, her hair hidden under a terrycloth turban and her face smeared with a pea green paste the precise shade of the foliage of the Carolina allspice (*Calycanthus floridus*). Although he was unsure of the chemical basis of the substance, he had encountered it in the past and been informed it did something quite astounding to her complexion. Of that, he had no doubt.

"I wondered if I might interrupt you long enough to engage in a small experiment," he said. He entered the room and carefully closed the door. "I'm still pondering the mystery of the film."

A slit formed in the pea green mask. "It's not in here, Uncle Theo. Those beastly policemen searched every nook and cranny, not to mention every cosmetic bag, beach bag, suitcase, lingerie drawer, and bottle of shampoo. Bitsy was an absolute basket case by the time they were finished. It was almost—but not quite—worth it."

"I presume the police would have found it if it were in the

villa. What has been bothering me is that set of prints. I cannot believe Eli would be murdered over such photographs."

"Yeah," she said, smoothing the paste along her nose with a practiced swoop of her index finger. "Mary Margaret's not all that hot. So what's this experiment? In six minutes I have to scrub this off and move on to the moisturizing base. If I'm delayed, the consequences may be devastating."

"It will take only a second. I was wondering about the camera angle from the balcony." He went across the room and out onto the balcony. Shading his eyes with a hand, he looked down at the terrace immediately below and the pool beyond it. Bitsy was seated in the chair he'd taken that first afternoon, when Mary Margaret had caught him by surprise. Although he had a clear view, the angle was clearly wrong. He then glanced at the side of the pool where Mary Margaret had retreated to continue her sunbathing. The edge of the terrace extended into his view, blocking off most of that area of the deck.

Dorrie tapped him on the shoulder. "Four minutes and counting. What's the conclusion, Uncle Sherlock? Did Eli shoot that roll of film from my balcony?"

"No, he did not," Theo said pensively. "Sergeant Stahl was behaving in such an adolescent manner that he would not listen when I tried to make the point that Eli could not have been on the balcony at that time. I certainly would have seen him. Bitsy was upstairs changing and would hardly fail to remark on the intrusion. And in any case, the angle is wrong." He swiveled his head to look over the fence at D'Orsini's pool and patio. The area around the bar was visible, as was the grouping of rattan furniture and most of the pool. "This does offer a reasonable view, however. Under cover of darkness, one easily could creep out here, set up a tripod, and take all the photographs one wished of activities next door."

"Three minutes and counting. Maybe Mary Margaret went over there to sunbathe. She seemed terribly possessive about dear Uncle Billy's old school chum—and he is male, over fifteen, titled, and wealthy. Any one of those qualifications could have sucked Magsy over the fence like a two-ton magnet."

"But I was on our deck," Theo reminded her. "And although D'Orsini is indeed male and over fifteen, I'm not at all sure his title is credible. I doubt he's wealthy."

"Poor Mary Margaret's in for a shockeroo, then. First believing Sitermann was a hotshot Hollywood producer, and then salivating all over Count D'Orsini and his yacht. Did he rent it from Hertz for the day?"

"He's tending it for friends, along with the villa. And he is involved in the transportation of cocaine, although he claims only in a small fashion. He admitted it to me early this afternoon."

"Two and one-half minutes. Then did he murder Eli when he learned he was a narc?"

Theo related the highlights of the blackmail attempt and the reasons why he felt fairly certain D'Orsini had not poisoned Eli. He was in the midst of stressing the necessity of finding the notorious roll of film when Dorrie glanced at her watch, shrieked, and ran toward the bathroom. The slam of the door was followed by the splash of water in the sink. The conversation, for all intents and purposes, seemed to be at an end.

Theo went out to the landing and started toward his room. But after a single step in that direction, he turned on his heel, marched the few feet down the hall, and rapped on Biff and Sandy's door. Biff, dressed in boxer shorts and socks, opened the door. "Yes, sir?"

"We need to talk, my boy," Theo said. "I think we will realize more enlightenment if we do so in private."

"Sure, sir. Sandy's in the shower, and I was waiting my turn. I don't understand why there's this urgent need for privacy." When Theo continued to regard him through unblinking eyes, he stepped back and held open the door. "I am totally in the dark, Mr. Bloomer, but, sure, come on in. Sandy won't be able to hear anything while the water's running. He takes incredibly long showers, because he's only allowed a minute or two at the academy and he swears hot water is almost as nifty as cold beer. Would you like to sit down, sir? We have some ice if you'd like a drink. The potato chips are stale, but—"

"I would like to look out your window," Theo said firmly. "I am interested in the potential camera angles."

"Wow, sure, help yourself." Biff's face turned scarlet as he busied himself with the ice bucket and glasses. "Ah, does this have anything to do with Dorrie, Mr. Bloomer? I mean, you're her uncle and I know she really dotes on you, but you don't have to get involved—"

"A charming view, charming. Why, you can see the Caribbean, the tops of the villas below us, the street, the yard—and the patio around the pool. The view is amazing, if somewhat unexciting at the moment. A nude sunbather would add an element of interest, don't you think?"

"Yeah, the view's super." He gave Theo a glass of Perrier, then sat down on the bed and sighed noisily. "You're not going to tell Dorrie, are you? She'll work herself up to such a snit that she won't speak to me for a month. I'll have to send flowers, buy presents, call her ten times a day so that she can hang up on me, and literally crawl around on my knees until they bleed. We have a really good shot for the mixed doubles title in the Labor Day tournament at the club. God, I'd hate to let Akinson and his sister win it for the third straight year. Akinson is such a prick.”

“It may occur to her without any assistance on my part. However, I won’t say anything, in that I am also aware of her probable reaction to the news that you took a series of photographs of another woman. The additional fact that your subject lacked clothing will not help you plead your case. But how did your roll of film end up in Eli’s room below the pool?”

“Beats me, Mr. Bloomer. Dorrie always insists I take the film to one of those one-hour places so that she can see the results as soon as possible. Somehow, I figured it might be smarter to wait until we got home to take that roll to some little hole of a place where they don’t know me. I just stuck the film in my camera case and started a new roll. Until I realized what those prints were, I had no idea it wasn’t in my case.”

“Have you examined the case? It’s possible someone exchanged the two rolls, thinking it would be a safe hiding place. Poe did that sort of thing with a letter once, and it worked well.”

“I was here when the police searched the room. I was floored when they found no used film in the camera case, since I was preparing to explain why they didn’t want to confiscate that roll. You know,” he said, bristling a bit, “someone must have taken that film.”

“Very good, Biff. The most obvious suspect is Eli, who did prowl in the villa when we were gone, but I cannot imagine why he would take a roll of film from your room. Although in reality the subject matter was less than ordinary, he would have anticipated nothing more interesting than palm trees and beaches, with Dorrie smiling in the center.”

“Yeah, it’s totally mind-boggling.” Biff went to the

window and looked down at the pool. "What have the police found out about Mary Margaret? Do they have any theory about what might have happened to her? I mean, it's been less than twenty-four hours since she vanished, but something could have happened to her."

"I have the feeling that they're not especially worried about her, that they continue to believe she disappeared for her own reasons," said Theo. He noted the tautness of Biff's shoulders as he added, "I have not yet told them that her father received a ransom demand this morning."

Biff spun around, a shocked expression on his face. "Holy shit! She's been kidnapped? What does that mean, Mr. Bloomer? Shouldn't we do something? Is she in danger?"

"Kidnap victims are usually in some danger," Theo said, wondering how Biff had made it through the entrance exams for his school—or even primary school. Nursery school. "I have some doubts that she was taken against her will, however. We were all sitting on the terrace, and we would have heard something had she been grabbed from behind. Count D'Orsini would have heard a scuffle, or even a muffled cry. He claims to have heard nothing, and Sitermann says he saw no traffic along the street."

"But, wow, a ransom note . . ." Biff sank down on the bed and stared blankly at the small pink hearts sprinkled on his shorts. "How much? Did old Win have a coronary when he saw the figure? Has he sent the money?"

"Dorrie's mother told him to ignore the demand, and she would not have tolerated a coronary in the breakfast room. She told me to deal with the situation from this end, and to bring Mary Margaret home intact."

"Have you figured out what you're going to do, Mr. Bloomer?"

"Not with any sense of direction. Any suggestions?"

227

"No, sir. This is just an absolute mess, isn't it? I think I'm going to start locking my door at night. But now that Eli's dead, we won't have anyone to keep the gate locked. It could be dangerous without any security system."

"Are you proposing to take charge of security?" Theo asked curiously.

Biff gave him a bewildered look. "Me? No, sir. But I will call the police and tell them to station a man at the gate. If they're toads about it, we can have that real estate woman send over a new man. After all, we're paying for a full package of servants. There's no reason why we ought to settle for anything less than that."

"Of course not," Theo said. He put down his glass and went downstairs to see if Amelia and Emelda had returned. They had not. He considered calling Gerry, but opted instead to retreat to the terrace and let things proceed of their own accord. They seemed to be doing so despite his best efforts.

When Dorrie joined him, he pointed to a photograph in one of the brochures Gerry had left for them. "I am thinking about taking the tour of Rose Hall," he said. "It's not far, and it promises to be interesting. Would you care to join me?"

"A guided tour of an old house?" Her complexion, charmingly radiant, paled. "Uncle Theo, you know how much I detest being led around old places with a herd of sweaty tourists right off the street. I always get tired, and those guides absolutely expire if you so much as glance at a chair. It's not as if I haven't sat on Chippendale since I was a toddler. My high chair was Regency."

"This house has quite a legend, my dear. It seems the mistress murdered three husbands, took numerous lovers, had slaves beheaded, and generally spilled a lot of blood until her slaves revolted and murdered her in her bed."

"Really?" Dorrie said, covering a yawn.

"Rose Hall is a restored plantation great house, built in the late-eighteenth-century Georgian style. Also, it is rumored to be haunted," Theo persisted. "Annie Palmer's grave is in the East Garden. I would like to catch a glimpse of a garden, even one marred by a grave."

"Oh, I am being beastly! I swore I'd go to all those gardens, didn't I? You were a dear to come with us, and I ought to be a good sport and go with you." Her lower lip crept out in a delicately girlish pout. "It's just that I've made no progress to speak of on my tan. With all these policemen stomping around, I haven't had any time at all to relax and work on that hideous white line across my back. But I will go with you if you wish, because you're my very favorite uncle." She studied him through her eyelashes as she produced a coy smile intended to disarm him.

"Good," Theo said, picking up the brochure and tucking it in his coat pocket. "Get your purse; I'll meet you at the car." He went down to the driveway and bent over to examine the air pressure of the tires, being careful to avoid any glances in the direction of the terrace. He did hear a sharp exhalation of breath, followed by a despondent word or two, and footsteps that seemed to drag across the surface of the terrace and ultimately into the dining room beyond.

"How long will this take?" Dorrie asked as Theo parked behind a tour bus.

"The tour lasts only half an hour, unless we chance upon a ghost or two. You can compare the furniture here with that of your mother's, or simply sit in the shade while I explore the garden."

Dorrie eyed the group of tourists coming around the corner of the house. "Schoolteachers from Iowa," she said under her breath. "I'm going to spend hours and hours and hours in the company of schoolteachers from Iowa. I should have made Biff come along, but he was acting very odd when I went by his room. He was as nervous as a junior golfer at his first tournament. What on earth could be wrong with him, Uncle Theo?"

"He might be upset about the murder of someone he knew," Theo suggested as they walked toward the house.

"We're all upset about that. I'm hardly accustomed to spending the night in dreary, grimy police stations, or having my lingerie pawed by policemen in Bermuda shorts. But I haven't allowed that to cast a nasty shadow on my spirits, have I?" She caught Theo's arm and stopped him. "Do you think he's all distraught about Mary Margaret's disappearance?"

"I told him of the ransom note," Theo said, nudging her back into motion as a tour bus bore down on them. "It's quite normal to be concerned when one of your friends may be in danger."

"Friend," she muttered under her breath, sending a malevolent look at the group spewing forth from the bus.

They followed a guide dressed in a print skirt through the great house, obediently eyeing the furniture when instructed to do so, then went to the East Garden to ponder the grave of the Witch of Rose Hall. Dorrie had been quiet the entire time, and Theo was not surprised when she suggested they find a place to sit in the shade for a serious conversation.

"What do you think is going on, Uncle Theo?" she asked once they were perched on a low rock wall. "Who left the poisoned rum for Eli? If Count D'Orsini didn't, then someone else did. I can't imagine either Amelia or Emelda having any reason to do him in, but it has to be someone with access to the villa. Do you suppose that real estate woman is involved?"

Theo tugged at his beard for a moment. "She is a very

good friend of Count D'Orsini and might do almost anything to save him from the clutches of the police. But the murder of Eli increased D'Orsini's peril, rather than alleviated it."

"But it alleviated someone's peril. The exchange of the film protected the identity of D'Orsini's so-called associate. Don't you think it was the same person?"

"We have at least three unknown factors. Someone took an ackee from the kitchen and used it to poison a bottle of rum. We shall assume, for simplicity's sake, that the same person then either presented it to Eli as a gift or left it in his room. That's one person." Theo held up a finger. "Someone exchanged the film from Eli's camera with another. That's two." As he held up a second finger, he caught her sudden frown. Hurriedly, he added, "The mysterious business associate was implicated by the film Eli shot and might have chosen extreme measures to avoid blackmail. That's three— unless any of the said factors are one in the same."

"Let's go back to number two," Dorrie said. "Eli couldn't have taken that film; you yourself said as much earlier this afternoon. He was probably on my balcony that night to photograph the goings-on next door, but he didn't take the shots of the unclad walrus." She took a deep breath and let it out slowly. Her voice grew icy as she continued, "There's only one other person at the villa with a camera, Uncle Theo. That person has been behaving very strangely lately. That person—"

"Hey, could you do us a favor?" A woman in shorts, a T-shirt, and a straw hat approached them. "I hate to interrupt, but we're, dying to get a group shot of all of us, so we can show it to our colleagues in the teachers' lounge when we get back to Boise. Would you take a picture of us in front of the witch's grave?"

"I would be charmed," Theo said, standing up to accept the proffered camera. He abandoned his niece, who was now growling with the vehemence of a pit bull terrier, and trailed the woman across the garden. He waited patiently as the group, identified through their chirps as Carolyn, Mo, Belinda, Angela, and Esther, jostled each other into position. When they had satisfied themselves, they produced bright smiles and Theo took the shot.

"Let's do a really goofy one," one of them suggested. "After all, this witch was a first-class murderer, and we ought to go for the drama of the locale. How about if I'm strangling Esther in front of the house, while the rest of you cringe in the background? Mr. Wooten would love it."

"You're perfect as the witch," another said, laughing, "but I'm not sure I can play one of your husbands. Let Belinda do it—her voice is deeper and she does have that darling little mustache."

"I beg your pardon! I do not have a darling little mustache. I spent a fortune on electrolysis, and you couldn't find a hair on a bet."

"How much do you want to bet, sweetie?"

"How about your pension, honey?"

With a vague smile, Theo returned the camera to its owner and went to find Dorrie. She was in the same position, as if made of marble, although he could detect a faint line across her forehead. Her expression was as stony as the wall on which she sat.

"Biff took those photographs, didn't he?" she said as Theo sat down beside her. "He took a whole roll of Mary Margaret in the flesh, so to speak."

Theo nodded. "Once I examined the angle from your balcony, it became obvious the photographer was stationed in the center of the upstairs story, rather than the corner. I confronted your young man, and he admitted it."

"And you didn't tell me?"

"He asked me not to," Theo said apologetically. "He did not want to upset you any more than necessary."

"How totally considerate of him." Dorrie snatched up her purse and began to stalk toward the parking lot. "I wouldn't be surprised if he had kidnapped Mary Margaret and stashed her in a love nest in some seedy hotel," she added as Theo caught up with her. "They arranged for the ransom note to be delivered to dear old Daddy, hoping to take the money and elope to South America or some such primitive place. Eat tamales and watch the sun set over the ocean. Servants to bring those icky drinks with umbrellas in them. Silk sheets and—" She broke off with a gulp, then ducked her head to wipe her eyes with a trembling hand.

"Now, Dorrie," Theo said, alarmed at the un-Caldicottish public display of emotion. "It was a boyish prank, very typical of the mentality. Boys do buy magazines with photographs of . . . of women in disarray, but it hardly implies they're sex maniacs or conspirators in kidnap schemes."

"Right." She got in the car and slammed the door. "I'd prefer to return to the villa now, if you don't mind."

"How about a nice drive along the coast? It might give you an opportunity to cool off before we go to the villa."

"Why ever would I want to cool off, Uncle Theo? I'm perfectly composed at this moment."

In that her words had been spat from between clenched teeth, Theo was less than convinced. He saw no way to divert her, however, so he put the key in the ignition and turned on the engine. He was fumbling with the gear shift when a hand rapped on his window. A florid face loomed over the windshield, grinning gleefully.

Theo reluctantly rolled down the window. "What, Sitermann? We were about to leave, and it's too warm for idle discussions."

"I saw you with those lovely ladies with the dimpled knees and luscious rumps, you old Romeo, you. Are you trying to set a record for wooing women in paradise?"

"They requested that I take a group photograph. I did. Now, if that's all, we're leaving. You may follow us if you wish, since it seems to be your favorite hobby these days. Perhaps it will help you to know our destination—the villa."

"Me following you?" Sitermann put his hand over his heart as he gave Theo a pained look. "Is it not possible that I am visiting the touristy highlights of the island, attempting to soak up some sense of history and culture, exploring the traditions and lifestyles of the natives?"

"No." Theo began to roll up the window, risking a glance across the car at his niece. She still resembled a marble statue, her face frozen and her jaw extended to an ominous angle that forebode ill for Biff. If she had heard any of the previous remarks, they had not interested her.

"Well, Bloom," Sitermann yelled through the glass, "I guess I'll see if your lovely lady friends over there need any technical assistance from a real, live Hollywood producer."

Theo rolled down the window a cautious inch. "What they need is a male to portray a husband being throttled. Would you like me to scribble a recommendation for you to play that part? I would be more than delighted to arrange for your death scene, mock or real."

"If I didn't know you better, I'd let my tender soul be wounded by that, old man. But I know you have a genuine fondness for me, so I'll let your petty little ripostes go right over my head."

"I would like to leave now," Dorrie said.

"A wonderful idea." Theo rolled up the window, gave

Sitermann a small wave, and backed around the tour bus. They bumped down the rutted road to the highway, also rutted, and drove back toward Harmony Hills. The name seemed increasingly incongruous with each hour that passed.

They drove to the villa in cold, cold silence. Once Theo had parked, Dorrie got out of the car and swept inside, her expression the essence of Caldicottian fury. Theo hesitated for a moment, wondering if the walls were apt to come tumbling down, then eased through the side door and listened intently. Nothing. He checked the kitchen, but it was exactly as he had left it and still quite unpopulated. He returned to the dining room and listened once again for sounds of conversation or violence from upstairs. It was, he thought soberly, very much like the calm before the storm. If he had judged Dorrie's mood correctly (and he feared he had), then the storm would be a full-blown hurricane, worthy of both name and notoriety in the annals of meteorology.

Feeling a little silly, he tiptoed across the dining room and went out to the terrace. Bitsy was occupying the chair under the umbrella, the magazine replaced by a paperback novel. The boys were nowhere to be seen, and Dorrie was likely to remain upstairs, sharpening both her tongue and a fingernail file.

"Are you enjoying the sun?" he called as he went down to the pool. "Would I be disrupting your solitude if I joined you?"

Bitsy glanced up with only a flicker of annoyance. "No, I'd love some company, Mr. Bloomer," she said as she closed her book and put it in her lap. "Sandy and Biff walked down the hill to the golf course, although Biff didn't look very excited about the prospect of a round of golf. Now that I think about it, the poor baby looked rather distraught. Sandy must have been desperate for company. Some man from the real estate office came by with a key; it's on the dining room table. Where did you and Dorrie go?"

He told her about the jaunt to Rose Hall and a synopsis of its legend. He mentioned the group of schoolteachers who had asked him to take their picture, but his voice trailed off before he finished the story. He was staring at the wall beyond the pool when Bitsy tapped him on the shoulder.

"Are you okay, Mr. Bloomer? Would you like a glass of water?"

"No, thank you," he said, still perplexed by a surprising . . . a thoroughly bewildering idea. Heretical. No, not heretical. Hard to believe, but not impossible. That sort of thing did happen. Not in the ordinary daily progression of life, of course. He caught himself wishing he could find the schoolteachers and hug them, but instead he turned to Bitsy. "Where is Trey?"

"I have no idea. For that matter, I couldn't care less if he has been dragged off by Rastafarians to be sacrificed over a barbecue spit. I'd gladly chip in for the sauce."

"They don't do that anymore," Theo said drily. "Do you think he might have gone to his room to change for dinner?"

"Are we having dinner? The kitchen is rather bare, and I'm not about to whip up ackee quiches for everyone. I'm on vacation. I doubt you can convince Trey to carry so much as a glass of water to the dining room table; he's so stoned these days he can't find the dining room, not to mention the table. It's simply disgusting, but exactly what one would expect from his sort."

"Dorrie mentioned that you and he were once engaged. If you'll excuse the curiosity of a snoopy old man, what did he do to cause you to terminate the relationship?"

She snatched up her book and opened it. "I really don't care to discuss it, Mr. Bloomer. I can assure you that it was disgusting. The very thought of it makes my skin crawl to this day."

"Goodness," Theo murmured. "It wasn't anything illegal, was it?"

"Just disgusting." She flipped a page and pointedly began to read. Several pages flipped by at an improbable rate. Then, with a martyred sigh, she closed the book and looked at Theo. "I came back to my dorm room one evening and found him there. He was prancing around the room in . . ." She gulped several times, and her eyes filled with tears. "He was wearing my underwear, if you can imagine such a thing. My new black bra and panties, both trimmed with lace, panty hose, a half-slip, and my best black pumps that I wore all the time. They were stretched hopelessly out of shape. I put all of it in a bag and threw it away in the trash can behind the dorm."

"What did Trey say when you caught him?"

"He said it was practically a family tradition," she said, beginning to sniffle. "He said almost every male in his family did it. Not his father, of course, but all the black sheep branches." The sniffling increased, until she was forced to blot the tip of her nose with a towel. "It's one of the reasons he's forever being booted out of school." The sniffling evolved into a deluge. "It was so humiliating," she sobbed. "What if one of my friends had caught him? I would have died, literally died, right there on the dorm floor. My parents would have had to bury me in a pine box out behind the stables. The obituary wouldn't have made the *Penny Saver*, much less the *Times*. It was just so totally icky."

Theo waited quietly until the sobbing had run its course and her composure had returned, at least to some extent. He then said, "Some men do like to dress in women's clothing. It's rare, but perhaps not as rare as we presume. It doesn't mean that he's a homosexual, however."

"I just couldn't go through with the marriage. What if he wanted to wear the garter at the wedding? A bridesmaid's dress rather than a tuxedo? My analyst and I agonized for days over it, but he agreed that I would never overcome my phobia that Trey might be a homosexual—or at least a bisexual. There's no way I could deal with that; my analyst says I have a very fragile ego due to a lack of parental warmth during my formative years. I don't intend to rear children who can't tell Daddy from Mommy without a scorecard."

Theo reached across the table to pat her hand. "I understand your reaction to the disturbing scene and your decision to break off the engagement."

"When I gave him back the engagement ring, he had the nerve to ask for my half-slip. He said it was awkward to shop for that sort of thing, especially in the finer stores, and that he adored silk. It was so disgusting that I almost barfed."

"I truly do understand. However, my dear, you might do well to put that behind you and continue with your life. There are many other men in the world; I'm confident you will encounter a more conventional one—if you cease this obsession with Trey's behavior."

"Like Sandy?" She let out a short laugh. "He may be Biff's best friend, but he's hardly a suitable match. Once he graduates, he'll have to do some dreadfully tedious stint in the Navy, on an aircraft carrier or a submarine. After that, he'll stay in the Navy as his father did. The best he can aspire to is admiral; the prestige is not unpalatable, but the salary certainly is. Sandy does not come from a wealthy family, and there is no possibility of a trust fund from some obscure relative. He's forever scrambling about for mere pocket money. He even works in the summer doing unskilled labor. Biff almost has to kidnap him to have him crew at the regattas."

Theo could sense it was not a match made in heaven.

"There will be others along the road, but you must be careful not to judge them too quickly."

"You're absolutely right, Mr. Bloomer. I'm going to ask for transcripts, credit references, bank account statements, potential trust situations, and prenuptial contracts. I fully intend to protect my personal and family wealth. My father worked hard for our money; I am not going to allow some callous fortune hunter to take advantage of my naiveté."

"So I see. Well, please don't let me disturb you further. I suspect we'll go out to dinner tonight, since the servants haven't returned. I suggest we meet on the terrace in an hour to discuss where we might want to go." He went around the pool and tapped on the sliding glass doors of Trey's bedroom. After a muffled grunt that he assumed indicated permission to enter, he opened the door and went in to be met by an acrid cloud of smoke.

The figure sprawled on the bed flapped a hand in greeting. Theo opened both windows, remaining near one in order to savor the air. Trey pulled himself up partway and aimed a finger in the direction of a chair. "Have a seat, Mr. Bloomer. Have a toke, for that matter, or a martini if you prefer the more staid vice of alcohol."

"I shall stay where I am, thank you. I thought the police had confiscated your marijuana."

"They sure did, the arrogant bastards. I had to go all the way across the street to buy some from the gardener. It's pretty good, but not nearly the quality of the stuff those damnable policemen stole from me. They're probably higher than kites by now—on my designer ganja."

"From whom did you make your original purchase?"

"From Eli. No problem, he kept telling me. He got hot and bothered the day I flashed it on the street, but other than that he was a real cool dude. We mustn't speak ill of the dead, you know."

Eli was seeming less and less the ideal policeman, Theo thought with a grim smile. Selling ganja, blackmailing the neighbors. One could only speculate where his career might have headed, had his career had the opportunity to head anywhere. "When did you purchase it?" he asked.

"About ten minutes after we arrived. Service with a smile. Old Eli had a damn discount store in his room, although his quantities weren't impressive. He offered to put us in touch with major retailers. He was a real sport—humble, polite, eager to serve in any capacity. Damn shame he kicked off like that."

"Did he subsequently put you in touch with major retailers?"

Trey rolled his eyes. "No. I figured he would double-cross us. Dealers have been known to pocket the money from the sale, then report their clients to the customs officials and make a little more change. And," he said, wiggling a finger through the smoke, "I figured that out before we found out he was a narc. I really have no intention of passing a few years in some tropical dungeon. I think I'll do the Grand Tour this fall, see how many European women I can lay in seventeen countries, seven days, ground transportation and gratuities included."

"While shopping for lingerie in Paris?" Theo said softly.

"Ooh la la, the fancy silks and satins of Paris. I suppose Bitsy has been spilling her icy little heart to you? How like her to confide in any male who remembers her name for more than fifteen seconds. She's just a little kitten waiting to curl up in her daddy's lap and purr out all her troubles."

"I'm not interested in your private amusements. I am curious about your Uncle Billy's fond memories, though.

What did he tell you of his antics with D'Orsini during their days at Harvard?"

"Uncle Billy didn't much go for dressing in drag," Trey said pensively, lighting what Theo prayed was a conventional cigarette. "Not to say that he didn't have a certain fondness for polyester pants suits, but he was a mere youth and we must forgive him his minor sins. He made it through without the big boot, but only by the seat of his skivvies. D'Orsini wasn't as fortunate. Both of them were caught in bed, but at different times and with decidedly different people. Uncle Billy was with a dean's wife, which is why it was hushed up. D'Orsini was, if I remember correctly, coupling on a regular basis with the janitor's son. He was booted across the state line. That's what one deserves if one insists on coupling with the lower classes."

"I wondered if he might be a homosexual," Theo said. "Despite the implication that he lavishes love and attention on single women, I suspected it might be of the platonic variety. Not that it alters much of anything. It does lend credence to a somewhat fanciful theory, though."

"A fanciful theory? I am impressed, sir. My theories are no better than mundane, idle, hazy fragments of speculation."

Theo told him to be prepared to go to dinner in an hour, then escaped from the cloying miasma of smoke and bitterness. After he showered and changed into a light gray suit, he went to the terrace to enjoy the pinkish hues of the clouds as the sun began to set. A foursome of strolling minstrels wandered by the house, laden with their island instruments. Theo shook his head when they called to him. As they moved along, he heard them call to Count D'Orsini next door, who apparently also declined a private performance.

It was not difficult to understand why D'Orsini was in no mood for music, Theo told himself. The pertinent roll of film was still missing, but might well surface at any moment, followed by flashing blue lights, sirens, handcuffs, and a lengthy session in the hot, grimy interrogation room at the police station. His associates would be identified and included in the unpleasantries. And Theo was beginning to think he knew the identity of one of them—the one he'd heard the first night.

But that individual was not apt to have murdered Eli. D'Orsini had admitted that he had entertained a Colombian businessman; he also had claimed that the same had departed the next morning—and would not have stooped to poison in any case. That implied the existence of yet a third person, someone who had negotiated a drug deal beside the pool. Someone who might have objected to being blackmailed and had been willing to take extreme action to avoid it.

Trey was a candidate. He had a fondness for drugs and a disinterest in either the legality or the morality of using them. But the police had searched the villa most thoroughly, uncovering Trey's baggie along with Bitsy's lingerie and Dorrie's skin conditioners. None of the young people could have hidden a significant quantity of cocaine in the villa, and they had no contacts outside the villa with whom to leave a package.

Except for Mary Margaret, Theo amended with a frown. She seemed to have made quite a few friends in the few days they'd been in Jamaica. Male friends. He glared at the driveway, down which she'd vanished. He glared at the pool, in which Eli's corpse had been discovered. He glared at the fence, behind which D'Orsini had conducted illegal business. When he again glared at the driveway, he found himself glaring at Sergeant Stahl. Which wasn't at all friendly, although somewhat appropriate since the sergeant appeared to be in an equally foul mood.

"No film, Mr. Bloomer," Stahl said as he sat down. "We

checked every place on the island; no one had the roll of film we're looking for. I know D'Orsini's a dope dealer, but I don't have a damn bit of evidence. I know somebody murdered one of my men, but I don't have the faintest lead as to the identity of the murderer. I'm still getting calls from the ex-governor and the island elite assuring me that D'Orsini is a splendid chap." He banged his fist on the table. "I don't have shit."

"Officer Staggley was a bit more of an entrepreneur than we'd realized," Theo said, repeating what Trey had told him about the so-called discount store below the pool. "His offer to put Trey in touch with a major dealer leads me to think he might have been encouraging his investigation by providing his suspect—D'Orsini—with a purchaser. It is not entertaining to run surveillance on someone who's failing to do anything worthy of said surveillance. Eli must have decided to recruit a purchaser in order to facilitate progress."

"And did he succeed?" Stahl asked.

"I don't see how it could be anyone from this villa. Your men searched every inch of it and found nothing beyond Trey's small bag of ganja." Theo glanced up at the balcony, then added in a lowered voice, "I do know the identity of the photographer who took the shots of the . . . ah, the nubile sunbather. It seems one of our young men noted the opportunity from his bedroom window. He claims he put the used film in his camera case, and was flabbergasted when your men did not come across it during the search."

Stahl took out a notebook and flipped through the pages. "Yeah, I have a notation that Bedford Hartley has a camera and a case. So he put the film in his case . . . and someone put it in Staggley's room. It certainly threw us off the track. This Hartley doesn't have any idea who stole his film?"

"He claims no knowledge whatsoever," Theo said, still

keeping an eye on the balcony. "He is a rather oblivious type, unaware of anything that doesn't directly concern his immediate personal well-being. Egotism is a common malaise within this group. Of epidemic proportions."

"So I noticed," Stahl said in a rueful voice. "I've never before taken down so many statements that centered on hair conditioners, wardrobe changes, and manicures—from both sexes. What about the Ellison boy? What's his problem?"

"It is deep-seated and complex, but I'm not convinced he has anything to do with this muddle. As one of the girls commented, he's been too stoned to do much of anything. You don't seem surprised to learn that one of your officers was selling dope."

"I wish I were surprised. We found some stuff in his room, but we were assuming it was evidence, that it had something to do with the investigation. Hoping, anyway. But a lot of my officers—most of them, to be frank—smoke ganja in their time off. It's readily available, cheap, and grown in most every backyard. We discourage them from showing up high or dealing, but that's the best we can do. It's the island."

"Have you done anything about the missing girl? I realize it's been less than twenty-four hours, but I am increasingly concerned about her."

"I had the patrolmen check the beaches, the hotels, and the bars for her. There're about a hundred private parties at any given hour, though, and she's likely to be at one of them—or on a boat, or shacked up in a hotel room, or in a private residence, or in a Jeep, or simply moving around. Jamaica's got more than four thousand square miles, man. Maybe she went to Kingston to prowl or to the Cockpit country to look at those crazy folks. Or maybe she's next door in D'Orsini's hot tub. As you said, it's been less than twenty-four hours—and I've got a murder on my hands."

Theo considered the wisdom of relating the existence of the ransom note, but decided once again to delay the revelation. Sitermann might come up with information from his Connecticut cohorts. The information was apt to be damning for one of his sextet. And there wasn't much Stahl could do about it, anyway, Theo concluded with an admittedly minuscule edge of justification. "Have you had an autopsy report?"

"This is Jamaica, not Los Angeles. We won't hear anything from Forensics for weeks. We're assuming Staggley came back from the railroad station in MoBay, ate lunch and teased the women, visited D'Orsini, then came back over here. He made a pitcher of rum punch, went to the pool, drank the lethal stuff, and eventually collapsed and fell into the pool. Several of the boys who do yard work in the neighborhood swore they didn't see anyone go in or out of the gate here. That means the rum was laced with ackee pulp and given to Staggley sometime before noon yesterday. He had the pertinent roll of film when he visited next door, and he didn't go anywhere else after the visit. Someone made the exchange before we searched his room this morning."

"D'Orsini couldn't have climbed the fence or come through the back?"

"We thought of that, but the Greeley woman said she was there all afternoon. She swears she drove up just as Eli came down D'Orsini's driveway, and she didn't leave until almost seven o'clock. Even though we're aware of the friendship between the two, we're operating on the premise that she wouldn't lie to cover a murder." Stahl's teeth flashed for an instant. "It's not to say that we didn't check out her story. The boy across the street saw her famous flamingo wagon arrive, and he saw it leave about the time she told us. There's no gate in the back, no way to force a path through the thicket of thorns and overgrowth there. The vines on the fence haven't been disturbed."

"D'Orsini could have given the rum to Eli during the blackmail attempt," Theo said, yanking at his beard hard enough to pull out a hair. "I don't think he did, though— since Eli didn't have the film in his possession. He could have talked his way out of verbal allegations, but not out of black-and-white evidence."

"Which we don't have."

"The film is missing," Theo agreed. "Mary Margaret is missing, evidence of D'Orsini's criminal activity is missing, and the identity of his associates is missing. As are the cook and the maid, for that matter. The real estate agent is trying to persuade them to return, but seems to have had no success thus far."

"I'm missing dinner. I'll be missing an ear if I don't get home and apologize to my wife. If you run across a roll of film, give me a call."

Stahl went down the driveway, nodded to Sandy and Biff as they came through the gate, then drove away. Sandy had his golf bag over one shoulder, and his face was pink from the exertion of carrying the weight. Biff was also carrying a golf bag, but his face, in contrast, had the milky whiteness of a hibiscus Diana.

"Has Dorrie said anything?" he asked softly.

Once again Theo prudently glanced at the balcony. "She arrived at the correct premise over an hour ago. She did so with no hints from me."

"Is she totally pissed off?"

"That would be a mild description of her initial reaction and present mood."

"Did she resemble her mother?"

Theo nodded. Biff ran his fingers through his hair, peeked at the balcony, and then, with a shudder, went through the dining room and up the stairs. To the lion's den.

"Wow," Sandy said, "what was that about? Old Biff looked as if he might roll over and die."

"Dorrie has determined the identity of the photographer who took the shots of Mary Margaret beside the pool. She was not amused."

Sandy leaned his golf bag against the rail and joined Theo at the table. "And she's gone into melt-down mode over that? God, we thought it was a stitch. Biff said he was going to pin up the prints all over his room at school, and tell everybody how hot she was for him. But it wasn't totally serious or anything. He knows which side of the toast the caviar's on, and he was just using Mary Margaret to make Dorrie jealous."

"The sergeant and I were discussing the girl's disappearance. The police are somewhat more concerned, and have gone so far as to make a desultory search of the public beaches and bars, but they seem to continue to treat it as a lark on her part. I am still perplexed and more than a little worried. Count D'Orsini was extremely agitated when he returned with you. Think back to the trip, Sandy. When you first went to his villa, was there anything at all that struck you as the slightest bit peculiar?"

"Well, he did have company. Some guy was sitting on the sofa in the living room. I only got a glimpse of him, because D'Orsini closed the door when he came out on the porch."

"Although he didn't actually say so, he certainly implied he was alone," Theo said thoughtfully. "Perhaps he was agitated because he did not want anyone to know about this midnight visitor."

Sandy's eyes narrowed. "Do you think D'Orsini and this guy grabbed Mary Margaret and stuffed her in a closet? Neither one of them looked like he'd been in a struggle. I think Mary Margaret would have struggled, don't you? She's a healthy sort; I sure as hell couldn't wrestle her down unless she cooperated."

"Mary Margaret is indeed a healthy, robust girl with functional lungs and very long fingernails. Can you describe the man you saw?"

"Not really, sir. Ordinary height, short brown hair, regular build, middle-aged, dressed in normal clothes. Like I said, I only had a glimpse of him, and I wasn't paying much attention. I was worried about Mary Margaret."

"He had brown hair? You're positive it wasn't a swarthy man or someone with white hair, along the lines of our pet CIA agent?"

"The guy was normal," Sandy said apologetically. "He sort of jumped when he saw me in the doorway, but he didn't yell or pull a gun or anything. That would have made me suspicious. As it was, I forgot about him until you asked me."

"What precisely did D'Orsini say when you asked him if he'd seen the girl?"

"He looked as though I'd pulled up to the door on the U.S.S. *Constitution*, sir. I mean, his jaw dropped and his eyes got really wide. He asked me to repeat the question, then he shook his head and said he hadn't seen or heard anybody at his door."

"Did you believe him?"

"Yeah, he really seemed floored. He told me to wait while he went inside for a minute. As we walked back over here, he made me tell him once more what had happened. He kept staring under the bushes and glancing over his shoulder all the way over."

"It sounds as if D'Orsini was indeed surprised by your question. I doubt he and this friend had time to deal with the girl, mix drinks, and appear composed in the few minutes from the time she left until the time you knocked on the door.

If her disappearance is voluntary, her motivation is impossible to determine." Theo felt like throwing up his hands in despair, but he instead put them in his lap and sighed. "One would almost wonder if the White Witch of Rose Hall had swooped down to carry the girl away. It makes as much sense as anything I've hypothesized."

"What did the police say about the murder, sir? Have they made any progress?"

"No, they seem stymied by the missing film. Eli had it in his possession yesterday afternoon. He remained at the villa, and no one was seen visiting. Therefore, the rum was already poisoned and the film has to be here somewhere. You and Biff are sharing a room. Do you have any idea how someone might have taken the film from Biff's camera case?"

"It's creepy, isn't it? The police found it in Eli's room, so I guess I thought he'd taken it for some obscure reason. He did go into the girls' room and onto the balcony. He might have sneaked into our room, too, although I don't know why he'd take a roll of used film."

"Someone did," Theo said peevishly. "Someone also mashed up pulp of the ackee plant, mixed it in a bottle of rum, and either gave it to Eli or left it as an anonymous present. The means are not insurmountable, but the motive escapes me—unless our poisoner was D'Orsini's associate."

Sandy looked nervously at the fence between the villas. "Was he really dealing dope right over there? The authorities are pretty lax, but I'd be more cautious than that. I thought he used the yacht for that sort of thing."

"He went out in the yacht to make the transfer on the open seas. He saw himself in the role of a twentieth-century buccaneer, I suspect. But he couldn't use the yacht to take the cocaine to Florida, where he would receive the best return on his investment. He knew he was being watched very carefully by the DEA agents, so he had to make other arrangements to export the cocaine."

"What about the real estate woman?" Sandy asked in a hoarse whisper, as if the bougainvillea vine were a telegraph cable to the opposite side of the fence. "She said something about going to New York for travel fairs, and she seems really chummy with Count D'Orsini."

"The authorities are aware of their friendship. I would imagine her possessions are searched thoroughly each time she enters the United States." Theo finished his coffee and stood up. "We're going out to dinner in forty-five minutes or so. Would you be so kind as to relay the information to those upstairs? I think I shall take a walk."

Sandy looked less than delighted, as though torn between an instinct for self-preservation and an unwillingness to disobey an order, no matter how politely couched as a request. "I was going to practice a few pitch shots in the yard before I change for dinner. I managed to find every sand trap on the course earlier this afternoon, along with the egrets, cows, cow patties, and other assorted hazards. The PGA players don't have to putt around livestock. Biff didn't survive the first three holes; he went down the road to a hotel and hung out in the bar for a couple of hours." He glanced at the balcony. "I hope the drinks helped calm him down. He's been in a flap ever since you nailed him, because he knew a confrontation with Dorrie was inevitable. At least she hasn't thrown him through the window—yet. Do you really think it's wise to interrupt them, sir?"

"Just relay the message before too long," Theo said with a jaunty wave. He went down the driveway and walked along the curving road, admiring those yards that were particularly tidy and looking up when the occasional jet roared across the distant water to return sunburned tourists to their homes, offices, factories, and schoolrooms. He had little time left before he would be obliged to pack up his charges and put them on such a jet. Six of them.

All the villas had fences and gates. Mary Margaret could not have darted up a driveway to hide in someone's yard. D'Orsini had said he noticed no unfamiliar cars parked along the street. Sitermann had noticed no suspicious activity in the neighborhood—or so he'd said. However, Theo thought for not the first time, Sitermann did lie.

And why was Sitermann so interested in the comings and goings of the occupants of Harmony Hills? He'd claimed it merely offered an opportune cover to observe D'Orsini in the next villa. That might explain why the spy had popped up like a dandelion in the market the day they'd taken the yacht back to the local pier. It did not explain why Sitermann had been lurking in the area the previous evening, when Mary Margaret had vanished and Eli's body was discovered. Theo began to stride more rapidly as irritation stirred within him. He studied each villa for signs of illicit behavior, but saw only plastic flamingos (a symptom of yuppie influx), lush foliage, manicured grass, and a handful of residents moving about their patios.

By the time he returned to the villa, he was quite as red-faced as Sandy had been. Sandy's condition had been the result of lugging a golf bag up the hill from the golf course. Theo's was the result of a desire to throttle the man from the CIA. At that moment in time, given the opportunity and despite his distaste for violent interaction, he very well might have.

They had gathered on the terrace for dinner, the boys in suits and the girls in dresses. When Theo arrived, he found them sitting around the table. Glasses of untouched rum punch were grouped near the pitcher; a plate of cheese attracted the attention of only a fly and a sprinkling of gnats. No one spoke as he pulled out a chair and sat down. Theo realized he had attended tax audits more jovial than the present scene. "Does anyone have a suggestion for a restaurant?" he asked. Dorrie stared at the Caribbean in the distance. Biff cleared his throat, then looked at Dorrie for a second, shrugged helplessly, and opted to study his feet. Trey produced a dazzlingly blank smile. Bitsy glanced at him, sniffed, and began to twist a ring on her finger. Sandy slithered farther down in his chair and shook his head.

"I have a travel guide," Theo continued valiantly. "Does everyone think seafood sounds good? Or barbecue? If no one has a preference, we could try one of the hotels or just pick a place out of the book."

"It does not matter to me," Dorrie said. "Yeah, any place will be swell." Biff tried a smile, but conceded defeat when Dorrie gazed through him at the pool. "Yeah, any place," he added weakly. Bitsy and Sandy nodded without interest. Trey nodded without comprehension.

Theo managed to herd them into the car, drive to a hotel, unload them, and get them all into the restaurant, feeling as though he were the trainer of a circus of zombies. Everyone mumbled a selection from the menu, sat until the food arrived, and ate. The few attempts at conversation were briskly squelched.

At least they had ceased the incessant bickering, Theo told himself as he drove them back to the villa. The silence was not disagreeable, although the tension was thick enough to be served on crackers. He was relieved when each announced he or she was going to bed, thank you for dinner, it was lovely, good night. Social amenities were too instinctive to be overlooked. Theo soon found himself the sole occupant of the terrace.

He heard a low murmur of voices from D'Orsini's villa, much as he had the first evening he'd been in Jamaica. He now was confident he knew the identity of the male speaker who'd sounded vaguely familiar, but for the moment he could devise no way to use the knowledge.

Sitermann hailed him from the bottom of the driveway. Theo went down to the gate and stopped. "What's new?" he inquired through the bars.

"I thought I'd come by and have a drink, Bloom. Why don't you unlock this contraption?"

"I think not. I'm having a lovely time alone on the terrace. Dorrie and her friends have stopped quarreling, in that they've stopped speaking to each other for various reasons. We had a peaceful dinner, and they've all retired for the evening. It's remarkably nice to have a period of serenity; I see no reason to mar it with your loquacity, most of which is mendacious and without the redeeming virtue of wit."

"There you go again—pretending you don't love me. Open the gate and I'll tell you what I learned about the Connecticut connection." Sitermann took out a handkerchief and wiped his neck. "I walked all the way up the hill, and I can tell you it's steamier than a casting couch. I could use an icy martini while we talk on the terrace."

"I can hear you quite well here, and there's something comforting about seeing you behind bars. What did you learn?"

"I'm too thirsty to remember, old boy."

"You mean you can't lie without a drink in your hand," Theo said, taking the key from his pocket to unlock the gate. He locked the gate behind Sitermann and trudged up the driveway, adding, "No, that's not true. You could lie while dangling from one foot upside down from a mango tree. You spies study prevarication in your freshman year at spy school."

"Required course," Sitermann agreed. "But you have firsthand knowledge of the curriculum, don't you?" When Theo merely smiled, he plopped down at the table. "As Bond, my boyhood hero, would say, shaken—not stirred, my good man. You might as well make a pitcher while you're at it."

For lack of anything better to do, Theo went to the kitchen and mixed a pitcher of martinis. After stirring it to his heart's content, he returned to the terrace and set the tray in front of the spy.

"May I presume you have learned something of value?" he asked.

"Maybe, maybe not. The ransom note was in an envelope, the words cut out of *The New York Times*. That narrows it down to ten or twenty million people right there. If some of them didn't have access to scissors and glue, then we can narrow it down even further." Sitermann poured the martini down his throat and refilled his glass. "And if we exclude all the folks that didn't know Mary Margaret Ellison dropped off the face of the earth last night around midnight—why, that shoots down most everybody."

"You are a veritable cerebral machine. Did you discover anything concerning the identity of the deliverer of the note?"

"We did, and we didn't. Do you have any olives?"

"I have no idea, but if we indeed have olives, I would rather roll them down the driveway in a primitive version of bowling than offer them to you. Would you please continue?"

"Holy major studio release, you are testy this evening. Here I am, offering to tell you information gleaned by the largest covert agency in the world—except for the KGB, since they're on the same scale as the readership of *The New York Times*—and you won't give me a measly olive. I swear, Bloom, I'm likely to get my feelings hurt once and for—"

"Would you please continue?"

"Okay, okay. Well, the note was stuck in Ellison's mailbox about seven o'clock this morning. The cook was just coming in to fix breakfast, and she spotted this suspicious character darting up the road."

"How suspicious?" Theo said, resigned to the necessity of playing straight man to Sitermann's self-perceived wit.

"Dressed in navy blue sweats and a knitted cap. Wearing designer sneakers, wrist and ankle weights, and one of those portable radios with a headset. The cook said that the figure looked mighty suspicious."

"Why did the figure look mighty suspicious?"

"Jogging is passé these days. It's considered more civilized to exercise at one's health club, where one will not be assaulted by dogs, bird droppings, motorcyclists, swerving BMWs, or the possibility of sweat. One can go directly from the low-impact aerobics session to the whirlpool and the sauna, where one will be in the company of the right sort of people. The sidewalks are public, you see, and the clubs are exclusive."

"How kind of you to explain the intricacies, Sitermann. I suppose this was gleaned from a yup-spy in a spandex trenchcoat? Please get to the point. Is there any way to identify this jogger?"

"Nope. The cook wasn't even sure of the gender, much less anything more descriptive. There could have been a crewcut under the cap, or waist-length hair pinned up. The sweats were baggy. Youngish, but that's not extraordinary. In good shape. Designer outfit, standard issue in that neighborhood. Sorry, Bloom."

"For this I mixed a pitcher of martinis? And you had the audacity to request olives? You are a treacherous devil." Theo poured himself a martini and leaned back with a sigh.

"There's been no sign of the girl for almost twenty-four hours now. Sergeant Stahl had his patrolmen check beaches and bars, but he listed several dozen places she might be. Understandably, he is more concerned with the murder investigation, which seems to be galloping toward a brick wall."

Sitermann's expression sharpened. "I spoke to him a while ago. He said the film is not to be found anywhere on the island, and that it's his only hope to solve the murder. What do you think?"

"I've thought about it quite a lot in the last few hours," Theo admitted. "It seems logical to assume the film is here at the villa, but the police surely would have come across it. This joint is clean, as they're inclined to mutter in old movies."

Sitermann nodded. "Whoever swiped it might have simply tossed it out a window or buried it under a banana bush. There's no reason to think the police'll ever find it. It's challenging to hide a busty young woman, but it's easy to dispose of a cylinder less than two inches long." He paused long enough to refill his glass. "So it looks like D'Orsini's going to get away with his drug trafficking for the time being, and the murderer's going to get away with murder. Hardly seems sporting, does it?"

"I hope the kidnapper doesn't get away with kidnapping —if that's what happened," Theo said in a discouraged voice. "I have not yet mentioned the ransom note to Stahl, but I shall feel obliged to do so tomorrow if the girl does not return. We may well be in Jamaica for Memorial Day, if not Thanksgiving. My tomato seedlings will not plant themselves in the garden without assistance. I am relying on my sister to water them and see that they are not burnt should there be an unseasonable warm spell, but she is less concerned about their welfare than about her performance at the bridge table and might forget to drop by my greenhouse. Were I at home, I would be planting beans and potatoes by now, but instead I have been thrown involuntarily into all sorts of distasteful events. I am not a happy man, Sitermann."

"Finish off the pitcher," Sitermann said graciously. "It'll do wonders for the old spirit. We're plowing through the island telephone records, but it's needle-haystack stuff to think we can isolate one call from the entire island to the state of Connecticut. No international calls from here, by the way." He wiped his neck with a handkerchief, drank the last few drops in his glass, and rose. "You don't have to walk me to the door, Bloom. I'll let myself out."

"I locked the gate."

"Picking locks, sophomore year. Have you forgotten already?" Laughing, Sitermann went down the driveway, paused in front of the gate for a few seconds, his bulk blocking the view of the formidable lock, then exited and strolled down the hill. His laughter drifted back in the now cool breeze from the Caribbean.

Theo ascertained that the gate was secured. He carried the tray to the kitchen and rinsed the glasses and pitcher, locked doors, checked windows, turned out the downstairs lights, and went upstairs to bed. He was in the midst of a most complex dream, in which Mary Margaret was the mistress of Rose Hall and Biff a husband with a limited future, when the ring of the telephone awakened him.

He grabbed his bathrobe and hurried downstairs, praying he would not stumble in the dim light. He switched on the light in the kitchen and snatched up the receiver. "Yes?"

"It was beginning to become quite tedious waiting for you to answer the telephone, Theo. I considered hanging up."

"And how are you, Nadine?"

"Not well. Pookie played the second session with all the

acumen of a trustee at a psychiatric facility. She then refused to listen to a single word about the string of ghastly errors she made, although I did make every effort to temper my criticism with a few kind words. It was not easy to find those kind words, and I was most irritated when she abandoned the table to dance with that orthodontist who thinks he's the Charles Goren of Hartford."

"Oh, really?" Theo said, having learned in sixty-one years that his sister could not be diverted once she had been launched.

"I told Pookie that if she insisted on dancing half the night with Mr. Straight Teeth, then she would have to find another partner for the team event tomorrow. Of course, Betty Lou and Adele will be livid if we cancel on such short notice, but I shall tell them it is entirely Pookie's fault. She has not been stable since her last divorce; I don't know why I attempt any serious bridge with her. She is adolescent, at best."

"Indeed. Was there anything else, Nadine? It is well past midnight, and I was asleep."

"I am aware that it is nearly two o'clock in the morning. The evening session was not over until after eleven, and we stayed to have a drink and discuss the hands. I did, anyway. Pookie seems to have stayed in order to gyrate on the dance floor with the kingpin of orthodontia. I simply left her there and drove home alone. I cannot repeat some of the things I said to myself along the interstate; I simply cannot."

"Has Ellison had any word about his daughter?" Theo hazarded.

"Why else would I call? This is not an inexpensive conversation, Theo. I had to deal with all sorts of operators whose enunciation is less than crisp, and Charles will expire when he sees the telephone bill next month. If you will cease chattering, I will tell you what Win said when he came over during the cocktail hour this afternoon. There has been a second demand."

"You waited nine hours to tell me this? Really, Nadine, it is vital that the girl be found—"

"I could hardly call you during the second session of the women's pairs, could I? Tournament bridge is a timed event, and I am not the egotistical sort to demand that everyone sit in limbo because I need to make a personal call. Yesterday afternoon a woman from Philadelphia had a coronary at the table, and the game was halted only long enough to allow the paramedics to wheel her out of the room. Pookie completely forgot the bidding and leapt to six spades, then preceded to go down three."

"What was the substance of the demand?"

"A muffled voice on the telephone instructed Win to place fifty thousand dollars in small bills in a suitcase and leave it in a Salvation Army collection box in the shopping center. He was to do so by midnight. If he refused to cooperate, all sorts of dreadful things would be done to Mary Margaret."

"Did he follow the instructions?" Theo asked, blinking.

"He asked me for my opinion. I told him it was absurd, that you were seeing to the situation down there, wherever it is. Besides, the banks were closed and the idea melodramatic and utterly preposterous. Win doesn't know a Salvation Army box from a hat box. One has a maid call them to come along in their battered truck to pick up whatever one is discarding; it's their responsibility, after all. Win would have had a sporting chance had the demand involved safe deposit boxes or even cigar boxes."

"Oh, dear," Theo said. He sank down to the floor and leaned against the refrigerator, which rumbled against his spine in a comforting way. "Did Ellison tell this muffled voice that he intended to comply with the demand?"

"I really couldn't say, Theo. Pookie and I had to leave before he finished the little story. You have found Mary Margaret, haven't you? Although her monetary value seems to be decreasing, this ransom business is still disturbing Win."

"I am looking for her," Theo said, looking at the baseboard. "I have every hope I shall find her soon. If there is another communication from the kidnappers, I would like to be informed immediately. Is that possible?"

"The first session of the team event begins at eleven tomorrow morning, and the second at five. If I hear from Win either before or after the sessions, you may rest assured I shall spare no expense to call you, Theo. I am not heartless."

She hung up before Theo could offer an opinion. He remained on the floor, this time fairly certain he would not be caught by Amelia and Emelda, should they ever return. The floor was cool. The view was almost as familiar as the verdant sweep from the terrace to the Caribbean. He had done a reasonably competent job of tidying up after the police search, although from this perspective he could see a wisp of flour underneath the table. "Tut, tut," he said dispiritedly.

The kitchen door swung open. "Who's here?" Dorrie demanded as she came into the room, a golf club clutched in her hand. She looked around wildly.

"Down here, my dear."

"What on earth are you doing, Uncle Theo? I heard a noise and came down to investigate, but I hardly expected to find you on the kitchen floor."

"I've been on the telephone to your mother. Once we got through the latest adventures at the bridge table, she told me there'd been a second ransom demand. Midnight—or else. It seems we got 'else,' for better or worse."

Dorrie propped the golf club (a five iron, Theo noted) in a corner and sat down beside him. "You mean something has happened to Mary Margaret? You don't believe someone would actually do . . . something to her, do you? But that's terrible—totally terrible. I know I said some catty things about her, but she's one of my best friends, for pete's sake."

"I don't know. I would have hypothesized that the situation was losing momentum, since the film has not been found. The police seem discouraged and rather at a loss to determine the next move, but for some reason the pressure has intensified for our unknown player—or players. Mary Margaret is now worth only fifty thousand, although it was to be paid within a matter of hours after the demand was made."

"She's down to fifty thousand? She'll be furious when she learns that." Dorrie gulped several times. "She will learn that, won't she? Uncle Theo, we've got to do something. This is no longer amusing, and I want you to get her back immediately so that I won't have to worry about her." She held out her hand for his inspection. "Look at that. I've chipped two nails since this morning."

Theo found himself wishing he had not sworn off cigarettes thirty years ago; it was the perfect time to light a cigarette, blow a cloud of smoke at the ceiling, and ask his niece what precisely she thought he ought to do. About Mary Margaret, about the murderer, or even about her manicure predicament. He was about to inquire when the door opened and Sandy, dressed in pajamas dotted with red and blue sailboats, came cautiously into the kitchen, a golf club in his hand.

"Who's here?" he demanded in a fierce whisper.

"We're down here," Dorrie said, fluttering her fingers.

"My God, are you okay? Did Mr. Bloomer fall? Did he break his hip? Can I get him a glass of water or something?"

"Uncle Theo didn't fall and he didn't break anything. He's just sitting here thinking about what to do next."

"Are you sure he's not dizzy or weak? He's an old guy,

Dorrie." Sandy put down the golf club (a seven iron) and bent over to peer at Theo. "He looks pale, too."

"He's not that old," she said in an indignant voice. "Well, he's not all that young, either, but he's not so gaga that he wouldn't know if he were dizzy or weak-kneed."

The dizzy, weak-kneed, gaga topic of conversation patted the floor beside him. "Have a seat, my boy. If I feel a sudden compulsion to drool, I'll give you ample warning. Dorrie and I were discussing Mary Margaret's whereabouts."

"They want fifty thousand for her," Dorrie added, her eyes wide. "They might do something totally awful to her if her father doesn't pay."

"Wait a minute," Sandy said. "Maybe you're the one going gaga. What the hell are you talking about?"

Dorrie related the tale of the ransom demands. "So," she concluded, patting Theo's knee, "Uncle Theo and I were trying to figure out what to do in order to rescue Mary Margaret from the clutches of the kidnappers—if there really are kidnappers. Right, Uncle Theo?"

Theo had been pondering the criteria each of them used in the selection of a golf club. "Yes, indeed," he said, "we are pondering which course of action would prove most beneficial to the girl."

Sandy scratched his chin. "Do we have options, sir? I mean, do you have any idea where she might be? I don't see how we can snatch her away from the kidnappers if we can't find them."

"A keen observation," Theo said. "We cannot retrieve her if we don't know where she is. Have you any theories?"

"She could be anyplace on the island. It's a big island."

"What if," Dorrie said slowly, "she really is a conspirator in the kidnap plot? I doubt she's met any strangers crazy enough to help her, so it's liable to be someone she already knew. I can't see her working up a scheme with the cook or the maid, and Eli's dead. That leaves Count D'Orsini and the real estate woman."

"The real estate woman has a name," Theo said, trying not to sound irritable.

"Everyone has a name, Uncle Theo; I simply do not clutter my mind with names of short-term employees. Heavens, we had a chauffeur for six months and I never could remember if he was John or James. He could still drive."

Sandy leaned forward, his expression animated. "If Mary Margaret cooked up this disappearance with D'Orsini, then she might be hiding in his villa. We could go pound on the door and demand that we be allowed to search every room. He's not a big guy; I could hold him while you—"

"The police have already searched his villa," Theo interrupted before Sandy could leap to his feet, grab his seven iron, and storm the neighbor's bastion.

"Oh," he said, sinking back against the refrigerator. "I guess they would have found her."

"One would assume so," Theo murmured.

Now Dorrie leaned forward. "But did they search the yacht? Knowing Mary Margaret, she'd absolutely die to hide out on a zillion-dollar yacht stocked with champagne and caviar."

"Wow," Sandy said, "she really might think that was a riot. But wouldn't the police have searched the yacht?"

"They didn't mention it," Theo said. He absently took off his bifocals and polished them on the hem of his bathrobe. "I suppose it is possible, but we shouldn't get our hopes too high."

"I think it's a totally wonderful theory," Dorrie sniffed, offended by his lack of enthusiasm. "I think we ought to go right down to the marina and see if she's there. We ought to do it this very minute, before the kidnappers have a chance to . . . to do things."

"We might call the police," Theo said.

Sandy shook his head. "If the kidnappers see the police, they'll panic and shoot Mary Margaret. Dorrie's right. We can sneak up on the yacht and try to determine if anyone's on board. The captain gave me an extensive tour the other day, and showed me all the staterooms and the equipment below decks. I can get us on board, then we can explore the rooms where Mary Margaret might be a prisoner."

"Calm down," Theo said. "The theory that led to all this was that she is a conspirator, rather than the hapless victim of kidnappers. According to Dorrie, Mary Margaret is guzzling champagne and munching caviar, not hog-tied in the bilge. We don't need to dash down to the pier, brandishing golf clubs and tiptoeing across the deck. We—"

"Good idea, Uncle Theo—we'll take the golf clubs. I'll meet you two by the car in five minutes. I have on no makeup whatsoever." She glanced at Sandy's pajamas and Theo's bathrobe. "You might want to change into something more appropriate yourselves." She picked up the five iron as she left the kitchen.

"It's a genetic problem," Theo said. When Sandy looked bewildered, he sighed, stood up, and went upstairs to change into something appropriate for yacht skulking and kidnapper bashing. Two of his least favorite hobbies.

They met by the car. Theo gave Sandy the key and told him to open the gate at the bottom of the driveway. With Dorrie breathing heavily beside him, he let the car roll to the street, then waited until Sandy had locked the gate and climbed in the backseat before starting the engine.

"I am not at all sure we ought to do this," he said as the car lurched forward. He started the engine again and reminded himself of the necessity of using left when right felt—well, right. He drove down the hill and turned toward the city of Montego Bay, where they would, with luck and a certain amount of divine guidance, find the harbor.

Dorrie turned the rearview mirror to examine her lipstick. "Come on, Uncle Theo, we're rescuing Mary Margaret, not holding up a bank. If she's on the yacht, we'll bring her back to the villa and call Mother. If she's not, then we'll just slip away and admit defeat."

"And if we're arrested for trespassing?" Theo asked.

Sandy patted Theo on the shoulder. "Just think of it as a school prank, sir. We'll tell the police that D'Orsini told us we could use the yacht whenever we wanted to. The captain explained all the equipment to me; I could take us out for a moonlight cruise."

"Could you really?" Dorrie asked. "You know enough to operate the yacht after one quick tour?"

Theo realized the situation was careening out of control. "We are not going to steal the yacht for a moonlight cruise," he said firmly. "We are going to take a quick look for Mary Margaret while praying we are not spotted by the harbor security men. If we are arrested, I can assure you that Sergeant Stahl will not be amused and will not release us with a little slap on the wrist. There has been a murder, you know. It was not a school prank."

He kept up the lecture, although he could see Dorrie was craning her neck to search the sky for moonlight. He suspected Sandy was envisioning himself at the helm of the *Pis Aller*, the wind ruffling his crewcut as he opened the throttle or whatever one did in the nautical sense.

The streets of the city were dark, the last of the tourists safely abed at their hotels and the natives abed at their homes. There were no cars, no motorcycles, no pedestrians wandering from bar to bar. The stores were black boxes. A dog came out of an alley to stare at them as the car lurched by, then ducked back into the shadows to root through garbage cans.

A streetlight gleamed dimly over the gate to the marina. Theo parked across the road and cut off the engine. "Well," he said, trying to sound disappointed, "there's no way we can get inside the fence, so I suppose we ought to go home and call the proper authorities."

Dorrie eyed the fence. "I am not about to climb that thing. I have on new jeans, and I have no intention of ripping them on barbed wire."

"I can open a regular lock with a credit card," Sandy said from the backseat. "The guys at school are getting locked out of their dorm rooms all the time, and I charge a buck to get them in. But that's a padlock."

"A shame," Theo said. He reached for the ignition key, but Dorrie's fingernails cut into the back of his hand.

"You can open that padlock, Uncle Theo. We'll wait in the car until you've opened the gate, then I'll drive the car through and park where we can't be seen by a patrol car." She gave him a beady Caldicott look. "Go on, Uncle Theo. I'd hate to be arrested now, since we haven't even accomplished anything. Just imagine what Mother would say."

It was not a difficult chore to imagine Nadine's reaction. Nor was it difficult to open the padlock, swing back the metal gate, and wait while Dorrie drove through and found an inky shadow in which to park. She and Sandy joined him, both armed with golf clubs and determined smiles.

"That wasn't too bad, was it?" Dorrie said, slipping her arm through Theo's. "Now we'll simply find D'Orsini's yacht, slip aboard, and search for Mary Margaret. I find this rather exciting; it's like pouring detergent in the fountain by the library, or drinking wine in the dorm."

Sandy pointed at a long pier lined with boats of all sizes. They were rocking silently, their masts and wires etched against the dull matte of the sky. Things creaked like unseen tree frogs. Water slapped softly against hulls.

"Ooh," Dorrie whispered, "this is straight from some creepy movie, isn't it? All we need is for some hulk to leap onto the pier in front of us, lunging and snarling. Sandy bashes him with a golf club, Mary Margaret stumbles out from the yacht, her eyes glazed from dope, and the credits roll while she babbles gratitude and hugs everybody."

Theo could not find the precise words to convey his reaction to her scenario. It did bring to mind Sitermann, however. Theo was unable to resist a quick peek over his shoulder, prepared to see a flash of white hair and a glowing red nose. He saw only a flurry of insects around the streetlight and a solitary cat ambling along the top of the fence.

Sandy pointed his golf club at the boat at the end of the pier. "That's D'Orsini's yacht. We'd better hurry. I think I saw a flashlight on the far side of the building; it could be a security man making rounds."

The three went down the pier and stopped in front of the *Pis Aller.* It was dark, as to be expected at three in the morning, Theo thought with a sigh, and its deck smooth and glinting. Sandy helped Dorrie scramble over the rail and onto the deck, then turned to Theo with a hesitant look.

"Shall I give you a hand, sir? The deck should not be wet, but it might be slippery and I wouldn't want you to fall."

"I shall be careful," Theo said. He joined Dorrie, who was giggling, and they waited as Sandy stepped soundlessly over the rail in his rubber-soled shoes.

Sandy looked around for a moment, then pointed at a doorway. "She's likely to be asleep in one of the staterooms," he hissed. "Follow me, and watch your head. Keep a hand on the wall to steady yourself, sir."

Before Theo could point out that he was hardly in the doddering stage, Sandy ducked through the doorway. Dorrie followed, leaving Theo alone on the deck. No, he told himself, Nadine would harp well into the twenty-first century if he simply returned to the car and drove to the villa. He ducked his head and went down the stairs.

As the yacht rocked gently under their feet, Theo, Dorrie, and Sandy began to ease open doors and peer into the dark staterooms. Tunnels of dull reddish light streamed through the portholes, allowing them to ascertain the vacancy factor, which seemed to be a tidy one hundred percent.

"This is the dining room," Sandy whispered. "The galley's beyond it, but I can't believe Mary Margaret would be there. She's not in any of the staterooms. Maybe your theory was crazy, after all."

"My theory?" Dorrie hissed. "It was your theory, buddy. Uncle Theo and I just came along to be polite." She put down her golf club in order to fold her arms arid stare at him. "You were the one who knew how to find the yacht and how to creep aboard like a wharf rat. You and Biff seem to feel you know everything, as if the two of you have a direct line to God. But you're just little boys, snickering over Mary Margaret's boobs and taking silly little pictures out the window. Did you punch each other on the shoulder while you giggled and goggled?"

Theo looked down at the golf club, which threatened to slide down the wall and hit him on the foot. In a metaphorical sense, it did. Taking Dorrie's arm, he tugged her backward. "Let's save the vituperation for another time, my dear. Sandy is not responsible for Biff's conduct in the minor issue of his choice of models. Mary Margaret is not here, so we really ought to leave before a security guard comes to investigate."

"Minor?" she said, her lip curled and her eyes glittering. "Biff gave me a locket, Uncle Theo, and intends to give me an engagement ring as soon as he inherits money from some comatose old aunt in Boston. We've spent entire afternoons together in Tiffany's. He is supposedly above pubescent, slobbery voyeurism now that we're practically engaged."

"Of course, of course," Theo said. He tugged at her arm again, but it was much like trying to nudge a mountain into motion. "But there's no reason to rail at Sandy. Let's return to the villa; you can awaken Biff and rail at him for the rest of the night, if you so desire."

"I am no longer speaking to him. I do not rail at anyone, including servants, children, and shopkeepers. It is unforgivable to be rude to those less fortunate or in less desirable circumstances."

"Indeed, my dear. Shall we leave now?"

Eyeing her with trepidation, Sandy picked up her golf club and handed it to her. "Are we going to call it a night and split? Your theory was reasonable; it just didn't pan out. As they say here, no problem."

The Caldicott jaw inched out. "The theory was more than reasonable, Sandy. I would like to point out that we have not yet searched the storage rooms or the facilities below this deck. The theory may be proven correct. Now, which way do we go?"

Theo wondered if they had a problem—a very big problem —but he could see no way to extricate his niece without literally jerking her down the corridor to the door that led to the deck. Somehow, it was Biff's fault, he thought grimly as he followed the two through the dining room and galley. Had Biff kept his camera aimed in the proper direction, Dorrie would not be in such a mood. Her moods were written in stone.

They reached another door. "This is a pantry," Sandy said. "It's locked, though—I guess to keep the crew out of the booze. It's stuffy in here; I could go for a cold brewski right now. Too bad the door's locked."

"Uncle Theo can open it."

Theo gave her an exasperated look. "My dear, we're operating under the premise that Mary Margaret came here willingly, as a conspirator in this ransom business. She would hardly lock herself in a cramped little storage room. I truly think we should leave before we're arrested for trespassing or burglary."

"I am not going to be dragged all the way down to this yacht and then not make a proper search, Uncle Theo. What if she's in there, tied up or drugged—or worse? We'd feel pretty silly, wouldn't we? You've already unlocked Eli's door, the gate at the villa, and the gate at the marina. I fail to see why you're being so mulish about one more teeny little lock."

Cursing Biff's perfidy under his breath, Theo took the metal strip from his pocket and moved toward the door. Sandy suddenly flinched, then peered over Theo's shoulder at the galley.

"I think I heard something, sir," he said, frowning. "And the boat seemed to rock as if someone had come aboard. Do you think I ought to investigate?"

"Oh, stop dithering and go see who it is," Dorrie snapped.

"It might be a good idea," Theo said, still intent on the pantry lock. "If it's a policeman, tell him we'll be there in a minute or two."

Sandy tiptoed through the galley and around a corner. Dorrie began to hum, although to Theo it sounded more like the drone of a hornet than a melody. He inserted the metal strip in the lock and twisted it, allowing his fingertips to sense the ridges of the tumblers. Whoever selected the lock had spared no expense to keep the crew out of the caviar, he thought testily.

"What is taking so long?" Dorrie said.

"It's a delicate procedure. By the way, there's something you need to be told, and Sandy's absence provides a propitious moment. I fear he's involved in this situation."

"Of course he's involved. He came with us, and if we're arrested, he'll be singing hymns in the back of the paddy wagon with us."

"Yes, but more deeply than that. There—I do believe I've got it. Here, Dorrie, go in and see if you stumble over an inert body on the storeroom floor."

"But what about Sandy?" she said, staring at him.

"We need to complete our search as quickly as possible and return to the villa. Once we are there, I shall take you aside and explain a few puzzling things that have occurred to me. Speed is of the essence."

Something in his voice stirred her into action. Clutching the golf club, she edged past him and stepped across the threshold into the dark room. "I don't see anything, Uncle Theo. I actually don't much like this anymore, but I'll look behind the shelves and then we can go." She vanished around the ceiling-high metal shelves stacked with cases of supplies. "It's really rather dark back here," she added in a small voice. "This is dumb; I wouldn't find anyone unless I tripped over—"

There was a thud and a muffled shriek, followed by a great deal of rattling, clanking, and banging. A metal bucket skidded across the floor and rolled out the door. Brooms fell one by one, clattering like drumsticks against the metal edges of the shelves.

"Dorrie?" Theo hesitated in the doorway, aware his vision would improve as his eyes adjusted to the darkness. Falling

271

over his niece would not improve the situation. "Are you harmed in any way?"

"I skinned my knee," she wailed. "I hit my head on one of these damn cases of champagne, and who knows what my chin will look like in the morning. Good Lord, I broke a nail!"

"What caused you to stumble?"

"I don't know, but it had better be worth a fingernail. I'll have to crawl over and . . ." There was a moment of silence. "Oh, Uncle Theo," she added, her volume increasing until the wailing seemed to be of banshee origin. "It's Mary Margaret. She's dead!"

Abandoning caution, Theo flipped on the light and hurried around the end of the shelves. Dorrie was on her hands and knees, crouched up against a wall and as far as she could move away from the body on the floor. Tears streamed down her cheeks. Her teeth were chattering as she said, "I—I stepped on her, Uncle Theo. I didn't mean to. I really couldn't see. I really didn't mean to step . . . to step on her like that."

"I know," he said soothingly, as he dropped to his knees and bent over Mary Margaret. He touched her face, which felt warm, then felt the side of her neck for a pulse. "She's not dead, Dorrie. Her pulse is quite regular and strong. I would surmise that she's been drugged."

Dorrie took a frayed napkin from a box and wiped her nose. "Are you sure? You're not just saying that to make me feel better?"

"No, my dear. There are needle marks on her arm, which would make it most probable that she was given some sort of sedative. Other than that, she appears to be unharmed."

"Really?" Dorrie crawled forward to join Theo next to the body. "I lost my head, I guess. Finding Eli's body like that did

272

me in to the max. I'm fully expecting to have nightmares for the next year. Then to feel flesh again, and not hear any breathing . . ." She began to cry, more quietly now.

Theo put his arms around her and waited until she broke off with a series of hiccups. "There, there, you had a horrible experience and it would be perfectly normal to panic when encountering what you assumed was another corpse. Mary Margaret is alive, however."

Dorrie dried her cheeks with the napkin, unaware of the black smudges she was applying simultaneously to her face. "What's she doing here, anyway? I was being whimsical earlier when I said all that nonsense about drugs and all. I didn't think I was hitting quite so close to reality."

"I would think that she was lured down here by someone, but came freely. Once she was here, perhaps hiding in a stateroom with champagne and caviar as you suggested, the game turned ugly. Her co-conspirator decided to increase the urgency of the demands while making the sum low enough so that Mary Margaret's father had a fighting chance to arrange for the cash."

"Who?" Dorrie whispered.

"Sandy is the most likely suspect." Theo took Mary Margaret's hand in his own and lightly slapped her wrist. Mary Margaret's Rubenesque proportions would make it more than a little difficult to carry her out of the yacht and to the car—if they were permitted to attempt it. "Sandy was the leader of the impromptu search party. He and Biff were the only ones in the villa who were out when the telephone call was placed to the girl's father this afternoon. Biff is hardly the type to arrange this sort of thing. I was worried when Sandy had no problem identifying D'Orsini's yacht in the darkness."

"But why, Uncle Theo?"

"For money," Sandy said as he came around the corner of the shelves. His golf club had been replaced with a nasty-looking revolver. "I'm dreadfully sorry about the weapon, sir. I found it in the master cabin. Mary Margaret and I thought this little ruse might be an amusing way to earn enough money to do something really wild and crazy. The idea of the yacht did appeal to her, as you said, and it seemed like a harmless little scheme. The captain mentioned that he and the crew were off-duty for the week. It seemed like a heaven-sent opportunity."

"How did she vanish in the driveway?" Theo asked, trying to avoid looking directly into the barrel of the gun, which seemed to be aimed at the center of his forehead.

"She crouched under a shrub in the backyard and waited. When you sent Biff and me to search for her, I told him to check the front while I checked the back. He's not exactly a candidate for Mensa. Once he and I came back to report, Mary Margaret walked down the road to a hotel and called a cab to bring her here. I happened on a stray key the other day while being given a tour, and it almost leapt into my pocket when the captain turned his back to explain the computerized navigational system."

Dorrie raised an eyebrow. "I thought Biff was your best friend."

"He's been useful. He introduced me to the right people and funded a few trips when I was broke. My father is not a generous man; he's very big on discipline and erect posture and all that military malarkey. I did enjoy those summers on the Cape, the snooty rich kids, the food and wine, the mindless hospitality. I never had to spend a penny for anything. But when Mary Margaret and I cooked up this scheme, we were talking real money for a change. Good-bye academy, hello Rio. The only flaw in the plan was that we've missed

Mardi Gras this year. A year's a long time to wait for a party of that magnitude, but we had to be flexible about some things."

"What a tragedy you were found out," Dorrie sniffed. She stood up and brushed at the stain on her knee. "At least you won't have to pay for prison food."

Theo jabbed an elbow in his niece's calf. "Let's not discuss prison, Dorrie. I doubt Sandy and Mary Margaret have done anything too serious thus far. No money has passed hands. Her father can hardly prosecute her, which means nothing is likely to happen to either of them."

"He drugged her, didn't he?"

"Yes," Theo conceded, wishing Dorrie would consider the wisdom of her words, "but she'll recover with no ill effects. The entire affair can be kept quiet, I would imagine."

Sandy waved the gun at them. "To be candid, sir, I'm still hoping that Mary Margaret's father will cough up the money. This is a nice, well-stocked craft, and the navigation system is state-of-the-art. I'm seriously thinking about taking it to Rio."

"Oh, that's totally darling," Dorrie said. "Just run up the Jolly Roger and slap on a gold earring. Maybe you can overtake a garbage scow and board it, Captain Hook. When you're caught, you'll be hanged from the mast, but you'll have had so much fun playing pirate."

"It may be entertaining," he said coolly. "I really must do something with you two while I wait to hear from my partner in Connecticut. The drop was to be made by midnight, but I'll give Ellison an extra twelve hours to scoot down to the bank and pack the cash."

Dorrie studied her broken fingernail. "What does that mean? I don't have twelve hours to sit around while you make devious, guttural telephone calls to Connecticut. I've faced

275

the fact that I cannot get a decent manicure on this island, but I shall presume they've heard of adhesive nails for emergencies like this. I need to try a few stores in the downtown area."

Sandy blinked at her. "For the moment, I think you and your uncle ought to stay here and take care of Mary Margaret. She became restless this afternoon and implied she was ready to forget the plan and work on her tan. I'm afraid I was forced to insist she continue to participate." He began to back away from them. "Help yourselves to caviar and champagne; I'm sure D'Orsini would not begrudge you a few bites."

"How totally gracious of you," said Dorrie. "You do realize any champagne in here will be hot, don't you?"

Theo grabbed her ankle as she started forward. "Sit down," he commanded in a low voice. "We'll be fine for a few hours. We don't want to panic the boy. He has a gun; it would be foolhardy to presume he wouldn't use it."

"You're absolutely right, sir. I don't wish to do anything to hurt either of you, but the game is afoot and we must all obey the rules. I learned that much at the academy. Also, if it's not too much of a bother, would you please let me have that little thing you use to unlock doors? It rather defeats my purpose if you unlock the door in ten minutes." Theo obliged. Sandy then backed around the metal shelves. Seconds later the door closed and the lock clicked into place.

"Congratulations, Uncle Theo. Now we're locked in here for who knows how long, and expected to survive on hot champagne and tins of caviar. We don't even know if there's a can opener in here." She looked down at Mary Margaret, who was stirring. "Oh, keep your porch lights out. This is aggravating enough without having to deal with you."

Despite Dorrie's request, Mary Margaret opened her eyes. Theo and Dorrie helped her sit up and explained several times where she was before a flicker of comprehension flashed across her face.

"So Sandy drugged me," she said through a yawn. "That boy is something, isn't he? Why, he'd steal the arch supports out of his grandmother's orthopedic shoes. Did Daddy deliver the money?"

Theo gave her a grave look. "No, and I fear he has been instructed by a well-meaning third party to ignore any further ransom demands."

"Maybe Sandy will reduce it again," Dorrie said. "You're already more a selection from a Bloomingdale's sale rack than a Saks designer outfit. If it continues, you'll be ransomed as a blue light special."

Mary Margaret observed her through heavily lidded eyes. "Whatever have you done to your face, Dorrie? You look like the coal miner's daughter."

Dorrie took a silver tray from a shelf and held it up to examine her reflection. "Oh, my Lord," she said hollowly. "I look dreadful."

Theo handed her his handkerchief and watched with only a few winces as she scrubbed the black smears off her face. Once she finished, he suggested they partake of a bottle of champagne. They all agreed there was no reason not to, in that it was Dom Perignon and the room was warm. During the second bottle, the engines below them rumbled to life and the yacht began to move.

"Now what's he doing?" Dorrie demanded from behind the metal shelves, where she was making a casual inventory of their potential rations. "Does anyone want to try a can of paté? It's French and real goose liver."

"No, thank you. I would guess Sandy's moving the yacht to a different location while he awaits word from his cohort in Connecticut," Theo said. He looked at Mary Margaret. "Who is it, by the way?"

"The cook. She pasted up the original note for a five-hundred-dollar fee and agreed to say she saw some mysterious sort at the mailbox. At eleven o'clock she was supposed to hide in some charity box and wait for a suitcase to fall on her head." Mary Margaret yawned once again, still fighting the last vestiges of the drug in her system. "I hope she doesn't get canned for it; she does a divine chocolate mousse."

They sat for some time as the floor vibrated beneath them. Dorrie opened a tin of caviar and a packet of crackers, but no one did more than nibble. When Dorrie asked Mary Margaret about possible destinations, the red-haired girl yawned a disavowal of knowledge, leaned back, and fell asleep against a case of very good scotch.

"If he dumps us on a deserted island, he'll be sorry," Dorrie said, breaking off a corner of a cracker to scoop up some caviar. "I am not the sort to find it romantic. Beaches are fine when there's a bar with iced drinks and perhaps a small band playing native music, but basically they're sandy. I absolutely hate sand between my toes. Doesn't that drive you dotty, Uncle Theo?"

"Quite dotty," he agreed in a distracted voice. The girl was found, and that mystery resolved, although the conclusion to the drama was still unknown. Sandy was a greedy sort. Mary Margaret was simply too self-centered to consider the repercussions of the scheme, or to deal with the complications that were inevitable at some point in time. But how did any of it relate to Eli's murder?

"I do wish we had found the roll of film," he said. "Its disappearance is more troubling than Mary Margaret's, in that I had suspected some degree of collusion on her part. The film, however, did not walk down the hill and call a cab from a hotel."

"Did you ask D'Orsini about it?" Dorrie gnawed on the broken fingernail.

"I did, but he refused to discuss the identity of his associates. One he described as a Colombian businessman who left Jamaica before the murder occurred. He has chosen to protect a second visitor, but for other reasons. The third is likely to be our poisoner. D'Orsini has every reason not to identify the person, since this person, once charged with first-degree murder, will have no reason not to implicate D'Orsini in the drug dealings. Until either the murderer is caught or the film found, there is no evidence against him."

"Surely Count D'Orsini would put personal considerations aside to help solve a murder. He's not all that bad. He prepped at Andover."

"Eli admitted to being a narcotics agent and then attempted to blackmail him. D'Orsini was not devastated when Eli was removed from the scene. Were I in a similar situation, I might feel that way myself."

"Maybe he did poison Eli," Dorrie said, still occupied with her fingernail. "Maybe he got the film and used it for a champagne cork or a golf tee. He probably has ackee trees all over his yard and a cabinet full of rum. Damn, I've got a hangnail now; it's going to drive me wild until I get back to my manicure kit at the villa. We are going to get back to the villa, aren't we? He isn't going to dump us on some mosquito-ridden lump of sand in the middle of the ocean. I really can't face the idea of twenty years on an island with both a hangnail and Mary Margaret. I don't know which would be worse."

The engine roared and the yacht began to roll back and forth. Dorrie grabbed at the champagne bottle before it fell on the canapés. Theo eased Mary Margaret to the floor and placed his jacket under her head as a pillow.

"This is too much," Dorrie snapped. "I have a delicate stomach, and all this rolling about is liable to make me feel quite ill. You're going to have to make him stop, Uncle Theo. You know how I hate to barf." The rolling stopped. "That's better," she said, taking a drink from the bottle. "It's one thing to be kidnapped, but another to be abused in the process. I should have told Sandy that I'd write him a check for however much Magsy's worth these days."

Before Theo could comment on the likely reaction, the lock clicked on the door. He took the champagne bottle by its neck and gingerly rose, doubting that the weapon would be effective against more modern techniques. He crept to the edge of the metal shelves and raised the bottle above his head. The door opened. Theo stepped out, prepared to wreak what havoc he could with an empty bottle of Dom Perignon.

"Holy Metro-Goldwyn, Bloom!" Sitermann said, leaping back as the bottle swung near his head. "You're supposed to drink it, not attack with it. Do you know how much that stuff costs?"

"It would be worth every penny of it," Theo said with a twinge of regret for having missed his target. His fingers tightened around the neck of the bottle as he watched uniformed men swarming through the corridor of the yacht. A second swing would not be politic, he warned himself.

"Did you have a nice cruise?" Sitermann continued, grinning at the tray of canapés.

"It was hardly my idea of a jolly outing. I presume you came aboard earlier, while we were still at the marina. At one point Sandy suspected he heard something and went to investigate. The only thing he stumbled into was a gun in the master cabin. Did you consider the possibility of overpowering him before he locked us in here and set sail?"

"Of course I did, Bloom. But I was just following you three

out of idle curiosity, and I was by my lonesome. I lurked on board long enough to figure out I needed assistance, then hopped off and went to make a couple of telephone calls. The locals do like to be included, especially in the dramatic stuff. Makes 'em feel important."

"You forgot your gun, didn't you?"

Sitermann gave him a pained look. "As a matter of fact, I did. I spent most of the evening with an enchantress from Idaho, and I left my weapon in my hotel room so's not to unduly alarm the little lady. I wasn't prepared for you and the two youngsters to go charging into the night, waving golf clubs and looking just a mite silly."

"Because of your dalliance, the girls and I were subjected to several hours of unpleasantness," Theo said coldly. "Sandy was clearly desperate enough to do something irrational in the name of self-preservation. Then you pop up like a clump of crabgrass and tell me you could have prevented all this, but you left your gun at home. Really, Sitermann, you CIA boys ought to take lessons from the Boy Scouts. Or even the Cub Scouts."

"As long as you still love me, Bloom." He began to bark orders in a very un-Sitermannish voice. Theo and Dorrie were escorted to the dining room for questions from a grim-lipped Coast Guard officer. Mary Margaret was carried to a stateroom, where she might sleep more comfortably. Sandy was led past the doorway to another room; he gave Theo a mock salute and Dorrie a polite nod.

The sun had risen by the time they arrived at the marina. Mary Margaret was transported to a hospital to be examined for any residuals from her ordeal, although Dorrie pointed out several times that the kidnap victim was most likely faking sleep to avoid questioning. A uniformed man drove Theo and Dorrie to the villa in their car, and left in a police car that had escorted them. Bitsy, Biff, and Trey were on the terrace, the remains of breakfast on the table. Theo left Dorrie to explain as best she could and went to the kitchen, where he was heartened to find Amelia and Emelda washing dishes.

"How kind of you to return," he said.

"Weren't my idea of a good time, not with all the murdering and stealing and searching going on," Amelia said with a shrug. "Missus Greeley is paying double-time, and I've had my eye on a compact disc player in a store in MoBay."

Emelda chuckled. "I need a new television set. I love 'Dallas' on Friday evenings, but the reception's bad."

Their loyalty was touching. Theo again thanked them for returning, then went upstairs to shower, shave, and find clean clothes. He was very tired, he realized as his knees began to quiver. First the night at the police station, and now a second night on the kitchen floor and in the storage room of D'Orsini's yacht. He was, he thought glumly as he studied a gray hair in his beard, too old for such things. He toyed with the idea of a telephone call to Nadine, but decided she was by this time flinging cards and vitriolic comments across the bridge table.

He laid out a clean shirt and his pin-striped pajamas and was indecisively studying both when there was a tap on the door. "Uncle Theo?" Dorrie called. "Sergeant Stahl is here and he wants to talk to us about what happened. He's frothing again." Theo picked up the folded shirt and replaced it in a drawer. "Please tell him that I will discuss this entire business at five o'clock this afternoon," he said through the door. "He needs to bring Sandy, D'Orsini, and Gerry Greeley with him, so that we can explore all the nagging little details of the last week. In the interim, I shall sleep." Theo put on his pajamas, closed the curtains, pulled back the covers on the bed, and slept.

Chapter Four

"Can I offer you a glass of punch, Uncle Theo?" Dorrie said as he came out to the terrace. "It's a little bit crowded out here, but we'll find room for you to sit at the table, and I've asked the maid to serve hors d'oeuvres. Nothing complicated, mind you—just crackers, cheese, and a tin of pâté." She gave him a bright smile as she pulled back a chair and gestured for him to sit down.

The terrace was indeed a little bit crowded. Count D'Orsini and Gerry sat at one end of the table, both solemn and wary. Sandy sat beside Sergeant Stahl; the presence of several uniformed men at a discreet distance seemed adequate to deter any attempt to escape. Stahl's eyes were narrowed and his lips pressed together in a tight line. Trey, Bitsy, and Biff stood against the railing; the former was smiling but the latter two were cautiously observing the stage, waiting for the drama to begin.

Dorrie sat down and filled a glass from the pitcher. "There you are, Uncle Theo—unless you'd prefer something from the kitchen?"

Theo shook his head. "No, this will be fine, dear. How is Mary Margaret? Has she not recovered from the sedative she was given?"

Stahl glanced at Sandy. "No, she's doing fine, but the doctor wants to keep her in the hospital overnight for observation. I don't know what'll happen next. Her father's thinking about pressing charges for attempted extortion. I've told D'Orsini what happened on the yacht. He can decide if he wants to file charges for trespassing and theft."

"How delightful." Trey chortled. "If Daddy has Magsy thrown into prison, I shall move into her bedroom at home."

"And her closet?" Bitsy said, edging away from him to the far end of the railing.

Stahl gave her a perplexed look, then said, "I haven't had any final word about the charges from that end. What D'Orsini does is up to him."

"No harm done, my good man," the count murmured. "I'm relieved the gal was found and is now safe. That was my only worry, although I shall have to fire my captain for negligence. He's a reliable sort, but altogether too eager to give guided tours and leave keys lying about."

Smiling indulgently, Gerry patted his shoulder. "He's not precisely your employee, you know. He came with the craft."

"So he did, so he did." D'Orsini crossed his legs and gazed at Theo. "I understand we're all here to find out who murdered Eli. I don't want to rush you along, but I have a dinner engagement and I need time to change into proper evening clothes."

Theo ignored the low rumble from Stahl. "Yes, I think that if we all cooperate, we'll be able to produce an explanation for the various mysteries that arose in the last few days. The situation is this: Eli Staggley posed as a pool boy in order to observe certain transactions that took place beside D'Orsini's pool. Eli had good reason to suspect these transactions were illegal, and indeed they were. One evening, while we were out at a hotel, he drove back here. He then went upstairs and through the master bedroom to the balcony, where he had an unobstructed view of the pool area next door. Using a camera equipped to take photographs under limited lighting conditions, he shot a roll of film he felt was most incriminating."

"We know this," Stahl said. "Are you going to tell us he ate the film and it'll show up in the autopsy?"

"Patience," Theo murmured. "Two days ago we went on an all-day outing on the Governor's Coach, which gave Eli a golden opportunity to go next door and discuss the possible sale of the film to one of its featured stars. Negotiations were begun and further discussions planned once D'Orsini determined how much cash he could put his hands on. Eli was pleased with himself. He returned here, made a pitcher of rum punch from a bottle given to him, went to the area beside the pool, and eventually died. Therefore, he was not available to pick us up at the train station."

"Now that would have been disgusting," Trey said, lighting a cigarette and tossing the match over his shoulder. "A ghostly driver appears from the fog, his white teeth—"

"Will you shut up!" Bitsy hissed. "You're what is disgusting."

Theo took a deep breath. "To continue, in the middle of all this, Sandy and Mary Margaret cooked up a scheme to extort money from her father. The girl took the first opportunity to wander next door with a fanciful invitation, then simply hid until she could walk down the hill to the relative sanctuary of a hotel. She called the cook in Connecticut and made certain arrangements, then took a taxi to the marina and made herself comfortable on the yacht. A ransom note demanding a fantastic amount of money was delivered to her father yesterday morning."

"I'm surprised it wasn't stuck in chocolate mousse," Dorrie sniffed. When Biff smiled at her, she gave him a look withering enough to damage the hardiest perennial, and turned away. "We're waiting, Uncle Theo."

"Ransom note?" Stahl inserted in a mild voice. "I don't recall anything about a ransom note. Seems to me I asked if there'd been any word on the girl. Seems to me I asked a couple of times, while sitting in this very same chair."

Theo began to polish his glasses. "Yes, you did, and I apologize for keeping the information from you. I told you we hadn't had a peep from the girl, and that was basically true. The communication came second-hand from my sister, who's a friend of the Ellison family, and it was obvious from the beginning that the kidnapping was more complex than it appeared to be. I was waiting to see further developments before I took any action."

"Oh, Mr. Bloomer," Stahl said sadly, "and to think I trusted you with all of my confidences."

Count D'Orsini tapped his watch. "It's inexcusable to keep a lady waiting, chaps. The good sergeant has told us what occurred early this morning, and we now seem to know everything there is concerning this mock extortion. Are we or are we not to discover who murdered the policeman in the swimming pool?"

"We are," Theo said. "I initially assumed the two events were related in some obscure way, then I began to wonder if they were indeed entirely separate. But let us return to Eli's last afternoon. When he mentioned blackmail, he had not yet developed the roll of film, had he?" When D'Orsini nodded, Theo added, "Nor did he specify on which night he took the incriminating shots. Those of us living on this side of the fence knew, because Dorrie found the lens cap the next morning. You, however, were not privy to that knowledge and Eli saw no reason to mention the precise night. Am I right?"

Count D'Orsini removed a slender cigar from his pocket and took what seemed like several minutes to clip the ends and light it to his satisfaction. "That's right. There were many evenings that might have provided photographs which would cause me a certain amount of disagreeableness with the authorities. I did stop to wonder which evening he found so ominous, but I didn't have a chance to inquire. He was dead by then, you see."

"The first night we arrived, I heard you having an argument with a man whose voice sounded familiar, although I had met only four people at the time. Three were women—Gerry, Amelia, and Emelda—and one a male—Eli. Would you care to tell us with whom you argued that night?"

"I see no reason to do so," D'Orsini said through a cloud of smoke. "It has nothing to do with anything that happened afterwards. Nothing at all. My lips are sealed with epoxy; I shall carry his identity with me to the grave, should subsequent revelations indicate I'm headed in that direction."

Theo gazed at Gerry, who gazed back with a level expression. Now that he was confident he knew her secret, he could see the mannish aspects of her features—the face too large, the jaw too broad, the cheekbones too flat, the forehead too wide. The hint of a mustache on the upper lip, the insidious blue tinge of her cheeks where whiskers lurked even after the most methodical session with a razor.

"But," Theo said slowly, "it does have something to do with the problem of exporting illicit substances to the United States, I fear. Neither you nor any of your known associates, such as Gerry or a swarthy Colombian, could pass through customs without a rigorous search. A man with whom you are never seen would not have such problems, would he?"

Count D'Orsini's expression grew alarmed. "This hypothesis of yours may have had some validity in the past, but I can assure you it is no longer remotely true. The courier service has been terminated."

Dorrie produced an emery board and began to file her nails. "Well, who is it, Uncle Theo? We're all simply expiring

287

of curiosity." Across the table, Stahl was nodding.

"Let's move on for the moment," Theo said. "Count D'Orsini has assured us that this particular associate had nothing to do with Eli's murder. On another night, he claims to have conducted business with a Colombian who promptly left the island. On yet another night, we must presume there was a third visitor. Who was that?"

Twirling the cigar between his fingers, D'Orsini smiled. "But surely you see, Bloomer, it's not in my best interests to tell you that."

"It was the night Eli took the photographs," Theo said in a cold voice. "Whoever was with you was also approached to purchase the film."

"Well, you can't pin this one on me," Trey inserted. "I was dancing, although I'm sure I was disgusting, too. Whatever I do, I do disgust."

Theo turned to look at him. "Yes, you were at the hotel, as were Dorrie, Biff, Mary Margaret, and Bitsy. Sandy remained here, and slept so soundly he heard nothing—not the car come up the driveway nor Eli come upstairs and enter the adjoining bedroom."

"Yeah, I was blitzed," Sandy said. "All that booze did me in."

Theo shook his head. "No, I don't think you were sleeping so soundly that nothing disturbed you. I don't think you were in the villa."

"Sure I was," he said, his freckles darkening against his suddenly pale face.

"Part of the time, perhaps. Before you went next door to discuss a major cocaine transaction, and afterwards, when you wanted to be found asleep should we have returned at an early hour from the hotel."

"Where would I get that kind of money? I can't buy a kilo

of coke with my allowance, sir. Maybe Biff or the others could, but I sure as hell couldn't."

"Not with your allowance, no. We might conjecture that you went over to discuss a minor purchase. Larger quantities were suggested as a possibility. You suddenly realized you could make a major deal—if you could get your hands on some cash. Is that when the extortion scheme came to mind? Were you led to believe you would receive a substantial sum of money from Mary Margaret's father, especially if you kept the pressure up and were amenable to compromise? I doubt you expected a million dollars, but a fifty-thousand investment might result in a fortune via resale, would it not? And with Mary Margaret involved, it would seem a stupid prank if it fell apart and the two of you were caught. You might be able to talk your way out of serious charges."

"Dear old Magsy is such a good sport," Trey said, smirking. "Promise her oodles of booze and a round of hanky-panky, and she'd think it was a stitch and a half."

"She may have found it amusing at first," Theo said. "But after twelve hours of solitude and idleness, she was apt to grow bored with the game. Sandy was worried that she might back out of the scheme, and he couldn't let that happen. With a fortune dangling within reach, he was determined to continue —with or without her compliance. He needed to get to the marina without incurring suspicion, so he coerced Biff into a game of golf and then encouraged him to go sulk at a hotel bar. Those unencumbered hours resulted in a quick visit to the yacht, a needleful of sedative, and a once again cooperative co-conspirator."

"Until I figured out where she was hiding," Dorrie pointed out modestly. "Poor Sandy must have thought he had everything under control, but I intuitively put the pieces of the puzzle together and insisted we go to the yacht. He had no choice—either he took us, or Uncle Theo would telephone the police and they would go. He even tried to hurry us past the storeroom door by belittling my intellectual abilities. Despite everyone's lack of faith in me, I persuaded Uncle Theo to unlock the door. Voilà. Mary Margaret, unconscious but alive."

Theo managed not to wince during the narrative. "Where did you locate the sedative?"

"Eli had a few downers for sale, and I bought the needle at a drugstore. He was quite a pharmacist."

"For the lesser purchases, anyway," Theo said. "You had to go elsewhere for larger quantities, didn't you?"

Sandy shrugged. "He said to try D'Orsini for that. Initially, I went over to see what I could buy for a thousand dollars. I intended to buy ganja as a favor for the guys at the dorm, who all chipped in what they could."

D'Orsini glanced over his shoulder at the policemen in the driveway and the police car parked on the street. Clearing his throat, he said, "I'd like to contribute to this, if I may. The young man did come over to discuss a purchase. Once terms were agreed on, he said he wouldn't have the money for several days. Nothing changed hands. It was merely fanciful talk; I was amusing myself at his expense."

"You said you'd have the coke by Saturday morning," Sandy said, knocking over his glass as he jabbed his finger at D'Orsini. "Eli told me you were one of the biggest dealers in Jamaica, and you didn't deny it. In fact, you said you'd arrange for the shipment the next night. I'm not taking a fall alone. I'm just a misguided kid who wanted a few kilos of ganja; you asked me if I might prefer something with more potential."

D'Orsini held up his hands. "All we did is talk, my boy. Sticks and stones and so forth. Had I known that Eli captured that innocent conversation on film, I would have laughed off his blackmail attempt. I was . . . protecting someone else."

"Indeed," Theo said. "But Sandy suddenly found himself in serious trouble. The lens cap was discovered on the balcony the next morning, and he quickly deduced its significance. Although the film might not prove anything that would stand up in court, he could not allow himself to be implicated in the drug bust. Any association with a drug dealer would be enough to have him kicked out of the Naval Academy and cause a serious rift with his parents. He did not intend to be called as a witness, or to even have his face in a photograph."

"Not even on the cover of *People* magazine?" Trey interrupted. "Magsy would have killed for less."

Theo silenced him with a look. "In order to eliminate the possibility, Sandy purchased several ackees at the market and left them in the kitchen. During the night, he mashed one and put the pulp in a bottle of rum. He often went to Eli's room to send him out for a newspaper; it would not have been difficult to leave the bottle in an inviting place and cross his fingers. He did so the morning of the trip on the Governor's Coach, which distanced him from whatever happened later that day. It was an alibi of sorts, I suppose."

Dorrie fluffed her hair. "And while on the train, he and Mary Margaret finalized the bogus kidnapping scheme. I wondered why the two were so cozy. She sat in his lap for half the trip back; I was deeply concerned about the circulation in his legs."

Theo nodded at her, then turned back to Sandy. "After sending Eli on an errand, you left the bottle in his room. You did not, however, have an opportunity to search for the roll of film, since Gerry and I were on the terrace. Dorrie heard you later that night, when you crept down to Eli's room and

291

crawled through the window to search for the film. Biff assumed the screams had awakened you and that you'd subsequently gone to investigate. In reality, you were already in the driveway when the girls encountered Eli's body in the pool. When I saw you by the terrace door, you were on your way back upstairs, the film safely tucked in your pocket."

"I can't believe it," Dorrie said, staring at Sandy as if he were a lab specimen. "You heard the screams, but you went right on with your little mission. You probably guessed that we'd discovered a dead body in the pool. For all intents and purposes, you put it there, didn't you? And then let us find it! That is unforgivable."

"Disgusting," Bitsy sniffed.

"Yeah," Trey said with a laugh. "Now look who's Mr. Disgusto."

Biff opened his mouth to say something, but a look of pain crossed his face and he hastily stared down at his shoes. After a moment, Dorrie moved next to him and put her hand on his arm. He covered her hand with his, and they moved closer together.

Stahl cleared his throat. "Then what about this damn film? We can assume he replaced the film with a used roll from his friend's camera case; that's not all that tough. But we searched every inch of the villa and didn't find it. Did he throw it away?"

Theo looked at Sandy, who was sitting with a politely interested smile. "I think he's too much of a businessman to dispose of something with potential value. He might have wanted to have the film developed so that he himself could use it against D'Orsini."

"So where is it?" Stahl demanded. "It's still our only real evidence. We'll make a case once we have proof he was at D'Orsini's villa."

"In the one place your men didn't search—his golf bag. He had it with him during the search, and in fact stuck it under our noses while we sat on the terrace yesterday and lamented its disappearance. You might send a man at this time to investigate the contents of the bag."

"So develop the film; it will prove that I went over for a chat," Sandy said, shrugging. "I don't see how it proves anything else."

Theo waited for a minute, then in a soft voice said, "But how do you explain its presence in your golf bag? You really should have thrown it away, young man."

"Well, that's settled," Dorrie said, clasping her hands together. "Who would like some crackers and pâté?"

It took a while before hors d'oeuvres could be served. Stahl told D'Orsini and Gerry to come to the station the next morning for further discussion, then took Sandy and his golf bag away. Biff and Dorrie went to one side of the pool to talk, their heads bent close together. Trey ambled down to the opposite side and stared into the distance; after a moment, Bitsy joined him.

D'Orsini winked at Theo, then excused himself to change clothes. Gerry moved to the chair beside Theo and filled her glass with punch.

"Given a choice, this would not have been my lifestyle," she said, smiling ruefully. "A conventional lifestyle would be much simpler, but there's something within me that necessitates the pretense. I stopped fighting it a long time ago. After some horrid things happened in New Jersey, a conservative place where men don't eat quiche and women don't pump gas, I fled down here, where the sun is constant and the trade winds cool. Should I ever come into a great deal of money, I'll pack my bags and find a clinic in Switzerland to have extensive surgery. Thank you for not exposing my private situation to these young people."

"I shall be obligated to discuss it with the authorities. Sergeant Stahl will be discreet, I hope, and there is no hard evidence concerning your participation in the drug smuggling. I simply guessed at that. If you desist, I should imagine nothing will happen to you or to D'Orsini."

"Hal realizes that the only reason he's not going to prison is that the young man had to wait for his money to be wired. Hal made arrangements to acquire the cocaine the following night, but that had not been completed either. I think he'll turn to other occupations, now."

"Escorting single women?"

Laughing, she stood up. "It keeps him busy, and for rather obvious reasons, it does not threaten me." She went down the driveway and drove away in her flamingo station wagon.

Amelia came onto the terrace. "I'm glad that's over with," she said, eyeing the clutter on the table with a disapproving look. "I never did trust that boy—he was too polite to be real. You want me to serve dinner?"

Theo looked at the twosomes on either side of the pool. "No, they can dine at a restaurant tonight. I'll fix myself something."

Dorrikin and Biffkin were enthusiastic about the opportunity to dine at a hotel and dance until dawn. Bitsy agreed to go along with Trey and even swore not to say the word "disgusting" unless the group agreed it was justified. They drove away in the beige car.

Humming a reggae tune, Theo fixed himself a cup of tea and took it out to the terrace, where he sank down to watch the lights of the jets cutting across the sky.

"Yo," Sitermann called as he came onto the terrace. He wore fuchsia-colored Bermuda shorts and a shirt that threatened to either bloom or explode. "You got everything worked out, I hear. Nailed the boy, pussyfooted around certain folks' private lives, and told Stahl where to find the film. Scared D'Orsini into cleaning up his act in perpetuity. Not bad for an old guy, Bloom. I must admit I was impressed."

"Thank you," Theo said, sipping his tea. "I suppose you followed us to the marina last night. Sandy heard you come on board. You're lucky he had not yet fetched the gun, or he would have caused you grief."

"No, not this old boy. I had a transmitter on my person, and the coastal police were tagging along behind us all the way. I just wanted to hear what all he said to you and that sweet little niece of yours." Sitermann snorted as Theo picked up his teacup. "How about a pitcher of something with a little more oomph?"

"If you want to fix yourself something, please do," Theo said. He accompanied the spy to the kitchen and opened the cabinet where the liquor supply was kept. While Sitermann prepared a martini, Theo said, "Mary Margaret walked down the hill the night she opted to disappear. Could the worst-dressed movie mogul on the West Coast have failed to see someone of her proportions—even in the dark?"

Sitermann slapped his forehead. "Oh, yeah, I remember now. She practically knocked me down. While I was steadying her with a grandfatherly hand, she begged me not to tell anyone that I'd seen her. You know me, Bloom—I'm just a lamb when some future starlet bats her eyelashes and whispers in my ear. But I didn't know where she was going, so I didn't lie to you."

"Sitermann," Theo said, "you are—"

The telephone rang, interrupting what might have been a diatribe of astounding length and depth. Theo picked up the receiver. "Yes?"

"I would like to be kept informed of the situation, Theo.

Apparently Win received all sorts of absolutely bizarre telephone calls and communiqués from wherever it is you are. Considering the tribulations I was forced to endure during the second session, I feel I deserve a full explanation."

With a smile, Theo handed the receiver to Sitermann. "It's for you."